DATE DUE		

Introduction to Automation for Librarians
THIRD EDITION

Introduction to Automation for Librarians

THIRD EDITION

William Saffady

American Library Association

Chicago and London   1994

Composed by Publishing Services, Inc., Bettendorf, Iowa, on a Xyvision/Linotype L330
in Century Schoolbook and Helvetica

Printed on 50-pound Glatfelter, a pH-neutral stock, and bound in Holliston Roxite cloth
by Braun-Brumfield

The paper used in this publication meets the minimum requirements of American National Standard for Information Sciences—Permanence of Paper for Printed Library Materials, ANSI Z39.48-1984. ∞

IBM is a registered trademark of International Business Machines Corporation.

Apple is a registered trademark of Apple Computer, Inc.

Macintosh is a registered trademark of the Apple Computer, Inc.

MS-DOS and Windows are registered trademarks of Microsoft Corporation.

WordPerfect is a registered trademark of the WordPerfect Corporation.

1-2-3 is a registered trademark of Lotus Development Corporation.

Library of Congress Cataloging-in-Publication Data

Saffady, William, 1944–
    Introduction to automation for librarians / William Saffady. —
3rd ed.
        p.   cm.
    Includes bibliographical references and index.
    ISBN 0-8389-0628-1 (alk. paper)
    1. Libraries—United States—Automation.   2. Information
technology—United States.   I. Title.
Z678.9.A4U67   1993
025′.00285—dc20
                                                                    93-32749

Printed in the United States of America.

98 97 96 95 94   5 4 3 2 1

Contents

Introduction

This book is intended for librarians, information specialists, library school students, and others who want a tutorial survey of those aspects of information technology that are most significant for library operations. Like its predecessors, this edition is divided into two parts, each consisting of four chapters:

Chapters 1 through 4 discuss fundamental aspects of computers and related technologies, emphasizing concepts and terminology that are essential to librarians who must communicate with data processing personnel, equipment vendors, or other persons involved with the design and implementation of automated information systems.

Chapter 1 provides a tutorial introduction to computer hardware. It has been completely updated to reflect recent developments in information processing equipment, including the proliferation of powerful microcomputers and desktop workstations, and the availability of high-capacity optical and magnetic storage technology.

Chapter 2 provides a tutorial treatment of computer software. Compared to its counterpart in previous editions, it includes an expanded discussion of programming languages and prewritten software packages.

Chapter 3 discusses various modes of data processing, including online computing and distributed processing. It also contains a survey of data communications terminology and concepts. The section on local area networks has been expanded for this edition.

Chapter 4 surveys recent developments in automated office systems, including such noncomputer technologies as micrographics and facsimile. This edition features greatly expanded coverage of electronic document imaging systems and an overview of multimedia technology.

Chapters 5 through 8 survey library applications for which information processing equipment and computer software have been specifically developed.

Chapter 5 describes historical and current trends in automated circulation control, one of the first library applications to be automated.

Chapter 6 discusses the various facets of, and approaches to, the automation of cataloging, including both descriptive cataloging and the production of library catalogs.

Chapter 7 discusses automated reference services, emphasizing online information services and CD-ROM information products.

Chapter 8 deals with automated acquisitions and serials processing systems.

Before discussing specific systems, each chapter presents a brief introduction to the operations that relate to a particular library under discussion, and an analysis of the problems or other motives that have led to the development of automated alternatives to manual work procedures. Because this is a survey of the current state of the art, footnotes are omitted. Each chapter, however, includes a list of suggestions for additional reading, emphasizing more detailed conceptual treatments of specific topics. The reading lists combine newer books and articles with valuable older titles.

Throughout the book, specific products, systems, and services are discussed as examples of particular approaches to automation. Mention of a particular product or service does not constitute endorsement, nor does the omission of a particular product imply lack of value in it.

It should also be emphasized that this book is a survey of technology only. It intentionally omits some very important aspects of library automation—most notably, the interrelationship of automation and human resources, and the implications of automation for staff development, utilization, and training. Readers seeking a comprehensive understanding of the nature, implications, and consequences of automation should consult books and articles that deal with those subjects. Several titles are cited in the chapter bibliographies.

Part One

The Fundamentals

1

Computer Hardware

A computer system consists of three major groups of components: hardware, or equipment; software, or the programs that cause the equipment to perform specific operations; and data, or the information that the hardware and software process, store, retrieve, or otherwise manipulate. From the hardware standpoint, a computer system may contain hundreds of thousands or millions of electronic components, the nature and functions of which need not be individually understood in order to effectively apply computers to library operations. For purposes of simplified description, hardware components are customarily divided into two broad groups:

1. The computer itself, variously called the central processor, the central processing unit, or simply the CPU; and
2. The peripheral devices, which are functionally associated with the central processor but are not a part of it.

Peripheral devices may, as their name suggests, be located around the central processor in a computer room or other installation. If a given peripheral device is physically connected to a central processor, it is said to be operating "online" to it. If a peripheral device is not so connected, it is described as "offline." Most peripheral devices are designed to operate online. While offline operation is characteristic of certain older peripherals, some offline devices can play a limited but occasionally important role in library applications.

The categorization outlined above is, incidentally, applicable to other types of information processing equipment, including word processing systems, micrographic systems, video systems, and other technologies to be discussed in chapter 4. As a group, the various peripheral devices are designed to perform one or more of the specialized information processing tasks—input, output, and storage—discussed later in this chapter.

THE CENTRAL PROCESSOR

The term *computer* is widely and somewhat loosely used to denote a variety of information processing machines. The more descriptive phrases "central processor" or "central processing unit" better suggest the computer's role as the most important functional component in an information processing system. Paradoxically, the central processor is the hardware component that librarians need to know the least about. From the technical standpoint, computer operations generally are, and ought to be, transparent to the user—that is, the user should be aware of the results of particular operations rather than the manner in which they are performed.

In many library applications, such as searching of subject-oriented data bases offered by online information services or retrieval of cataloging records maintained by bibliographic utilities, the central processor is geographically remote from the user who works directly with one or more peripheral devices. Consequently, the discussion of central processors that follows is restricted to brief explanations of only those technical terms and concepts that are essential to an understanding of the application-oriented material presented in subsequent chapters. Emphasis is placed on the functional organization of the central processor and on the types of computers encountered in library applications. Later sections of this chapter will describe the various types of peripheral devices and their significance for library operations.

Functional Components

In terms of its internal composition, or architecture, the typical central processor consists of three interrelated sections: a control section, an arithmetic/logic section, and a memory section. The control section, as its name implies, directs the operation of the other two sections, as well as the relationship of the central processor to its associated peripheral devices. A description of typical control tasks is presented in the discussion of operating systems in chapter 2.

The arithmetic/logic section contains the specialized electronic circuitry essential to computation. Electronic computers were originally developed for scientific applications requiring extensive mathematical calculations based on elaborate combinations of such simple arithmetic operations as addition, subtraction, multiplication, and division. But computers, of course, are capable of more than mere calculation. Although scientific computing remains important, most computers today are used to process business data. In such applications—collectively described as electronic data processing (EDP) or, within federal government agencies, automatic data processing (ADP)—calculation requirements are often modest, but the central processor must perform repetitive logical operations involving the testing of specified conditions or the comparison of data. In most library-oriented information storage and retrieval applications, such logical operations are more important than arithmetic calculations.

The memory section provides storage for data and programs within the central processor itself. It is sometimes described as "main" or "primary" memory to distinguish it from the "auxiliary" or "secondary" storage devices and media described later in this chapter. Descriptive terminology aside, the memory section is typically reserved for data and programs that are being utilized by the central processor at a given moment; data and programs that will be used at some later time are relegated to the storage peripherals. Information stored in main memory is recorded in a specially coded form called "machine-readable" form. For purposes of this discussion, the term *machine-readable* is synonymous with *computer-processible*. It should be noted, however, that the term can be applied to other information technologies; audio and video recording systems, for example, also rely on machine-readable information.

As used in this context, the term *machine-readable* denotes information that is represented by a purposeful alteration of computer components —in this case, main memory circuits—in a manner that the central processor can "read" or detect. Most available computers are digital devices that process information represented by discrete electrical signals. Analog computers, which process continuously varying signals, have been used to monitor and control industrial processes or scientific experiments in technical and manufacturing applications. Such devices, which have no library applications, are omitted from this book.

The active conversion of information to digitally coded, machine-readable form is accomplished by input peripherals described later in this chapter. This section will describe the way in which information is stored in memory. It is assumed here that the information consists of characters— that is, letters of the alphabet, numeric digits, punctuation marks, or other symbols that might be encountered in data or computer programs. A coding pattern is established for each of the characters to be represented by a computer system. Although various coding schemes have been used since the inception of electronic information processing, most computer systems now employ either the American Standard Code for Information Interchange—the so-called ASCII (pronounced "askey") code—or the Extended Binary Coded Decimal Interchange Code, typically abbreviated as EBCDIC. These codes are delineated in charts that use the symbols one and zero to represent the code patterns for individual characters. This coding method is termed "binary" because it uses only two symbols to represent the various characters. Each of the symbols in the code chart is called a binary digit, or bit, and the accumulation of bits that encode a given character is commonly called a byte. The number of bits per byte varies with the coding scheme employed. The EBCDIC code, for example, uses eight bits to represent each character, while the ASCII code uses seven. Often, however, an extra bit is appended to each ASCII-coded character, bringing the number of bits per byte to eight.

Regardless of the number of bits involved, the important equivalence is that between a byte and a character. The capacity of main memory, and of auxiliary storage media as well, is customarily measured in bytes. It is expressed as a number followed by an alphabetic abbreviation that denotes a specific quantity of bytes. The abbreviation KB, for example, stands for 1,024 bytes. A computer described as having 640KB of main memory can store 640 times 1,024 bytes or 655,360 characters. For con-

Comparison of Bit Configurations in Two Standard Coding Schemes

Character	ASCII	EBCDIC
A	1000001	11000001
B	0100001	11000010
C	1100001	11000011
D	0010001	11000100
E	1010001	11000101
F	0110001	11000110
G	1110001	11000111
H	0001001	11001000
I	1001001	11001001
J	0101001	11010001
K	1101001	11010010
L	0011001	11010011
M	1011001	11010100

Computers store information in machine-readable encoded form in which individual characters, numeric digits, and other symbols are represented by a predefined pattern of bits. The above excerpts from ASCII and EBCDIC code charts indicate the standard coding pattern for given characters.

venience, the value of KB is often rounded down to 1,000, and the resulting memory capacity is described in thousands of characters, or kilobytes.

Because the amount of available memory affects the types of tasks a given computer system can effectively perform, main memory configurations have steadily expanded to meet the increasingly complex requirements of information processing applications. Central processors with main memory capacities measured in millions of characters, or megabytes (MB), were once encountered only in the largest computer installations; such memory capacities are now routinely supported by desktop computers. Main memory capacities of some large computers are measured in billions of characters or gigabytes (GB). Main memories with capacities measured in trillions of characters, or terabytes (TB), may be encountered in future computer configurations. Gigabyte and even terabyte capacities are characteristic of some of the auxiliary storage peripherals described later in this chapter.

Although the byte is the most common unit of computer storage capacity, main memory sizes are occasionally measured in words. More often, however, the term *word* is used to describe a central processor's data manipulation capabilities. That usage bears no relationship to words as grammatical units. As applied to computers, a word denotes the number of bits that can be processed—that is, retrieved from main memory or otherwise manipulated—in a single operation. An 8-bit word computer can manipulate eight bits, or one byte, of data at a time; a 16-bit computer can manipulate 16 bits, or two bytes of data at a time; and so on. Although 12-bit, 18-bit, and 24-bit word sizes have been employed by some computer systems, the word lengths of most central processors are fixed at a power of two; eight bits, 16 bits, 32 bits, and 64 bits are currently available configurations. As discussed in the next section, word length has a direct impact on a computer's operating speed; other things being equal, the longer the word, the faster the device. As an added advantage, computers with longer word lengths can generally support greater amounts of main memory.

To determine the character storage capacity where the size of main memory is expressed in words, multiply the number of words by the number of bits in each and divide by 8 (the number of bits per byte). Thus, a computer with 256K 16-bit words of main memory can store 256 times 1,024 times 16 bits or 4,194,304 (4,096K) bits. Dividing by 8 bits per byte, the equivalent character capacity is 524,288 (512K) bytes.

The discussion to this point has focused on the concept of bits and bytes, and their symbolic representation by combinations of the binary digits one and zero. The actual storage of bits and bytes, as previously noted, involves the physical alteration of memory components. Since the 1940s, computers have employed memory circuits that are capable of being altered in either of two ways for purposes of representing individual bits. The physical composition of main memory, however, has varied over time, and such variations are typically viewed as among the most important features that distinguish successive "generations" of computers.

In the earliest computers, for example, vacuum tubes were selectively turned on and off to represent the combinations of one and zero bits that encode individual characters. The memory sections of central processors developed during the 1960s and early 1970s consisted of small, circular-shaped metal cores capable of being magnetized in either of two directions. Individual characters were represented by the pattern of magnetization in a specified combination of cores. Although the phrase "core memory" is still occasionally used as a synonym for main memory, the memory sections of newer computers store information electronically rather than magnetically. They are composed of large numbers of highly miniaturized circuits that are consolidated or "integrated" on crystals or "chips" of semiconductive material.

Main memory circuits are typically categorized into two groups: random-access memory (RAM) and read-only memory (ROM). Random-access memory, the most widely encountered type of main memory circuit, is blank when purchased. Information, in the form of data and programs, is entered into RAM circuits when it is required by the central processor. In many cases, the information is transferred from an auxiliary storage peripheral, such as magnetic disk drive, on which it was previously recorded; alternatively, it may be entered directly into random-access memory from a keyboard or one of the other input devices described later in this chapter. When their contents are no longer needed, RAM circuits are released for other uses.

Read-only memory circuits, in contrast, are purchased with prerecorded information. As their name implies, the contents of ROM circuits can be read—that is, retrieved for use by the central processor—but not deleted, added to, or otherwise modified. ROM circuits are typically reserved for programs or, occasionally, data that must be immediately and continuously available to the central processor. The several forms of ROM circuits are variously described as programmable read-only memory (PROM), erasable programmable read-only memory (EPROM), and electrically alterable read-only memory (EAROM). While these names suggest recordability, their contents can only be altered by special mechanisms that are typically unavailable to computer users. In most computer configurations, read-only memories are used much more sparingly than RAM circuits. When undifferentiated main memory sizes and requirements are indicated for a given central processor or computer program, they typically apply to random-access rather than read-only memory.

Silicon is currently the most important and widely publicized semiconductor for integrated random-access and read-only memory circuits, but there has been much research interest in other semiconductive and superconductive materials. Also being studied is cryogenic technology, in which materials cooled to absolute zero can be switched between normal and superconductive states, and optical main memories, in which combinations of bits that encode individual characters are represented by the presence or absence of deformations that reflect light in a given manner. These alternatives to silicon offer potential advantages in compactness, processing speed, and cost, but significant theoretical and practical problems must be resolved before they can be readily utilized by integrated circuit manufacturers.

With existing semiconductive materials, individual memory circuits can assume one of two states—conducting electricity or not conducting electricity. One of the states represents the one bits in digitally coded information; the other represents the zero bits. In a manner similar to that employed with magnetic cores, individual characters are represented by the presence or absence of electrical current in a specified combination of circuits. Introduced in the late 1950s, the earliest silicon chips contained a few dozen electronic components and could store less than 1K bits of data. The manufacturing technology that produced such chips is today termed small-scale integration (SSI). During the 1960s, medium-scale integration (MSI) technology produced memory chips with several hundred components and several thousand bits of storage capacity. By the early 1970s, large-scale integration (LSI) had produced chips containing thousands of circuits with 16K to 64K bits of storage capacity. Since the mid-1980s, very large-scale integration (VLSI) manufacturing technologies have produced chips containing hundreds of thousands of components. VLSI chips capable of storing 256K bits were introduced in the early 1980s. Memory chips with megabit densities are now available, and chips that can store several hundred megabits are in development. Because many manufacturing and marketing costs are fixed, increased storage densities are an important factor in lowering the cost of a given memory configuration. Ongoing improvements in circuit etching, pattern registration, line-width reduction, and other aspects of chip fabrication have produced laboratory prototypes containing millions of components, but the routine manufacturing of such densely integrated circuits is not expected for some time.

Full-size Computers and Minicomputers

While available devices share the functional components described in the preceding section, central processors are typically categorized as full-size computers, minicomputers, microcomputers, and workstations, depending on such factors as physical size, processing power, the types of peripherals supported, intended applications, and cost. Because recent advances in electronics technology have reduced the physical size and cost of all types of central processors, differences among the four categories are increasingly difficult to delineate. The lack of precision inherent in these designations is further reflected in the development of such subcategories as mini-midi, midi-mini, and maxi-mini to represent gradations of processing power within a given product group. While some industry analysts contend that the terms used to denote the various categories of computers are more meaningful as advertising and marketing concepts than as informative product descriptions, a brief review of the development of the various types of central processors may help to clarify their distinctive features.

Through the early 1970s, computer system designers emphasized the economies of scale inherent in powerful, large-scale computing machinery serving many users from a centralized facility. Such large-scale devices are often termed full-size computers. They are also described as "main-

Type of Computer	Main Memory	Word Size	Typical Installation Pattern
Large-Scale	16MB-512MB+	64-bits or 32-bits	Centralized in large library government agency, corporation, or other organization; shared by many departments
Minicomputer	2MB-64MB+	32-bits or 16-bits	Centralized in medium-size library, government agency, corporation, or other organization; decentralized at division or department level in larger organizations; sometimes dedicated to specific applications, such as circulation control
Microcomputer	64K-16MB+	32-bits, 16-bits, or 8-bits	Decentralized at office or desk-level in organizations of all types; and sizes; may serve as sole computer in very small libraries and other organizations; sometimes dedicated to specific applications, such as circulation control

Types of computers can be categorized by memory size, word length, and intended application.

frames," although that term has no precise definition. Once used to distinguish the central processor as the most significant piece of hardware in a computer installation, the "mainframe" designation may be loosely applied to the largest, most powerful computer at a given site. In that sense, it differentiates full-size and minicomputers from the smaller and presumably less powerful desktop devices described below. Throughout this book, however, it will be used in its most common sense—as a synonym for full-size computers.

Terminology aside, the philosophical and economic foundation for centralized implementation of large-scale computing resources is derived from a principle called Grosch's Law, which, although never formally published, became a fundamental precept of computer engineering. Formulated by the computer scientist Herbert R. J. Grosch in the late 1940s, it contended that larger, and consequently more expensive, computers provide significantly greater information processing power per dollar than smaller, less expensive machines. Assuming that considerable processing power is required, Grosch's Law implies that consolidation of an organization's computing capabilities in a single, relatively large computer rather than in several smaller ones reduces the unit cost of computing. By the mid-1960s, the development of time-sharing operating systems and telecommunication facilities for remote access made such consolidated computing resources possible and practical. Since that time, advances in electronics, combined with market demands, have resulted in the development of several subcategories of full-size computers, each distinguished by such factors as word length, operating speed, memory size, and cost.

At the low end of this product group, relatively small full-size computers are virtually indistinguishable from—and in some cases less powerful than—the largest minicomputers. Widely used in businesses, government agencies, and schools, such devices can support a variety of online peripheral devices, including disk drives and dozens of terminals. They access 32-bit words, and their operating speeds are usually measured in microseconds (millionths of a second). Typical memory capacities range from 10 to 100 megabytes. At the other end of the full-size computer group are so-called supercomputers—very powerful, special-purpose machines designed for scientific research, computer simulations, and other applications requiring rapid execution of a high volume of complex calculations. Their word size is 64 bits, their operating speeds are measured in fractions of a nanosecond (a billionth of a second), and their main memory capacities may attain gigabyte levels. Supercomputers typically employ parallel processing techniques in which multiple mathematical calculations associated with a particular problem are performed simultaneously rather than sequentially. Supercomputers are not important for automated library operations, since such activities do not involve extensive mathematical calculations.

Falling between the two extremes cited above, most full-size computers are properly characterized as medium- or large-scale devices. Designed to perform commonly encountered scientific and data processing tasks, medium-scale computers are generally faster and support a more varied

Mainframes and minicomputers are available in a variety of sizes and configurations. (Courtesy: Hewlett-Packard)

group of peripheral devices than the small full-size computers described above. They access 64-bit words, are typically configured with several hundred megabytes of main memory, feature operating speeds measured in nanoseconds, and can support several hundred online terminals as well as high-capacity auxiliary storage devices. As their product designation suggests, large-scale computers are bigger and faster than their medium-scale counterparts. They access 64-bit words, have gigabyte-level main memories, feature operating speeds measured in nanoseconds, and may support hundreds or even thousands of online terminals. Measured by market share, IBM Corporation is the world's leading manufacturer of large-scale computers, although its product line also includes small- and medium-scale mainframes as well as minicomputers, microcomputers, and workstations. Several other companies—including Amdahl, Hitachi Data Systems, and NEC—offer full-size computers that can support the same peripheral devices and run the same software as IBM processors. Such computers are collectively described as plug-compatible mainframes (PCMs); they can be viewed as the large-scale counterparts of the IBM-compatible microcomputers described below. Other full-size computers are manufactured by companies such as Unisys, NCR, Bull Worldwide Information Systems, Fujitsu, Tandem, and ICL. Such products are based on proprietary technology and are not IBM-compatible. Supercomputer manufacturers include Cray Research, Hitachi, Fujitsu, and NEC. Several companies, including Convex Computer Corporation and Alliant Computer Systems, market smaller, less expensive models described as "mini-supercomputers."

As discussed in later chapters, full-size computers are used by bibliographic utilities, online search services, and other organizations that provide automated reference and technical services to libraries. In addition, some library-oriented software products are designed for full-size central processors. A few large libraries and library systems have purchased mainframe computers for that purpose. Many more libraries have access to full-size computers operated by municipal, institutional, or corporate data processing centers. Often, libraries are encouraged to use such centralized, shared facilities to automate their applications. In such circumstances, computer resources are typically allocated to individual agencies according to a predefined set of priorities. Many library applications require considerable input, output, and storage resources; involve a high volume of transaction-processing activity; and must be continuously available well beyond a typical eight-hour workday. Although centralized data processing facilities can provide good service, a number of libraries have expressed dissatisfaction with an arrangement that forces them to relinquish control over work scheduling. Such dissatisfaction is not unique to libraries. In the early 1970s, many business users began complaining about the difficulties of dealing with seemingly unresponsive computing center personnel, indicating a strong preference for more direct control over increasingly indispensable computing resources.

Coincidentally, developments in electronics technology—specifically, improvements in the manufacturing of integrated circuitry—made such direct control possible through drastic reductions in the cost of smaller computers. Such smaller devices were termed "minicomputers" because of their smaller physical dimensions when compared to mainframes. They had been available since the 1950s, but high prices limited their use to specialized applications in such fields as aerospace and process control, where sharing of computing resources was impractical and the cost of a dedicated computer could be justified. By the mid-1970s, however, many businesses and government agencies were using minicomputers to decentralize, or distribute, their computing resources, thereby placing computers under the control of operating divisions or departments. Today, many minicomputers operate in office environments, close to the workers who use them. Others are installed in centralized computing facilities within medium-size organizations for which full-size computers are too powerful or too expensive. In some applications, as described in chapter 3, geographically scattered minicomputers may be linked electronically in a distributed processing network.

While the earliest minicomputers were intended for specialized scientific or industrial applications, most newer models are general-purpose devices designed to perform a wide range of information processing tasks. As with full-size computers, the term *minicomputer* encompasses products of diverse capabilities. The most powerful models—manufactured by such companies as Digital Equipment Corporation, IBM, Hewlett-Packard, and Data General—are virtually indistinguishable from some full-size computers. Their operating speeds are measured in nanoseconds. Their main memory capacities approach gigabyte levels. They may support hundreds or even thousands of online terminals and can be configured with a variety of input, output, and storage peripherals. Reflecting their impressive performance characteristics and the imprecise nature of much data processing terminology, such high-end minicomputers are often described as "mainframes" by their manufacturers and owners. Their categorization as minicomputers largely reflects the fact that they are manufactured by companies historically associated with the minicomputer segment of the data processing industry.

Less powerful minicomputers are measurably slower, have less memory capacity, and support fewer online terminals. Manufactured by the companies listed above, they are sometimes described as "midrange" machines because their position in the hierarchy of computer performance places them between the most powerful full-size machines and somewhat slower desktop systems. Most models process 32-bit words, although some older 16-bit machines remain in use. Midrange minicomputers enjoyed their greatest customer acceptance between the early 1970s, when decentralized computing concepts first gained prominence, and the mid-1980s, when high-performance microcomputers began eroding traditional minicomputer markets. While no longer considered leading-edge technology, midrange minicomputers can perform very effectively in a variety of business applications where they typically support many users and a broad mix of information processing tasks. In library installations, in contrast, midrange minicomputers are often dedicated to a particular activity, such as circulation control or online catalog access.

Microcomputers and Workstations

Like the minicomputer, the microcomputer defies precise categorization. Its historical definition, now two decades old, remains accurate but only marginally useful; it describes a microcomputer as a computer that incorporates a microprocessor as its central processor. The most dramatic end product of the LSI and VLSI manufacturing techniques described earlier in this chapter, a microprocessor is a single-chip integrated circuit device that is capable of performing the operations typically associated with the control and arithmetic/logic sections of a central processor.

It is important to note, however, that the mere incorporation of microprocessors and related components does not make a device a microcomputer. Since the 1970s, microprocessors have been increasingly used in many consumer products, including automobiles, television receivers, audio systems, kitchen appliances, and thermostats, as well as such computer-like devices as handheld calculators and digital watches. While they make extensive use of electronic circuitry, such devices are designed by their manufacturers to perform specific tasks. They lack the programmability of the computer systems discussed in this book. More relevant to this discussion, microprocessors are incorporated into computers of various types and sizes; most minicomputers and full-size computers, for example, employ microprocessors in some capacity. Some minicomputer manufacturers have introduced microprocessor-based models at the low end of their product lines, and it has been suggested that mainframes of the

Desktop systems bring significant computing power to libraries, offices, laboratories, schools, and homes. (Courtesy: Tandy Corporation)

future will consist of integrated configurations of microprocessors, each performing specialized information-processing tasks. Several computer companies, for example, have demonstrated parallel processing machines with thousands of microprocessors.

Internal architecture aside, microcomputers' intended applications and implementation patterns distinguish them from larger central processors. From the standpoint of data processing operations, most mainframes are installed in centralized facilities operated by corporations, government agencies, universities, hospitals, or other institutions. Minicomputers are widely installed in centralized data processing facilities operated by medium-size organizations. In addition, as noted above, they are often decentralized at the division or department level in larger organizations. Microcomputers permit a further decentralization of computing power at the office or even the desk level, where their entire information-processing capabilities are at the complete disposal of individual workers—a role that is reflected in the widespread use of the phrase "personal computers" as a synonym for microcomputers. Portable microcomputers—variously categorized as "laptop," "notebook," or "palmtop" systems—provide self-contained data processing capabilities outside of traditional work environments.

Portable computers, like this notebook model, provide self-contained data processing capabilities outside of traditional work environments. (Courtesy: NEC)

The foregoing description of microcomputers as personal information processing machines is accurate but potentially misleading; as will be described in chapter 3, microcomputers are increasingly linked in networked configurations that promote electronic communication and resource sharing. In a startling and widely publicized reversal of Grosch's Law, it has been suggested that such networked microcomputers can cost-effectively replace minicomputers or even mainframes in centralized data processing configurations. A relatively small but growing number of organizations have switched from full-size computers to microcomputers for certain information processing tasks. That approach to computer utilization is variously termed "downsizing" or, more optimistically, "right sizing" by its proponents. More philosophically, some sociologists and futurists view the advent of powerful desktop computers as the basis for an information processing revolution that will drastically alter the character of our society and economy. Certainly, the development of microcomputers has made computing power available to many libraries that otherwise could not afford it.

Microcomputers have historically been categorized by the word sizes of the microprocessors on which their computing capabilities are based. Introduced in the mid- to late 1970s, the first popular microcomputers

Palmtop computers combine a typewriter-style keyboard with a small screen. (Courtesy: ZEOS International)

featured 8-bit microprocessors, such as the Intel 8080/8085, the Zilog Z80, and the 6500 series developed by MOS Technology. While such microprocessors continue to be utilized in some consumer products, they are no longer attractive as microcomputer components. The installed base of 8-bit microcomputer systems has declined steadily and significantly since the early 1980s, as equipment manufacturers, software developers, and customers have moved on to newer, more advanced devices based on 16-bit and, most recently, 32-bit microprocessors. Once-popular 8-bit microcomputers—such as the Radio Shack TRS-80 series, Atari 800, Kaypro II, Xerox 820, Hewlett-Packard HP-125, and Zenith Z90—have long since been discontinued and are rarely encountered.

The long-lived Apple II product line is a notable exception. While its underlying technology is two decades old, it has incorporated enhanced models, such as the Apple IIgs, with its impressive graphics and audio processing capabilities. Many Apple II systems remain in use, particularly by elementary and secondary schools which have made substantial investments in Apple-compatible educational software. Apple II computers are likewise encountered in school libraries, and several library-specific software packages are available for them.

Customer interest in 8-bit technology faded quickly with the introduction of the IBM Personal Computer, the first commercially successful 16-bit microcomputer, in the early 1980s. Their larger word sizes gave 16-bit microprocessors several significant advantages over 8-bit devices. As previously noted, larger word structures generally result in faster operation, as data and instructions can be manipulated in larger increments. In addition, most 16-bit microprocessors feature timing circuits that operate at much faster clock rates than their 8-bit counterparts. Computationally intensive tasks are consequently performed more quickly. Sixteen-bit microprocessors support longer instructions which facilitate the development of complex programs; larger, more versatile instruction sets; and larger memory configurations. In scientific and technical applications, 16-bit words can represent larger numbers for greater computational range and accuracy. Many 16-bit microprocessors also support explicit multiplication and division instructions, thereby incorporating capabilities that most 8-bit microprocessors must simulate through software.

The original IBM Personal Computer and IBM PC/XT utilized the Intel 8088, a 16-bit microprocessor with an 8-bit data bus. It performed calculations and other data manipulations in 16-bit units but transported data between system components in 8-bit increments. IBM-compatible microcomputers—so-called clones—variously employed the Intel 8088 or the Intel 8086 microprocessor, which featured a 16-bit internal architecture and a 16-bit data bus. IBM also incorporated the 8086 into entry-level models in its PS/2 series. The Intel 80286 microprocessor, an enhanced version of the 8086, was first utilized in the IBM PC/AT and was quickly adopted by manufacturers of compatible devices. It was also incorporated into certain early models in the IBM PS/2 product line. By the late 1980s, the 80286—often simply described as the 286—had virtually replaced the 8088 and 8086 as the microprocessor of choice for entry-level, IBM-compatible microcomputers. At the time of this writing, 80286-based microcomputers were widely installed in various work environments, including libraries.

Since the late 1980s, however, microcomputer manufacturers have emphasized higher performance equipment configurations based on 32-bit microprocessors. Compared to 16-bit devices, 32-bit microprocessors feature more complex instruction sets, faster operating speeds, and much larger main memories. Timing circuits associated with such microprocessors operate at eight to 12 times the rate of those employed in 16-bit machines. Thirty-two-bit microcomputers with four to eight megabytes of random-access memory—seven to 14 times the maximum RAM configuration supported by the original IBM Personal Computer—are routinely encountered. Such powerful capabilities are essential for networked installations or for downsized implementations of the type described above. Prewritten software packages, including microcomputer-based library automation programs, increasingly require 32-bit machines; 80286-based systems cannot execute many newer programs. Most IBM-compatible microcomputers now incorporate the Intel 80386 and 80486 microprocessors, popularly termed the 386 and 486, respectively. So-called 386-class machines, once viewed as leading-edge devices to be reserved for the most complex microcomputing requirements, are now widely regarded as entry-level products. The narrowing price differential between 80386- and 80486-based systems makes the latter an attractive alternative for many libraries. At the time of this writing, their successor—popularly described as the Pentium processor—had been announced but not yet incorporated into commercially available microcomputers.

Macintosh and Amiga computer systems have utilized 32-bit microprocessors since their inception. The most powerful models employ the Motorola 68030 and 68040 microprocessors, which offer capabilities that are comparable to the Intel 80386 and 80486. They are increasingly supplanting older models based on the 68000 and 68020 microprocessors.

An increasingly important group of high-performance desktop computing devices are collectively categorized as "workstations." They are sometimes described as "technical workstations" or "Unix workstations" because they were initially utilized for computer-aided design (CAD) or other engineering applications, and they usually employ the Unix operating system described in chapter 2. Such products are manufactured by a growing number of companies, including Sun Microsystems, Intergraph, Silicon Graphics, and such traditional mainframe and minicomputer manufacturers as IBM, Hewlett-Packard, and Digital Equipment Corporation. As a group, workstations differ from microcomputers in their use of so-called RISC processors. The acronym RISC stands for Reduced Instruction Set Computing. As their name suggests, RISC processors support a relatively small repertoire of instructions. When compared to conventional computing devices, however, RISC processors can execute instructions more quickly. For added speed, some models feature "pipelining" techniques in which the next instruction to be processed is retrieved from main memory and decoded while the current instruction is being executed. Others incorporate multiple processors and employ parallel processing techniques.

The execution speed of RISC-based workstations is an important characteristic for computationally intensive scientific and technical applications. Their advantages over powerful 32-bit microcomputers are more difficult to determine for business and library implementations, where large amounts of data must be processed but calculation requirements are modest. Compared to IBM-compatible microcomputers and Macintosh systems, a relatively small selection of prewritten business software packages is available for workstations. Library-oriented programs are virtually nonexistent.

INPUT PERIPHERALS

As noted earlier, a computer system, as opposed to merely a computer, consists of a central processor and its associated peripheral devices, each of which is dedicated to one or more of the following specialized information-processing tasks: input, output, or storage. The function of the input peripherals is to convert human-readable information to the machine-readable form required by the central processor. The information to be converted is usually contained in typewritten or handwritten documents, called source documents, and the conversion process is variously called input or data entry.

Available input peripherals are customarily categorized by the conversion methods they employ. In library applications and business data processing, two types of equipment account for the majority of all input activity: keyboard-oriented devices and optical scanning equipment. Other, more specialized input peripherals, such as speech-recognition devices, are currently limited in capabilities and consequently in application. While they may play an important role in future computer systems, their library potential is unclear.

Keyboard-oriented Devices

As their name suggests, keyboard-oriented devices feature a typewriter-like keyboard at which the information to be converted is typed, character by character. Used in this context, the term *character* denotes a letter of the alphabet, numeric digit, punctuation mark, or other symbol encountered in books, journal articles, technical reports, business correspondence, and other textual documents. The first generation of keyboard-oriented input equipment recorded typed characters in machine-readable form on paper media such as cards or tape. Keypunch machines, which are

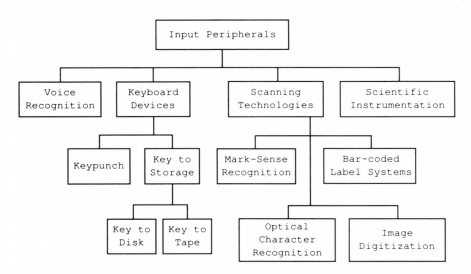

Although customarily categorized by the conversion method employed, the input peripherals collectively convert information to the machine-readable form required for computer processing.

still occasionally encountered in some computing installations, convert individually typed characters to a specified pattern of holes punched in successive columns of a specially designed card. In most cases, the cards are the familiar tabulating size (3.25 by 8.375 inches) and can contain up to 80 characters each, although other card sizes and character capacities have been utilized.

Typically, the cards are both punched and interpreted—that is, human-readable representations of individual characters are printed at the top of the column in which punches are recorded. Once punched and interpreted, the cards are taken to a card reader, a peripheral device that operates online to a computer. The card reader detects the pattern of holes punched in successive columns of each card and converts them to computer-processable form for immediate processing or transfer to other computer media, such as magnetic disks or tapes. The card reader may be located in the computer room itself or with related equipment in a separate facility called a remote job-entry (RJE) station.

Although it dominated data entry activity through the mid-1970s, keypunching is now considered an archaic input methodology. It survives only in those applications where a replacement system has not been implemented and is discussed here only for the sake of completeness. Reflecting the technology of the 1960s, keypunch machines are relatively large devices that occupy more floor space than some complete computer systems. Compared to conventional typing, keypunching procedures are cumbersome. The keypunch machine employs a somewhat different keyboard layout. The keyboard, being mechanical, responds slowly to key depression. Error-correction routines—which require repunching all or part of a card—are inconvenient and time-consuming, and waste card stock. Punched cards themselves are relatively expensive, vulnerable to mishandling or other damage, and sensitive to changes in temperature and humidity. They can also require considerable storage space.

Key-to-storage methodologies can address these limitations and reduce the cost of data entry. In the key-to-storage approach to data entry, typed characters are recorded in encoded form directly on magnetic storage media; punched cards are not created as intermediaries. Depending on the computer installation, character coding and recording may be based on the

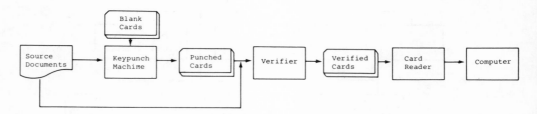

Keypunch machines are keyboard-oriented input devices that convert individually typed characters to a specified pattern of holes punched in successive columns of a paper card. The information is subsequently retyped to verify the correctness of the punched holes, and the verified card deck is inserted in a card reader for input to a computer.

ASCII or EBCDIC codes described above. In either case, key-to-storage methodologies are commonly divided into two groups: key-to-disk and key-to-tape. Key-to-disk is the methodology of choice for most data-entry applications.

The simplest key-to-disk configuration consists of a display terminal—that is, a video monitor and keyboard, to be described more fully in chapter 3—which operates online to a computer. Characters entered at the keyboard are transmitted to the computer, where they are first captured in random-access memory, and then transferred to magnetic disks for storage, pending later processing. The keyboard typically features a typewriter-style layout. Being electronic, it can accept characters as fast as the operator can enter them. Errors detected during keystroking can be corrected by simply backspacing and overtyping with the correct character or characters. In many applications, a key-to-disk terminal displays a formatted screen or template with labeled areas designed to prompt and guide an operator in the entry of specific data. The operator "fills in the blanks" by typing appropriate information into designated spaces, using the tab key or carriage return to advance from one labeled area to the next. As discussed in chapter 6, such formatted screens are used by bibliographic utilities and CD-ROM systems to simplify the entry and editing of cataloging records. Labels, consisting of words or special numeric codes, identify screen areas where the author, title, and other bibliographic information are to be typed. As a useful enhancement, some key-to-disk configurations in mincomputer and full-size computer installations utilize microcomputers as "intelligent" data-entry devices that can be programmed to perform various error-detection and entry-validation procedures prior to transmission. Such microcomputer-based equipment configurations may also provide temporary local disk storage for entered data which will subsequently be transmitted to a remote computer.

As their name suggests, key-to-tape systems use magnetic tape as a recording medium. Like key-to-disk systems, the typical key-to-tape unit features a video display and keyboard. Characters typed at the keyboard are captured on magnetic tape cassettes or cartridges for later transfer to a remote computer. In some cases, the data are transferred electronically; in others, the cassettes or cartridges are carried to a tape reader attached to the computer on which the data will be processed. The role of this tape reader is analogous to that of a card reader in keypunch installations. Key-to-tape devices were popular in the 1970s and early 1980s, when disk storage was much more expensive than it is today. In recent years, key-to-tape units have been largely supplanted by key-to-disk systems.

While key-to-storage equipment configurations can simplify typing tasks, keyboard-oriented input remains an error-prone activity. Depending on operator skill, as much as 5 percent of typed characters (over and above those errors detected and corrected during data entry) may be incorrect. While this percentage may seem relatively low, it is considered unacceptable in most applications. In the case of bibliographic data, for example, an erroneous character in an author's name, title, or subject heading will affect sorting operations. Where retrieval operations are based on exact matches of specified character strings, keystroking errors can render information unretrievable. For libraries making a long-term investment in machine-readable data to support online catalog access, circulation control, and similar applications discussed in later chapters, it is important that incorrectly typed characters be detected and corrected.

Several error-detection methods are possible. A computer program, for example, can print a listing of all entered data for proofreading. Items on the list can be compared to the contents of the source documents from which the information was entered. Similarly, in key-to-disk and key-to-tape systems, entered data can be displayed on a video screen for operator examination. Unfortunately, such visual verification techniques may leave incorrect characters undetected. Furthermore, proofreading is generally an ineffective method of detecting errors in numeric data. While it is conceptually appealing and easily applied, proofreading can rarely be recommended with confidence.

The preferred alternative is called keystroke verification. It is best explained with reference to punched card systems, where a keypunch-like device called a verifier is loaded with previously punched cards and the characters to be verified are retyped from the original source documents. The verifier detects the presence of holes in the successive columns of each punched card. When a discrepancy is detected between a retyped character and the previously punched pattern of holes, an alarm sounds; the card in question is removed for examination and, if necessary, a replacement card is punched. The same principle can be applied to key-to-storage systems. The character content of source documents is retyped and compared with characters previously entered and recorded on magnetic media. As noted above, one of the advantages of key-to-disk and key-to-tape systems is the ability to correct errors by overtyping. Keystroke verification is a highly effective method of error detection, since it is unlikely that the same errors will be made during both initial data entry and retyping.

As an obvious disadvantage, keystroke verification doubles the already substantial time and labor required for data entry. Consider, as an example, a library application involving the conversion of borrower identification data to machine-readable form for use in a computerized circulation control system. Assuming that the library has 30,000 registered borrowers and intends to record 125 characters of information about each of them, the initial data entry effort will involve 3.75 million keystrokes. Since the typical data entry operator can generate 7,000 to 10,000 keystrokes per hour, an estimated 375 to 535 hours will be required for the initial keystroking. Assuming an operator wage of $10 per hour, including fringe benefits, the estimated cost of labor for this initial work effort will be $3,750 to $5,350, exclusive of any supervision, equipment costs, or overhead charges. Allowing for keystroke verification of the entered data, the estimated labor cost will increase to $7,500 to $10,700.

Optical Scanning

The cost of data entry and verification should not be underestimated. Library systems analysts and others responsible for planning and implementing computer-based systems must calculate such costs and include them in their implementation budgets. In some installations, the labor cost for data entry and verification can exceed the cost of computer hardware and software. This is often the case in retrospective conversion projects involving large numbers of bibliographic records. In such situations, data-entry costs can be significantly reduced by purchasing or otherwise obtaining existing machine-readable data from bibliographic utilities or other sources discussed in later chapters. Where the local conversion of data is required, however, optical-recognition technologies can minimize data-entry labor by substituting scanning for keystroking.

Broadly defined, optical recognition uses reflected light to determine the information content of source documents. Once identified, the information is encoded and transferred to a computer, where it is typically recorded on magnetic media in the manner of the key-to-storage systems described above. Several types of optical-recognition technologies have been developed for special situations. Mark-sense recognition, for example, relies on specially designed input documents with demarcated spaces to be filled in by pencil. Completed documents are scanned by a machine which determines the meaning of individual marks by their locations. While library uses are limited, mark-sense recognition is widely employed in educational testing and survey applications where the source document is a specially designed answer sheet or questionnaire.

In barcode-label recognition, a specially designed label consisting of closely spaced lines of varying widths is used to encode a numeric identifier. A typical barcode label measures 1.5 to 2 inches wide by 0.6 to 0.75

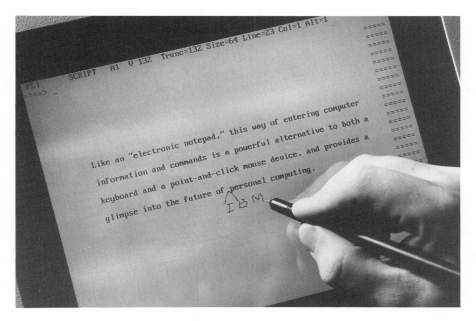

In the future, computers may accept handwritten input from penlike instruments.
(Courtesy: IBM Corporation)

inches high. In addition to the barcode itself, the label may contain the barcode number in human-readable form and other printed information. Various types of barcode patterns are available. Popular examples include Code 3 of 9, sometimes described as Code 39; Codabar; and Interleaved 2 of 5. Most barcode formats employ a 14- to 16-digit number. Barcode labels, which may be affixed to documents or other objects, are read by specially designed scanners that interpret the numbers they represent and transmit them to a computer.

The least expensive barcode scanner is a handheld light pen, sometimes described as a "barwand." It may be configured with a calculator-style keyboard that is used to activate commands and enter numbers from unreadable barcodes. Other configurations—which permit faster operation as well as more reliable reading of barcodes of marginal quality—include a CCD scanner, a handheld device that resembles a hair dryer, and a laser scanner, which is a desktop unit. As an advantage, laser scanners can read barcodes without contact, thereby preventing damage to the labels. Barcode labels are commonplace in supermarkets and other retailing operations. Their use to simplify the entry of item and borrower identifiers in library circulation control systems is discussed in chapter 5.

An interesting group of optical scanning devices—variously described as "document scanners," "page scanners," "document digitizers," or "image digitizers"—convert documents to electronic images for computer processing and storage. The scanning process is properly termed "document digitization," and the resulting electronic images are described as "digitized images." Document scanners are available in floor-standing,

Document scanners, like this desktop model, generate digitized images suitable for computer processing and storage. (Courtesy: Xerox Imaging Systems)

desktop, and handheld configurations. Intended for very high-volume applications, floor-standing models are typically equipped with high-speed automatic page feeders. Desktop scanners can be subdivided by mode of operation into flatbed and sheetfed varieties.

Flatbed models, as their name indicates, feature a flat surface on which pages are individually positioned for scanning. Because they can accommodate books, technical reports, and other bound volumes, flatbed scanners are particularly well suited to library applications. Most flatbed desktop scanners, like the photocopiers they closely resemble, feature a glass platen on which source documents are positioned face down. An optical head assembly and light source move across the glass beneath them. Sheetfed desktop scanners are sometimes described as "pass-through" or "pull-through" scanners. Source documents, inserted into a narrow opening, are transported by rollers across a stationary optical head assembly and light source. An automatic feeder, which can accommodate a stack of perhaps five to 50 pages, may be a standard or optional feature. Depending on equipment design, scanned pages are ejected at the back or at the bottom of the machine. Handheld scanners must be manually moved, slowly and in a straight line, across a page that is positioned face up on a desktop or other flat surface. Measuring approximately four inches across, most models are partial-page scanners.

Regardless of equipment design, a scanner divides a subject document into a series of small scannable units termed "picture elements," "pixels," "pels," or "dots." A given scanner's resolution is defined by the number of pixels per horizontal and vertical inch that it employs. The possibilities range from fewer than 75 pixels per inch to more than 1,000 pixels per inch, although not all scanners support that broad range. The scanning resolution selected for a particular application determines the sharpness of digitized images. As resolution increases, the size of each pixel decreases, and the amount of detail captured by the scanner is increased. While scanning resolutions of 75 to 100 pixels per inch are often adequate for graphic documents, 200 pixels per inch is the minimum resolution required for consistently legible digitization of typewritten office documents and typeset publications.

Resolution aside, a scanner exposes a document to a light source, such as a fluorescent lamp or a light-emitting diode (LED) array. Light reflected from individual pixels passes through a lens and onto a photosensor, which generates an electrical voltage that is proportional to the intensity of the light that strikes it. Light areas of a scan line, which are reflective, will generate the strongest voltages; dark areas, which absorb light, yield relatively weak voltages. The scanner creates an electronic image by converting the resulting electrical output into digital bit patterns that represent the tonal values of successively encountered pixels.

The simplest case of document digitization involves binary-mode scanning of black-on-white textual documents, with one bit being used to encode each pixel. Pixels that reflect light in excess of a predetermined threshold amount are considered white and are each encoded as zero bits. With most textual documents, such white pixels constitute the background areas of a page. Where light reflectance values and their associated voltages are lower than the predetermined threshold value, the corresponding pixels are considered black and are each encoded as a one bit. Such pixels typically represent the textual areas of a page. In most cases, the voltage threshold is set midway between black and white. Gray or colored pixels are treated as black or white, depending on their relative lightness or darkness. Some document scanners, however, support a gray-scale mode, which uses multiple bits to encode individual pixels, thereby representing gray tones within photographs or other documents. By using eight bits to encode each pixel, the scanner can differentiate among 256 shades of gray. An increasing number of document scanners support a color mode, which employs 24 bits to encode each pixel. Such devices can represent more than 16.7 million colors.

Document scanners are routinely employed in several applications of interest to libraries. In desktop publishing, for example, they can digitize photographs and illustrations for resizing, cropping, or other manipulation by image editing or page composition software. The images can then be inserted into page layouts. As described in chapter 4, electronic images of books, journal articles, technical reports, and other library documents can be recorded on optical disks or other computer storage media as an alternative to paper formats or microfilm. Assuming an appropriate equipment configuration, electronic images generated by document scanners can also be transmitted to facsimile machines, which are themselves examples of special-purpose document digitizers.

Optical character recognition (OCR), the most sophisticated and important type of recognition technology, uses document scanning and image analysis to identify characters contained in documents and convert them to the machine-readable form required for computer storage and processing. In a typical OCR implementation, a scanner converts paper documents to electronic images in the manner described above. An OCR program, which may operate within the scanner itself or on a computer to which the scanner is attached, analyzes the digitized images and attempts to identify the characters they contain. The recognized characters are represented by predetermined combinations of bits, just as if they had been typed at a keyboard. The encoded characters are usually transferred to a computer for recording and storage on magnetic disks or other media.

0123456789
ABCDEFGHIJ

1 2 3 4
H Y
d P H b

Some OCR products require that source documents be prepared in specially designed fonts, such as those depicted here. (Courtesy: MSI Data Corporation)

Because document scanning is an essential preliminary to optical character recognition, the terms *OCR* and *scanning* are often used interchangeably—but that usage is imprecise and misleading. Document scanning is merely one work step in an OCR system; the digitized images generated by document scanners must be analyzed by OCR programs and the recognized characters converted to computer-processable codes. As previously noted, a document scanner may incorporate processing circuitry with recognition programs stored in read-only memories. Such scanners are sometimes described as "OCR readers." Alternatively, the images generated by a document scanner may be transmitted to an external computer on which OCR programs are executed. Such software-based OCR implementations are increasingly popular. Since the late 1980s, the availability of relatively inexpensive document scanners and microcomputer-based optical character recognition programs has made OCR an attractively priced data-entry methodology.

Optical character recognition's potential for library applications is obvious: it offers a faster, more automated, and presumably less expensive alternative to the keyboard-oriented input devices described above. In theory, an OCR system should be able to accept a library's existing source documents—catalog cards, bibliographic lists, borrower rosters, and so on—and convert their contents to machine-readable form for computer processing. In actual practice, however, the range of acceptable input varies from system to system. Some OCR programs require that source documents be prepared according to rigid format specifications and in certain type fonts, such as OCR-A and OCR-B, that are optimized for machine recognition. Such devices have been utilized successfully for two decades in transaction processing applications involving specially designed business forms. To be useful for library applications, however, an OCR system must be able to recognize a variety of typeset, typewritten, and computer-printed fonts in different sizes and styles. Such OCR products are typically described as "multifont," or, for those that impose no significant restrictions on type styles, "omnifont" systems.

Most omnifont recognition capabilities are based on feature extraction methodologies which identify characters by their distinctive features. An uppercase letter "A," for example, is recognized as a character with two diagonal lines, joined at the top and bisected by a horizontal crossbar, while an uppercase "D" is recognized as having one vertical line joined at the ends by a loop. As their principal advantage, feature extraction methodologies transcend ornamental differences associated with particular type fonts, sizes, and styles; presumably, the letter "O" will be recognizable as a continuous loop whether it is printed in the Courier or the Times Roman font, boldface or italicized, large or small. A less versatile recognition technique, called matrix matching, compares the characters in source documents to reference sets or templates. The most sophisticated group of OCR products, sometimes described as Intelligent Character Recognition (ICR) systems, employ contextual clues, spelling dictionaries, and other tools as supplements to feature extraction.

OUTPUT PERIPHERALS

The function of output peripherals is to convert machine-readable, computer-processed information to human-readable form. They present the results of computer processing to users. As with input peripherals, there are a number of available output options, but some are inappropriate for library applications. Indicator lights and audio alarms, for example, are widely used as output mechanisms with computer-controlled instrumentation, in computer-assisted aviation, and in many automobiles, but they have no utility for bibliographic applications. Similarly, synthesized voice output has little significance for libraries. Instead, library automation relies on those output peripherals that print information onto paper, record it on microfilm, or display it on a screen.

Paper Output Devices

Although the use of computers to implement "paperless" information systems has been widely discussed, paper printers remain indispensable output devices. Even those computer systems that are heavily oriented toward screen displays rely on paper output for reference copies of selected information, for backup, or for the production of supplemental reports. As with other types of peripheral devices, available paper printers vary considerably in technology, output characteristics, operating speeds, and intended applications. As might be expected, large, centralized computers support fast, high-volume printing devices. In the past, impact-type line printers dominated such installations; increasingly, however, centralized computing facilities rely on nonimpact page printers.

A commonly encountered type of line printer, sometimes called a chain printer, features a printing chain that consists of characters represented on embossed metal slugs linked in an endless loop. The simplest devices

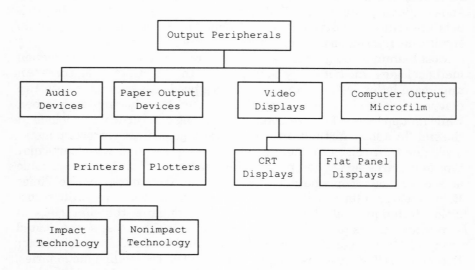

Subdivided above by the medium produced, the output peripherals convert the machine-readable results of computer processing to human-readable form.

can generate 60 to 64 different characters, including the uppercase roman alphabet, the numeric digits zero through nine, and the most widely used punctuation symbols. The most commonly used characters may appear multiple times within a chain, band, or belt. Sometimes the printable character set is extended to include the lowercase roman alphabet as well as European characters and accent marks. Special extended print chains have been developed for applications involving bibliographic data, the most famous being the so-called ALA print chain for IBM line printers.

Specific character content aside, a line printer's chain rotates horizontally at high speed. Paper and an inked ribbon move vertically between the print chain and a bank of hammers, one for each position on a line where a character can be printed. In most applications, the line printer accepts continuous, fanfolded paper stock. Each page measures 11 by 14 inches and contains up to 64 lines with as many as 132 characters or print positions per line. The line printer operates online to a computer which transmits information indicating the print positions for specified characters. As characters on the printing mechanism rotate to their designated print positions, individual hammers are activated to strike the paper, driving it against the inked ribbon and embossed characters. Since multiple hammers may be activated simultaneously, the device appears to print entire lines at one time, hence its name. Other line printers may utilize belts, bands, or drums rather than printing chains, but their output characteristics are similar to those of chain-type printers.

The nominal or rated speeds of available line printers range from several hundred to several thousand lines per minute, which is equivalent to a typing rate of about 4,000 to more than 40,000 words per minute. As might be expected, the fastest machines are typically encountered in mainframe installations. Slower line printers are commonly used with minicomputers or desktop systems. While they are many times faster than typewriters, line printers record data at a much slower rate than computers can process it. As a further complication, a printer's rated speed is typically degraded by such variables as line lengths, page lengths, and—most notably in library applications—the size of the printable character set. Thus, a printer capable of 1,000 lines per minute with an uppercase print chain may operate at only half that speed if the printable character set is extended to include the lowercase alphabet. Output speeds will be even further degraded by the addition of foreign characters or special symbols. Among other disadvantages, the quality of line printer output—which depends on ribbon condition, mechanical adjustments, and other factors—is, at best, fair. Carbon-interleaved paper is used to produce multiple copies, with resulting variations in quality from copy to copy. Line printers' output repertoire is limited to text; they cannot generate graphics. Many users find 11-by-14-inch fanfold paper cumbersome to handle, even when the pages are separated and bound.

Nonimpact page printers are designed to address these problems. Like line printers, they are intended for the high-volume applications encountered in centralized computer installations; but rather than using metal printing mechanisms, which strike a paper and inked ribbon, nonimpact

Typically designed for centralized mainframe and minicomputer installations, line printers can generate paper output at high speeds. (Courtesy: Mannesmann Tally)

printers employ other methods of generating characters. The most widely installed models use a combination of lasers and electrophotography. Based on definitions stored in electronic memory circuits, latent images of individual characters are generated as pixel patterns on a photosensitive medium. The latent images, which consist of closely spaced electrical charges, are developed through the application of finely powdered ink particles called toner. The resulting visible images are then transferred to paper at speeds ranging from two to five pages per second (approximately 7,200 to more than 20,000 lines per minute). As an alternative to lasers, some page printers employ light-emitting diodes. Other nonimpact technologies capable of high-speed hardcopy production include ion deposition printing, in which latent images are formed by negatively charged ions, and magnetographic printing, in which magnetic charges attract a toner that contains iron particles.

In addition to their substantial speed advantages, page printers offer more extensive typographic and document formatting capabilities than their line printer counterparts. They print onto single sheets of letter-size

Page printers like this midrange model offer a more versatile, nonimpact alternative to conventional line printers. (Courtesy: Printronix)

bond paper rather than onto the fanfolded stock used by line printers. The most powerful devices can print on both sides of a sheet of paper. Alternatively, the output can be reduced to fit four or even eight pages on a two-sided sheet. Page printers store character definitions for multiple type styles which can be printed in various sizes. Type styles and sizes can be interchanged within a single page. In a book catalog, for example, the body and tracings portion of a catalog record can be printed in one size and the collation and notes in another. Specified information, such as the main entry, can be emphasized by boldface printing or shading. Vertical and horizontal spacing can be adjusted to meet special application requirements. Because multiple copies are created by successive printer runs rather than carbon paper, quality is uniform from copy to copy. Images of business forms are stored by computer programs and superimposed on data at printing time, thereby eliminating the need to maintain inventories of preprinted blank forms for specific applications.

Slower impact and nonimpact printers are intended for desktop computer installations where workloads are lighter and speed requirements are less stringent. Operating speeds for such low-volume printers are typically measured in characters per second or pages per minute. Among low-volume impact printers, the most common device is a dot matrix printer, so called because it prints individual characters from a matrix of closely spaced dots created by selectively driving a set of needles—sometimes described as pins—into an inked ribbon. Depending on the model, the output speed ranges from 30 to more than 400 characters per second. A related group of nonimpact printers employs selectively heated needles to print dot matrix characters on thermally sensitive paper; popular in the 1970s, such thermal printers are now seldom encountered.

Because individual characters are generated from predefined needle patterns stored in internal memory circuits, a given dot matrix printer may have a large typographic repertoire, including accented characters and, in some cases, entire nonroman character sets. Output quality varies with the number of dots used to shape individual characters. The least expensive models use a nine-pin printing mechanism that yields satisfactory legibility for proof listings, charge-out slips, lists of books on order, and working copies of reports or similar documents. A more expensive group of dot matrix printers features 24-pin printing mechanisms. Their output is often described as "near letter quality," meaning that it approaches but does not quite equal the quality of a typewriter. For a library's correspondence, management reports, and important bibliographic documents, a true letter-quality printer is preferred. Introduced in the late 1960s, the earliest examples of such devices were based on the popular IBM Selectric typewriter. Since the mid-1970s, impact-type letter-quality printers for desktop computer installations have relied on interchangeable wheel-shaped printing elements. Commonly described as "daisywheel" printers, such devices are slower than their dot matrix counterparts. Speeds range from 10 to 50 characters per second. Some models feature wide carriages and automatic feeders for letter-size paper and envelopes.

Typewriter-like impact technology dominated low-volume desktop printer installations through the late 1980s. Since that time, microcomputer and workstation users have increasingly turned to nonimpact inkjet and laser printers. Inkjet printers create characters by spraying microscopic ink pellets at a sheet of paper. Output speeds of one to two pages per minute are typical. Desktop laser printers are the low-volume counterparts of the nonimpact page printers described above. They employ electrostatic printing technology based on a combination of lasers and xerography. Typical operating speeds range from four to 12 pages per minute. The fastest devices are intended for network installations where several microcomputers share a printer. As a group, inkjet and laser printers are well suited to microcomputer-based word processing and desktop publishing installations. They offer typewriter-like quality and excellent typographic versatility. Most models support multiple type styles and sizes. While individual characters are formed from dot matrix patterns, the dots are so closely spaced that the characters appear to be fully formed; a printing resolution of 300 dots per inch is typical.

Most of the paper output devices discussed to this point are principally designed to print textual documents that contain alphanumeric characters, punctuation marks, and perhaps some special symbols. Dot matrix printers, inkjet printers, and laser printers can also generate bar charts, line graphs, pie charts, and other diagrammatic information. Reflecting these capabilities, such devices are sometimes described as "graphic printers." They offer acceptable performance for business and library applications involving relatively straightforward graphic presentations. Some

Desktop laser printers, a type of nonimpact printer, provide high-quality output capabilities. (Courtesy: Hewlett-Packard)

graphic printers offer color printing as an output option. Of limited library utility, digital plotters are a special class of paper output devices designed for scientific, engineering, and other applications with complex graphic output requirements. Available plotters range from sophisticated and expensive electrostatic devices, which are employed in large-scale computer-aided design (CAD) installations, to the comparatively simple and inexpensive desktop machines, which use mechanized pens to draw graphs, diagrams, and charts. Plotters for engineering applications can often reproduce drawings in large formats.

Computer-Output Microfilm Recorders

Computer-output microfilm (COM) is a variant form of nonimpact output technology in which textual or graphic information is recorded on microfilm rather than printed on paper. Actually, a computer-output microfilmer—often described as a COM recorder—is both a computer peripheral device and a high-speed microfilmer. As a computer peripheral, a COM recorder can be configured for either online or offline operation. In the latter case, data generated by a computer must be brought to the COM recorder on magnetic tape. In either operating mode, COM recorders—like page printers—can generate document images at rates ranging from 7,000 to more than 20,000 lines per minute. Like line printers and page printers, COM recorders are designed for centralized operation in large data processing facilities. Many libraries use COM recorders operated by computer or micrographics service bureaus. Several companies—including Auto-Graphics, Brodart, and General Research Corporation—offer specialized COM services to libraries.

Regardless of the COM equipment's location, two recording technologies are available: (1) in CRT photography, information displayed on a cathode-

A compact, portable printer designed specifically for use with notebook computers.
(Courtesy: Eastman Kodak)

ray-tube screen contained within the COM recorder is microfilmed by a specially designed camera that uses conventional silver-gelatin photographic film as its recording medium; (2) in laser beam recording, a laser writes alphanumeric characters on thermally sensitive microfilm. With either method, document images are recorded in greatly reduced size on rolls of 16mm or 35mm microfilm or, more commonly, on 105mm by 148mm microfiche. As with all photographic processes, the film or fiche must be processed following exposure. An increasing number of COM recorders include a microfilm processor as an integral component.

In the typical application, a COM recorder is used to make a master roll or fiche from which multiple working copies will be produced, using a duplicator that may be attached directly to the recorder itself or operate as a separate device. The working copies are distributed for use in display devices called readers. Where paper enlargements of displayed images are required, combination units called reader/printers are available. Once a

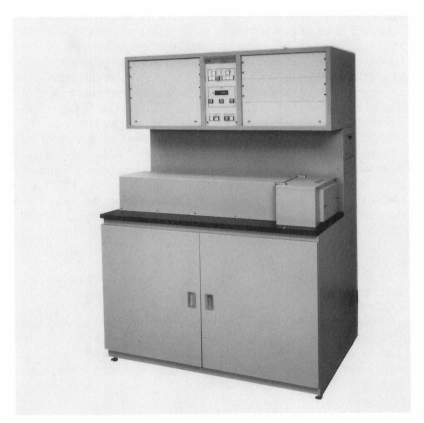

A COM recorder is a variant form of computer printer that generates human-readable information on microfilm or microfiche, rather than in hard copy. (Courtesy: Image Graphics)

master microfilm roll or microfiche is created, its information content cannot be updated or otherwise changed. For updating, a replacement roll or fiche must be produced.

Image capacities vary with the type of microform and amount of reduction employed. A single microfiche, for example, can contain the equivalent of 270 computer-printout-size (11-by-14-inch) pages reduced 48 to 1; 208 computer-printout-size pages reduced 42 to 1; 420 letter-size (8.5-by-11-inch) pages reduced 48 to 1; or 325 letter-size pages reduced 42 to 1. The capacity of a 100-foot roll of 16mm microfilm ranges from 1,800 computer-printout-size pages reduced 24 to 1 to 7,200 computer-printout-size pages reduced 48 to 1. With some COM recorders, page boundaries can be eliminated altogether, so that information is recorded as a series of continuous lines on roll film or fiche.

The typographic characteristics of available COM recorders resemble those of line printers. Using a sans serif type font that is well suited to legible microrecording at high reductions, most models can print the lowercase alphabet, accented characters, and other symbols used in bibliographic data. The earliest COM recorders were introduced in the late 1950s as high-speed alternatives to mechanical plotters in scientific and technical applications requiring the high-volume production of engineering drawings, maps, circuit diagrams, and similar computer-generated graphics. Alphanumeric COM recorders, designed for business data processing, were introduced in the late 1950s but were not widely utilized until the early 1970s. Initial, limited library interest in COM followed the introduction of machine-readable bibliographic data bases in the mid-1960s. The first library application—a computer-produced microfilm catalog—was reported in 1967 by the Lockheed Technical Information Center. As discussed in chapter 6, such applications became commonplace in the late 1970s and early 1980s. In addition to library catalogs, COM has been successfully utilized for serials holdings lists, various technical services reports, and popular micropublications, including the Magazine Index and the National Newspaper Index.

Video Display Units

Rather than printing human-readable information on paper or microfilm, a third class of output peripherals displays the results of computer processing on a screen. Such devices are collectively called video monitors or video display units (VDUs). As described in chapter 3, they are most often configured with a keyboard for operation as interactive computer terminals. Video display units without keyboards are widely encountered, however, in airports, public buildings, and other locations where computer-generated schedules, messages, and similar information may be viewed by groups of persons.

With or without a keyboard, most video display units incorporate a television-like cathode-ray tube (CRT) mounted in a plastic or metal case. Display sizes range from nine to 19 inches, diagonally measured, with 12 to 14 inches being the most common size; larger displays are usually employed in special situations, such as computer-aided design or computer-based page composition, where large documents must be displayed in their entirety. Screen size aside, a CRT employs a rapidly deflected electron beam to write information on a phosphorescent faceplate. The electron beam scans the faceplate in a series of horizontal lines composed of illuminable picture elements. In most cases, the displayed image lasts only a fraction of a second, and the phosphorescent picture must be repeatedly reilluminated or "refreshed."

While it has been criticized for bulkiness, high power consumption, and health hazards associated with radiation, CRT technology is well developed, readily available, reasonably priced, and well suited to a broad range of computer applications, including those requiring varied visual attributes and color display capabilities. The simplest, least expensive CRT-based video monitors are monochrome devices that display light characters on a dark background—a screen presentation described as standard video. Depending on the particular screen phosphor employed, the characters themselves may be white, green, or amber. For flexibility in application development, most devices give the user the option of displaying dark

Most video display units employ CRT technology. Display sizes typically range from nine to 19 inches, diagonally measured. (Courtesy: NEC)

characters on a light background—a screen presentation described as reverse video. Many computer programs rely on reverse video display of selected information for emphasis, although some applications utilize it as the normal display mode. Color video monitors, once regarded as a rarity, are now commonplace. Most devices are properly described as Red-Blue-Green (RBG) monitors because they provide separate input lines for each of the three primary video colors, plus an additional line for synchronization signals. Simpler composite video monitors employ an interleaved signal for color and synchronization signals. They typically lack the color clarity and image sharpness of RBG devices.

Alphanumeric video monitors, as their name indicates, can display textual information, including letters of the alphabet, numeric digits, and punctuation marks. Some models can also display accented characters, a potentially useful capability for certain library applications. Conforming to a de facto industry standard, most alphanumeric video monitors display 24 or 25 lines of textual information with 80 columns or character positions per line, although some computer terminals can display up to 132 characters per line. Special models, designed primarily for word processing applications, feature letter-size, vertically oriented screens that can display as many as 60 lines of text.

Bit-mapped CRTs offer both textual and graphic display capabilities. They generate graphic images by illuminating picture elements in a specified pattern. Available in both monochrome and color versions, low-resolution bit-mapped video monitors are commonly encountered in microcomputer installations. Examples include VGA displays for IBM-compatible microcomputers and Macintosh-compatible displays; both feature a display resolution of 640 (horizontal) by 480 (vertical) pixels. Higher resolution bit-mapped video monitors are available for desktop publishing and electronic imaging applications. Measuring 17 to 19 inches diagonally, they can display digitized document images or full pages of

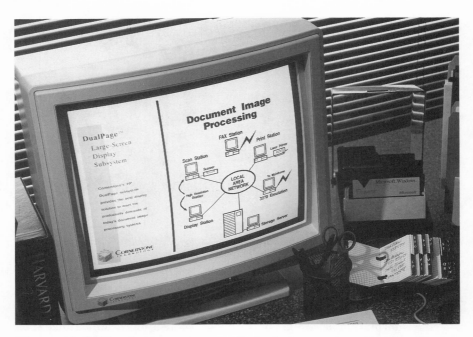

Bit-mapped, CRT-based video monitors can display both text and graphics. (Courtesy: Cornerstone Technology)

typed text to simplify page composition. The horizontal and vertical resolution of such displays exceeds 1,000 pixels. A special group of graphic CRT displays is designed for computer-aided design and other technical applications.

Despite the relative economy, varied visual attributes, and other significant advantages of CRT-based video monitors, alternative display technologies have attracted considerable attention among equipment designers and prospective customers. Collectively called "flat panel displays," these alternative technologies have characteristics and capabilities that CRTs lack. As their name indicates, flat panel displays offer a compact alternative to bulky cathode-ray tubes. Depth is their smallest dimension, and their light weight and low power consumption are particularly appropriate for portable computer configurations. As additional advantages, flat panel displays can withstand considerable vibration and shock. They can operate reliably under a wider range of environmental conditions than CRT devices, are less susceptible to magnetic or electrical interference, and emit no radiation. On the other hand, available flat panel displays are more expensive than their CRT counterparts and, while their display attributes have improved, they do not offer the quality and versatility of CRT devices.

Commonplace in portable computers, liquid crystal displays (LCDs) are currently the most widely utilized flat panel technology. LCDs use electricity to alter the light reflectance properties of liquid chemical compounds. Because they consume relatively little power, they are well suited to battery-operated equipment configurations. Display quality has improved steadily and significantly since the mid-1980s. The newest models provide highly legible, attractive monochrome or color displays. Alphanumeric and bit-mapped versions are available.

Among other flat panel technologies, electroluminescent (EL) displays feature a thin, polycrystalline film that glows when energized at specific points. The resulting images are bright and pleasing, with sufficient contrast for textual information plus grayscale capabilities for straightforward graphics applications. Alternating current (AC) flat panel devices are employed in large displays. First demonstrated in the early 1960s, AC gas plasma displays utilize an electric current to energize gas trapped between glass plates. The glowing gas forms a bright, high-contrast image. Because the display retains its image until erased, screen refreshment is eliminated. Display characteristics are unaffected by size. AC gas panels with one-meter screens were introduced in the 1980s, and displays measuring up to three meters diagonally have been demonstrated. As their name suggests, DC gas plasma displays utilize direct electrical current to display information by energizing trapped gas. Compared to their AC

Liquid crystal displays are widely utilized in portable computer configurations. The newest models can display bit-mapped graphics in gray tones and colors. (Courtesy: Tandy Corporation)

counterparts, they feature smaller screens which require refreshing. DC gas plasma video terminals have been available since the 1960s.

AUXILIARY STORAGE PERIPHERALS AND MEDIA

Auxiliary storage peripherals and media are designed to retain information in machine-readable form, pending computer processing. As such, they supplement the necessarily limited capacity of main memory, the latter being reserved for the storage of programs and data that the computer is processing at a given moment. Consequently, auxiliary storage is sometimes described as "secondary" storage to differentiate it from the "primary" storage provided by main memory. If auxiliary storage peripherals and media did not exist, data would have to be reentered before each incident of computer processing, and applications involving large amounts of information could not be computerized successfully.

Although early computer systems used paper media, such as punched cards or punched tape, for the recording and storage of machine-readable data, magnetic media have dominated auxiliary storage technology since the early 1970s. Even where punched cards continue to be used for input, data from cards are typically transferred to magnetic media prior to computer processing. Of the several types of magnetic storage media, magnetic tapes are the most economical, while magnetic disks offer the highest performance.

Magnetic Tape

Magnetic tapes have been successfully utilized for information storage since the 1920s. Audio recording was their initial application. Magnetic tape systems for computer installations date from the 1940s. Broadly defined, a magnetic tape is a ribbon or strip of plastic film coated with a magnetizable recording material, such as gamma ferric oxide. For computer use, magnetic tapes may be packaged on open reels, in cartridges, or in cassettes of various sizes and shapes. A given tape is recorded (written) and played back (read) by an auxiliary storage peripheral variously known as a magnetic tape drive or a magnetic tape unit. It incorporates a motorized mechanism that moves the tape past a specially designed electromagnet called a read/write head. Unrecorded tapes contain magnetic particles that are randomly aligned. A read/write head records individual bits by aligning the particles in a predetermined direction; recorded information is read by sensing the direction of previously aligned particles. While magnetic tape drives operate online—that is, connected to a computer—the tapes themselves are typically stored offline, on shelves or hanging from racks when not in use.

Half-inch magnetic tapes mounted on open plastic reels have been widely used in mainframe and minicomputer installations since the 1950s. The most common open reel measures 10.5 inches in diameter and contains 2,400 feet of tape. Such media are typically described as nine-track tapes because the bits that encode individual characters are recorded in nine parallel tracks across the tape's width. Data bits are

Half-inch magnetic tape, mounted on plastic reels of various sizes, has been widely utilized in mainframe and minicomputer installations for decades. (Courtesy: Verbatim)

recorded in eight of the tracks; the ninth track is reserved for a parity bit that is used to reduce recording and playback errors. Storage capacity per reel varies with recording density, which is measured in bits per inch (bpi). High-performance reel-to-reel magnetic tape drives operate at 6,250 bpi. They can record approximately 160 megabytes of data per 2,400-foot reel. The theoretical reel capacity is higher, but nine-track magnetic tape drives operate in a start/stop mode that requires blank spaces, called inter-record gaps, between blocks of recorded data. The gaps—which can occupy considerable space—reduce the data storage capacity of magnetic tape reels by 10 to 50 percent, depending on the size of data blocks. Other magnetic tape drives, including some older models, record data at 800 or 1,600 bits per inch. Allowing for inter-record gaps, they can store 21 megabytes or 40 megabytes per 2,400-foot reel. Regardless of media capacity, individual characters recorded on tape are usually represented in either the ASCII or EBCDIC code.

In 1984, IBM introduced the 3480 Magnetic Tape Cartridge Subsystem as a more compact and convenient alternative to magnetic tape reels in mainframe computer installations. 3480-type cartridge tape systems have since been introduced by other mainframe and minicomputer manufacturers and peripheral equipment suppliers. A 3480-type cartridge, sometimes described as a half-inch data cartridge, measures four inches by five inches by one inch. Data are recorded on half-inch magnetic tape in 18 parallel tracks. The most common tape length, 550 feet, provides 200 megabytes of storage capacity. Extra-length cartridges are available, and several vendors employ data compression methodologies to further increase cartridge capacity. Such methodologies, which are supported by various types of computer storage products, use special codes to reduce the amount of space required to store a given quantity of information.

Quarter-inch magnetic tape cartridges are principally intended for small computer systems, including desktop computer installations and microcomputer networks. Quarter-inch cartridges are actually cassettes, since they contain both a tape supply and a take-up spool. The half-inch cartridges described above contain only a supply spool; tape passes out of the cartridge during use and must be rewound before the cartridge is removed from the drive. Imprecise descriptive terminology aside, quarter-inch data cartridges are available in two sizes: the regular version measures 4 inches high by 6 inches wide by 0.625 inches deep and contains 150 to 1,020 feet of magnetic tape; a mini data cartridge measures 2 inches high by 3 inches wide by 0.5 inches deep and contains 140 to 308 feet of tape. At the time this chapter was written, capacities ranged from 45 megabytes to two gigabytes for regular-size data cartridges, and 40 megabytes to 128 megabytes for mini data cartridges. As with half-inch data cartridges, some vendors utilize compression methodologies to increase these capacities.

The magnetic tape systems described to this point employ longitudinal recording and playback methods in which stationary magnetic heads record and read data in parallel tracks running down the length of the tape. Among recent advances in computer storage peripherals, an increasingly popular group of magnetic tape products utilizes helical scan technology to record data in narrow tracks that are positioned in diagonal stripes across the width of the tape. Precise head positioning permits very close spacing of tracks and yields high storage capacities. Helical scan data recorders based on videotape technology have been commercially available since the 1970s. The newest models can store more than 10 gigabytes of data per VHS-type cassette. Since the late 1980s, a growing number of computer peripheral suppliers have offered helical scan recording systems based on 8mm videocassettes or four-millimeter digital audiotape. Eight-millimeter data cartridge systems support media capacities of 2.5 or five gigabytes, depending on the model selected. Digital audiotapes can record up to two gigabytes of data. Equipment manufacturers expect media capacities to increase significantly through a combination of improved recording densities and data compression.

Magnetic Disks

In computer installations, magnetic tapes are utilized for several purposes, including the storage of duplicate data files (file backup), the offline storage of information transferred from online media (data archiving), and the physical distribution of information in machine-readable form. In library applications, as described in later chapters, magnetic tape is widely employed for the sale or exchange of bibliographic data. Among their

Magnetic tape cartridges (top) offer a compact, convenient alternative to open reels. As an additional advantage, cartridge tape drives (bottom) are smaller than their open-reel counterparts.

Eight-millimeter data cartridges offer very high recording capabilities in a compact format. Autochanger devices can provide unattended access to large quantities of data. (Courtesy: Exabyte)

advantages, magnetic tapes offer high recording capacities at reasonable costs relative to other computer storage media. As a significant limitation, however, the recording or reading of data onto or from a particular portion of a tape requires that preceding portions be moved past the tape drive's read/write heads. Because this process is time-consuming, magnetic tape is typically reserved for applications in which data will be processed serially—that is, in the same order in which the data are recorded on tape. It is not a suitable storage medium for interactive computing applications in which data must be accessed rapidly and in more or less random order with respect to their recorded sequence. Such applications must use more expensive direct-access storage devices and media, of which magnetic disks are the most widely encountered and important example.

Magnetic disks, as their name implies, are platter-shaped media. For recording and playback purposes, magnetic disks are divided into concentric tracks, with successive bits stored in linear fashion within each track. The tracks are divided into sectors. Like the tape drives described above, disk drives incorporate electromagnetic read/write heads for recording and playback. The read/write heads are mounted on retracting

Fixed, rigid magnetic disks, shown here in a cutaway view of a hard drive, are the primary form of online auxiliary storage for machine-readable data. (Courtesy: Seagate)

access arms. To read data from, or record data onto, a given portion of a disk surface, the drive positions the read/write head above a designated track, while the rotating platter brings the desired sector under the electromagnetic mechanism. Reading or recording occurs at very high speed as the indicated sector location passes by. Actual recording, as described above, is performed by aligning the recording material in predetermined directions. Alignment toward the north pole of a magnetic field, for example, may record the one bits in digitally coded information, while alignment toward the south pole records the zero bits. Playback of recorded bits involves the detection of alignment patterns. Because the drive's access arm can move the read/write head directly to a given track without passing serially through all data recorded in preceding tracks, magnetic disk systems can read and record data at significantly faster rates than is possible with magnetic tape.

Magnetic disks may be fixed in or removable from their drives. Their platters—the substrates on which a magnetizable recording material is coated—may be rigid or flexible. Fixed magnetic disk drives, popularly termed "hard disk drives," have rigid aluminum platters. They are the auxiliary storage peripherals of choice in high-performance computing applications requiring rapid, online access to recorded information. Most models are configured with a stack of five or more platters and one read/write head for each recording surface. Storage capacities vary with platter size and recording densities. Since the 1950s, platter sizes have decreased steadily, while technological innovations and improved product designs have significantly enhanced recording densities and capacities. Magnetic disks that measure nine to 12 inches in diameter are widely encountered in mainframe and larger minicomputer installations. Storage capacities of such devices routinely exceed several gigabytes, and multidrive configurations can provide online access to hundreds of gigabytes.

Reflecting the trend toward smaller media, some 5.25-inch fixed magnetic disk drives offer storage capacities that approach or exceed those of larger platters. Models with several gigabytes of storage capacity are available. Some manufacturers offer arrays of high-capacity 5.25-inch hard disk drives as alternatives to larger fixed magnetic disk systems in full-size and minicomputer installations. For microcomputer installations, typical capacities of 5.25-inch fixed magnetic disk drives range from 40 megabytes for low-priced units intended for entry-level personal computers to more than 500 megabytes for drives suitable for powerful desktop workstations and networked microcomputers. Obviously, 3.5-inch fixed magnetic disk drives are well suited to portable computer systems. They also address the increasingly strong preference of microcomputer purchasers for desktop devices with small dimensions. Storage capacities of 3.5-inch hard disk drives are necessarily constrained by a combination of small recording surfaces and low height, which limits the number of platters they can contain. Capacities exceeding 200 megabytes are available, and continuing improvements are expected. The 2.5-inch hard disk drives, which have capacities of 40 to 80 megabytes, are principally intended for portable computer configurations.

Fixed magnetic disk drives, as noted above, are the principal storage peripherals in computer applications requiring rapid, online access to machine-readable information. As a potentially significant constraint, however, fixed disks can become full, necessitating the purchase of additional drives, the deletion of information, or the transfer of data to magnetic tape or other media. Addressing this limitation, magnetic disk systems that utilize removable media provide infinite storage capacity with a given hardware configuration, although some data will necessarily be stored offline at any given time. Where confidential or otherwise sensitive or valuable information is involved, removable magnetic disk systems offer a potentially attractive security advantage, since media can be stored in safes, vaults, or other locked repositories when not in use.

Introduced in the 1960s, the earliest removable magnetic disk systems were intended for computer installations that could not afford enough fixed disk capacity to meet their data storage requirements. Such devices, which were widely encountered in full-size and minicomputer installations through the early 1980s, featured removable disk packs consisting of multiple rigid platters mounted on a common spindle. While no longer popular, drives that accept removable disk packs are still available for sale, and some older devices remain in use. When not mounted in their drives, the disk packs are stored under a protective translucent plastic cover that resembles a hat box. A newer group of removable rigid magnetic disk drives employs 5.25-inch cartridges as recording media. Principally intended for desktop computer installations, such hard disk cartridges can store from 40 megabytes to more than 100 megabytes of information.

Whether fixed or removable disks are involved, a hard disk drive's read/write head is suspended aerodynamically above the surface of a spinning platter. Should the drive become contaminated by dust or pollutants, or should its power supply be momentarily interrupted, the read/write head will make contact with the disk surface, eradicating some or all of the recorded data. This malfunction, commonly called a "head crash," necessitates the implementation of backup procedures for the protection and recovery of data stored on hard disks. The usual protection method involves the periodic copying of data onto magnetic tape for offline storage. Depending on the frequency with which data are generated, this copying procedure may be performed one or more times daily. In the event of a disk system failure, stored data can be reconstructed up to the point of last

Hard disk cartridge systems provide removable online storage for desktop computer installations. (Courtesy: SyQuest)

copying. For more comprehensive protection against disk system failures, some computer installations employ redundant architecture in which data are simultaneously recorded onto two hard disk drives. Should the system's primary drive fail, the backup drive is automatically activated.

Floppy disk drives are the most widely used examples of removable magnetic disk devices. Floppy disks—variously called flexible disks or, simply, diskettes—are circular pieces of polyester coated with a magnetizable material. Media diameters range from 2 inches to 8 inches, with 5.25 inches and 3.5 inches being the most widely encountered varieties. The 5.25-inch diskettes are enclosed in square paper envelopes that offer some protection against contaminants and rough handling; 3.5-inch media are encapsulated in protective plastic cartridges. Storage capacities vary with media size and recording formats. In IBM-compatible microcomputer configurations, for example, 5.25-inch double-sided/double-density (DS/DD) diskettes can store 360 kilobytes. Their 3.5-inch counterparts can store 720 kilobytes. Double-sided/high-density (DS/HD) diskettes can store 1.2 megabytes in the 5.25-inch configuration and 1.44 megabytes in the 3.5-inch configuration.

Compared to hard disk systems, floppy disk drives are simpler and less expensive. Because those drives' read/write heads are normally in contact with the diskette's surface, crashes are not a problem. As potentially significant disadvantages, however, floppy disk drives operate much more slowly and provide online access to smaller amounts of data than do their hard disk counterparts. Addressing this limitation, several manufacturers have introduced floppy disk drives that support higher media capacities. Perhaps the best-known example is the Bernoulli Box product line developed by Iomega Corporation. Available for various types of desktop computers, it can record more than 100 megabytes of data on specially designed 5.25-inch diskettes. "Floptical" disk drives, a recent innovation in floppy disk technology developed by Insite Peripherals, combine magnetic data recording with optical control signals. A 3.5-inch floptical diskette offers 21 megabytes of storage capacity. As an advantage, floptical drives can also read conventional double-sided/double-density and double-sided/high-density diskettes.

Optical Storage

While the disk and tape systems described in preceding sections utilize magnetic fields to orient metallic particles in desired directions, optical storage systems use lasers to record information by selectively altering the light reflectance characteristics of specially designed media. The laser-induced alterations may take any of several physical forms, including light-scattering holes, bumps, or bubbles. Regardless of form, optically recorded information is read by a laser and pickup mechanism which detects variations in reflected light, much as magnetic read/write heads sense variations in the alignment of metallic particles. The playback laser operates at lower power or a different wavelength than the laser used for optical recording.

As their most attractive and significant characteristic, optical storage media support very high areal recording densities and offer much higher storage capacities than magnetic media of comparable size. Optical media can consequently accommodate huge quantities of character-coded text, quantitative data, and graphic images. Optical disks, the most important and fully developed type of optical storage product, can be divided by technology and intended application into two broad categories: read-only optical disks, which are produced by a mastering process and contain prerecorded information, and read/write optical disks, which are purchased blank and permit the direct recording of information by end users.

In the typical production cycle for read-only optical disks, the information to be recorded is submitted in a prescribed format to a production facility. The information is usually submitted on magnetic tape. In some cases, a premastering system or service bureau reformats, edits, indexes, and otherwise processes the information prior to submission. At the optical disk factory, a laser beam recorder creates a glass master disk from which one or more stampers are generated. Individual plastic copies are produced from the stampers, usually by injection molding. The stamper's surface contours, which represent information encoded as combinations of microscopic pits and spaces, are impressed on the plastic copies, which are then distributed or sold to end users. The copies themselves have no recordable properties; they are designed to be read in playback devices that have no recording mechanisms. The copies have a protective coating, but they are not encapsulated in cartridges.

Derived from technologies originally developed for consumer applications, read-only optical disks can be subdivided into two broad groups: those based on video disk technology, and those based on compact disc technology. As their name suggests, read-only video disks contain television images. The images are encoded in analog, rather than digital form, with accompanying stereo sound. As discussed in chapter 4, read-only video disks have been effectively utilized in a variety of interactive display and training applications. Compact disc is the generic designation for a group of read-only optical disk formats based on specifications developed jointly by Sony and Philips. The most widely encountered type of compact disc is a rigid plastic platter that measures 12 centimeters (approximately 4.75 inches) in diameter. A nine-centimeter (approximately 3.5-inch) version is also available. The various compact disc formats are typically categorized by the type of information they contain. The best-known formats are intended for music and/or video recording. They include Compact Disc-Digital Audio (CD-DA), Compact Disc-Video (CD-V), and Compact Disc-Interactive (CD-I). Pertinent to this discussion, Compact Disc-Read Only Memory (CD-ROM) is the compact disc format for computer-processable information. A 4.75-inch CD-ROM can store approximately 540 megabytes; the approximate storage capacity of a 3.5-inch CD-ROM is 180 megabytes. The recorded information is read by specially designed drives which typically operate as microcomputer peripherals. In library applications, CD-ROM technology is utilized for data base publishing,

*CD-ROM is a read-only optical disk format for computer-processible data.
A recordable variety, described as CD-R, is also available. (Courtesy:
Verbatim)*

including the preparation of library catalogs. Examples are discussed in chapters 6 and 7.

Read/write optical disks, as defined above, permit direct recording of information in the manner of magnetic media. They are available in write-once and rewritable varieties. Write-once optical disks are sometimes described as WORM media, the acronym variously standing for Write Once Read Many or Write Once Read Mostly. Write-once optical disks feature a recording material that is capable of absorbing laser light, converting it into thermal energy, and producing localized, detectable reflectivity transformations in areas irradiated by the laser. The recording material, which varies from product to product, is coated on platter-shaped substrates which measure 5.25, 12, or 14 inches in diameter. Capac-

Optical disk jukeboxes can provide unattended access to very large quantities of information recorded on multiple WORM or rewritable cartridges. (Courtesy: Aquidneck Systems International)

ities range from 600 megabytes to more than 10 gigabytes per double-sided disk.

Write-once media are not erasable. Once information is recorded in a given area of a write-once optical disk, that area cannot be reused. Such disks can consequently become irrevocably full. With rewritable optical disks, in contrast, the contents of previously recorded media segments can be erased and replaced with new information. Like their magnetic counterparts, rewritable optical disks are reusable. The majority of rewritable optical disk systems employ magneto-optical (MO) recording, a hybrid technology that uses specially designed magnetic media for storage, and lasers for recording and playback. Rewritable optical disks are available in 3.5-inch and 5.25-inch sizes. Media capacities range from 128 megabytes to more than one gigabyte.

Like floppy disks, optical disks are removable storage media. Write-once and rewritable optical disks are encapsulated in protective cartridges. Optical disk drives are available for computer configurations of all types and sizes. Autochangers, sometimes described as jukebox units, can provide unattended access to large quantities of information recorded on multiple optical disk cartridges. The cartridges, which are stored on shelves or in bins, are automatically located and mounted in an optical disk drive when required by a particular computer program.

While optical disks are the most fully developed type of optical storage product, optical cards and optical tapes also exist. Optical cards—sometimes termed "optical memory cards" or "optical digital data cards"—are wallet-size media coated with a non-erasable optical recording material. Intended for microcomputer installations, the best-known example can store approximately 2.8 megabytes. The information is recorded and played back by a peripheral device called an optical card reader/writer. Although optical card technology was introduced in the early 1980s, commercial implementations have been limited to demonstration projects and field tapes, principally because reader/writers have not been routinely available. Among potential library applications, optical cards offer an electronic alternative to microfiche for document image storage, as well as a portable publishing medium for books or other textual documents.

Optical tape, as its name suggests, is a ribbon of film coated with an optical recording material. Compared to magnetic tape, it offers much greater recording capacity. A 12-inch reel of optical tape, measuring 35mm wide by 2,400 feet long, can store one terabyte (one trillion bytes) of data—the equivalent of over 6,000 reels of nine-track magnetic tape recorded at 6,250 bits per inch. Such high-capacity media are obviously intended for large computer installations. They are of particular interest in scientific and technical applications where large quantities of data are generated by instrumentation. Several companies have announced plans to develop lower-capacity optical tapes packaged in cartridges and cassettes, but such products were not commercially available at the time of this writing.

Reels of optical tape offer terabyte-level storage capacities. They are of particular significance for scientific and technical applications involving voluminous amounts of data generated by instrumentation. (Courtesy: ICI Imagedata)

SUMMARY
A computer hardware system consists of a central processor and its associated peripheral devices. The central processor, which performs the actual work of computation, contains interrelated arithmetic/logic, control, and memory circuitry, the last of these being designated for the storage of the data and programs with which a computer system is working at a given moment. These data and programs are encoded in machine-readable binary form, each character being represented by a predetermined pattern of bits. The physical representation of bits varies with the type of memory component utilized. Newer computers feature semiconductor memories in which individual characters are represented by the presence or absence of electrical current in a specified combination of circuits.

Historically, central processors have been categorized as full-size computers, minicomputers, or microcomputers, depending on such factors as physical size, processing power, intended application, and price. Recent advances in electronics technology, however, have blurred whatever clear distinctions previously existed between these categories. Smaller full-size computers, for example, are indistinguishable from the most powerful minicomputers, while the most powerful microcomputers offer capabilities that equal or exceed those of certain minicomputers. A relatively new group of desktop computers, collectively described as workstations, is particularly difficult to categorize; such devices offer powerful information processing capabilities that are particularly attractive for scientific and engineering applications.

While generalizations are necessarily subject to exceptions, full-size computers are usually operated by centralized data processing facilities within large organizations, while minicomputers may be installed in decentralized departments or in medium-sized organizations. In libraries, minicomputers are often dedicated to a specific task, such as circulation control or online catalog access. Most microcomputers are designed for installation at the office or desk level, although there has been much recent interest in microcomputer networks as alternatives to larger systems for complex information processing tasks.

While central processors perform the actual work of computation, the peripheral devices provide specialized input, output, or auxiliary storage capabilities. The input peripherals convert human-readable information to the machine-readable form required by the central processor. In library applications, most input operations rely on keyboard devices at which information is typed, character by character. Key-to-storage technology, particularly key-to-disk systems, is currently the dominant keyboard-oriented data-entry methodology. As an alternative to keystroking, optical recognition technologies scan documents, converting their content to machine-readable form automatically. Barcode label recognition, a limited form of optical recognition, is used in many library circulation control systems. Optical character recognition (OCR), which uses reflected light to identify the individual characters contained in documents, is of more general utility. Document digitizers convert textual or graphic documents to electronic pictures for computer processing and storage. They are encountered in desktop publishing and image storage and retrieval systems, among other applications.

The output peripherals convert machine-readable, computer-processible data to human-readable form. In library applications, the resulting information may be printed on paper, recorded on microfilm, or displayed on a screen. Available paper printers range from very expensive devices with operating speeds measured in lines per minute or pages per second to relatively inexpensive character printers designed for decentralized installations. In both groups, individual models vary considerably in their typographic capabilities; some devices are capable of printing accented characters, nonroman alphabets, and other symbols encountered in bibliographic data. A special class of paper printers, digital plotters, is designed for graphic output, principally in scientific and engineering applications. A COM recorder is a variant form of computer printer which transfers machine-readable data to human-readable information on microfilm or microfiche rather than paper. The resulting miniaturized document images can be enlarged for display on a readerscreen or copied onto paper using a reader/printer.

Video display units likewise present the results of computer processing on a screen. Most models incorporate a television-like cathode ray tube (CRT) as the display mechanism. Display capabilities vary considerably from model to model; a number of available units can display accented characters and other special symbols. Among flat panel alternatives to CRT technology, liquid crystal displays (LCDs) are widely used in portable computers.

Auxiliary storage peripherals and media are designed to retain information in machine-readable form, pending computer processing or reprocessing. They thus serve as extensions to the central processor's necessarily limited memory section. While early computer systems used paper storage media, magnetic tapes and disks have dominated auxiliary storage since the 1970s. Magnetic tape offers the advantages of high storage capacity and reasonable media cost, but it is typically reserved for applications in which data will be processed serially rather than randomly. To access a particular portion of a tape, all preceding portions must be traversed.

Magnetic disks are the preferred storage media in applications where data must be continuously available for rapid access in an unpredictable manner. Magnetic disks are available in fixed and removable varieties. Fixed magnetic disk drives, so-called hard disk drives, are the storage peripherals of choice in high-performance, online computing applications. Removable magnetic disks may have rigid or flexible substrates; the latter include conventional floppy disks, which are widely employed in small computer installations.

Compared to magnetic media, optical storage products offer very high recording capacities. Optical disks are available in two varieties: (1) read-only optical disks, including video discs and compact discs, contain prerecorded information; (2) read/write optical disks permit direct recording. Read/write optical disk drives and media are available in write-once and rewritable models. Optical card and optical tape systems offer higher storage capacities than their magnetic counterparts, but commercial implementations have been limited.

ADDITIONAL READING

ANCHORDOGUY, M. *Computer, Inc.: Japan's Challenge to IBM*. Cambridge, Mass.: Harvard University Press, 1989.

ASPRAY, W. *John von Neumann and the Origins of Modern Computing*. Cambridge, Mass.: MIT Press, 1990.

ASPRAY, W., ed. *Computing before Computers*. Ames: Iowa State University Press, 1990.

BASHE, C, et al. *IBM's Early Computers*. Cambridge, Mass.: MIT Press, 1986.

BENIGER, J. *The Control Revolution: Technologies and Economic Origins of the Information Society*. Cambridge, Mass.: Harvard University Press, 1986.

BERNSTEIN, J. *The Analytical Engine: Computers—Past, Present, and Future*. New York: Morrow, 1981.

BRANDON, D., and HARRISON, M. *The Technology War: A Case for Competitiveness*. New York: Wiley-Interscience, 1987.

BRAUN, E., and MacDONALD, S. *Revolution in Miniature*. New York: Cambridge University Press, 1982.

BROD, C. *Technostress: The Human Cost of the Computer Revolution*. Reading, Mass.: Addison-Wesley, 1987.

BURKS, A., and BURKS, A. *The First Electronic Computer: The Atanasoff Story*. Ann Arbor: University of Michigan Press, 1988.

CERUZZI, P. *Reckoners: The Prehistory of the Digital Computer from Relays to the Stored Program Concept, 1935–1945*. Westport, Conn.: Greenwood Press, 1983.

CHPOSKY, J., and LEONSIS, T. *Blue Magic: The People, Power, and Politics behind the IBM Personal Computer*. New York: Facts on File, 1988.

DeLAMARTER, R. *Big Blue: IBM's Use and Abuse of Power*. New York: Dodd, Mead, 1986.

DERTOUZOS, M., and MOSES, J., eds. *The Computer Age: A Twenty Year View*. Cambridge, Mass.: MIT Press, 1979.

FERGUSON, C., and MORRIS, C. *Computer Wars: How the West Can Win in a Post-IBM World*. New York: Times Books, 1992.

FISHMAN, K. *The Computer Establishment*. New York: Harper and Row, 1981.

FLAMM, K. *Creating the Computer*. Washington, D.C.: The Brookings Institution, 1987.

GASSE, J. *The Third Apple: Personal Computers and the Cultural Revolution*. San Diego: Harcourt Brace Jovanovich, 1987.

GOLDBERG, A., ed. *A History of Personal Workstations*. New York: ACM Press, 1988.

GOLDSTINE, H. *The Computer from Pascal to von Neumann*. Princeton, N.J.: Princeton University Press, 1972.

JORGENSEN, F. *The Complete Handbook of Magnetic Recording*. Blue Ridge Summit, Penn.: Tab Professional and Reference Books, 1988.

KEMENY, J. *Man and the Computer*. New York: Scribner's, 1972.

LAVINGTON, S. *Early British Computers: The Story of Vintage Computers and the People Who Built Them*. Bedford, Mass.: Digital Press, 1980.

MALLINSON, J. *The Foundations of Magnetic Recording*. San Diego: Academic Press, 1987.

MOREAU, R. *The Computer Comes of Age: The People, the Hardware, and the Software*. Translated by J. Howlett. Cambridge, Mass.: MIT Press, 1984.

NORA, S., and MINC, A. *The Computerization of Society*. Cambridge, Mass.: MIT Press, 1980.

NYCE, J., ed. *From Memex to Hypertext: Vannevar Bush and the Mind's Machine*. Boston: Academic Press, 1991.

RANADE, S. *Mass Storage Technologies*. Westport, Conn.: Meckler Corporation, 1991.

RANDELL, B., ed. *The Origins of Digital Computers: Selected Papers*. 2d ed. New York: Springer-Verlag, 1975.

RITCHIE, D. *The Computer Pioneers: The Making of the Modern Computer*. New York: Simon and Schuster, 1986.

ROSE, F. *West of Eden: The End of Innocence at Apple Computer*. New York: Viking, 1989.

SAFFADY, W. *Optical Storage Technology 1992: A State of the Art Review*. Westport, Conn.: Meckler Corporation, 1992.

————. "Stability, Care, and Handling of Microforms, Magnetic Media, and Optical Disks." *Library Technology Reports* 27 (1): 5–116 (1991).

SEADLE, M. *Automating Mainframe Management: Using Expert Systems with Examples from VM and MVS*. New York: McGraw-Hill, Intertext Publications, 1991.

SIERRA, H. *Introduction to Direct Access Storage Devices*. Boston: Academic Press, 1990.

SMITH, D., and ALEXANDER, R. *Fumbling the Future: How Xerox Invented, Then Ignored the First Personal Computer*. New York: William Morrow, 1988.

TANENBAUM, A. *Structured Computer Organization*. Englewood Cliffs, N.J.: Prentice Hall, 1990.

WATSON, T., and PETRE, P. *Father, Son & Co.: My Life at IBM and Beyond*. New York: Bantam Books, 1990.

WHITE, R. *Introduction to Magnetic Recording*. New York: IEEE Press, 1985.

YOURDON, E. *Nation at Risk: The Impact of the Computer Revolution*. Englewood Cliffs, N.J.: Prentice Hall, 1986.

2

Computer Software

The term *hardware,* as defined in the preceding chapter, denotes the equipment components in a computer system. The term *software* denotes the programs, or predefined sequences of instructions, that a computer executes to accomplish information processing tasks. The software concepts discussed in this chapter are normally applicable only to the central processor in a computer system. Most peripheral devices operate under the control of the central processor and are not programmable in the conventional sense.

The hardware components in a computer system are visible, tangible, and readily comprehensible; software, on the other hand, is an intellectual product. It does have a tangible manifestation: the individual instructions that make up a computer program may be written or printed on paper in the more or less human-readable form described later in this chapter. Such human-readable instructions, however, must be converted to machine-readable form for computer execution. As with data, this conversion is typically accomplished by typing the instructions, character by character, at a computer input device, such as a key-to-disk system. The resulting machine-readable program is typically maintained on a magnetic or optical storage medium from which it is loaded into the central processor's random-access memory for execution. This is most obviously the case with prewritten software packages for microcomputers, most of which are distributed on floppy disks. Prewritten programs for mainframes, minicomputers, and workstations are typically distributed on magnetic tape reels or data cartridges. Taking advantage of the high storage capacity of optical disks, several publishers employ CD-ROM as a distribution medium for large software collections.

In some computer configurations, frequently executed programs—and, occasionally, data—may be permanently recorded in the read-only memory circuits described in chapter 1. This approach to information storage is typically used for programs that must be immediately and continuously available to the central processor. Programs stored in this manner are termed "firmware" to reflect their embodiment in hardware components and to distinguish them from conventional software, which is maintained on auxiliary storage media for transfer to the central processor's random-access memory when required. Among the most important uses of firmware are "bootstrap" programs, which start a computer system and instruct it to load control programs located on a disk, and diagnostic programs, which check the operating status of specific hardware components when a computer is first turned on. In most computer configurations, however, firmware is used sparingly, principally because read-only memory circuits are relatively expensive storage media. As an additional constraint, programs stored in firmware must be updated by replacement of hardware components. Conventional software, in contrast, is easily updated by issuing replacement diskettes or tapes.

It is possible to build computing equipment with fixed electronic circuitry designed to perform one or more specific operations; certain calculators and electronic typewriters are examples of such products. The power and versatility of computers, however, are largely derived from their general-purpose, programmable nature. However, at a time when a varied and flexible range of hardware components is readily available and increasingly affordable, problems of software development constitute the most significant impediment to the implementation of computer systems in both library and nonlibrary installations. This chapter discusses the characteristics and problems of computer software, beginning with a description of the two basic types of software and the role of system software and programming languages in computer systems. Later sections deal with application software, the software development process, and prewritten software packages. Throughout the chapter, emphasis is placed on concepts and terminology essential to librarians who must purchase programs from software developers or communicate their software requirements to data processing personnel.

SYSTEM SOFTWARE

Historically, the computer industry has distinguished system software (programs that enable a computer to function and control its own operations) from application software (programs that perform some user-specified task, such as the printing of purchase orders in an acquisitions application, the computing of fines for overdue materials, or the production of bibliographic lists). Until recently, the computing industry viewed the development of application software as the user's responsibility. As discussed later in this chapter, mainframe and minicomputer installations continue to rely heavily on customized programming for specific applications. Since the 1950s, however, most computer manufacturers have provided prewritten system software for use with their equipment. In addition, some software development companies specialize in system programs for specific types of computers.

Operating Systems

The most important category of system software is a group of multi-functional supervisory programs variously called an operating system, executive system, or system monitor. At the most fundamental level, an operating system identifies users and determines whether, and to what extent, they are to be given access to particular computer resources. It responds to user-entered commands that initiate the execution of specific programs, allocates required hardware and software resources to those programs, and controls their progress and termination. An operating system must also act on exceptional conditions that arise during the execution of a program and alert the user with appropriate messages.

As software products, operating systems are typically given initialed or acronymic names. Most operating systems have been developed and sold by computer manufacturers for use with their equipment. Popular examples likely to be encountered in library installations include the MVS and VM operating systems for IBM mainframes; the GCOS 8 operating system for Bull mainframes; the OS/1100 operating system for Unisys mainframes; the VMS operating system for Digital Equipment's VAX product line; the MPE operating system, developed by Hewlett-Packard for its HP-3000 series of minicomputers; SunOS for workstations manufactured by Sun Microsystems; and the Macintosh System and Finder developed by Apple Computer for Macintosh installations.

As a supplement or alternative to manufacturer-supplied products, several popular operating systems have been developed by companies or other organizations that specialize in systems software. Rather than being limited to a specific manufacturer's hardware, such third-party operating systems are often designed for computers that share certain hardware components or other characteristics. The best-known and most widely installed example is the MS-DOS operating system, which was developed by Microsoft Corporation for IBM-compatible microcomputers. The Unix operating system has attracted considerable attention in a broad spectrum of applications, including library automation. An outgrowth of software research conducted at Bell Telephone Laboratories during the 1960s and 1970s, versions of Unix are available for hardware configurations ranging from notebook systems to supercomputers. They are marketed by many companies under a variety of names, including Unix System V, AT&T's own implementation; Xenix, which was developed by Microsoft Corporation for IBM-compatible microcomputers; SCO Unix, which is likewise intended for microcomputer installations; Ultrix, Digital Equipment Corporation's Unix implementation for VAX minicomputers; A/UX, Apple Computer's version of Unix for Macintosh systems; and AIX, IBM's Unix implementation. While several organizations have initiated efforts to standardize the Unix operating system, available versions differ from one another in significant or subtle ways that can affect their compatibility.

Several library automation systems have employed minicomputers equipped with the Meditech Interpretive Information System (MIIS), an expanded version of the Massachusetts Utility Multi-Programming System (MUMPS) that combines the characteristics of an operating system and a programming language. In some cases, operating systems for specific computers have been developed by universities. Although such operating systems played an important role in the 1960s, when satisfactory vendor-developed products were not readily available, they are seldom encountered today. Examples that remain in limited use, principally for mainframe computers, include the MULTICS operating system, developed at the Massachusetts Institute of Technology, and the Michigan Terminal System (MTS), developed at the University of Michigan.

Specific hardware configurations and implementations aside, an operating system serves as an interface between a computer and a user. In the most primitive implementations, it accepts and responds to commands submitted in a special job control language (JCL). Since the inception of data processing, conventional operating systems have relied on an often cryptic repertoire of terse textual messages combined with uninformative prompts which indicate that the computer is ready to receive a command. In IBM-compatible microcomputer installations, for example, the MS-DOS operating system displays "C:/>" or a similar prompt with no explanation of the commands available at a given moment. The user must understand the prompt's significance and know the responses required to initiate desired operations.

As a further complication, the commands that make up a specific operating system's job control language may have many variations and can prove difficult to memorize. This poses few problems in mainframe and minicomputer installations where most system functions are initiated by trained operators and end users have little or no direct contact with system software. Microcomputer users, however, must learn the operating system commands necessary to activate programs, store and load data, format disks, and perform other routine tasks. To support such users, several vendors have developed special interfaces that rely on menus and other features to activate specific functions and minimize or eliminate the memorization of commands. Designed as operating system extensions, such interfaces are often described as "user friendly" because they simplify the learning requirements associated with particular work routines.

Based on ideas originally developed at the Xerox Palo Alto Research Center (PARC), the Macintosh interface is one of the most successful and fully realized examples of a graphical user interface (GUI). Treating the video display as a "desktop," it combines menus of commands with small graphic symbols called icons which represent the programs and data normally listed in disk directories. The interface supports "point and click" initiation of computer operations; a mechanical/optical device called a mouse is used to activate menus and icons by positioning a displayed arrow over them and pressing a designated button on the mouse itself. Mouse alternatives, such as arrow keys or trackballs, may also be employed. Some menu selections activate dialog boxes with additional lists of options or blank spaces for the entry of specific values. Individual application programs are displayed in one or more windows which can be scrolled, moved, enlarged, reduced, or otherwise manipulated. Similar graphical user interfaces have been developed for other computers. Ex-

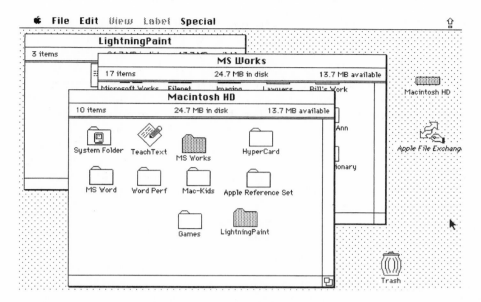

Graphical user interfaces rely on symbols to represent programs and data.

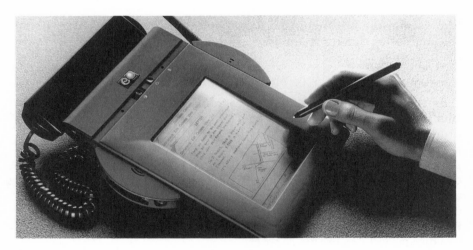

Computer systems increasingly rely on pointing devices, such as a mouse or a handheld pen, to activate programs and select commands. (Courtesy: EO Systems)

amples for IBM-compatible microcomputers include Microsoft Corporation's Windows program, which adds a graphical component to the MS-DOS operating system, and IBM's Presentation Manager for the OS/2 operating system. Graphical user interfaces for Unix-based computer systems include Open Look, Motif, and SunView.

The simplest operating systems are designed for standalone microcomputers. They can handle one task submitted by one user at a time. MS-DOS is the most widely encountered example of a microcomputer-based, single-user, single-tasking operating system. At the time of this writing, it was installed on tens of millions of desktop and portable machines. Single-user, multi-tasking operating systems permit concurrent execution of multiple programs. A microcomputer user can utilize a spreadsheet program, for example, while a spelling verification program is being applied to a word processing document. Tasks that do not require continuous computer-user interaction are performed in an unattended "background" mode. If a graphical user interface is provided, multiple programs typically occupy separate windows within a video display. The OS/2 operating system for IBM-compatible microcomputers and the MultiFinder for Macintosh systems are examples of a single-user, multi-tasking operating system.

Operating systems for mainframes and minicomputers must support multiple users simultaneously. Such operating systems are typically capable of multiprogramming (maintaining two or more programs in main memory at the same time) and multitasking (the concurrent execution of two or more tasks). Multi-user operating systems are likewise described as timesharing in that they can support multiple terminals in a manner described more fully in the next chapter. Some mainframe and minicomputer operating systems are also capable of multiprocessing in which the resources of two or more central processors are applied to a given program. Specific processing modes aside, a successful operating system must perform its work in a manner that is largely transparent to the user, giving the impression that its capabilities are inherent in the computer hardware itself.

Utility Programs

As their name suggests, utility programs perform tasks that are routinely required by computer users. As with other types of systems software, utility programs may be obtained from computer equipment manufacturers or from companies specializing in software development. Some utility programs are implemented as operating system extensions. This is the case, for example, with microcomputer operating systems which routinely include utility programs to format disks, selectively copy files between disks, and perform other commonly encountered tasks. Alternatively, utility programs may be custom-developed by local programmers in the manner discussed later in this chapter.

Among the most important types of utility programs are those that copy data from one medium to another, such as from magnetic disks to tape, in order to remove inactive data from online storage or to provide offline security for data that are maintained online. This activity, commonly known as data archiving, is an indispensable aspect of computer systems management. Other common utility programs are designed to recover data in the event of a system failure, determine the unused storage capacity of a given disk, consolidate unused areas within a disk for more efficient operation, sort data into a predefined sequence, or merge two or more files of previously stored data. Several types of utility programs are specifically designed to facilitate the software development process by simplifying the work of programmers. Editor programs, for example, allow other programs to be conveniently entered into online storage and modified as required. Other utility programs assist in the detection and correction of errors or "bugs" encountered during program testing. The most important category of software development tools, however, consists of the assemblers, compilers, and interpreters discussed in the following section.

Programming Languages

A program is a predefined sequence of commands or instructions that a computer executes to accomplish one or more tasks. All computers are built to respond to a predetermined set of instructions that initiate the execution of arithmetic calculations, logical comparisons, or other data manipulations, as well as the transfer of data between various system components. For a given information processing task, the number and nature of required instructions vary with the size and power of the central processor and, for processors of a given type, from model to model. As noted in chapter 1, some workstations employ Reduced Instruction Set Computing (RISC) processors that support a relatively small repertoire of instructions which are optimized for rapid execution. The central processors encountered in conventional computer systems are sometimes described as Complex Instruction Set Computing (CISC) devices. Compared to RISC processors, they support a much larger repertoire of executable instructions.

Regardless of the number of instructions supported by a given computer configuration, programming is that activity in which executable instructions are selected and combined in an appropriate sequence. The term properly denotes the development of either system software or application software, although it is most often used to denote the latter—that is, those programs that perform user-defined tasks. A programming language consists of syntactical and semantic rules that specify the manner in which particular instructions are to be used and combined.

As with data, computers can only process instructions that are encoded in machine-readable, binary form. Programs coded in binary form are said to be written in machine-level language, the only type of programming language immediately executable by a computer. In machine-level programming, binary-coded instructions may be written initially in hand-printed form on a programmer's worksheet. The instructions, which consist of the human-readable symbols "1" and "0," must then be converted to the machine-readable form required for computer processing. This is usually accomplished by typing them, line by line, at a key-to-disk device. An editing utility or word processing program is typically used to simplify the entry, insertion, modification, and deletion of instructions. Manuals prepared by the computer's manufacturer provide syntactical guidelines and tell the programmer which binary codes represent particular information processing operations.

Within machine-level programs, instructions consist of two parts: a code for an arithmetic, logical, or other operation to be performed is followed by the binary-coded address within main memory of the intended operand—that is, the object of a specific operation. Thus, an instruction of the form:

01000001110

might cause the data stored in memory location number 14 to be brought into an accumulator register within the central processor's arithmetic/logic unit, while the following instruction sequence:

01100001111
00110010000

may cause the contents of memory location number 15 to be added to it, and the result stored in memory location 16.

Historically, there has been an unfortunate disparity between the computer industry's ability to manufacture sophisticated hardware and the customer's ability to produce or otherwise obtain effective software to address his or her information processing requirements. Programming in machine-level language is a time-consuming, error-prone activity. Machine-level language is difficult to learn and produces programs that can prove very difficult to debug and modify. As a result, machine-level language is rarely used, even by experienced programmers. Instead, the software development process is better served by simpler methodologies that enable programmers to accomplish more work in a shorter amount of time.

In assembler language programming, for example, mnemonic commands and symbolic operands are substituted for binary codes. Thus, the three-instruction sequence:

MOV 14
ADD 15
STO 16

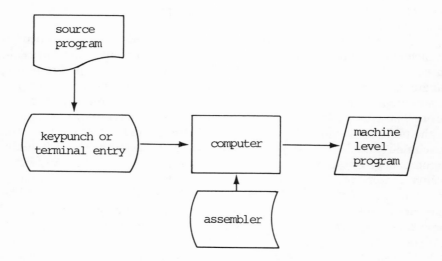

Programs written in assembler language are converted to machine-readable form and must subsequently be translated to the machine-level language required for computer execution. This translation is performed by a special program called an assembler.

is the assembler language equivalent of the binary-coded, machine-level instructions presented above. From the standpoint of programmers' productivity, mnemonic assembler language commands are much easier to remember than their machine-level counterparts, and the resulting programs are obviously easier to read and correct. In most cases, assembler language programming can be further simplified by substituting mnemonic names for numeric memory locations and combining frequently used instruction sequences into programmer-defined "macro" instructions that can be invoked with a single command.

While they are easier to write, the individual instructions that comprise an assembler language program must eventually be translated into machine-level language for computer execution. This translation is performed automatically by the computer itself, using a special program called an assembler—another example of system software. The assembler program, which is usually obtained from the manufacturer of the central processor, may itself be written in machine-level language. All available computers support an assembler of some type, although assemblers designed for different machines are typically incompatible with one another.

Assembler language is most often used when a programmer requires very close control over the internal operation of the central processor in order, for example, to optimize the allocation of memory space or the speed with which a given program is executed. Consequently, assembler language programming is a useful methodology for writing operating systems, sort/merge programs, and other systems software. Its general-purpose character, combined with its efficient utilization of computing resources, makes assembler language highly suitable for writing application programs. In many applications, however, speed of software development is more important than efficient program execution. As a result, application software is often written in one of the higher-level programming languages.

While they differ in ease of use, machine-level and assembler languages are collectively categorized as lower-level languages because the programmer must pay close attention to the specific central processor components used in a given operation. The higher-level languages, in contrast, allow a programmer to encode successive instructions in a comparatively abstract notation with little concern for details of machine design. Thus, a sequence of three instructions designed to add the data contents of two specified memory locations and store the results in a third may be simply expressed in the algebraic form:

$$C = A + B.$$

When higher languages are used, the programmer can devote full attention to the problem to be solved, rather than to the computer on which a given program will be executed. As a further advantage, each instruction written in a higher-level language is typically the equivalent of several machine-level language instructions. In short, higher-level language programs are easier, faster, and less expensive to develop than those written in assembler languages.

The resulting programs, however, must be translated into machine-level language prior to execution. As with assembler language programs, this translation is performed by the computer itself, using a special program called a compiler. Before its initial execution, a higher-level language program (sometimes called a source program) is translated by a compiler into a machine-level object program. A variant form of compiler called an interpreter does not generate a formal object program but, instead, translates individual instructions into their machine-level equivalents as they are encountered during the execution of a higher-level language program. As a rule, higher-level languages that use interpreters execute more slowly than those that use compilers, since instructions that initiate repetitive operations must be retranslated each time they are encountered. The relative economic advantages of assemblers, compilers, and interpreters and their significance in library applications are discussed later in this chapter.

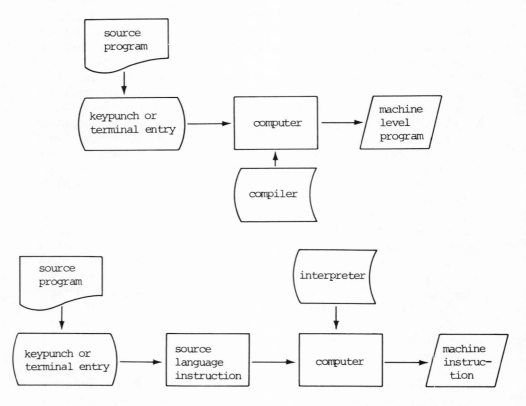

Compilers and interpreters are examples of system software that translates programs written in higher-level language to the machine-level language required for computer execution. A compiler translates the entire source program before execution. Interpreters translate individual program instructions and execute them immediately. In either case, the program must be first converted to machine-readable form through keypunching or other entry techniques.

Like assemblers, both compilers and interpreters are examples of system software and may be obtained from computer equipment manufacturers or from software development companies. Compilers and interpreters have also been developed by research laboratories and universities. Compilers and interpreters of the latter type often incorporate special features to assist student programmers.

Regardless of source, the nature and number of higher-level programming languages available in a particular situation vary with the type of central processor utilized and the mission of the computing facility that operates it. Although hundreds of higher-level languages have been developed, some are intended for special situations and only a handful are widely encountered. From the late 1950s through the mid-1970s, higher-level languages were typically categorized by the types of applications for which they were originally developed, although programming languages that are principally intended for a specific purpose may also be used for other types of tasks. Paralleling the development of computer hardware, the earliest higher-level languages were designed for technical applications. Of these, FORTRAN (an acronym coined from the phrase formula translator) is the best known.

FORTRAN instructions are written in an algebraic notation that is well suited to the mathematical problems encountered in the sciences and engineering. It can also be used in social science and business applications involving statistical analysis. Beneficially affected by more than two decades of enhancement, FORTRAN compilers are available for computers of all types and sizes, although FORTRAN programs written for execution on a given computer system will not necessarily execute on other hardware configurations. In fact, a given computer installation may maintain several different FORTRAN compilers, each supporting a different version or dialect of the language. Although FORTRAN standards have been developed by the American National Standards Institute (ANSI), most compilers deviate from the standards in offering additional features that are designed to both enhance the language's utility and bolster a given compiler's competitive position.

ALGOL is another programming language suitable for scientific applications. It was originally developed as a vehicle for the expression of the algorithms, or sequences of operations, which computers must execute to solve particular problems. As such, a knowledge of ALGOL is essential to an understanding of much of the professional literature of computer science. ALGOL compilers and interpreters have been developed for most full-size computers, but for practical programming purposes, ALGOL is more often encountered in Europe than in North America. Worldwide, however, its use is diminishing. In the future, ALGOL is most likely to be remembered for its considerable impact on the development of other programming languages, particularly PASCAL and other structured programming languages described below.

COBOL (the Common Business Oriented Language) has long been the most widely used higher-level programming language for business data processing in full-size computer installations. Unlike scientific comput-

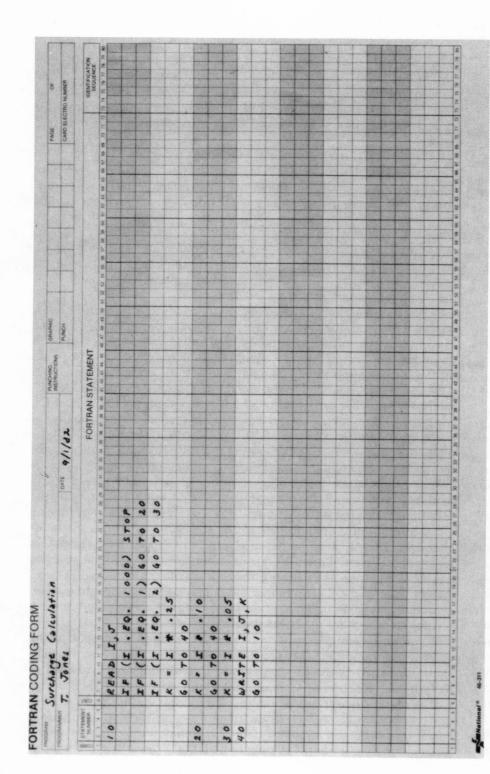

FORTRAN, a programming language developed for scientific and engineering applications, features a mathematical syntax. FORTRAN programs are typically written on special coding sheets which help the programmer observe the spacing required within individual lines.

ing, with its complex mathematical calculations, business applications are typically characterized by the repetitive performance of fairly simple computations involving large amounts of data. As a result, COBOL instructions emphasize data handling and report production. The language's mathematical capabilities are generally limited to the straightforward arithmetic operations required in such applications as general ledger maintenance or the writing of payment orders.

COBOL instructions themselves are written in an English-like notation designed for simplified readability. As originally developed by a committee of computer manufacturers and users, COBOL was intended to be as machine-independent as possible. COBOL standards have been adopted by the American National Standards Institute, but various versions offer enhancements not included in the language. While COBOL compilers are available for virtually all full-size computers and most smaller hardware configurations, a COBOL program written for a particular computer system cannot usually be executed on others without modification.

While circulation control, book ordering, and other aspects of library work share many of the characteristics of business data processing, applications involving information retrieval or the production of indexes and bibliographies require the ability to perform complex operations on character strings (finite, ordered sequences of alphabetic characters, numeric digits, punctuation marks, or other symbols) without regard to numeric values. Programs written in conventional higher-level languages, such as FORTRAN or COBOL, can do little more than store such character strings for later printing as headings or identifying lines in tables or reports that are otherwise heavily numeric.

Where more complex manipulations are required, a group of string processing programming languages features special instructions that permit such operations as the concatenation, or joining, of two character strings to form a third; the bifurcation of character strings into their component parts (sentences into words or words into characters, for example); and pattern matching, or the examination of a character string for the occurence of a specified substring. The most important example of a string processing programming language, SNOBOL, was originally developed by Bell Telephone Laboratories for the manipulation of formal algebraic expressions and the writing of compilers. It can, however, be used for other purposes, including the development of information retrieval and text analysis programs. During the 1970s, it received considerable attention from library educators and automation specialists. Other string processing languages—notably, COMIT and LISP—are more specialized in application than SNOBOL. COMIT was originally developed for computer-based linguistic analysis and automatic language translation, but it has been used in information retrieval applications. Although LISP was designed specifically for list processing, its symbol-handling capabilities have received much attention in artificial intelligence applications and "expert" simulation projects in which computer programs attempt to emulate human thought processes. PROLOG, a programming language derived from LISP, is likewise used for expert system development.

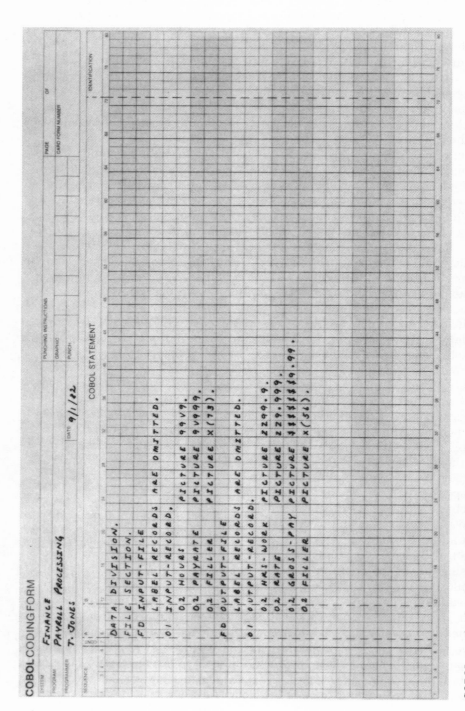

COBOL was developed specifically for business applications. COBOL programs are notable for their English-like syntax. As this program excerpt indicates, the COBOL programmer must provide the computer with a detailed description of the data to be processed. As with FORTRAN, special coding sheets are available for the preparation of COBOL programs.

```
 1              &TRIM = 1
 2              ALPHA = "ABCDEFGHIJKLMNOPQRSTUVWXYZ-'*"
 3              DELIM = '";,'
 4              DIGITS = '0123456789'
 5              TOTAL = INPUT
 6              AUTHOR = ARRAY(TOTAL)
 7              TITLE = ARRAY(TOTAL)
 8              SOURCE = ARRAY(TOTAL)
 9              PERMTITLE = ARRAY(TOTAL*5)
10 CLEAR        ITEM = LT(ITEM,TOTAL) ITEM + 1    :F(PERM)
11              CITATION =
12 READ         CITATION = CITATION ' ' INPUT
13              CITATION RPOS(1) '.'      :F(READ)
14              CITPAT = BREAK(ALPHA) BREAK(DELIM) . AUTHOR <ITEM>
   + SPAN(DELIM) BREAK(DELIM) SPAN(DELIM) $ D BREAK(*D) . TITLE <ITEM>
   + BREAK(ALPHA) REM . SOURCE <ITEM>
15              CITATION CITPAT       :(CLEAR)
16 PERM         ITEM = 1
17              PERMPAT = BREAK(ALPHA) . SAVE SPAN(ALPHA) . FWORD
18 NLOOP        N = N + 1
19 MORE         TITLE   ITEM    PERMPAT =      :F(ILOOP)
```

The SNOBOL4 language was developed expressly for string-processing operations. Despite its unusual notation, SNOBOL4 is easy to learn and is especially well suited to a wide range of library applications. The example given here is excerpted from a program that generates a keyword-in-context index from conventional footnotes punched on cards.

Despite their attractiveness, string processing programming languages are not widely utilized. Historically, they have played a minor role in computer science curricula; consequently, many professional programmers are unfamiliar with them. As an additional impediment to widespread acceptance, applications requiring extensive string processing capabilities are rarely encountered in business data processing. SNOBOL, COMIT, and LISP have not been implemented on all computers and, even when implementations are available, they may not be offered at a particular computer installation. They are most likely to be encountered in large university computer centers which routinely support a broad range of programming languages to address the varied requirements of administrative, research, and instructional computing. Microcomputer implementations, while available, have not been widely publicized, despite their potential attraction for librarians and information specialists who might like to experiment with string processing in a reasonably priced hardware environment. As a further constraint, most string processing languages use interpreters rather than compilers to translate instructions into machine-level language required for computer execution. As previously noted, programs written in interpreted languages tend to execute slowly and can prove costly where computing charges are based on the amount of central processor time used.

Several well-known higher-level languages have played an important role in the development of computing activities, but their limited significance in library applications places them beyond the scope of this discussion. Examples include JOVIAL, an ALGOL-like language developed for the United States Air Force; MUMPS, which was developed specifically for data processing and clinical applications in hospitals and other medical environments; RPG, a specialized language for report production; and DYNAMO, GPSS, SIMULA, and SIMSCRIPT, which are scripting languages for computer-based simulations. The LOGO and PILOT programming languages were developed specifically for educational applications. While their library significance is limited, they may be encountered in school libraries which operate computer resource laboratories in support of classroom instruction. LOGO, a list processing language that resembles LISP in design, was developed in the mid-1960s to teach reasoning and problem-solving skills through a series of straightforward programming procedures and operations. PILOT was created in the late 1960s as a simple authoring system for computer-aided instruction. Both languages are available in microcomputer implementations. To broaden their educational appeal, most versions support graphic and audio capabilities.

While the higher-level programming languages discussed to this point were developed for specific types of applications, the PL/1 programming language was designed with generality in mind. Introduced in the 1960s, it combines FORTRAN-like mathematical capabilities with COBOL-like data handling features. Some string processing facilities are also included. The resulting broad applicability proved conceptually attractive to computer center managers interested in simplifying their staffing and training requirements. PL/1 is principally a programming language for IBM mainframe computers. It enjoyed its greatest popularity during the 1960s and 1970s, when computing activities were dominated by mainframe systems. Although compilers have been developed for other hardware configurations, including IBM-compatible microcomputers, PL/1 has not been widely adopted in such installations. In recent years, it has been increasingly employed as a language for systems programming rather than application software development.

Programming languages developed during the 1950s and 1960s were designed for work environments in which the individual instructions that make up a program were punched on cards and submitted to a computing facility for execution. The programmer or user would return to the computing facility at some later time to obtain a paper printout containing the results. With the development of online systems during the 1970s, programmers and users began working at terminals, and programming languages were introduced that returned results immediately. BASIC (the Beginner's All-Purpose Symbolic Instruction Code) was the best known and most widely used of such "online" languages. Developed at Dartmouth College in the mid-1960s as a pedagogical device rather than a practical programming language, BASIC has since been implemented on a wide range of computers, including most microcomputers. Although it employs a FORTRAN-like algebraic notation, it can be used for both scientific computing and business data processing.

Easy to learn and widely taught in entry-level computer courses, BASIC is generally viewed as a language for so-called user programmers—that is, persons who write programs for their own use, as opposed to professional programmers who write programs for use by others. In fact, some professional programmers (in an extension of an attitude that earlier opposed the use of FORTRAN and other higher-level languages as an alternative to assembler and machine-level programming) are often contemptuous of it. BASIC is available in so many different versions that programs developed for one computer configuration cannot usually be executed on others without modification. Both interpreted and compiled implementations are available, the latter being preferred for speed of execution. Most versions of BASIC have been steadily augmented by their developers to incorporate new capabilities and take advantage of the latest developments in computing technology. Visual BASIC, for example, facilitates the development of programs with windows, pulldown menus, dialog boxes, and other graphical user interface components.

APL (A Programming Language) was, like BASIC, developed for online applications in which programmers work at terminals. Its most distinctive feature is its unusual notation, which employs a specially designed set of characters—represented by mathematical operators, Greek letters, and other symbols—to initiate particular programming instructions. While initially employed in scientific and engineering applications, APL is a multipurpose programming language with useful string processing facil-

```
5      PRINT 'TYPE DAYS OVERDUE AND BORROWER STATUS:'
10     INPUT DAYS
20     INPUT STATUS
30     IF STATUS=1 GOTO 90
40     IF STATUS=2 GOTO 70
50     FINE=DAYS*.25
60     GOTO 95
70     FINE=DAYS*.10
80     GOTO 95
90     FINE=DAYS*.05
95     PRINT 'THE FINE IS $'; FINE
100    PRINT 'DO YOU WISH TO CONTINUE?'
110    PRINT 'ENTER 1 FOR YES, 2 FOR NO.'
120    INPUT X
130    IF X=1 GOTO 5
140    END
```

While its notation resembles that of FORTRAN, the BASIC programming language is easier to learn. Originally developed as a pedagogical device for use in introductory computer science classes, it has become the most widely implemented programming language in small computer systems.

ities. Although not particularly suited to business applications involving extensive data handling, its powerful computation capabilities have contributed to its successful utilization in financial analysis, forecasting, operations research, and management decision-support systems. APL is primarily encountered in full-size computer installations, although minicomputer and microcomputer versions have been developed.

Since the mid-1970s, managers responsible for computing operations have been increasingly concerned about the maintainability of programs —that is, the ease with which programs written by one person can be corrected, enhanced, or otherwise modified by others. As organizations computerize greater numbers of applications, such "maintenance" programming accounts for an increasingly large percentage of the software development workload. Given the changing requirements of users and the high programmer turnover rate that characterizes many computer operations, the availability of readily maintainable programs is of great importance.

From the standpoint of maintainability, the rather abstract notations employed in higher-level languages represent a significant improvement over the machine-specific code employed in assembler language programming. COBOL programs, as previously noted, feature a readable English-like notation in which individual instructions take the form of imperative sentences. Critics of conventional higher-level languages, however, contend that their procedures for sequencing instructions greatly increase the potential for error and result in programs that can prove very difficult to maintain. These critics advocate the use of "structured" programming techniques that simplify and clarify the development of programs. Specifically, structured programming replaces the most troublesome logical constructs found in conventional programming methodologies with simpler sequences of instructions that are claimed to produce more accurate, readable, and maintainable programs.

While FORTRAN, COBOL, BASIC, and other conventional languages can be modified or otherwise adapted to the requirements of these improved programming techniques, several higher-level languages have been specifically developed for structured programming. The best known of these, PASCAL, organizes programs into self-contained blocks that facilitate the development of software for complicated applications, and simplify the detection and correction of errors. Developed in the early 1970s as a language for teaching computer programming as a systematic discipline, PASCAL has largely replaced BASIC as the language of first instruction in college-level computer science courses. It has also evolved into a popular tool for practical programming. Strongly influenced by ALGOL, PASCAL has been implemented on computers of all types and sizes. Although PASCAL was originally designed to produce "portable" programs that could be executed on different computers with very little modification, most PASCAL compilers, like their counterparts in other programming languages, incorporate special features that promote incompatibility and complicate portability.

Other structured programming languages were directly influenced by PASCAL and, through it, ALGOL. The C Language, which was developed at Bell Telephone Laboratories, is a structured programming language that combines the attributes of higher-level and assembler languages. Like the latter, C gives programmers considerable control over machine operations, memory allocations, and the speed of program execution. While C is widely regarded as an effective programming language for operating systems and other system software—the Unix operating system, for example, is largely written in C—it can be used to create application software as well. C compilers are available for many popular microcomputers. The language is widely used by professional software developers, who prize its ability to produce faster, more compact, more efficient programs that are highly portable.

Among other structured programming languages, ADA was developed by the United States Department of Defense as a standard software development tool that incorporates a variety of desirable capabilities, including structured programming facilities. ADA compilers are available for various types of computers. MODULA-2, a PASCAL-like language, has never gained the widespread popularity originally predicted for it, although versions are available for microcomputers.

Since the late 1980s, software developers have given considerable attention to object-oriented programming (OOP) languages and methodologies. Object-oriented methodologies describe arithmetic calculations, logical comparisons, and other computing operations as self-contained data structures, called objects, which can be combined and reused by programmers. An object consists of information accompanied by directions for manipulating it. The information might be a number, for example, and the description might tell how to multiply or divide it by other numbers. The manipulation of objects is often facilitated by a graphical user interface of the type described above. Advocates of object-oriented methodologies claim that they simplify programming procedures and produce accurate, readily maintainable programs. Examples of object-oriented programming languages include SMALLTALK, C++, OBJECT PASCAL, and IRIS.

APPLICATION SOFTWARE

The assemblers, compilers, and interpreters described above support the development of application software, which consists of those programs that perform one or more user-specified tasks. For most users, including librarians who want to automate particular operations, such application software is the most important computer system component.

Unlike system software, which is customarily obtained from computer manufacturers or other sources, the development of application software has historically been viewed as the user's responsibility. While an increasingly substantial amount of application software is purchased prewritten, custom-developed programs continue to play an important role in many installations. Although the automated library systems described in later chapters make extensive use of prewritten software, customized enhancements may be developed for specific situations. This section describes the software development process, emphasizing those aspects most important to librarians who must explain their application requirements to data processing professionals. Even where a library installation relies completely on prewritten software, familiarity with software development methodologies and procedures can facilitate an understanding of a given program's operating characteristics and limitations.

Systems Analysis

In most applications, the software development process begins with a detailed study of the existing operations or combinations of operations that accomplish the task or tasks to be computerized. This study is called a systems analysis. In the broadest sense, its purpose is to gather and evaluate the information necessary to improve an existing system or replace it with a new one. Over the past several decades, systems analyses have emphasized the evaluation of manual operations for possible improvement through computerization. Increasingly, however, attention is being given to the analysis of previously automated applications. This is the case, for example, in those libraries that are considering the replacement of previously implemented computer systems, particularly those that incorporate older technologies.

Whether its subject is manual or automated, a systems analysis is typically conducted by a person, aptly called a systems analyst, who determines what is being done in an existing system; whether, and to what extent, it is deficient; and what alternatives for improvement exist. The process of developing a modified or alternative system, sometimes called systems design, is discussed later in this chapter. Although it is the customary first step in the development of an automated system, a systems analysis need not invariably result in the recommendation of a computerized alternative. Systems analysts trained in industrial engineering, for example, often recommend the simplification of manual work steps or the routinization of procedures previously performed in a discretionary manner. Some systems analysts specialize in the application of technologies other than computers, such as micrographics, facsimile transmission, or voice communication systems. Computer systems analysts, while necessarily predisposed to computer-oriented alternatives, are presumably alert to problems that computers cannot effectively address or to situations for which other technologies or procedural approaches will prove more useful.

Although some large academic and public libraries employ one or more computer systems analysts, most librarians interested in automating a given activity will hire a consultant or work with a systems analyst employed by their organization's computing center or an external service bureau. Some systems analyses are of sufficiently narrow scope to be conducted by a single person. Complex problems may require a team of analysts working under the direction of a project leader or principal investigator. Such teams customarily consist of one or more entry-level analysts who are assigned to various data gathering tasks, while more experienced senior analysts assume responsibility for project planning, data evaluation, the formulation of recommendations, report writing, and oral presentations. In some applications, the systems analysis team may employ consultants with expertise relevant to specific phases of a project.

Although individual analysts may vary somewhat in their formal training and experience, the typical systems analysis is based on rather straightforward investigative and evaluative techniques. A series of preliminary meetings establishes major objectives, specifies the constraints within which the analysts must work, and provides a useful opportunity for "pre-analysis familiarization," in which the analysts can examine background documents and ask questions about the organization's mission and structure. The formal analysis begins with an intensive data-gathering phase that is designed to reveal the characteristics of the system under study and the requirements for a replacement system. Potentially useful data are generally obtained from a combination of sources:

1. Systems analysts will invariably inspect any available handbooks, manuals, policy and procedure statements, organization charts, and other written documents pertinent to the existing system. Standardized forms, such as catalogers' worksheets or purchase requisitions, are a particularly important class of documents that reveal both the types of information collected in a given activity and the flow of information through a given system. In addition, some libraries have collected data or compiled statistics pertinent to circulation control, acquisitions, or other activities. Such information can prove useful to the systems analyst, as can previously prepared studies or reports.

2. In most systems analyses, the data-gathering effort relies heavily on personal interviews as a means of identifying an application's requirements, as well as eliciting opinions about the strengths and problems of an existing system. In a well-planned system study, interviews will involve a representative cross-section of workers, including professional and clerical personnel. In some library applications, users may be interviewed as well. In studies of large systems or where personnel are geographically scattered, questionnaires often serve as a supplement or alternative to personal interviews.

3. Most systems analysts agree that personal observation is essential to verify data collected from the study of existing documentation, interviews, and questionnaires. Personal observation may take several forms, including site visits; equipment inventories; desk audits, in which the work of one or more persons is closely monitored; transaction walk-throughs, in which the flow of forms or other paperwork involved in transactions is traced; and work-volume measurements, in which the volume of work is sampled for given periods of time.

The systems analyst uses data gathered by the above methods to prepare a narrative description of the tasks performed within the system being studied. This narrative description, which may be embodied in a formal report or in informal working documents, is often supplemented by tabular or graphic presentations. Tables are usually the preferred format for summaries of such system features as equipment and file characteristics, transaction frequencies, or resources allocated to particular tasks. Organization charts are commonly used to depict the interrelationships among human resources in a given system. Similarly, the movement of documents or information is usually depicted through the use of charts consisting of interconnected, labelled symbols which represent various system components or work steps.

The flowchart is the most firmly established and widely encountered example of such graphic analytical tools. Program flowcharts, as described later in this chapter, are essentially logic diagrams used by programmers to prepare problems for computer solution. System flowcharts, the subject of this discussion, are of two types: task-oriented flowcharts, which depict

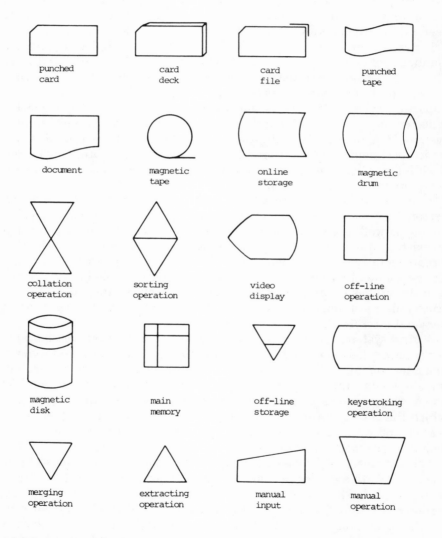

punched card	card deck	card file	punched tape
document	magnetic tape	online storage	magnetic drum
collation operation	sorting operation	video display	off-line operation
magnetic disk	main memory	off-line storage	keystroking operation
merging operation	extracting operation	manual input	manual operation

The flowchart is the most common of the graphic tools employed by systems analysts. Standard flowcharting templates contain a wide range of symbols that can be used to represent the work steps or equipment components in a given system.

the flow of data in terms of a given activity; and forms-oriented flowcharts, which trace the movement of forms or other documents through a system. With both types, a plastic template may be used to draw the symbols that represent various activities and components. Alternatively, flowcharting programs—several of which are available for microcomputers—can generate appropriate symbols for display or printing. In either case, most flowcharts employ a subset of the available symbols to depict such basic operations as input, output, processing, and storage.

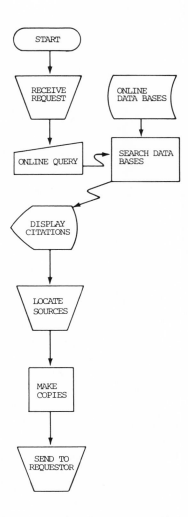

Task-oriented flowcharts depict flow of data in terms of a given activity. In the above example, requests for library materials on a given subject are received. Online data bases are searched for relevant citations, the appropriate sources located, and copies made for distribution to the requester.

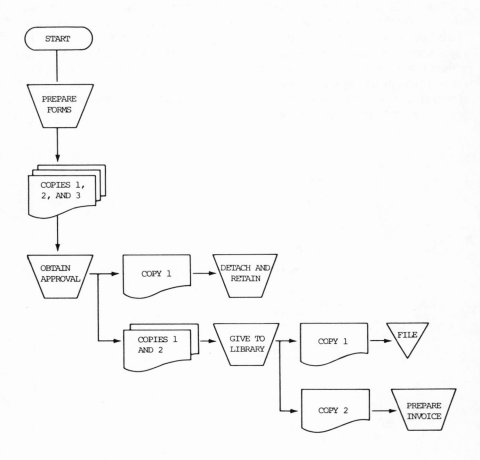

Forms-oriented flowcharts trace the movement of forms or other documents through a given system. In the above example, requests for book orders initiated by a library user are prepared in triplicate. The required approvals are obtained. The requester retains the first copy and submits the other two to the library, which uses one to prepare an invoice and retains the other for its files.

As alternatives or supplements to flowcharts, some systems analysts employ graphic representations variously known as data flow diagrams, data flow graphs, Petri networks, or bubble charts. Rather than concentrating on tasks or documents, as in conventional flowcharting, data flow diagrams trace the movement and transformation of data through a system. These diagrams use combinations of interconnected circles, boxes, lines, and arrows to represent various system operations. They are often preferred by data processing personnel who employ a variant form of systems analysis called structured analysis. Proponents of structured analysis contend that data flow diagrams and related techniques better

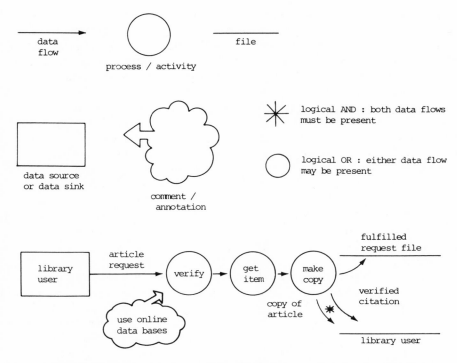

As an alternative to conventional system flowcharts, some analysts employ data flow diagrams which use combinations of interconnected circles, boxes, lines, and arrows to represent various system operations. In the above example, typical data flow symbols are depicted and their combined use indicated in an application involving the fulfillment of user requests for journal articles.

facilitate the design and development of computer applications when compared to conventional analytical methodologies.

Program Development

While some systems analyses confirm the appropriateness of an organization's existing work procedures, most culminate in a series of oral presentations and written reports that present recommendations for improvement or replacement of the system under study. If the existing system is to be replaced, a design is presented for an alternative. If the proposed alternative involves computers, the design includes specifications that describe the types of hardware to be used and the required application programs. The amount of detail presented in the software description varies but usually includes a discussion of the purpose of each required program, system flowcharts, descriptions of the data to be used as input and reports to be produced as output, and an indication of the frequency of program execution as well as the nature and amount of required machine-readable storage.

Assuming that management accepts the systems analyst's recommendations, this information will be given to one or more programmers who will expand the software specification by defining the application's requirements in greater detail and converting them into coded programs. In some cases, especially those involving small applications, the systems analyst is also responsible for program writing. Such information professionals are often described as analyst/programmers or programmer/analysts.

Complex software development projects, which can prove very difficult to manage, increasingly rely on teams of programmers and support personnel. An application's software requirements are usually conceptualized as a series of hierarchically interrelated modules, each of which is assigned to a team headed by a chief programmer. Using a "top-down" development approach to facilitate integration, lower-level modules are not programmed until the higher-level modules that invoke them have been coded and tested. This method produces logically structured programs while optimizing the deployment of computing resources and personnel.

Regardless of the specific developmental approach employed, the programmer must define the algorithms, or sequences of work steps, that a computer must perform to accomplish the information processing tasks specified by the systems analyst. Like systems analysts, programmers have historically relied on a combination of narrative description and flowcharts for this purpose. As noted earlier, program flowcharts are essentially logic diagrams that use predefined symbols to graphically depict a sequence of operations and decisions. Flowchart symbols may be drawn with the aid of templates or software. The range of symbols used in program flowcharts is usually narrower than that employed in system flowcharts.

Programmers typically prepare flowcharts in several levels of detail, ranging from an overview of general program logic to detailed specifications of individual work steps that can later be translated into coded instructions. Some computer specialists, however, question the value of contentional program flowcharts and advocate the use of alternative graphic presentations, such as Hierarchical Input-Process-Output (HIPO) charts, which depict the hierarchical arrangement of input, processing,

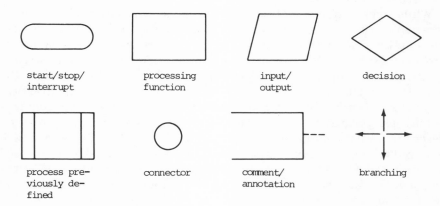

Program flowcharts are logic diagrams that graphically depict a sequence of operations and decisions. Special symbols, different from those employed in system flowcharts, are used in program flowcharts.

and output functions in a given system. Some software specialists reject all graphic presentations in favor of narrative descriptions which use indentations to reflect the hierarchical interrelationships among program operations. To formalize the preparation of software specifications, computer systems analysts and programmers may use specially developed specification languages, such as PSL/PSA (Problem Statement Language/Problem Specification Analyzer) or RSL (Requirements Specification Language). Such languages produce software specifications which resemble hierarchically structured programs, but they replace actual programming language instructions with English statements that describe the operations to be performed by specific program segments.

Once the algorithms that specify the operations necessary to accomplish particular tasks have been developed, the programmer uses an appropriate programming language to represent them as coded sequences of instructions for computer execution. The selection of a programming language for use in a particular application depends in large part on the nature of the operations to be performed. Some higher-level programming languages, as previously noted, are designed for specific types of applications. Thus, programs developed for such business-like, transaction-oriented library applications as circulation control and acquisitions may be written in CO-BOL, while a program designed for statistical analysis of library data might be written in FORTRAN.

In all cases, however, language selection is constrained by the programmer's knowledge and the availability of appropriate compilers and interpreters. Thus, for example, circulation or acquisitions programs designed for microcomputer implementations might be written in PASCAL or even BASIC because of the widespread availability of microcomputer-based compilers for those languages. Although they are well suited to the manipulation of bibliographic data, SNOBOL, COMIT, and other string processing languages are seldom used to program library applications, partly because appropriate compilers and interpreters are not widely available for such languages but, more important, because most application programmers are unfamiliar with them. As an additional constraint noted above, programs written in interpreted languages tend to execute more slowly than those written in FORTRAN, COBOL, PASCAL, or other compiled programming languages.

The desire for speed of program execution and efficiency of computer performance is an important consideration in a programmer's decision to use assembler language in preference to one of the higher-level languages. Because the automatic translation inherent in compilation and interpretation can introduce inefficiencies into the resulting machine-level object code, a program written in higher-level languages will usually execute more slowly than its assembler language counterpart. In addition, compilation itself is an extra processing step that requires computing resources. Once compiled, however, an object program can be stored on disk or tape and be executed repeatedly without recompilation.

The extent of assembler language's speed advantage is subject to debate and varies with the particular compiler or interpreter with which com-

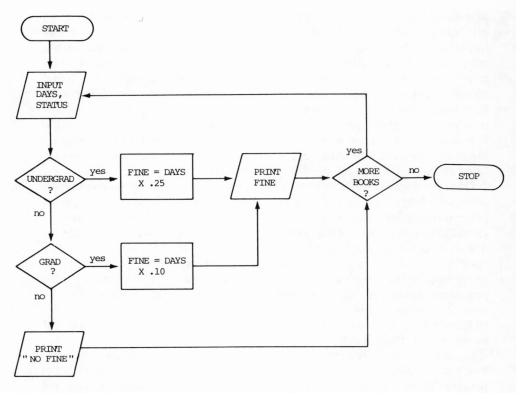

The algorithm coded as a BASIC program:

```
 5   DIM RESPONSE$(1), STATUS$(1)
10   PRINT "ENTER NUMBER OF DAYS OVERDUE:"
15   INPUT DAYS
20   PRINT "ENTER BORROWER'S STATUS -- UNDERGRAD, GRAD, FACULTY:"
25   INPUT STATUS$
30   IF STATUS$="U" THEN GOTO 50
35   IF STATUS$="G" THEN GOTO 60
40   PRINT "NO FINE"
45   GOTO 70
50   FINE = DAYS * .25
55   GOTO 65
60   FINE = DAYS * .10
65   PRINT "THE FINE IS $";FINE
70   PRINT "ARE THERE MORE BOOKS? TYPE YES OR NO:"
75   INPUT RESPONSE$
80   IF RESPONSE$="Y" THEN GOTO 10
85   END
```

Computer programming essentially consists of the formulation of algorithms and their encoding as sequences of instructions or computer execution. In the above example, a program flowchart is used to depict the algorithm which computes fines for overdue books in an academic library. The algorithm is then encoded as a BASIC program.

parisons are made. Because a single instruction written in a higher-level language is often the equivalent of several assembler language instructions, the higher-level languages permit a significant reduction in software development time. Since the cost of computing hardware is falling while the salaries of programmers are not, the savings in software development costs attainable through the use of higher-level languages will often outweigh the disadvantages of less efficient processing for all but the most complex and frequently executed programs. In addition, speed of software development is of great significance in applications where a computer system will replace a more costly manual or automated system, since the anticipated economic advantages of computerization will be realized sooner. As a further advantage, programs written in higher-level languages are typically easier to maintain—that is, to correct or modify—than those written in assembler language.

The foregoing discussion gives the misleading impression that higher-level and assembler language programming are mutually exclusive software development options that cannot coexist in a given application. If requirements warrant it, the two methodologies can be combined in a single program. Most programs consist of a series of modules, called subroutines, that perform sequences of operations associated with particular program operations, such as input or output. While the bulk of an application program may be written in a higher-level language, certain frequently executed subroutines may be coded in assembler language for faster execution.

Maintenance and Documentation

Once the instructions required to accomplish desired information processing tasks are coded in assembler or a higher-level language, the resulting programs are tested and any detected errors are corrected. While this testing or "checkout" procedure attempts to confirm that a given program will function in the intended manner, the length and complexity of most programs, combined with budget and schedule constraints, make it impossible to verify the correctness of all facets of program execution. The reliability of a typical computer program is consequently uncertain. While a given program may operate appropriately for a period of time following implementation, most programs eventually fail when some previously unanticipated situation is encountered. When such failure occurs, the program must be reexamined, the problem diagnosed, and the incorrect instructions rewritten. This "repair" activity is commonly described as "maintenance programming."

Because the characteristics of most information processing applications are dynamic rather than static, a second important type of maintenance programming consists of the modification of previously written programs to incorporate enhancements or to accommodate changes in application requirements. In some computing installations, especially long-established ones, such maintenance programming may account for 80 percent or more of the total programming activity and is the most common type of work assignment for entry-level programmers. In recent years, many organizations have undertaken "re-engineering" projects which involve significant modifications or a complete rewriting of application programs. Such projects are based on an in-depth reexamination of specific business processes and a reevaluation of the objectives of computerization. Such projects often focus on so-called legacy systems—that is, programs that were developed in the 1960s and 1970s and that may have been modified, in patchwork fashion, on multiple occasions.

Whatever the reasons for maintenance programming, the successive corrected or altered versions of a given program are termed "releases." The counterparts of revised editions of a printed book, successive software releases are typically identified by number. The initial operational version of a program is numbered 1.0. Test versions are typically assigned numbers lower than one; a final test release, sometimes described as a "beta" version, may be numbered 0.90 or higher. Minor revisions of a given operational version are identified by decimal increments, such as 1.1 or 1.2. Minor adjustments to such modified releases are often identified by incrementing the hundredths decimal position to 1.15 or 1.25, for example. Such minor revisions usually involve the correction of specific errors reported by users or discovered by software developers. Major program revisions are typically assigned the next largest whole number—2.0 in the case of the first major revision—to indicate that the new version offers significant enhancements when compared to its predecessors. Vendors of prewritten software for general-purpose and library-specific applications use major revisions to keep their products competitive and broaden their market appeal. Release numbers greater than 3.0 usually indicate programs that have been in use for some time and undergone successive, substantial improvement and augmentation.

Because maintenance programming requires an understanding of the purpose, structure, logic, and operation of previously written programs, the availability of adequate documentation is critical to its successful completion. Documentation can be broadly defined as the written information recorded during the development of a system that explains pertinent aspects of that system. Its purpose is to ensure that the details of a system are understood by those persons who have a need to know about it. Such documentation may address either the hardware or the software characteristics of a given system. This discussion is primarily concerned with software documentation, which is typically divided into three categories: analytical, developmental, and operational.

As its name suggests, analytical documentation is prepared at the systems analysis stage of program development. As previously discussed, it provides narrative and graphic descriptions of the characteristics, advantages, and disadvantages of an existing manual system; delineates and analyzes the information processing requirements of a given application; evaluates alternative courses of action; and presents recommendations for the improvement of an existing system or the development of a new one. From the standpoint of maintenance programming, analytical documentation is useful in determining the rationale for particular features of the system to be maintained.

The actual work of program modification relies most heavily, however, on developmental documentation. Such documentation consists of detailed narrative and graphic descriptions of the programs that implement a particular computer application. It includes a general statement of purpose for a given program or set of programs; a discussion of the algorithms employed, with flowcharts or other graphic presentations of program logic; a listing of program statements as written in assembler or higher-level languages; a description of the hardware configuration on which the program was designed to be executed, including an indication of memory requirements, online and offline storage media, and input/output peripherals; a listing of required system software and related support programs, including operating systems, assemblers, compilers, interpreters, utility programs, and prewritten subroutines; and a discussion of the program's input and data requirements.

The third category, operational documentation, includes installation and operating instructions. User manuals, an extremely important class of documentation, are included in this category. The best user manuals include tutorial material, which provides a step-by-step discussion of all program operations, and a reference section, which contains alphabetically arranged descriptions of specific program commands. Drawings or photographs of typical screen displays can be used to clarify and supplement narrative explanations. To further facilitate learning and use of a given program, a user manual may be accompanied by summary command tables, keyboard templates, wall charts, or similar reference aids. Recognizing that many users do not read printed manuals carefully, if at all, an increasing number of programs include an online "help" feature which provides access to information about specific operations from within the program itself. The typical online help module displays excerpts from printed program manuals. In most cases, the user selects the desired information from a list of topics displayed when the help module is invoked. A "context sensitive" help system automatically displays information appropriate to the task being performed at the time a help command is activated.

The preparation of appropriate analytical and developmental documentation is normally the responsibility of the systems analysts and programmers involved in a given software development effort. For best results, operational documentation should be prepared by technical writers. While most computer professionals recognize the value of complete documentation, a programmer working under the pressure of a tight schedule may neglect to document software activities fully. When the actual cost of software development threatens to exceed the budgeted amount, the reduction or elimination of documentation-related activities is too often viewed as a means of achieving greater economy in program writing. Unfortunately, any reduction in documentation typically proves to be a false economy that results in significant increases in the time and costs associated with program maintenance and utilization.

Prewritten Software Packages

The discussion to this point has dealt with software that is custom-developed for a specific situation. At a time when hardware prices are falling steadily and significantly, the cost of such customized software development accounts for an increasingly large percentage of total computer system costs and can be a significant impediment to the automation of library operations. This is particularly the case in microcomputer installations where the procurement of customized programming services on a contract basis, whether from independent consultants or from computer services companies that specialize in contract programming, can cost several times the purchase price of the microcomputer equipment itself.

Even if cost were not an issue, many libraries do not have convenient access to programming expertise. Because of large software development backlogs and the increasingly significant burden of maintenance programming, most institutional and corporate data processing centers limit their customized programming activities to high-priority tasks. As further constraints, customized software development projects are rarely completed on schedule. They often exceed budget allocations, partly because customers routinely augment their original program specifications to incorporate additions and enhancements after software development has begun. Success is never assured; customized programming can result in a disappointing end product that does not meet all application requirements.

For computer applications with relatively straightforward requirements, prewritten software packages are invariably more economical than custom-developed programs, and they offer the significant advantage of faster implementation. As the name implies, a prewritten software package is a program or group of programs that is marketed as a finished product. Such packages can be divided into two broad categories: general-purpose programs and industry-specific programs. General-purpose programs are designed to automate accounting, word processing, data base management, and other commonly encountered computer applications in a broad range of work environments. Industry-specific programs, in contrast, are designed to automate one or more operations in a specific work environment, such as a school, an engineering consulting firm, a hospital, or a law office. Software packages for library automation fall into the industry-specific category.

As an alternative to custom-developed programs, prewritten software packages can effectively address the applications for which they are intended. The best examples are intelligently conceived and attractively implemented. Newer products typically incorporate the latest advances in software development, such as graphical user interfaces and context-sensitive help systems. It is important to note, however, that prewritten software packages are intended for a class of applications, of which any given user's application is but one example. In many applications, information processing requirements vary little among users who must perform the same tasks; the circulation control activity, for instance, is performed in a similar manner by libraries of different types and sizes. By studying the way in which specific tasks are performed in various work environments, software developers can write broadly useful programs to automate them.

While some variations in local practice may be accommodated, prewritten software packages necessarily address the operations and work requirements that many users share. Custom-developed programs, in contrast, are designed for a specific installation, to the exclusion of other environments where similar operations may be performed. They are tailored to the requirements of a specific application and the stated preferences of users who ordered the programs to be written. If properly developed, they will address those requirements and preferences exactly—albeit, at a penalty in cost and time when compared to prewritten packages.

Regardless of type, prewritten software packages, like all computer programs, are designed for use with specific hardware configurations. As previously noted, computer manufacturers routinely supply operating systems and other systems software for use with their equipment. Historically, however, mainframe and minicomputer manufacturers have demonstrated little interest in application software, although some computer vendors offer consulting services and contract programming to support their hardware installations. Since the 1960s, most mainframe and minicomputer manufacturers have marketed some prewritten programs, principally for such common business applications as general ledger maintenance, accounts payable, payroll, accounts receivable, inventory management, personnel management, and project scheduling. They may also offer one or more data management programs suitable for information retrieval, document indexing, and other applications that are directly relevant to professional library activities.

A large percentage of prewritten software for mainframes and minicomputers is developed by third parties—that is, by persons or companies other than the computer system manufacturer or customer. In most cases, such packages are developed by independent software companies—so-called software houses—or computer services bureaus. As might be expected, their products are usually designed for widely installed central processors. Most emphasize a particular type of equipment configuration, such as IBM mainframes, VAX minicomputers, or computers that employ the Unix operating system. Some software development companies offer general accounting and administrative programs; many, however, specialize in products for specific "vertical" markets, such as banking, insurance, manufacturing, engineering, and transportation. As described in later chapters, several companies offer library automation programs for mainframes and minicomputers. Such programs are often implemented on computers operated by a university, municipality, corporation, or other organization with which a given library is affiliated.

To further simplify implementation, some software developers offer complete "turnkey" systems that consist of preselected combinations of hardware and software designed to automate specific operations. In most cases, the hardware configuration includes a minicomputer as its central processor. The turnkey designation suggests that a customer need only add the data particular to a given application, turn the key, and begin immediately realizing the benefits of automation without the involvement of programmers or other data processing professionals. Although such effortless implementations are rarely encountered in actual installations, the turnkey approach has been widely and successfully applied to the automation of library circulation control, online catalog access, and similar activities.

To some extent, an emphasis on customized software development is inherent in installation patterns for mainframes and minicomputers; as noted in chapter 1, such systems are operated by centralized data processing facilities which employ professional programmers. Preferring to write application programs rather than purchase them, data processing personnel may be unfamiliar with the evaluation, selection, procurement, and implementation of prewritten software packages. Microcomputer installations, on the other hand, are typically controlled by end users rather than by data processing professionals. Lacking programming skill or access to programming talent, microcomputer users typically depend on prewritten software packages for rapid, economical implementation of information processing applications. Thousands of prewritten programs are currently available, principally for IBM-compatible microcomputers and Macintosh systems.

Like their mainframe and minicomputer counterparts, microcomputer software packages can be divided into general-purpose and industry-specific categories. General-purpose microcomputer programs, which are of considerable interest to library installations, address various types of applications:

1. Word processing software packages, to be discussed more fully in chapter 4, support the preparation of typewritten documents. While low-priced, entry-level programs are available for straightforward typing tasks, the most powerful microcomputer-based word processing software packages support a varied group of editing and formatting capabilities, supplemented by such special features as automatic spelling verification, the production of customized form letters from mailing lists, an integral thesaurus for simplified identification of synonyms, automatic thesaurus control, automatic table of contents preparation, and document indexing. Well-known examples include the WordPerfect product line from WordPerfect Corporation, Word from Microsoft, Ami Pro from Lotus Development, WordStar from WordStar International, Signature from Xyquest, Professional Write Plus from Software Publishing Corporation, PC-Write from Quicksoft, Textra from Ann Arbor Software, JustWrite from Symantec Corporation, and MacWrite from Claris Corporation. Some popular products are available in multiple versions for IBM-compatible microcomputers running under the MS-DOS operating system, for IBM-compatible microcomputers running under Microsoft Windows, and for Macintosh systems. A few microcomputer-based word processing programs, such as WordPerfect, are also available in minicomputer implementations, thus facilitating the exchange of documents created on various computer platforms.

2. A related group of prewritten software packages is designed for desktop publishing. They can compose text into pages for printing in multiple fonts, sizes, styles, and columns. In most cases, the text is created by a word processing program and transferred into the desktop publishing package, although some desktop publishing programs incorporate straightforward editing capabilities. Textual information can also be merged with graphics to produce attractively formatted documents. Examples of desktop publishing programs for microcomputer systems include PageMaker from Aldus Corporation, Publisher for Windows from Microsoft Corporation, Ventura Publisher from Ventura Software, FrameMaker from Frame Technology, and QuarkXPress from Quark.

3. Spreadsheet programs are designed for administrative and analytical workers with complex planning and decision-making responsibilities. Taking their name from the large sheets of paper that accountants have traditionally used to present financial information in a tabular format, spreadsheet programs permit the creation and subsequent manipulation of financial and statistical models represented as matrices of intersecting rows and columns. They can simplify the preparation of budgets, cost estimates, cost justification statements, income projections, statistical tabulations, and similar planning documents. Spreadsheet programs are particularly useful for applications where a variety of interrelated variables must be considered and repetitive calculations are required. The best packages—such as 1-2-3 from Lotus Development, the Excel product line from Microsoft, and Quattro Pro from Borland International—support a repertoire of predefined functions that can quickly perform a variety of mathematical, statistical, financial, and logical computations. Depending on the program and available hardware components, results may be displayed or printed in tabular or graphic formats. Originally developed for microcomputers, spreadsheet programs have proved so popular that versions have been developed for mainframe and minicomputer installations.

4. Data management software packages permit the creation and manipulation of machine-readable records stored in data files. They are useful in a variety of applications involving information retrieval and report generation. As explained in chapter 3, the majority of data management programs operate on records that are organized into user-defined data elements called fields. The simplest microcomputer-based data management software packages, sometimes described as "flat file" programs, can only process information contained in a single data file. Well-known examples include Q&A from Symantec Corporation and FileMaker from Claris Corporation. More sophisticated products, called data base management programs, can process several data files simultaneously and permit the implementation of complex applications. The most widely encountered examples are the dBASE and Paradox product lines from Borland International, the FoxPro and Access programs from Microsoft Corporation, dBFast from Computer Associates International, the R:base product line from Microrim, DataEase from DataEase International, 4th Dimension from ACIUS, FileMaker Pro from Claris Corporation, Inmagic from Inmagic Corporation, and Omnis7 from Blyth Software. Of particular relevance to this discussion of application software development, some data base management packages support a proprietary programming language that can address application requirements which exceed the package's preprogrammed scope.

5. While conventional data base management programs operate on structured records that are organized into fields, an interesting group of microcomputer software packages can manipulate unstructured text segments. Such programs are variously known as text storage and retrieval systems, text-based data management systems, text information systems, or full-text retrieval systems. The text segments may consist of complete documents or shorter document representations, such as abstracts or

annotations. In most cases, the text is imported from a word processing software package, although optical character recognition can be used to convert paper documents to character-coded text files. Regardless of input source, a text storage and retrieval program creates indexes to every significant word on every page within the stored documents. The indexes permit full text searches for rapid identification of text segments that contain specified character strings. The text segments, or the complete documents that contain them, can be displayed or printed to satisfy specified retrieval requirements. Examples of microcomputer-based text storage and retrieval programs include Zyindex from Zylab, DocWorks from Information Dimensions, BRS Search from BRS Software Products, Folio Views from Folio Corporation, Concordance from Dataflight Software, Personal Librarian from Personal Library Software, Magellan from Lotus Development, Star from Cuadra Associates, PC DOCS from PC DOCS Incorporated, and Search Express from Executive Technologies. Text storage and retrieval programs for mainframes and minicomputers are described in chapter 3.

6. Presentation graphics programs facilitate the creation of reports, slides, overhead transparencies, promotional materials, and other business documents that include charts, line graphs, diagrams, and similar graphic components. Such programs can generate very attractive graphic output in a broad range of styles and colors. In most cases, numeric data can be entered directly, and a straightforward text-editing module permits typing of word charts. Alternatively, the textual or numeric information on which graphic presentations are to be based may be transferred from word processing programs, spreadsheet programs, data base management programs, or other sources. Graphic images can also be imported from collections of clip art, some of which are distributed on CD-ROM. Most products provide drawing and annotation tools for editing and enhancement of presentations. Graphic images can be cropped, resized, rotated, or otherwise manipulated. Notes, labels, and legends can be appended to them. Headings can be changed or repositioned. Presentations can be displayed on graphics-capable video monitors as selected individual images or in a slideshow format. Hardcopy output can be generated by color printers. Examples of microcomputer-based presentation graphics programs include Aldus Persuasion from Aldus Corporation, CA-Cricket Presents from Computer Associates International, Freelance Graphics from Lotus Development, PowerPoint from Microsoft Corporation, Harvard Graphics from Software Publishing Corporation, Charisma from Micrografx Incorporated, and Claris Hollywood from Claris Corporation.

7. Communications software packages enable a personal computer to function as a terminal for purposes of communicating with a remote device. As described more fully in chapter 3, a communications program interacts with a modem and other hardware components. Examples of communications software packages for microcomputers include the Crosstalk product line from Digital Communications Associates, the SmartCom product line from Hayes Microcomputer Products, Relay Gold from Microcom, ProComm Plus from Datastorm Technologies, Microphone II from Soft-

ware Ventures Incorporated, SmarTerm from Persoft, White Knight from the FreeSoft Company, and VersaTerm from Synergy Software.

8. Integrated software packages (not to be confused with the integrated library systems discussed in later chapters) combine word processing, spreadsheet processing, data management, and communications in a single, modularized product. Presentation graphics capabilities may be included as well. Examples of microcomputer-based integrated software packages include Microsoft Works from Microsoft Corporation, Claris-Works from Claris Corporation, Symphony and LotusWorks from Lotus Development, GreatWorks from Symantec, PFS: WindowWorks from Spinnaker Software, WordPerfect Works from WordPerfect Corporation, and Enable from Enable Software Incorporated. Compared to an equivalent number of standalone programs, integrated software packages usually cost less, can prove easier to learn, and simplify the exchange of information between program modules. They are especially effective in applications where information manipulated by spreadsheet or data management modules must be incorporated into word processing documents. As a potential disadvantage, few integrated software packages offer the broad range of features supported by the best standalone software packages purchased separately. Most feature one strong module, supplemented by other more or less adequate modules.

While prewritten software packages are increasingly available for computers of all types and sizes, it can prove difficult to identify products suitable for a given application. There is, unfortunately, no single authoritative directory of such programs comparable to the directories available for books, periodicals, microforms, and related bibliographic materials. The problems inherent in the production of such a directory are formidable. Unlike book publishing, which requires a significant capital investment in production facilities, software can be produced by anyone with access to a computer. As a result, it is virtually impossible to produce a comprehensive, up-to-date list of available prewritten programs. Subject to this limitation, however, a growing number of useful sources can assist librarians and other computer users in identifying software packages that might satisfy their requirements.

Some computer manufacturers publish catalogs of prewritten programs that are available for use with their equipment. Useful as they are, such publications are usually limited to products sold by the computer manufacturer and affiliated companies. They often omit interesting programs developed by independent software companies, user groups, and other third parties. For a comprehensive software search, such manufacturer-produced catalogs must be supplemented by one or more cross-industry software directories produced by such independent publishers as Datapro Research, International Computer Programs Incorporated, Auerbach Publishers, and Ziff-Davis Publishing. Among online information resources, the BUSINESS SOFTWARE DATABASE produced by Information Sources Incorporated, the BUYER'S GUIDE TO MICRO SOFTWARE produced by Online Incorporated, the MICROCOMPUTER SOFTWARE GUIDE produced by R.R. Bowker, and the SOFTWARE DIRECTORY produced by Black Box Corporation provide useful descriptions of available programs and are updated more frequently than some printed publications.

Software product reviews, product profiles, and availability reports are included in such computer industry information resources as the COMPUTER DATABASE from Information Access Company, the MICROCOMPUTER INDEX from Learned Information, and COMPUTER NEWS FULLTEXT from IDG Communications. The NTIS data base contains directory-type descriptions for software produced by and for U.S. federal government agencies. The National Technical Information Service also publishes the same information in a printed directory. The programs it lists are available to the public, but they are sold without installation support or maintenance service. A related NTIS publication, entitled *Library and Information Sciences: A Directory of Computer Software Applications,* covers programs for the library field specifically.

Printed microcomputer software directories are so numerous that a detailed survey is beyond the scope of this discussion. Some publications, such as *The Software Encyclopedia* from R.R. Bowker, list programs for all types of microcomputers and many kinds of applications. In addition, almost every type of microcomputer has at least one comprehensive directory devoted to it. Several dozen publications list software packages for IBM-compatible and Macintosh systems, for example. Some computer-specific directories are further limited to particular applications, such as accounting or office automation. Of particular interest to libraries and other organizations with limited software budgets, several directories list public domain and user-supported programs that are available at nominal cost. Sometimes described as "shareware," most user-supported programs can be duplicated for distribution to others, provided that the distributing party does not make a profit from the transaction. Recipients who find a shareware program useful are asked to make a modest payment to its creators, in return for which they usually receive documentation, technical support, and access to future enhancements.

In addition to directory-type publications, useful information about prewritten software packages can be found in periodicals and journals that deal with computers and data processing. Microcomputer magazines, in particular, contain software descriptions and reviews as regular features. Examples of such magazines include *Byte, PC Magazine, PC World, MacWorld, MacUser, InfoWorld, AmigaWorld,* and *Dr. Dobb's Journal. Software Reviews on File,* a loose-leaf reference service published by Facts on File, provides convenient summaries of reviews from microcomputer periodicals. In the library field, Meckler Corporation's *Library Software Review* presents reports of library experience with prewritten and custom-developed software packages, as well as reviews of prewritten programs and books about software. Articles and reviews dealing with general-purpose and library-specific software packages can also be found in such library/information science journals as *Library Technology Reports, Library Computer Systems and Equipment Review, Library Hi Tech, Computers in Libraries, Microcomputers and Information Management, Online,* and *Information Technology and Libraries.*

SUMMARY

Software is a program, or predefined sequences of instructions, that a computer executes to perform information processing operations. The computer industry typically distinguishes between system software (those programs that enable a computer to function and control its own operations) and application software (those programs that perform user-specified tasks). Examples of system software include the group of supervisory programs called the operating system; various utility programs that perform housekeeping operations, sorting, or other tasks routinely required by computer users; and assemblers, compilers, and interpreters which support programming activities.

A computer can only execute programs that are presented to it in a binary-coded form called machine-level language. Because the writing of such programs is a time-consuming, error-prone task, the computer industry has developed various programming languages that employ nonbinary instructions, thereby facilitating the software development process. In assembler language programming, mnemonic commands and symbolic operands are substituted for binary codes. The resulting program is then translated into machine-level language by a special program called an assembler. The higher-level languages use an even more abstract notation that greatly simplifies the programming task. The resulting programs must be translated into machine-level language by a program called a compiler or an interpreter.

The various higher-level programming languages are often categorized by the type of information processing applications that they are designed to support. FORTRAN, one of the oldest higher-level languages, remains widely used in scientific computing and engineering applications. COBOL has long been the most important programming language for business applications. SNOBOL, LISP, and COMIT are examples of string-processing programming languages. PL/1 is a general-purpose, higher-level language that combines scientific, business, and string-processing attributes. Several programming languages, including BASIC and APL, were developed specifically for programmers working in an online environment. BASIC offers the additional advantage of being widely available in microcomputer implementations. Since the 1980s, programming language designers have emphasized structured features that foster improved programming practice and the creation of more reliable, more easily maintainable programs. PASCAL, C, and ADA are examples of such structured programming languages. Much recent attention has been given to object-oriented programming methodologies that describe arithmetic calculations, logical comparisons, and other computing operations as self-contained data structures that can be combined and reused by programmers. Examples of object-oriented programming languages include SMALLTALK, C++, OBJECT PASCAL, and IRIS.

While system software is often bundled with computer hardware, the development of application software has historically been considered the customer's responsibility. Properly undertaken, the software development process begins with a study by a systems analyst of application characteristics and requirements. The result is a report that presents recommendations for the improvement or replacement of the system under study, including specifications for any required computer equipment and application programs. These specifications are then given to one or more programmers who will formulate the required algorithms, select an appropriate programming language, and write and test the necessary programs.

Because most computer programs are not fully tested prior to implementation, the likelihood of future operational failure is high. When such failures occur, the program must be reexamined and any incorrect instructions rewritten. This activity, called maintenance programming, is greatly facilitated by the availability of adequate documentation—written information about the characteristics of a particular program prepared at the time the program was originally written.

As an alternative to the time and expense required for customized software development, prewritten application software packages are increasingly available for computers of all types and sizes. In mainframe and minicomputer installations, where data processing professionals have traditionally preferred custom-developed programs, software packages offer an increasingly popular approach to the implementation of commonly encountered administrative and accounting operations. Most microcomputer installations rely heavily on prewritten software packages, and a substantial number of programs are available for word processing, spreadsheet analysis, data management, presentation graphics, communications, and various industry-specific tasks. An increasing number of directories, guides, and other information sources can assist librarians and other potential users in the identification, evaluation, and selection of such prewritten software.

ADDITIONAL READING

BABICH, W. *Software Configuration Management.* Reading, Mass.: Addison-Wesley, 1986.

BASS, L., and COUTAZ, J. *Developing Software for the User Interface.* Reading, Mass.: Addison-Wesley, 1991.

BECK, L. *System Software: An Introduction to Systems Programming.* Reading, Mass.: Addison-Wesley, 1985.

BOHL, M. *Flowcharting Techniques.* Chicago: Science Research Associates, 1971.

BORENSTEIN, N. *Programming as if People Mattered: Friendly Software Engineering, and Other Noble Delusions.* Princeton, N.J.: Princeton University Press, 1991.

BROOKS, F., JR. *The Mythical Man-Month: Essays in Software Engineering.* Reading, Mass.: Addison-Wesley, 1975.

CUGINI, J. *General Purpose Programming Languages.* Princeton, N.J.: Petrocelli Books, 1987.

CUSUMANO, M. *Japan's Software Factories: A Challenge to U.S. Management.* New York: Oxford University Press, 1991.

DAVIS, C., et al. *Pascal Programming for Libraries: Illustrative Examples for Information Specialists.* New York: Greenwood Press, 1988.

DEITEL, H. *An Introduction to Operating Systems.* Reading, Mass.: Addison-Wesley, 1989.

DIUJKSTRA, E. *A Discipline of Programming.* Englewood Cliffs, N.J.: Prentice Hall, 1979.

DYER, M. *The Cleanroom Approach to Quality Software Development.* New York: Wiley, 1992.

FISHER, A. *CASE: Using Software Development Tools.* New York: Wiley, 1991.

FRIEDMAN, A., and CORNFORD, D. *Computer Systems Development: History, Organization, and Implementation.* New York: Wiley, 1989.

GEHANI, N., and MCGETTRICK, A. *Software Specification Techniques.* Reading, Mass.: Addison-Wesley, 1986.

ICHBIAH, D., and KNEPPER, S. *The Making of Microsoft: How Bill Gates and His Team Created the World's Most Successful Software Company.* Rocklin, Calif.: Prima Publishing, 1991.

JANSON, P. *Operating Systems: Structures and Mechanisms.* New York: Academic Press, 1985.

KAWASAKI, G. *The Macintosh Way.* New York: Harper Collins, 1990.

KESTIN, H. *Twenty-first-century Management: The Strategies That Have Made Computer Associates a Multibillion-dollar Software Giant.* New York: Atlantic Monthly Press, 1992.

KLERER, M. *Design of Very High-Level Computer Languages: A User-Oriented Approach.* New York: McGraw-Hill, 1991.

LABUDDE, K. *Structured Programming Concepts.* New York: McGraw-Hill, 1987.

LAMB, A. *Software Engineering: Planning for Change.* Englewood Cliffs, N.J.: Prentice Hall, 1988.

LEVY, L. *Taming the Tiger: Software Engineering and Software Economics.* New York: Springer Verlag, 1986.

LEWIS, T. *CASE: Computer-Aided Software Engineering.* New York: Van Nostrand Reinhold, 1991.

LOWELL, J. *Improving Software Quality: An Insider's Guide.* New York: Wiley, 1993.

MCGREGOR, J., and SYKES, D. *Object-oriented Software Development: Software for Reuse.* New York: Van Nostrand Reinhold, 1992.

MADDIX, F. *Systems Software: An Introduction to Language Processors and Operating Systems.* New York: Halsted Press, 1989.

MARCOTTY, M., and LEDGARD, H. *The World of Programming Languages.* New York: Springer Verlag, 1987.

MEYER, B. *Introduction to the Theory of Programming Languages.* Englewood Cliffs, N.J.: Prentice Hall, 1988.

MODELL, M. *Professional's Guide to Systems Analysis.* New York: McGraw-Hill, 1988.

MOLLER, K. *Software Metrics: A Practitioner's Guide to Product Development.* New York: Chapman & Hall, 1993.

NUTT, G. *Open Systems.* Englewood Cliffs, N.J.: Prentice Hall, 1992.

SAMMETT, J. *Programming Languages: History and Fundamentals.* Englewood Cliffs, N.J.: Prentice Hall, 1969.

SCHNEIDERMAN, B. *Software Psychology: Human Factors in Computer and Information Systems.* Cambridge, Mass.: Winthrop Publishing, 1980.

SHAMLIN, C. *The Other Side of Software: A User's Guide for Defining Software Requirements.* New York: AMACOM, 1990.

SILVERMAN, G., and TURKVIEW, D. *Computers and Computer Languages.* New York: McGraw-Hill, 1988.

SILVERSCHATZ, A. *Operating System Concepts.* Reading, Mass.: Addison-Wesley, 1988.

SIMPSON, H. *Developing Effective User Documentation: A Human Factors Approach.* New York: McGraw-Hill, 1988.

SMITH, C. *Performance Engineering of Software Systems.* Reading, Mass.: Addison-Wesley, 1990.

SMITH, D., and WOOD, K. *Engineering Quality Software: A Review of Practices, Standards, and Guidelines, Including New Methods and Development Tools.* New York: Elsevier Applied Science, 1989.

STEVENS, W. *Software Design: Concepts and Methods.* New York: Prentice-Hall International, 1991.

TOWNER, L. *CASE: Concepts and Implementation.* New York: McGraw-Hill Intertext Publications, 1989.

WALLACE, J., and ERICKSON, J. *Hard Drive: Bill Gates and the Making of the Microsoft Empire.* New York: Wiley, 1992.

WARD, M. *Software That Works.* San Diego: Academic Press, 1990.

WATSON, D. *High-Level Languages and Their Compilers.* Reading, Mass.: Addison-Wesley, 1989.

WEINBERG, G. *The Psychology of Computer Programming.* New York: Van Nostrand Reinhold, 1971.

WEXELBLAT, R., ed. *History of Programming Languages.* New York: Academic Press, 1981.

WHITE, B. *Programming Techniques for Software Development.* New York: Van Nostrand Reinhold, 1989.

WHITTEN, N. *Managing Software Development Projects: Formula for Success.* New York: Wiley, 1990.

WILLIAMS, P. *Writing Effective Software Documentation.* Glenview, Ill.: Scott, Foresman, 1990.

WILSON, L., and CLARK, R. *Comparative Programming Languages.* Reading, Mass.: Addison-Wesley, 1988.

YOURDON, E. *Decline and Fall of the American Programmer.* Englewood Cliffs, N.J.: Yourdon Press, 1992.

———. *Managing the System Life Cycle.* Englewood Cliffs, N.J.: Yourdon Press, 1988.

YOURDON, E., ed. *Classics in Software Engineering.* New York: Yourdon Press, 1979.

YOURDON, E., and CONSTANTINE, L. *Structured Design: Fundamentals of a Discipline of Computer Program and Systems Design.* Englewood Cliffs, N.J.: Prentice Hall, 1979.

3

Data Processing Concepts

The preceding chapters described the most common hardware and software components in a computer system. This chapter examines the ways in which those components interact to process, manage, and distribute data. In doing so, it presents descriptions of some additional hardware and software concepts and products. The chapter begins with a discussion of basic modes of data processing, emphasizing the significance and pervasiveness of online, real time, interactive computing. Later sections will discuss the organization and management of machine-readable data, the concept of distributed data processing, fundamental data communications terminology, and the characteristics of computer networks. As with the preceding chapters, the discussion emphasizes facets of these topics that are of greatest importance for library automation.

MODES OF DATA PROCESSING

The terms *online* and *offline* indicate, respectively, the presence or absence of an electrical or other connection between computing devices. As noted in chapter 1, the terms most often describe the presence or absence of connections between a central processor and its associated peripherals. Thus, an online peripheral, such as a line printer, is physically connected to the computer on which the information to be printed is processed, while an offline peripheral, such as a keypunch machine, is not so connected. In addition, the two terms are sometimes used to describe particular computer system configurations. In an online system, data are stored on direct-access media, usually fixed magnetic disk drives. Terminals are used to access the central processor for information retrieval or other purposes. An offline system, in contrast, typically relies on magnetic tape for data storage, while printed reports communicate the results of computer processing.

When used to describe particular computer configurations, the adjectives *online* and *offline* are often confused with two other terms: *real time* and *batch*. The two pairs of terms are not, however, interchangeable. Rather than referring to the presence or absence of electrical connections between computing devices, batch and real time denote modes of data processing. The essential characteristics of real time and batch processing implementations are described below.

Real Time vs. Batch Processing

Batch processing systems, sometimes described as "batch-oriented systems," dominated data processing implementations through the early 1970s, and some systems developed several decades ago remain in use. The essential characteristics and inherent limitations of batch processing can be introduced through an example involving computerized circulation control. As implemented by various public and academic libraries during the 1960s and 1970s, the typical batch-oriented circulation control system used keypunch or key-to-tape technology to record information in the machine-readable, computer-processible form required for automated charging and discharging of library materials. With some systems, specially prepared decks of tabulating cards—prepunched with such information as an accession number or other item identifier, an abbreviated author's name, and a truncated title—were stored in pockets affixed to books or other circulating items. The additional information required to charge or discharge an item—a borrower identification number, a date, and a transaction code, for example—was punched into blank portions of one of the cards as individual transactions took place. In other systems, blank cards were punched in their entirety in a predetermined format by circulation clerks at the time each transaction occurred. Alternatively, key-to-tape devices were sometimes used to record machine-readable data pertaining to successive circulation transactions on reels or cassettes of computer-compatible magnetic tape. During the early to mid-1970s, several companies marketed key-to-tape data collection equipment specifically for library circulation control applications.

Regardless of the recording medium employed, the machine-readable records pertaining to successive circulation transactions (charges and discharges) were accumulated at the circulation point on punched cards or magnetic tapes. At predetermined intervals, the cards or tapes were taken to an institutional computing center or computer service bureau for processing in a batch. The computer processing typically involved updating a master circulation file which contained one machine-readable record for each circulating item in the library's collection. The file was usually stored on magnetic tape, the records being arranged by accession number or in some other sequence. (The characteristics of such circulation files are described in chapter 5.)

After being sorted into the same sequence as the master file, records representing circulation transactions were read by the computer, and their corresponding master records located on tape. If a given transaction reflected a charge, the borrower's number and other identifying information were added to the master record for the indicated item; if the transaction reflected the return of an item, the previously recorded charge-out information was erased.

When all circulation transactions had been processed, one or more lists were printed. These lists—which were produced in paper form by a line or page printer, or on microfilm or microfiche by a COM recorder—provided information about items in circulation. Abbreviated lists, arranged by call number, included short titles and due dates for items in circulation. Such lists were customarily made available for reference by library users, enabling them to determine whether or not a given item was in circulation and when it was due to be returned. More detailed lists, which included borrower information, were usually produced for circulation department personnel. At predetermined intervals, the master circulation file was further processed to identify overdue items, produce recall notices, derive and report circulation statistics, or print special lists of delinquent borrowers or circulating items placed on hold.

The foregoing description reflects the operating characteristics of a typical batch processing system. In summary:

1. Machine-readable data are collected offline on punched cards or magnetic tape for subsequent processing at predetermined intervals.
2. In some cases, batches of data are physically transported to a computing facility. Alternatively, data may be submitted electronically through specially designed batch-input terminals or through remote job entry (RJE) stations.
3. The frequency with which batches are submitted for processing depends on several factors, including the user's information-processing requirements, the rate at which data accumulate, and the availability of computing resources.
4. Machine-readable data, organized in files as explained later in this chapter, are recorded on one or more magnetic tapes.
5. The tapes are maintained offline until the prescheduled processing time. When a given tape is needed, it is removed from its offline location and mounted on an online tape drive.
6. To accommodate the serial access requirements of magnetic tape, the input data are customarily sorted prior to processing into the sequence in which data are recorded on tape.

Variations in the above pattern are widely encountered. Online terminals may be used for data collection, for example. In such configurations, input data are key-entered at a terminal for direct transmission to a central processor and online disk storage. The input data are not processed immediately, however; they are merely batched up in a disk file awaiting processing against a master file at predetermined intervals. Similarly, data access through online terminals can be used as an output alternative to paper or microfilm listings. In such an approach, the master circulation file is maintained online on disks rather than tapes. Using a terminal and specially designed application programs, the file is queried to determine the circulation status of a given item or to retrieve other information. The file's contents, however, are still updated in the batch mode.

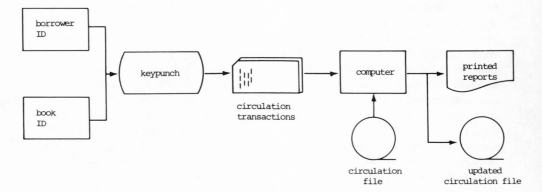

In the typical batch processing circulation system, information pertaining to individual transactions is punched on cards which are taken to a computer center at predetermined intervals. Information about transactions is processed against a master circulation file, which is typically maintained on magnetic tape. The master file is updated and various reports produced.

The batch processing methodologies described above have proved especially popular in transaction-oriented computer applications, such as accounts receivable, general ledger maintenance, payroll, and sales and order processing. When magnetic tape is used for the storage of data files and printed or microform reports are generated, batch systems are relatively simple and economical to implement and operate. The use of online terminals for input and/or output, however, can raise batch processing costs to a level approaching those of real time systems, although the costs associated with online terminals and disk storage have declined steadily and significantly over the past two decades.

Regardless of the particular equipment configuration employed, batch processing systems are invariably characterized by a potentially significant disadvantage: because data are accumulated for processing at predetermined intervals, there is a gap in time between the occurrence of a transaction or other event and the computer's processing of information about that event. Thus, in the circulation control example described above, the printed or microform lists that report the results of computer processing reflect the status of the library's circulating collection at the time when the latest batch of transaction records was taken from the library to the computing center for processing. Assuming that the library remains open, some of the information contained in such lists will necessarily be invalidated by circulation transactions occurring after a given batch was removed for processing.

As an example, a batch-oriented implementation may process records pertaining to circulation transactions at 5 p.m. each day, with updated lists being delivered to the library at 9 a.m. the following morning. Information about a given charge or discharge occurring at 5:01 p.m. on a Monday would not be reflected in a computer-generated listing until 9 a.m. the following Wednesday. In a transaction-based application of this type, some of the items appearing in a given computer-generated list of materials in circulation may have been returned, while other items not included in the list will have been checked out. Thus, unless a supplemental file is maintained manually, it is impossible to determine accurately the circulating status of a given item. The maintenance of such a manual file would obviously defeat the purpose of automating the circulation activity. The potential for inaccuracy inherent in batch processing systems can be minimized, of course, by processing batches and printing lists more frequently, but inaccuracy can only be eliminated entirely by real time data processing.

In computer implementations, the phrase "real time" can have several meanings. It is sometimes used to denote a type of computer system in which the results of computer processing are made available to the operator of an online terminal within a few seconds of the entry of a command or the submission of a task. As an example of such usage, online information services that allow users to search machine-readable data bases for bibliographic citations can be said to operate in a real time mode because the computer provides an immediate or extremely rapid response to entered search commands. For purposes of this discussion of modes of data processing, however, real time is used in a somewhat different sense: here it denotes a type of computer system in which information about transactions or other events is processed immediately after the transactions or events are initiated. Machine-readable data files are usually updated as an essential step in completion of a transaction or event. As a result, real time computer systems maintain data files that reflect the current status of a given application or situation, unlike batch processing systems, which reflect the status of an application or situation at some point in the past.

In a real time circulation control system, for example, charges, discharges, or other transactions are transmitted to and processed by a computer as they occur. The hardware and software characteristics of such

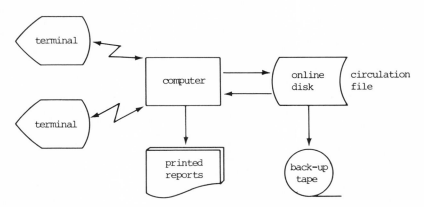

In real time systems, information pertaining to individual transactions is entered at online terminals and is immediately used to update master files, which are maintained on disks or other direct-access storage media. For security, data from disks are copied onto a backup magnetic tape. While online terminal inquiries are possible, various printed reports may still be produced.

systems are typically different from those required for batch processing. The data to be processed by real time systems are entered at online terminals and stored on fixed magnetic disks or other direct-access media. Unlike magnetic tapes, which must be mounted before use, fixed magnetic disks are continuously resident online. As an alternative to the printed lists employed in batch processing implementations, terminals are used for online inquiries and retrieval of data, such as the circulation status and due date of a given item.

Real time systems were originally developed in the late 1960s for processing airline reservations. They have since been utilized in a wide variety of applications where access to up-to-date information is essential. (Examples of real time systems for library applications are described in later chapters.) Although the cost differential is narrowing, real time systems have historically proved more expensive to develop and implement than batch processing systems. While meaningful cost comparisons are rarely reported in the literature of data processing, certain areas of potentially higher cost can be identified:

1. The online terminals and support equipment required in real time systems have no counterpart in the typical batch processing implementation, and consequently represent an added cost. Terminal equipment costs may be partially defrayed, however, by the elimination of costs associated with the production of paper or microform lists.

2. The magnetic disks required for online storage of data files in real time systems are more expensive than the magnetic tape used in batch processing applications. While magnetic disk storage costs are falling, they remain higher than magnetic tape costs. Data stored on magnetic tape are usually replicated on magnetic tape or other media for backup protection, thus further increasing the expense associated with real time systems.

3. Telecommunication facilities are required to link terminals and related local-site equipment with the computers on which data files are maintained and processed. No such costs are incurred in the typical batch processing installation, although there is a labor cost associated with the physical transportation of batches of cards or tape from a remote data entry site to the computer facility.

4. With many real time systems, a batch processing component is retained to produce printed reports as a backup information resource in the event of system failure or other unavailability. In addition, certain tasks related to real time operations may be performed in the batch mode. In circulation control applications, for example, charging and discharging may occur in real time, but overdue notices, hold notices, and other borrower communications are typically processed in batches.

The introduction to this chapter noted that the two pairs of terms—*online* and *real time, offline* and *batch*—are sometimes used interchangeably, even though they denote different concepts. The relationship between these terms requires further clarification. As described above, real time systems are invariably online systems, but batch systems may use online terminals to enter data. Similarly, data that are processed in batches may be maintained on magnetic disks for online retrieval through terminals. This is the case, for example, with most online library catalogs as well as with the data files maintained by online information services; such files are typically updated in batches at predetermined intervals. As a generalization, all real time systems are online systems, but a given online system may update stored information in either the batch or real time mode. Computer systems that use offline components are necessarily batch processing systems. It should further be noted that the two modes of data processing are not mutually exclusive, since most real time systems have one or more batch processing components.

Interactive Computing

Whether data are processed in the batch or the real time mode, computer specialists are increasingly emphasizing the development of online systems in which users, working at terminals, are prompted or otherwise guided by the computer in the performance of various information processing tasks. Such online systems are characterized as interactive because user commands and computer responses alternate in a more or less conversational manner. A computer program provides immediate information or instructions that may cause the user to modify work patterns. Such computer/user interaction is an obvious and indispensable component in online searching of library catalogs and other bibliographic data bases. A computer program responds to a user's search command with an indication of the number of potentially relevant citations or with a partial listing of bibliographic data. Depending on the computer's response, the user may decide to proceed with the search, modify the retrieval parameters to obtain more appropriate results, or take other action.

Although the advent of desktop computers permits the development of interactive computing applications in which a computer's entire resources are dedicated to a single user, interactive computing has historically been implemented in a timesharing environment. As the term suggests, timesharing is a method of operating a computer that allows two or more users to submit work for immediate processing. The computer's operating system employs a predetermined method to schedule and execute each job. Some timesharing operating systems use a straightforward first-in/first-out method of scheduling. Others employ a round-robin or "time slicing" approach in which the central processor interrupts and later returns to each job, devoting some predetermined amount of time—usually a fraction of a second—to it at each processing interval. In still another method, the timesharing operating system ranks jobs on the basis of their predetermined importance, estimated completion time, the status of the user submitting the work, or other factors.

Regardless of the particular job scheduling method employed, the operating system attempts to minimize the user's perception of the timesharing process, giving the impression that the computer's resources are entirely at a given user's disposal. Because full-size central processors and large minicomputers can perform millions of operations per second, a user might not perceive a delay in the execution of even a low-priority or complex task. The illusion that all computing resources are dedicated to a given user becomes extremely difficult to sustain, however, during peak work periods when many terminals are submitting jobs simultaneously. In such situations, the computer's response to a given user's commands may be measured in minutes rather than seconds. The degraded response times sometimes experienced by librarians who use online information services during mid-afternoon hours are typically attributable to the high demand associated with peak periods of terminal activity.

Appropriate response time, measured from the time a command is entered until information is displayed at the user's workstation, is one of several factors that ultimately influence a user's acceptance of online, interactive computing as an effective and comfortable alternative to familiar manual work methods. In any information processing system, user resistance can arise whenever established work habits must be changed. While it offers the substantial advantage of rapid response for retrieval or other information processing tasks, interactive computing may require significant user reorientation and retraining. Computer specialists have given considerable attention to the design of interactive programs that minimize problems associated with user adjustment. Such programs are often described as "user friendly." The computing industry's acknowledgement of their importance contrasts sharply with previous data processing practice in which users were too often required to have extensive familiarity with computer operations.

Simplicity and clarity are increasingly viewed as essential attributes of interactive programs. The best examples provide relatively few, but powerful, commands that enable users to perform significant amounts of work in a single step. A new user may be prompted or otherwise guided by one or more menus of alternatives or by unambiguous questions requiring the entry of a straightforward response. Microcomputer software packages, many of which are designed for first-time computer users, have done much to popularize such menu-driven interfaces. The graphical user interfaces described in chapter 2 are particularly noteworthy for their reliance on pull-down menu bars—horizontal lines of menu titles that expand to display lists of available commands when selected by the user. Menu titles and commands that do not apply to a particular program operation are usually displayed in a light shade and cannot be activated. Some menu selections activate dialog boxes with blank spaces for the entry of specific values or lists of options for operator selection. To maintain a consistent user interface and facilitate learning, software packages intended for a particular graphical user environment—such as a Macintosh system or an IBM-compatible microcomputer utilizing Microsoft Windows—may employ identical menus and dialog boxes for such commonly encountered tasks as file creation, page setup, and printing.

As noted in chapter 2, online documentation can often be consulted at any point in computer/user interaction without exiting from a given pro-

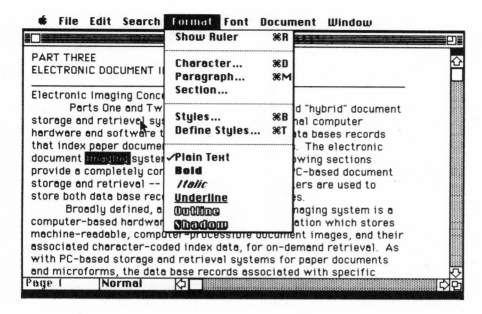

An increasing number of application programs make effective use of "pull-down" menus to facilitate command selection.

gram or invalidating work previously performed. Shortcuts or abbreviated commands are usually provided for experienced users who may be intolerant of the delay inherent in computer prompting. Well-designed interactive programs are forgiving of operator error and provide users with every opportunity to correct their own mistakes. When errors do occur, the best programs respond with a terse but clear explanation of the mistake and its correction procedure. Above all, a well-designed program makes users feel that they are in control of, rather than being controlled by, the interaction.

Online Terminals

While well-written programs offer an effective intellectual interface between the computer and the user of interactive systems, online terminals provide the required physical interface. For many libraries, online terminals are the single most important computer system component. When used in conjunction with appropriate telecommunication facilities, they provide a means of accessing a wide variety of computers and data processing services on a timesharing basis. Chapter 1 contained brief references to the hardware characteristics of online terminals. This section presents a more detailed discussion of their role in interactive computer systems, emphasizing those features and capabilities that are of greatest significance for library installations. It also provides an introduction to some fundamental telecommunication terminology and concepts.

An online terminal is a device that allows users to transmit data to, and receive data from, a computer or other information-processing machine by means of electronic digital pulses transmitted over connecting wires or other telecommunication facilities. This definition encompasses a wide range of data communication devices and must be refined to be meaningful. Terminal equipment can be subdivided, by mode of operation, into two groups: batch and interactive. Batch terminals are designed for the input of data or the production of output in applications for which interaction between the terminal operator and the computer is not required. Examples include card readers, magnetic tape input units, and high-speed printers that are typically located in remote job entry stations and that provide computer users with convenient local access to data entry or printing facilities.

Interactive terminals, the subject of this discussion, are designed for applications in which a user will interact with a computer in a more or less conversational manner. Rather than submitting a batch of data for later processing, interactive terminals allow users to enter commands, queries, or data one line at a time. Each line is acknowledged by the computer; the indicated action is taken, a rapid response produced, and the process repeated until the desired work is completed.

As a product group, interactive terminals can be categorized in four ways: (1) by their output capabilities, (2) by the combinations of components they include, (3) by their innate information processing capabilities, and (4) by the communications codes they employ. With respect to output capabilities, interactive terminals are commonly divided into printing and video display varieties. Printing terminals, sometimes described as teleprinters or teletypewriters, produce paper output as a record of computer/user interaction. They dominated interactive computing during the 1970s

With many Macintosh programs, dialog boxes solicit specific values or list options for operator selection.

but have since been replaced by video display terminals (VDTs) in most installations. Most video display terminals feature cathode-ray tubes (CRTs) as their display mechanisms. Most CRT-based terminals provide a 12-to-14-inch (diagonally measured) screen, although larger and smaller models are available. Small-screen models, which are designed for portability, utilize the flat panel display technologies described in chapter 1. Screen size aside, video display terminals are considered "soft copy" output devices, but they can be connected to an auxiliary printer in applications, such as online searching of bibliographic data bases, where paper output is desired.

The simplest video display terminals are alphanumeric devices. They can display the letters of the alphabet, numeric digits, punctuation marks, and other symbols encountered in textual documents. Depending on the model, the displayable repertoire may total 96 to 256 different characters and symbols. Most alphanumeric display terminals are dot matrix devices. They form individual characters by illuminating points on the video screen in a predetermined pattern. Such terminals are typically equipped with character-generation tables stored in read-only memories. On receipt of an incoming character code, the terminal looks up the appropriate dot matrix pattern for display. Of particular interest in bibliographic applications, some models are equipped with two or more character generation tables. The additional tables may contain foreign character sets, scientific character sets, or other special symbols.

Typographic capabilities aside, the most common alphanumeric display format provides 24 lines with up to 80 character positions in each, although some models can display up to 132 characters per line. Some video terminals provide one or two additional lines for prompts or the display of operating status information. Alphanumeric terminals capable of displaying as many as 60 lines at one time have been developed for special situations, such as word processing. Regardless of the display format employed by a particular VDT, a cursor—a special character in the shape of a rectangular block or underline—marks the position where the next character will be displayed.

In most cases, successive lines of entered or received data begin in the leftmost position of the first row and are displayed until the screen is filled, at which point the display typically scrolls upward to make room for additional lines. Normally, the data content of scrolled lines is lost as it disappears from the screen. Some display terminals, however, feature internal memories that are capable of storing one to eight screens of data. In such cases, the video display serves as a kind of "window" into memory, and special controls and commands allow the operator to recall previously displayed lines from memory to the screen. Such terminals are especially useful in library applications involving bibliographic searching where the screen may fill up rapidly with displayed citations.

Some video display terminals feature split-screen capabilities that allow ongoing computer interaction to be combined with the continuous display of data from one or more segments of memory. Thus, in a bibliographic searching application, the top portion of the screen might be dedicated to

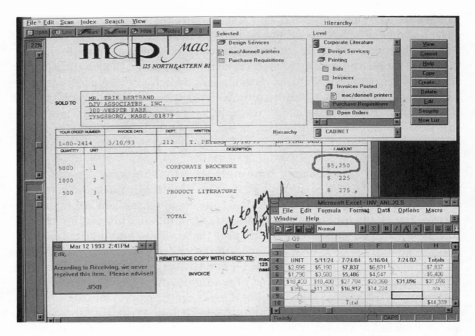

Interactive computer programs increasingly rely on special display capabilities, such as windowing.

the continuous display of a search strategy, while retrieved citations are displayed in the bottom portion. Several display terminals permit the simultaneous display of interaction with two or more application programs operating on one or more central processors. Interaction with different programs is displayed in separate windows.

As noted in chapter 1, the typical CRT-based alphanumeric video terminal displays light characters on a dark background, although most models allow the operator to select a reverse video presentation with dark characters on a light background. Reverse video is widely used for headings, data labels, and instructions requiring special emphasis. The most sophisticated alphanumeric video terminals allow the operator to selectively adjust the intensity and/or polarity of portions of the display in order, for example, to highlight certain data. With some terminals, this highlighting effect can be further enhanced by causing specified data to blink or by displaying selected characters in larger or smaller sizes. Color alphanumeric display terminals are available for applications where a multicolor presentation can effectively highlight important information and clarify relationships among displayed information.

Bit-mapped video display terminals, once reserved for scientific and engineering applications, are now commonly available in monochrome and color models. As described in chapter 1, such devices provide graphic as well as alphanumeric display capabilities. Sometimes described as "raster" displays, they draw graphic presentations as patterns of picture elements. In library applications, bit-mapped video terminals can be used to display business-type graphic presentations, such as line graphs and bar charts. Such graphics can be generated by various software packages described in chapter 2. Bit-mapped video terminals can also display digitized document images in desktop publishing and in the document storage and retrieval applications described in chapter 4. A special type of graphics terminal employs vector rather than raster display methodologies. Intended for computer-aided design and other engineering applications, such devices display geometric shapes by drawing lines between specified points.

With respect to the combinations of components that constitute an interactive terminal, three configurations can be distinguished. The most familiar, a keyboard send-receive (KSR) terminal, can both transmit and receive data. Its distinguishing feature is a keyboard that is used for the

Designed for scientific and technical installations, sophisticated graphic terminals can display drawings, diagrams, and plots in raster and vector formats.

entry of data or commands. The output mechanism may be a video display or a printer. The keyboard itself may be either integral to the terminal's chassis or connected to it by a cord. The latter design is preferred from the human engineering standpoint because it allows the operator to position the keyboard for maximum comfort during prolonged terminal use. The keyboard typically features a typewriter-like layout with additional keys to manipulate the cursor, simplify the entry of numeric values, activate functions associated with specific programs, and initiate and control the transmission of data.

A second terminal configuration, called receive-only (RO), is capable of displaying or printing data received from a computer but cannot itself transmit data. Physically, an RO terminal is distinguished from a KSR device by the absence of a keyboard. Receive-only display terminals are widely used for information dissemination in airports, hotels, and other public facilities. Receive-only teleprinters are most commonly attached to KSR display terminals in applications requiring selective paper output.

The third terminal configuration, automatic send-receive (ASR), was popular through the early 1980s but is rarely encountered any longer as newly manufactured equipment. It consists of a KSR terminal with peripheral attachments or internal electronic storage components that permit the preparation of machine-readable messages or other data before the establishment of an online connection with a computer. Most ASR terminals employed paper tape or magnetic tape units to prerecord messages or data. A few models featured expanded internal memories, including magnetic bubble memories. They were widely publicized during the 1970s but never enjoyed the commercial success that was predicted for them.

With respect to innate information processing capabilities, interactive terminals can be characterized as dumb, smart, or intelligent. Dumb terminals, the oldest and most primitive of the three varieties, derive all of their information processing capabilities from the computer with which they are communicating. They can perform effectively in a variety of library applications, but, aside from the ability to transmit and receive digitally coded signals, dumb terminals can perform no work unless they are operating online to a computer.

More an advertising concept than a precisely definable product group, smart terminals likewise lack self-contained information-processing capabilities, but they do incorporate certain microprocessor-based features that set them apart from simple dumb terminals. Such features include operator-selectable display attributes and transmission speeds, internal memory for simplified data preparation or the temporary storage of received data, and the ability to define or redefine the functions of specified keys to meet special application requirements. Given the economic and performance advantages of using microprocessors in the design and manufacturing of terminal equipment, most newer terminals are properly categorized as smart devices. Dumb terminals will cease to exist when the useful life of currently installed devices has elapsed.

As information-processing devices assume an increasingly important role in library operations, online terminals must compete with microcomputers for available desk space. While dumb and smart terminals are readily available and attractively priced, they do not offer the standalone information-processing capabilities—especially the ability to execute prewritten software packages—that many users want or need. Where such flexibility is required, an intelligent terminal is actually a microcomputer equipped with special hardware and software components that enable it to operate as a terminal for purposes of communicating with another computer. To function as a terminal, a microcomputer must be equipped with a communications program, examples of which were given in chapter 2. Originally designed as components in distributed processing networks, intelligent terminals can access remote computers to obtain data or programs for local processing. They can also be used in data entry applications to perform certain preparation and validation routines prior to transmission of information to other computers.

As a microcomputer, an intelligent terminal has self-contained information-processing capabilities. It can consequently be programmed by the user or can execute prewritten software packages when operating offline. In some installations, standalone computing is the equipment's primary application, and its ability to function as a terminal is reserved for occasional or supplemental communication requirements. As microcomputer prices have declined, intelligent terminals are increasingly the online devices of choice for many users.

As a significant performance advantage over conventional terminals, microcomputers equipped with appropriate communications software can exchange data and program files with other computing devices. If a communications software package is used to transmit one or more files to a remote device, the process is termed "uploading." When a microcomputer captures incoming information on a magnetic disk or other local storage media for later use, the process is termed "downloading." In the most common library application of downloading, bibliographic citations or other results of an online information search are recorded on a magnetic disk for editing by a word processing program following termination of the online session. Depending on the application, downloaded information may also serve as input to data base management or spreadsheet programs.

Whether dumb, smart, or intelligent devices are employed, an interactive terminal transmits and receives digital data in the form of an electrical signal consisting of a series of on/off pulses. Taken in combination, a predetermined number of these pulses, which represent binary digits or bits, form individual characters intended for transmission, printing, or display. Two coding schemes are widely utilized for terminal/computer interaction: the American Standard Code for Information Interchange (ASCII) and the Extended Binary Coded Decimal Interchange Code (EBCDIC). Both were described briefly in chapter 1.

The majority of available terminals transmit the ASCII code and employ serial asynchronous transmission techniques. In asynchronous transmission, the individual bits that represent a given character are framed (preceded and followed) by additional bits which separate successively transmitted characters from one another. The additional bits are required because such terminals are not synchronized with the computers with which they are communicating. In most cases, ASCII asynchronous terminals transmit an additional error-detection bit, called a parity bit, with each character. Terminals that transmit the EBCDIC code operate in the synchronous mode, sometimes described as the bisynchronous mode. Typically designed for communication with IBM mainframes, EBCDIC bisynchronous terminals are often described as 3270-compatible terminals. That designation refers to the IBM 3270 Display Station, one of the first video display terminals to employ the EBCDIC code.

In the field of data communications, transmission speeds are variously measured in bauds or bits per second (bps). While the two measures are sometimes used interchangeably, they are not identical. Terminals and computers transmit data by altering the amplitude, phase, or other condition of a telephone line or other communication facility. Successive alterations in line conditions represent the on/off pulses (bits) that encode individual characters. Bits per second, sometimes termed the "bit rate," is the most accurate and reflective expression of communication speed. It measures the number of bits transmitted by a terminal in a specified period of time.

Bauds, in contrast, measure fluctuations in the conditions of a telephone line or other communication facility. In the simplest case, successive telephone line fluctuations occur as the pulses representing individual bits are transmitted. In such cases, the bit rate and the baud rate are identical. For communication over voice-grade telephone lines at speeds exceeding 600 bits per second, however, most terminals employ coding schemes that transmit two or more bits per line fluctuation. In such cases, the bit rate will be higher than the baud rate, even though product descriptions and library literature often fail to observe this distinction. Terminals that transmit at 1200 bits per second, for example, usually operate at 600 bauds, although they may be advertised as "1200 baud" devices.

Available interactive terminals are capable of transmitting and receiving data at speeds ranging from 50 to 19,200 bits per second. The actual speed employed in a particular application depends on the telecommunication facility employed. Where dial-up, switched telephone lines are used for terminal-to-computer interaction, the most common speeds are 300, 1200, and 2400 bits per second. In ASCII asynchronous communications, each transmitted character is usually composed of 10 bits: seven bits to encode the character, two framing bits, and one parity bit. A terminal operating at 300 bits per second can consequently transmit 30 characters per second. The same coding patterns and character transmission rates apply at higher speeds. Thus, a 1200-bit-per-second terminal will transmit 120 characters per second and a 2400-bit-per-second terminal will transmit 240 characters per second. Some information specialists contend that transmission speeds greater than 2400 bits per second are inappropriate for interactive computing applications involving video display terminals, since incoming data will replace previously displayed information before it can be read and comprehended by the terminal operator. High data transmission rates can prove very effective in file transfer applications, however. At 9600 bits per second, for example, a word processing file containing 60,000 characters (the equivalent of approximately 35 double-spaced, typewritten pages) can be transmitted from one computer to another in a little over one minute. Transmission of the same file at 1200 bits per second would require more than eight minutes.

Transmission speed aside, most available terminals can operate in either of two line modes. In the half-duplex line mode, data entered at the terminal keyboard are both displayed locally and transmitted to a remote computer. Reception and transmission cannot occur simultaneously, however, and it is not possible to interrupt the reception and printing of data once they have begun.

In the full-duplex line mode, data entered at the terminal keyboard are transmitted to a remote computer, which echoes it back for display and verification of accurate reception. This usually happens instantaneously, giving the impression that the typed characters are being transferred directly to the terminal's screen as they are in the half-duplex mode. The full-duplex mode overcomes the indicated disadvantage of half-duplex communication by permitting simultaneous transmission and reception.

The decision to operate in the half- or full-duplex line mode is determined by the requirements of the computer system with which a given terminal is interacting. The user must know the mode required for communication with a particular computer and set the appropriate terminal controls, typically by positioning a switch on the terminal's chassis or selecting a command from a menu displayed by communications software. Selection of the incorrect line mode is the source of a common but easily corrected problem in terminal/computer interaction; if characters typed at the terminal's keyboard are not displayed on the screen, or if each character is displayed twice, the wrong mode has been activated.

Modems

As discussed above, online terminals communicate information in the form of an electrical signal that consists of discrete digital pulses. If a terminal is located in close proximity—typically, less than 1,000 feet—to the computer with which it must communicate, the digital signal can be transmitted over direct cable connections or other customer-owned wires. In such situations, the successive bits are represented by the presence or absence of an electrical current. For longer distance communication, however, the public telephone network is commonly utilized.

While it has been routinely employed for data transmission for several decades, the public telephone network was originally designed to transmit the continuously varying analog signals characteristic of the human voice. The discrete, digitally coded signals generated by online terminals and other computing devices must consequently be converted to analog form prior to transmission and reconverted to digital form following reception. This conversion process, which is termed "modulation and demodulation," is performed by modems. A modem—the term is actually a contraction for modulator/demodulator—is an electronic device that converts digital signals to and from the analog form required for transmission over telephone lines. In terminal-to-computer communication over analog telephone lines, both devices must be equipped with modems.

Conventional "industrial" modems are designed for use with dumb and smart terminals. While some terminals are equipped with internal modems, most are not. In such cases, an external modem and connector cable must be purchased separately. The connection of terminals to external modems is greatly simplified by widespread adherence to the Electronics Industry Association (EIA) RS-232C interface standard. So-called smart modems are designed specifically for installations where microcomputers will operate as intelligent terminals. They make extensive use of microprocessors and prewritten programs stored in read-only memory circuits to control operations, enhance flexibility, facilitate the diagnosis of equipment malfunctions, simplify repair, and reduce the number of component parts, with resulting improvements in reliability and heat dissipation.

In addition to converting data to a form suitable for online transmission and reception, smart modems can operate in a local mode in which they respond to commands entered at a microcomputer's keyboard or generated by communications software. These commands specify transmission parameters and initiate operations that would otherwise have to be performed manually or by the microcomputer itself. Most smart modems include automatic dialers and support unattended reception. In keeping with a growing tendency to have peripheral devices assume an increasing share of the information processing workload, some smart modems can even transmit and receive data when the microcomputer is turned off. Like their industrial counterparts, smart modems are available in internal and external configurations.

A modem converts digital signals to and from the analog form required for data communication over ordinary telephone lines.

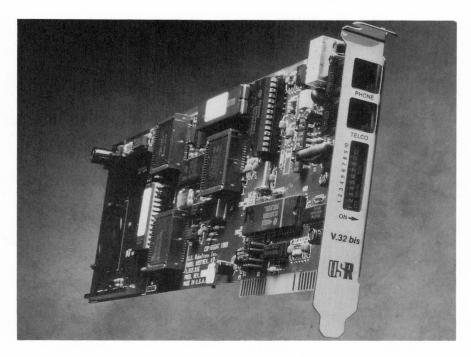

Internal modems, mounted on circuit cards, require no desk space and are usually less expensive than external models.

Regardless of the specific equipment configuration, communication protocols specify the procedures that industrial and smart modems observe when communicating with one another. Communication protocols are established by a combination of industry practice and standard-setting organizations. They provide the compatibility that is essential to effective communication between modems of different manufacturers. For terminal-to-computer communications over dial-up, switched (voice-grade) telephone lines, modems are commonly divided into three groups: low-speed devices, which transmit and receive at speeds up to 600 bits per second; medium-speed devices, which transmit and receive at speeds ranging between 600 and 9600 bits per second; and high-speed devices, which transmit and receive at speeds of 9600 bits per second or greater.

Within North America, the Bell 103A protocol governs low-speed data communication over voice-grade telephone lines. Taking its name from the modem that first utilized it, Bell 103A is one of several industry-standard protocols established by the American Telephone and Telegraph Company. Employed by terminals and microcomputers since the 1970s, it supports full-duplex communications at speeds of up to 300 bits per second. The CCITT Recommendation V.21, developed by the Consultative Committee on International Telephony and Telegraphy, is its international counterpart.

In North America, Bell 212A is the most important modem protocol for full-duplex communication at 1200 bits per second over voice-grade telephone lines. Unlike 103A-type modems, which transmit one bit at a time by altering the frequency of a carrier signal, Bell 212A modems operate at 600 bauds and transmit double bits by altering the timing of a carrier signal. To facilitate communication between computers equipped with different modems, 212A-type modems commonly support the Bell 103A protocol. The CCITT Recommendation V.22 is the international counterpart of the Bell 212A protocol.

Since the late 1980s, many libraries have replaced Bell 103A and 212A modems with devices that conform to the CCITT Recommendation V.22bis, the international standard for full-duplex data communication at 2400 bits per second over voice-grade telephone lines. Operating at 600 bauds, 2400-bit-per-second modems employ special phase modulation techniques to transmit four bits per baud. Modems that strictly observe the CCITT Recommendation V.22bis also support the V.22 international standard for data communication at 1200 bits per second. In North America, however, most modems that implement the V.22bis standard for communication at 2400 bits per second also support the Bell 212A and 103A protocols for slower operation.

Until recently, data communication at speeds exceeding 2400 bits per second required specially conditioned leased telephone lines. Advances in electronics technology, however, have permitted the development of modems that support the reliable transmission and reception of data over conventional voice-grade telephone lines. Early examples, which employed proprietary signaling schemes, have been replaced by modems based on standard protocols. Modems that conform to the CCITT Recommendation V.32 permit full-duplex communication over voice-grade telephone lines at 9600 bits per second. Based on telephone line conditions, these modems will automatically adjust the signaling rate downward to 7200 or 4800 bits per second to counteract the effects of line noise or other interference.

Even faster signaling rates are supported by the CCITT Recommendation V.32bis, which expands the V.32 standard to permit transmission and reception at 12,000 and 14,400 bits per second. Modems that conform to the CCITT Recommendation V.42bis employ data compression to raise the effective communication speed to levels approaching 38,400 bits per second. The extent of compression and the resulting data rate achieved in a particular situation, however, depend on the characteristics of the information being transmitted; data bases, spreadsheets, and graphic files will typically yield higher compression ratios than word processing documents. At the time of this writing, CCITT standards were being developed for uncompressed data transmission at speeds of up to 19,200 bits per second over voice-grade telephone lines.

Regardless of protocol, most modems establish a direct electrical connection to the public telephone network via modular jacks and cords. Through the early 1980s, many libraries employed terminals equipped with acoustic couplers as an alternative to modems. A variant form of external modem, an acoustic coupler consists of a microphone and speaker in rubber cups designed to cradle a telephone handset. When its speaker is aligned with the telephone's transmitter and its microphone is aligned with the telephone's receiver, the acoustic coupler converts the terminal's electrical signal to audible tones for transmission through the telephone network. Although acoustic couplers are compatible with most terminals and telephones, they are vulnerable to transmission impairments and have difficulty accommodating weak signals. Most of them have been replaced by conventional modems, which are less expensive and offer much better performance.

ORGANIZATION AND MANAGEMENT OF DATA

Whether it is accessed through online terminals for real time updating or submitted in batches for offline processing, computer-processible information is usually organized in a structured format for storage and processing. Chapter 1 discussed the various auxiliary storage devices and media on which machine-readable data can be stored while awaiting processing. The first part of this chapter briefly described the role of magnetic disks and tapes in real time and batch processing. In considering the organization of data on such media, it is necessary to distinguish between physical and logical storage structures.

Physical and Logical Data Structures

As defined in chapter 1, computer-processible information consists of a sequence of bits recorded on magnetic or other media. For a computer to update, retrieve, or otherwise process specified information, its physical location—that is, its position within a machine-readable storage medium—must be known. Once the information has been located by the central processor, its logical structure—that is, the method by which the recorded bits are combined to represent numbers, characters, words, or other information—must be understood. With both physical location and logical data structure, a hierarchy of organizational concepts is recognized, and certain terms are widely used to denote the various levels in the hierarchy. Some of these concepts and terms are most meaningful to programmers or other data processing specialists. The following discussion concentrates on those that are significant for library automation.

While specific physical storage structures are largely determined by the types of auxiliary storage devices and machine-readable media employed, a hierarchy of structural levels can be delineated in a general way. At the highest level, for example, information is stored on a particular disk drive, magnetic tape unit, or other hardware device. One level lower in the hierarchy, the physical medium on which machine-readable information is recorded is called the volume. Examples of such volumes include hard disks, floppy disks, magnetic tape reels or cartridges, and optical disk cartridges. In some hardware configurations, the physical storage device and volume are identical; this is the case, for example, with fixed hard disk drives. With removable media, however, the one-to-one correspondence between a device and a volume is temporary.

In either case, a given storage volume is further partitioned in a manner that varies with the type of auxiliary storage peripherals employed. With multiple-platter magnetic disk cartridges (removable hard disks), for example, each volume is divided into cylinders, which are, in turn, subdivided into tracks. Within individual tracks, information is recorded consecutively, bit by bit. The unit of stored information that can be read into, or written from, main memory in a single operation is called a physical record. Each physical record is composed of a sequence of bits. With floppy disks, optical disks, and magnetic tape, this structural hierarchy is abbreviated; each physical volume is subdivided into records, and the cylinder concept is eliminated.

While these physical storage structures denote the locations of computer-maintained information, logical storage structures are concerned with its content. Earlier in this chapter, the term *file* was used to denote a collection of machine-readable information to be processed by a given application. The term is derived from the manual information systems that computers typically replace. It is often preceded by a description denoting the physical storage medium on which information is recorded—hence, the expressions "disk file" and "tape file," for example. Alternatively, and more meaningfully, a given file may be described in terms of the content of the data it contains and the applications it serves. Computerization of circulation control, for example, typically requires a bibliographic file that contains information about a library's holdings, an item file that contains information about individual circulating copies, and a patron file that contains information about registered borrowers. Similarly, the computerization of library acquisitions activities requires the establishment of machine-readable files that contain information about vendors and items on order. Often additional adjectives, such as "master," "update," "temporary," or "backup," are used to reflect a given file's relationship to other files. Computer files may be further categorized as text files, data files, or image files, depending on the type of information they contain.

Text files are widely associated with word processing programs. They may also be produced by electronic messaging software, optical character recognition equipment and programs, text editors of the type furnished as utility programs with some operating systems, and various special-purpose information processing devices, including typesetters and telex machines. As their name suggests, text files contain computer-processible information in character-coded form—that is, each character is represented by a predetermined number and sequence of bits. The bit sequences that represent individual characters are determined by the digital coding scheme employed by a particular computer system; the ASCII and EBCDIC codes, as previously described, are the most widely encountered examples.

Text files store information in a relatively unstructured manner. In most word processing applications, for example, a text file usually consists of a single record—the machine-readable equivalent of a typewritten document consisting of one or more pages. Alternatively, a text file may contain several or many documents. In such cases, individual records may be separated by page break commands or other delimiting characters. Their physical sequence within a text file may be based on their order of creation or logical interrelationships. Word processing and other text-oriented programs typically place few significant restrictions on the lengths of text files or the records they contain, although limits may be imposed by available memory or other hardware characteristics.

If text files contain numeric digits, they are simply stored as characters, without regard to their quantitative significance. Data files, in contrast, store numbers as quantitative values. They can also store character-coded textual information, but they differ from text files in their more structured format. Data files contain records that are subdivided into one or more data elements, called fields, which store particular categories of information. As an example, a data file designed for bibliographic control of technical reports maintained by a special library will contain one record for each technical report in the library's collection. Within each record, designated fields may store such information as a report number, author, title, date the report was prepared, originating department, and subjects. Fields are sometimes divided into subfields. Within bibliographic records, for example, an imprint field may consist of subfields for publisher, place of publication, and date of publication. Similarly, the home address field in a borrower data file may be subdivided into street number and name, city, state, and zip code.

In the hierarchy of logical storage structures, a field is a component of a logical record used for a particular category of information. Fields may be of fixed or variable length. In the former case, a predetermined amount of storage space—sufficient to accommodate a specified number of alphanumeric characters, for example—is allocated for each field value. Long values are truncated to fit the predetermined allocation; short field values are padded with blanks to attain the desired length. In contrast, the space allocated to variable-length fields is dynamically adjusted to accommodate specific values. Fixed- and variable-length fields may be intermingled with records. This is often the case in library applications. As described in chapter 6, the MARC format for bibliographic records incorporates both fixed- and variable-length fields.

Within data files, records may be arranged in various sequences. Commonly encountered possibilities include sequential files, indexed-sequential files, direct data files, and indexed data files. Sequential arrangements are the simplest; records are ordered, or sorted, by values contained in a designated field, which is variously described as the "sort field," "key field," or "sort key." Records in a borrower data file, for example, may be arranged in alphabetical order by borrower name, while records in an acquisitions file may be arranged in ascending or descending numeric sequence by order number. In some cases, a secondary sort field must be used to differentiate records that contain identical values in the primary sort field; borrower records for persons with the same name, for example, may be sorted by zip code or borrower number. Sequential arrangements are typically employed in applications with straightforward processing characteristics and infrequent updating requirements. Sequential data files are updated by reorganization at scheduled intervals. In some applications, several versions of sequential data files, arranged by different sort fields, may be created for specific purposes.

In the indexed-sequential approach to data file arrangement, records are ordered sequentially as described above, but indexes indicate the physical locations—typically, the block numbers—of records that contain particular values in one or more designated fields. To process a given record, the appropriate index is first consulted to determine its block number. Individual records within that block are then examined sequentially until the desired record is located. Availability of an index improves access time by eliminating the time-consuming examination of all records, as is the case with conventional sequential files. In some implementations, multilayer indexes are created to improve access time.

With direct data files, the arrangement of records is determined by arithmetic calculations performed on designated field values. Typically, a computer program transforms specific field values—such as a borrower's social security number or a book's accession number—into physical storage locations on magnetic disks or other direct-access media. As an example, a field value may be divided by a specified number and the quotient utilized as the record's disk location. Such computational procedures are sometimes termed "hashing." Direct data files permit rapid access, but records can only be retrieved by the field values from which their storage locations were derived.

Where rapid retrieval by multiple parameters is required, indexed data files provide access to records through one or more indexes which contain pointers to records having specified values in designated fields. The indexes are stored in separate files sometimes described as inverted files. They may be created for all or selected fields. In the latter case, fields selected for indexing are termed "key fields." Indexed data files are invariably stored on magnetic disks or other direct-access storage media. Unlike the indexed-sequential method described above, the physical arrangement of records within indexed files is insignificant, since all access is based on index lookups.

Computer-processable, digitally coded images are an increasingly important type of machine-readable record. Computer-processable images may be created by a wide variety of programs and devices, including document scanners; computer-aided design (CAD) programs; computer painting, drawing, and other graphic arts programs; statistical and demographic analysis programs; geographical information systems; and spreadsheet programs which include graphic capabilities. Depending on their source, images may be encoded in object-oriented or bit-mapped formats.

Object-oriented images are described in terms of geometrical objects, such as points, lines, and circles. Sometimes termed "vector-based" or "shape-defined" images, they are generated by many computer-aided design and computer-based drawing programs. Bit-mapped images, sometimes termed "raster-based images," consist of dots that represent tonal values. Bit-mapped images are generated by document scanners and computer painting programs. They may be compressed to conserve storage space. Because they utilize different methods of representing images, object-oriented and bit-mapped files are incompatible with one another. Conversion programs exist, but they are not invariably effective.

The Data Base Approach

In many data processing applications, individual data files—based on the physical and logical structures outlined in the preceding section—are specifically designed to meet the requirements of particular application programs. Thus, a library that has computerized both circulation control and acquisitions activities will typically have separate bibliographic data files, each with record formats suited to the requirements of programs written to support those applications. This approach, which dominated data processing through the mid-1970s, poses several problems, the most obvious being data redundancy and its resulting wasted storage space and higher storage costs. It is likely, for example, that much of the same bibliographic data will be stored in both circulation and acquisition files. As an additional difficulty, the potential for inconsistencies and inaccuracies is increased when identical data are stored in separate files, since a change made in one file will not necessarily be replicated in other files.

As a further limitation, the maintenance of separate data files limits flexibility. Because existing file arrangements and records formats are optimized for processing by particular application programs, the writing of new programs requires the creation of additional data files formatted to address that specific program's requirements. Similarly, modifications to existing application programs often require changes in file structure, while changes in file structure—the addition of a new field, for example—may necessitate extensive program modifications.

Finally, and perhaps most significant for library automation, the separate data file approach ignores relationships between applications and activities. If the data maintained in separate files are integrated, the information captured by a computerized acquisitions system at the time an item is ordered can later be used and enhanced by computerized cataloging and circulation activities. Similarly, the same bibliographic data that support computerized circulation control can serve as the basis for an online catalog, and information about the circulation status of particular items can be incorporated into bibliographic data. This integrated approach is a major focus of various library automation systems described in later chapters.

While separate data files are still widely used, computer systems specialists increasingly recognize the advantages of the data base approach for the organization and management of machine-readable information. As used in this book, a data base can be broadly defined as an integrated accumulation of computer-processible information organized for use in various applications. The information itself may be numeric, textual, or even graphic in nature. Many librarians are familiar with data base services that provide online access to various types of bibliographic and nonbibliographic information. These services and their importance for library automation are discussed in chapter 7. This section will summarize some fundamental data base concepts.

Because terminology dealing with this facet of information processing is subject to considerable variation, it is important to distinguish data bases—as they are discussed in this section—from the data files described above. Unlike a data file, a data base is not established for use by any one

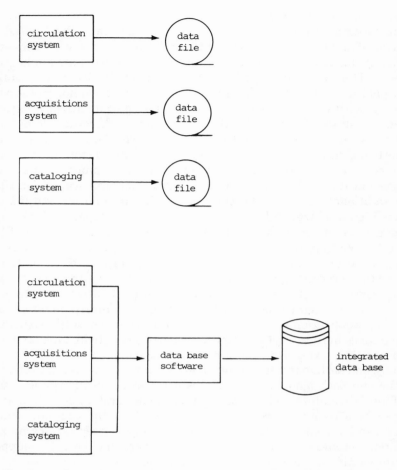

In older approaches to data management, individual but related applications were served by separate data files tailored to the requirements of specific application programs (top). The resulting problems of data redundancy and integrity have led many computer users to establish integrated data bases that can be used by several applications (bottom). Data base management systems, an example of systems software, provide the necessary interface between the data base and individual application programs.

application program. Instead, it is designed to be program-independent. It provides a common repository of information organized in a manner that various application programs can use. While data bases are typically maintained on fixed magnetic disks or other direct-access storage media for online availability, they can also be processed by programs operating in the batch mode. A given data base's organization and content are initially determined by systems analysts following a careful study of application requirements, users' expectations, and the types of information maintained in existing files.

Once a data base is established, continuing additions to, and refinements of, its structure and content are typically the responsibility of a data base administrator (DBA) who maintains close working relationships with application programmers and data base users. The data base administrator, usually assisted by a staff of data processing professionals and an advisory committee, monitors data base performance, supervises the preparation of documentation, and maintains a data dictionary. The data dictionary is itself a machine-readable collection of information about a data base, including its content, physical storage structures, authorization checks and validation procedures, and the utilization of particular data by specific departments. The data base administrator also develops strategies for backup and recovery of data in the event of a computer system failure.

Properly applied, the data base approach addresses the previously discussed problems associated with data files. The integration of separate files in a single data base eliminates redundancy, reduces storage requirements, and improves data integrity. Because an integrated data base is program-independent, changes can be made in its organization and content without requiring corresponding modifications in application programs. Similarly, changes in existing programs will not necessarily be accompanied by data base modifications.

The implementation of an integrated data base offering these advantages is accomplished through a data base management system (DBMS), a complex set of programs designed to facilitate the establishment and utilization of a data base. This definition, and the discussion that follows, applies mainly to data base management systems designed for mainframe and minicomputer installations. As discussed in chapter 2, a type of data management software package called a data base management system is also available for microcomputer installations, but such products may not offer all of the characteristics and capabilities of their mainframe and minicomputer counterparts. As their most significant difference, they typically maintain information in separate but linked data files rather than in a unified data base.

Data base management systems for mainframe and minicomputer installations customarily include programs that organize and load a user's data onto disks or other direct-access storage media, while establishing and maintaining various indexes to the stored data. Such data base management systems are properly categorized as examples of system software. While they can be custom developed to meet the requirements of a specific data processing installation, they are usually purchased as prewritten software packages. Examples include the IMS and DB2 data base management systems from IBM Corporation, ADABAS from Software AG, IDMS from Cullinane Corporation, INQUIRE from Infodata Systems Incorporated, System 2000 from MRI Systems, MODEL 204 from Computer Corporation of America, Supra from Cincom Systems, Rdb from Digital Equipment Corporation, Oracle from Oracle Corporation, INGRES from Ingres Corporation, Informix Online from Informix, and Sybase from Sybase Incorporated. While some vendors treat their data base management systems as operating system components, most design them as optional software packages to be purchased separately, often at substantial cost.

Available data base management programs differ in the method, or model, that they employ to organize stored data. Some systems employ a treelike hierarchy or network storage structure which reflects logical relationships among records. A field within each record contains a reference, or pointer, to the location(s) or subordinate record(s) elsewhere in the data base. Such data base management systems are sometimes described as physically linked because their pointers provide pathways along which the system seeks desired data. As an alternative to physical linkage, some data base management systems establish indexes to stored records. This approach, sometimes called the "inverted access method," is especially useful in applications requiring the retrieval of information by multiple parameters. In a third method, which is based on theories derived from relational mathematics, the data base management system uses a series of relatively simple tables to reflect relationships among stored records. This relational model has been widely publicized. In addition to mainframe and minicomputer implementations, it is often employed by data base management software packages designed for microcomputer installations.

Regardless of the particular organizational model employed, a data base serves as a common repository for computer-processable information. As described above, it replaces separate files that address the specific needs of individual application programs. Data base records must consequently be accessible to programs written in COBOL, FORTRAN, or other languages, and each program must be able to access only those parts of a data base that are appropriate to its purpose. From the programmer's standpoint, the processing of data base records is accomplished through procedural statements that can be embedded in application programs. Beyond the fact of its existence, this interface between computer programs and data base management systems is of little interest to librarians or other data base users.

More significant is the ability of many data base management systems to accommodate ad hoc information retrieval requests through a specially developed query language, sometimes called a fourth-generation language (usually abbreviated as 4GL). This nomenclature reflects the position of query languages in a chain of software development that began with first-generation machine-level languages and includes assembler languages as the second generation and higher-level languages as the third generation. Presumably, a fifth-generation approach to software development will emphasize natural language programming involving simple English-language instructions with few or no syntactic or semantic restrictions.

Unlike conventional programming languages, which require the specification of detailed instructions that a computer must follow to identify and retrieve data, query languages allow a nonprogrammer working at an online terminal to initiate searches and produce reports by entering a series of commands accompanied by specified retrieval parameters. Query languages are consequently classified as nonprocedural languages because their users tell the computer what data to retrieve rather than how the desired retrieval operation is to be performed. While they do not permit the unrestricted use of natural language in the expression of information retrieval requirements, query language commands are typically easy to learn. The use of query languages does not require the training in algorithmic thought and the memorization of elaborate sets of rules that characterize most conventional programming languages. In an application involving a bibliographic data base, for example, the entry of a specified sequence of commands might result in the rapid retrieval of books and articles indexed with a particular subject heading or written by a particular author. Query languages, which function at a higher level of abstraction than conventional programming languages, are an important feature of the information retrieval capabilities offered by the various online information services discussed in chapter 7. Support for query languages that can initiate complex searches involving the logical coordination of several or many retrieval parameters is an important feature of data base management systems. It enables such systems to satisfy information retrieval requirements which either cannot be anticipated or occur too infrequently to justify customized programming.

Text Storage and Retrieval Systems

The characteristics of text storage and retrieval programs as a special category of data base management system were briefly discussed in chapter 2. Like conventional data base management systems, such programs create, maintain, and manipulate files of computer-processible records, but the records contain the unstructured textual contents of complete documents. The documents, which are stored in character-coded form, may be generated by word processing programs, electronic messaging systems, or other computer applications capable of producing text files of the type described earlier in this chapter. Alternatively, existing paper documents may be converted to character-coded text by optical character recognition or, as a method of last resort, key entry. In any case, text storage and retrieval programs create indexes to every significant word in stored documents. The indexes permit the rapid identification and retrieval of text segments containing specified character strings. Some text storage and retrieval programs also support field-oriented records in the manner of conventional data base management systems. In a library application involving technical reports, for example, each bibliographic record might contain fields for such data elements as author, title, originating department, release date, and subject headings, plus an additional long field that contains the complete text of a report.

Experimental text storage and retrieval implementations date from the mid-1960s. Typically conceived as demonstration projects designed to test the efficacy of particular indexing and retrieval methodologies, they involved small numbers of documents, narrowly circumscribed applications, and tightly controlled user groups. Operational systems intended for library reference and research applications were implemented in the early 1970s when online information services introduced full-text retrieval capabilities. Such implementations were initially limited to relatively short bibliographic records, some of which contained abstracts. The LEXIS search service, which is discussed more fully in chapter 7, was the first operational system to provide online access to the complete text of large document collections.

Prewritten software packages suitable for in-house implementation of text storage and retrieval capabilities became available during the 1960s. The earliest examples, such as IBM's Storage and Information Retrieval System (STAIRS), were designed for mainframe installations. Product availability increased significantly during the 1970s and 1980s. Examples for mainframes and minicomputers include ASSASSIN from Associated Knowledge Systems, BASISplus from Information Dimensions, BRS Search from BRS Software Products, CC SEARCH from CC Software, Docu/Master from Document Systems Incorporated, Info DB+ from Henco Software, Inquire/Text from Infodata Systems Incorporated, QL/Search from QL Systems Limited, STATUS from CP International, TEXTDBMS from Data Retrieval, Textware from Unibase Systems, TOPIC from Verity Incorporated, and TRIP from Paralog AB. Microcomputer-based text storage and retrieval programs of the type described in chapter 2 have been available since the mid-1980s.

Libraries, archives, and related organizations have utilized text storage and retrieval programs to manage a variety of documents, including proprietary scientific, technical, and managerial reports; laboratory notebooks; patent case files; material safety data sheets; standard operating procedures; and conference presentations, preprints, and reprints. Most implementations have been in industrial, technical, medical, and law libraries where complex retrieval operations necessitate powerful search capabilities. Text storage and retrieval programs can search the complete texts of documents for specified words or, in most cases, word roots. Boolean operators can be used to broaden or narrow retrieval specifications. As a distinctive and useful alternative to Boolean operations, most text storage and retrieval programs support commands that can locate documents containing two or more words in a specified proximity relationship. Depending on the program, such commands may be able to retrieve documents containing two or more words in the same paragraph, in the same sentence, or within a specified number of words of one another. An increasing number of text storage and retrieval programs offer hypertext capabilities, which link interrelated documents and allow words in previously retrieved text segments to be used as search terms.

Depending on the program utilized and the operator's preferences, documents identified by a full-text search may be displayed or printed in their entirety. Alternatively, retrieval may be limited to sentences, paragraphs, or other text segments that contain specified search terms. Some text storage and retrieval programs rank documents or document segments by their presumed relevance and will display them in ranked sequence. Such rankings are usually based on the frequency and proximity of the search terms they contain.

As an unusual alternative to text storage and retrieval programs, several vendors offer hardware-based systems that are described as associative processors or text array processors. Such devices are special-purpose computers engineered specifically for high-speed, sequential searches through character-coded text files. Some associative processors are designed for self-contained operation. Others operate online to a mainframe or minicomputer; they receive retrieval requests formulated by application programs running on the computers to which they are attached. In either case, the requests specify words or phrases to be searched in specified text files. Rather than consulting indexes or employing other software access methods to determine the text file locations of records meeting the indicated retrieval requirements, the associative processor examines the specified text files sequentially, seeking a match for the listed items.

Associative processors are a logical extension of the much-publicized disparity between the dramatically declining cost of computer hardware and the rapidly rising cost of software development. They are less commonly encountered in North America than in Europe, where their proponents cite several advantages over text storage and retrieval programs, including reductions in disk storage requirements through the elimination of indexes, and savings in mainframe or minicomputer time for searches that are offloaded to an associative processor. In some respects, however, associative processors represent a reversion to older retrieval methodologies. Early information retrieval systems that employed sequential searching of magnetic tape files were ultimately replaced by high-performance software that relied on disk storage and indexed access. In returning to sequential searching, associative processors rely on the latest developments in computer technology to attain very rapid search rates. Capable of performing millions of comparisons per second, associative processors can effectively address certain information retrieval requirements for which indexed access is impractical. As an example, they have been utilized to continuously monitor newswire feeds or similar incoming data streams for records that contain specific subject terms, personal names, company names, or other text segments.

DISTRIBUTED DATA PROCESSING

Centralized computing facilities have often been criticized for failing to respond satisfactorily to users' information processing requirements. Decentralized computing configurations give individual departments or offices greater control over those data processing activities that affect their operations directly. The decentralization of computing resources gained considerable popularity during the early to mid-1970s. At that time, interest in decentralized computing was stimulated by the availability of relatively inexpensive minicomputers. It has intensified with the increasing availability and power of microcomputer systems. Autonomous decentralized systems can, however, create coordination problems in installations where related activities must have access to identical data. Properly implemented, distributed computer systems can effectively address such coordination problems.

Distributed System Concepts

Distributed data processing is a method of managing computing resources in which data processing capabilities are placed closer to the user while preserving the overall coordination of resources. In distributed data processing, two or more computers are used in combination to perform the work associated with a particular application. An integrated configuration of computers functioning in this manner is described as a distributed system. If the computers that constitute a distributed system are geographically dispersed, the system may be described as a computer network. The technology and organization of computer networks are discussed later in this section.

While the phrase "distributed system" was first used in the mid-1970s, the distribution of functions among multiple computers has been a familiar data processing practice since the 1960s. Mainframes and minicomputers, for example, can be configured for multiprocessing operations, in which portions of a given program are simultaneously executed by two or more central processors. Similarly, in multiprogramming configurations, multiple programs are simultaneously executed on two or more computers which share a common memory. Historically, however, the widespread implementation of distributed systems has been linked to the development of minicomputers and other small, relatively inexpensive computing devices. While the earliest minicomputers were most often configured as decentralized, self-sufficient computing devices dedicated to particular applications, the early 1970s saw their increased use as special-purpose processors operating online to larger computers. As an example, data processing centers often use a front-end minicomputer to perform time-consuming tasks associated with the control of online terminals in a timesharing system, thereby allowing the resources of the system's mainframe or large minicomputer to be deployed more efficiently. Similarly, a

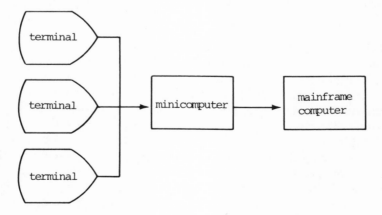

In a simple and commonly found example of distributed processing, a front-end minicomputer performs the time-consuming tasks associated with the control of online terminals in a time-sharing system, thereby allowing the resources of the system's mainframe computer to be used more effectively.

minicomputer may be used as a back-end processor dedicated to data base management, thereby freeing a larger computer of those operations.

While ideas about the interrelationship of distributed system components are still evolving, two different system structures—horizontal and hierarchical—are widely implemented. In a horizontal distributed system, two or more central processors are interconnected for purposes of data or resource sharing. By supporting computer-to-computer file transfers, such horizontal distributed configurations can minimize or eliminate the use of magnetic tape or other removable media for high-volume data exchange. They also allow specialized or expensive peripheral devices located at one computer site to be accessed by other computers with an occasional need for them. Often, horizontal distributed systems are used to spread a data processing workload over multiple machines. In a system composed of two computers, for example, one of the central processors may be used primarily for online computing; the other may perform batch processing while being prepared to shift to online work in the event that the first computer fails or becomes overloaded. Regardless of purpose,

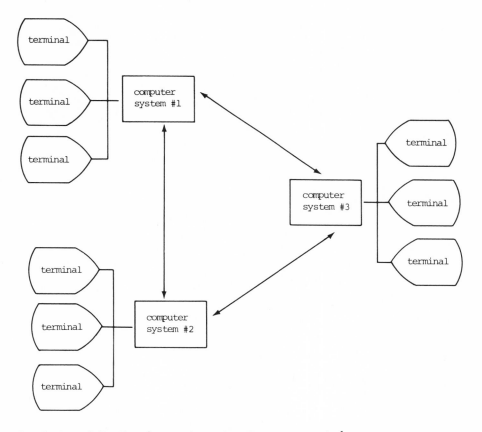

In a horizontal distributed processing system, two or more central processors are interconnected for purposes of sharing data or hardware resources. The central processors are considered peers, although they may vary in computing power.

however, the central processors employed in a horizontal distributed system are considered peers, although they may be of different brands and vary somewhat in computing power. Automated library networks in which one library's computer accesses the computers of other libraries in search of bibliographic data that are not available locally are based on horizontal distribution models.

In hierarchical distributed systems, certain computers are logically subordinated to other computers as application functions are subdivided in vertical fashion. The most common hierarchical systems feature a treelike structure in which data flow from and to the top. The computer at the apex of the hierarchy is termed the "host." It is usually, but not necessarily, a mainframe or large minicomputer. Computers that are subordinate to the host are described as "satellite processors." They may be microcomputers or minicomputers. Rather than enhancing the host's processing power in the manner of the multiple processors used in horizontal systems, the satellite processors in a hierarchical distributed system are often used to simplify the interface between the user and the host computer. In a data-entry application, for example, microcomputer-based intelligent terminals may be used to store and display various screen

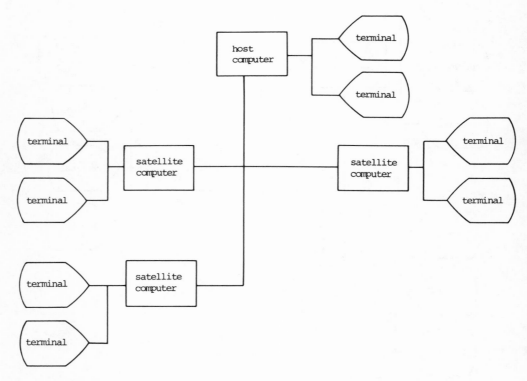

In a hierarchical distributed processing system, certain computers are logically subordinated to other computers. The subordinated computers are considered satellite processors, and they support the vertical distribution of work. Note that the host computer may support some terminals directly as well as through satellite processors.

formats, to prompt the operator for the entry of data in specialized fields, and to check data for such obvious errors as the entry of alphabetic characters in an exclusively numeric field or of numeric values that fall outside of a specified range. Detected errors are reported back to the operator for correction prior to transmission of data to the host computer.

In another example, users working at online terminals may enter a few sentences or a paragraph indicating their information retrieval requirements. This input might then be analyzed by a minicomputer- or microcomputer-based artificial intelligence program which determines appropriate search terms, initiates information retrieval operations, and returns the results to the user. In a simpler application, a microcomputer-based program can be used to translate the search commands required by one information retrieval system into those employed by others, thereby simplifying training requirements in libraries where one system is searched frequently but the others are accessed too occasionally to retain mastery of their search procedures. As a more commonly encountered application, a microcomputer operating as an intelligent terminal may be used to retrieve bibliographic citations or other information from data bases stored on one or more mainframes or minicomputers. The retrieved citations may then be processed by local software packages to combine them with information from other sources or to reformat them for input to data bases maintained by other computers.

While they differ in design, horizontal and hierarchical systems are not mutually exclusive distributed processing options. Some distributed systems feature a hybrid structure in which two or more hierarchical systems are linked horizontally at the host processor level. Alternatively, a given hierarchical system may have multiple host processors. Whether based on horizontal, hierarchical, or hybrid models, distributed data processing systems may employ distributed data bases which place required information closer to the hardware and software that will process it. A distributed data base is one that is partly or entirely stored in multiple locations. Data bases can be distributed in either of two ways: by partitioning or by replication.

A partitioned data base is one in which a given item of information is stored at only one location in a distributed system. Distributed systems designed for such applications as sales order processing, automated shipping, inventory control, and computerized reservation booking often partition their data bases geographically. Geographic partitioning is well suited to the horizontal distribution structure described above, but it is only practical where access to specific information is geographically determined. This is rarely the case with bibliographic data. A method that is perhaps more appropriate for library applications involves hierarchical partitioning in which unique local data bases are maintained by satellite processors. The totality of these local data bases forms the system's master data base. As an example, the online catalogs of individual libraries in a cooperative network might be maintained as local data bases controlled by satellite processors. The host computer could then handle requests from one satellite processor to access information maintained by others.

In the replicated approach to data base distribution, copies of all or parts of a data base are stored in two or more locations. As with partitioning, data bases can be replicated horizontally or, more commonly, hierarchically, with one or more satellite processors maintaining copies of those portions of a master data base that are most relevant for local operations. As an example, a master union catalog might be stored on a host computer located at a library system's headquarters, while satellite processors in the system's individual libraries maintain subsets of the master catalog corresponding to their own holdings.

Regardless of their structures or data base usage patterns, distributed systems offer potentially significant performance advantages when compared to conventional centralized or decentralized data processing configurations. By placing computer hardware and data bases closer to their users, problems and costs associated with long-distance communication facilities can often be minimized or eliminated. Problems of contention and delay are generally reduced in a distributed system. In addition, the use of minicomputers as satellite processors can eliminate the degraded response times that may occur under peak loads when many online terminals are directly connected to a single, centralized computer.

Compared to decentralized data processing, distributed systems offer improved coordination of computing resources. While users are often able to exploit their computing capabilities more directly and effectively than in centralized systems, distributed systems remain amenable to centralized enforcement of standard operating procedures. Furthermore, distributed systems offer somewhat greater resistance to failure, since the malfunctioning of any one component will only affect a subset of total system operations. Additional protection against the adverse effects of system failure is provided by redundancies in hardware and stored data.

As a cautionary note, distributed systems require careful planning involving multisite preparation. They can be more expensive to install and operate than centralized or decentralized data processing facilities. From the technical standpoint, the design and successful implementation of distributed systems require an understanding of principles of data communications and the fundamentals of computer networks.

Computer Networks

Broadly defined, a telecommunication network is a combination of equipment, transmission facilities, and, in some cases, software that supports the communication of information-bearing signals from one location to another. The most familiar telecommunication network, the public telephone network, was originally designed for the transmission of voice messages, although it is also used to transmit computer-processible information. Other telecommunication networks are designed to facilitate the transmission of messages between telex terminals and facsimile machines. A computer network is a specialized form of telecommunication network. It consists of various combinations of computers, terminals, and related equipment connected by data communication facilities. Computer networks are often categorized by their geographic spans: a wide area network (WAN) links geographically distant computers and related equipment, while a local area network (LAN) links computers and other devices that are located in close proximity to each other. In either case, the complex technical characteristics of computer networks are of primary interest to engineers and others responsible for actual network design and implementation. The following discussion is limited to terminology, concepts, and other facets of network design and function which are significant for librarians.

In computer network terminology, hardware components are called "nodes" and communication facilities are called "links." The specific types and combinations of nodes encountered in a given computer network will vary with the network's topology or structure. The simplest networks, common in timeshared mainframe and minicomputer configurations, feature a starlike topology in which terminals and other data communication devices are directly connected to a centralized host processor. In contrast, a more complex treelike network topology is better suited to the hierarchical structure characteristic of the distributed computer systems described above. With a treelike topology, terminals and related data communication devices are connected to intermediate nodes, which are, in turn, connected to a host processor or, in some cases, to other intermediate nodes. In most hierarchical distributed systems, the intermediate nodes are minicomputers that function as satellite processors. In some cases, however, the intermediate nodes may be special-purpose minicomputers or microcomputers functioning as communication controllers. To maximize the utilization of communication facilities and thereby reduce communication costs, several terminals may be connected to a single communication line, called a "multidrop" or "multipoint" line. In such equipment configurations, a minicomputer or microcomputer functions as an intermediate controller to resolve contention when two or more terminals want to communicate simultaneously.

Horizontal distributed systems, in which multiple computers function as peers, may be better served by a meshed network topology that provides direct connections between nodes. In a fully connected meshed network, each computer can communicate with every other computer. In a partially connected implementation, one node may serve as an intermediary between two other nodes. Compared to starlike or treelike topologies, the meshed network structure offers the advantage of alternative communication routes, so that a circuit failure in one part of the network will not invariably isolate a given node.

In a fourth network alternative, described as a ring topology, nodes are connected in circular fashion. Each node is linked to two others, and the last node is connected to the first. Information transmitted by a given node is passed around the ring until it reaches a designated recipient node. The ring topology is commonly encountered in local area networks. In a variation employed by the widely installed IBM Token-Ring Network, nodes are connected to hubs in starlike fashion, and the hubs are linked in a ring.

The linear bus, in which nodes are connected to a trunk cable, is another popular topology for local area networks. It is relatively easy to implement, uses less cable than some other topologies, and is readily expandable within limits imposed by the specific local area network in use. In a treelike variant of the linear bus topology, several nodes may be grouped for connection to the trunk cable. The daisy chain, a simpler variation suitable for small networks, connects individual nodes directly to one another. As in ring networks, information must be relayed from one node to another until it reaches its destination.

It is important to note that several topologies may be combined in a given network installation. For example, a timeshared mainframe or minicomputer that serves as the host processor in a starlike network may also be a node in a meshed network. Similarly, a local area network that uses a ring or linear bus topology to link microcomputers may provide a node for a minicomputer- or mainframe-based library automation system that supports online catalog access.

Communication links vary with network topologies and geographic spans. Wide area networks have traditionally relied on telephone lines in switched or dedicated varieties. With conventional dial-up telephone lines —properly described as "switched lines"—a communication circuit is established between two nodes for the duration of a given transmission. The connection is terminated when the transmission is completed. Subsequent transmissions between the same nodes require reconnections, which may employ different circuits of possibly varying quality. Switched telephone lines are customarily described as voice-grade rather than data-grade. Recognizing the potential for interference which can impede reliable transmission or reception, communication over switched telephone lines typically occurs at speeds of 2400 bits per second or lower. Although some modems described earlier in this chapter support faster transmission rates in certain circumstances, switched telephone lines are typically categorized as "narrowband" communication links because they respond to the bandwidth, or range of frequencies, characteristic of the human voice. Transmission speed is limited by available bandwidth; the narrower the bandwidth, the lower the speed.

Narrowband communication links are appropriate for terminal-to-computer interaction where the operator's typing rate and reaction time are limiting factors. "Wideband" communication facilities, which support faster speeds, are normally required for bulk transmission of large quantities of information between computers, as is the case in the distributed system implementations described above. Computer networks that support distributed systems typically employ dedicated telephone lines as communication links. Such lines are often described as leased lines because the customer pays a flat monthly fee for their unlimited use, as opposed to switched, dial-up lines for which monthly charges vary with the frequency, duration, and distance of specific calls.

As their name suggests, dedicated lines provide a permanent connection between two nodes in a computer network, thereby eliminating the quality variations associated with switched telephone lines. As an additional advantage, the reliability of dedicated lines can be improved through a technique called "conditioning," which minimizes interference and enhances the ability to transmit computer-processible information accurately at high speed. A single conditioned dedicated line can support communication speeds of up to 19,200 bits per second, while multiple conditioned lines can be combined to create wideband communication links capable of transmission rates in excess of 50,000 bits per second. In many computer networks, special-purpose computer-based devices called "multiplexers" and "concentrators" route traffic from low-speed to high-speed lines, thus permitting such relatively expensive facilities to be used in the most cost-effective manner.

Whether switched or dedicated, conventional telephone lines were originally designed for transmission of the analog signals characteristic of the human voice. As previously discussed, modems must be used to convert the digital signals generated by computers, terminals, and related communication devices to analog form prior to transmission. As computer networks have proliferated, there has been considerable interest in the development of communication facilities specifically intended for the transmission of digital signals. As its principal advantage, digital transmission is much less susceptible to interference and distortion than its analog counterpart. It is consequently better suited to reliable communication at high signaling rates. As an additional advantage, modems are not required.

AT&T, MCI, U.S. Sprint, and other companies offer several types of leased digital communication services that support domestic and international data transmission at rates of up to 56,000 bits per second. The so-called T-Series carriers provide even faster digital transmission facilities; T1 lines, for example, support data rates exceeding 1.5 million bits per second. Fractional T1 lines support lower signaling rates in increments of 64,000 bits per second. Integrated Services Digital Network (ISDN) services support digital transmission of data, images, and voice. ISDN technology is viewed as a comprehensive vehicle for a variety of telecommunication services, including enhanced telephony, high-speed data and message transmission, home telemetry, and the videoconferencing and videotext systems described in chapter 4. ISDN services and products have been available for several years, but their acceptance by businesses, government agencies, and other organizations has been slower than anticipated.

Some of the most interesting developments in telecommunication technology involve telephone lines only indirectly. As an example, some high-speed communication links employ fiber optics technology in which digitally coded signals are transmitted as pulses of light through thin strands of glass or plastic which serve as waveguides. Compared to copper wires, fiber optics offer the advantages of relatively low signal losses over long distances, compact size, durability under adverse environmental conditions, and immunity to external electromagnetic and radio frequency interference. Fiber optic links can support very fast transmission speeds. Data rates exceeding 100 million bits per second are routinely possible, and speeds of one billion bits per second have been demonstrated in experimental configurations.

Terrestrial microwave technology can transmit information at speeds comparable to those of leased telephone lines. Terrestrial microwave transmission facilities are not, however, as geographically wide-ranging or as versatile as the telephone network. To prevent deflection by obstacles in the communication path, microwave signals are usually transmitted by directional antennas spaced at maximum distances of 20 to 30 miles. This requirement for an unobstructed communication path necessarily limits the utility of terrestrial microwaves in long-distance communication. As a further complication, there is considerable congestion of currently allocated microwave frequencies in major metropolitan areas.

These problems can be minimized or overcome if microwave signals are first transmitted to satellites for amplification and retransmission to earth stations located at or near the intended reception point. Satellites suitable for data communication are positioned in the so-called geosynchronous or geostationary orbit located perpendicular to the equator approximately 22,300 miles above the earth's surface. In that orbit, the satellites revolve around the earth at the same speed at which the earth revolves around its own axis. They consequently occupy a constant position relative to earthbound antennas and serve as stationary relay devices in the sky.

Satellites have been used for international video broadcasting and voice communication since the 1960s. While underdeveloped countries, which lack a wire-based communications infrastructure, have long recognized their potential for domestic voice and data transmission, U.S. interest in satellites for those applications dates from the early 1980s. Since that time, several companies have introduced satellite communication services designed specifically for the transmission of business data at speeds ranging from several hundred thousand to several million bits per second. While they never experienced the spectacular growth that some industry analysts and entrepreneurs originally predicted for them, these satellite communication services offer effective, high-speed transmission capabilities suitable for high-volume applications.

The communication links described to this point are principally intended for wide area network installations. Such networks may be publicly accessible or intended for the private use of one or more institutions, government agencies, corporations, or other organizations. In the former category, a group of companies collectively called "value-added carriers" have created nationwide and international data communication networks that link computers, terminals, and various other data communication devices. Computer networks developed by such companies are termed "value-added networks." Examples include Tymnet, Sprintnet, and the CompuServe Network.

Unlike the conventional telephone network, which uses a single communication circuit to establish a transmission link between two points, value-added networks employ packet-switching technology. Information is subdivided into segments or packets, each of which may be transmitted to its intended destination by a different route. At the destination point, the packets are assembled into their proper sequence under computer control.

Packet-switching promotes the efficient use of available communication facilities with a resulting reduction in communication costs, especially in applications involving long-distance transmission. Many libraries utilize value-added networks to access the online information services and bibliographic utilities described in later chapters.

Perhaps the best-known example of a publicly accessible wide area computer network is the Internet. It is actually a collection of networks that interconnect computers in universities, government agencies, scientific laboratories, corporations, and other organizations. At the time of this writing, the Internet connected over eight million users to more than 8,000 networks consisting of more than 1.3 million computers of various types and sizes. Many library catalogs, as well as reference and research data bases on a variety of subjects, can be accessed via the Internet. It also supports international electronic messaging capabilities, bulletin boards, and computer conferencing services. Public domain software can be downloaded from various computers. Several organizations use the Internet as a publishing medium for electronic books and journals. Libraries associated with universities, government agencies, and corporations can gain access to the Internet through nodes operated by their host institutions. Other types of libraries can obtain Internet access through computer service companies at modest rates.

Local Area Networks

Since the late 1970s, local area network concepts and technologies have played an increasingly prominent role in the planning, implementation, and operation of computer networks in general and microcomputer networks in particular. As previously defined, a local area network connects computers and related devices located within a narrowly circumscribed geographic area, such as a college campus, an industrial park, a school, an office building, a military base, a warehouse, a factory, or a library. The geographic span of a local area network—defined as the maximum permissible distance between the furthest nodes—may be several miles, but most installations involve a much smaller area. Another essential attribute of local area networks is full intercommunication capability, meaning that every network node must be capable of communicating with every other network node. A local area network is a data communication network for independent devices capable of autonomous operation. LAN nodes may be computers or autonomous noncomputer devices, such as facsimile machines. Printers, disk drives, and other nonautonomous peripheral devices are not themselves considered nodes, although they may operate as LAN devices attached to nodes.

The autonomous node and intercommunication requirements distinguish local area networks from conventional timeshared systems that support online terminals linked to a host computer. While such timeshared systems may operate within a limited geographic area, they do not share the characteristics of local area networks described above. Although timeshared mainframe and minicomputer installations increasingly include autonomous microcomputers such as intelligent terminals, dumb

In local area network installations, powerful microcomputers functioning as servers supply resources to desktop workstations.

terminals are usually supported as well. Because dumb terminals, as previously discussed, require connection to a host computer in order to function, they do not qualify as autonomous nodes. The timeshared mainframe or minicomputer to which such terminals are attached may itself function as a local area network node, however. As a further limitation, conventional timesharing systems do not support communication between terminals without host computer intervention.

A number of libraries have installed local area networks; others have access to LANs implemented by universities, corporations, school systems, municipalities, or other organizations with which they are affiliated. Among their advantages for libraries, local area networks permit sharing of printers, disk drives, and other peripheral devices. Peripherals attached to one LAN node can often be accessed by other nodes, thereby promoting fuller utilization of available equipment and minimizing the total number of peripherals required at a given site. Such peripheral sharing is particularly effective where network participants have an occasional, rather than continuous, need for a particular output, storage, or communication device. In many local area network installations, designated nodes function as servers which provide particular resources to other network nodes. A print server, for example, provides shared access to printers, plotters, and other output peripherals attached to it. It receives requests for hardcopy output from other network nodes and directs them to the appropriate devices, queuing print jobs as necessary. Similarly, file servers provide shared access to high-capacity magnetic disk drives or other storage peripherals, while communication servers provide shared access to modems. Depending on the installation, a LAN server may be a microcomputer, a minicomputer, or a mainframe. LAN nodes which receive the services are variously called "workstations" or "clients." In some local area networks, specific computers function only as servers. In other cases, computers can function as both workstations and servers.

Local area networks also permit information sharing among nodes. Assuming proper authorization, data bases stored by a file server can be accessed by other LAN nodes. In an administrative application, for example, data bases of accounting, purchasing, payroll, or personnel information can be referenced, updated, or otherwise processed by LAN participants. Such capabilities are critical to downsizing initiatives in which LAN-based microcomputers support complex applications that were previously implemented on mainframes or minicomputers. The phrase "client/server computing" is sometimes used to denote downsized implementations in which processing tasks are shared by workstations and servers within a local area network. It is a form of distributed computing.

As a potentially attractive form of resource sharing, local area networks can provide multi-user access to prewritten application software packages stored on magnetic disk drives or other peripherals attached to designated file servers. Many software publishers offer LAN licenses that permit simultaneous use by a specified number of computers operating in a local area network. While they are more costly than single-user licenses, LAN licenses usually prove less expensive than the cost of purchasing an equivalent number of copies of a given program for individual microcomputers.

As described in later chapters, a growing number of library automation programs and CD-ROM information products are available in local area network versions. In LAN implementations, microcomputers can perform different tasks, thereby giving a library considerable flexibility in configuring an automated system. In a five-node microcomputer network that supports circulation control and public catalog access, for example, one microcomputer might be used to check books out, another to check books in, and the remaining three for catalog searches. In academic, school, government, and corporate installations, a local area network can make a library's computer-based information resources conveniently accessible to faculty, students, researchers, managers, and others working in offices, laboratories, classrooms, dormitories, or other locations within the library's parent organization, thereby improving communication with users and extending the reach of library services beyond the physical confines of the library itself.

Local area networks typically utilize telephone wires, sometimes described as "twisted-pair wiring," or coaxial cable as communication links. Long associated with the delivery of television signals, coaxial cable consists of a metal conductor surrounded by a nonconducting insulator and covered by shielding material. All layers are concentric and share a common axis, hence the coaxial designation. Coaxial cable is a reliable medium for high-speed communication. In local area network installations, transmission rates of up to 10 million bits per second are routinely encountered. Where higher transmission rates are required, fiber optic links can be utilized. As an alternative to conventional cabling, some local area networks use microwave, infrared, or spread-spectrum radio technology to transmit signals between nodes over the air. As a group, such "wireless" communication links are more easily installed than twisted-pair wiring or coaxial cable, but they are vulnerable to interference and their components can prove costly.

In LAN installations, the communication link—whether it is twisted-pair wiring, coaxial cable, or some other medium—is shared by multiple nodes. As noted above, LAN nodes are autonomous; there is no central processor to mediate among contending users, as is the case in timeshared systems. Instead, media access protocols determine how and when a given device can transmit information over a given network. Several protocols are widely encountered. In one approach, called Carrier Sense Multiple Access with Collision Detection (CSMA/CD), network nodes desiring to transmit information monitor the communication medium to determine whether it is in use by another node. If the medium is idle, a node may transmit immediately. If two or more nodes sense a clear channel and attempt to transmit simultaneously, a "collision" occurs as their signals interfere with one another. Transmission is immediately terminated, and all devices pause for a randomly determined amount of time before retransmitting. If another collision occurs, the procedure is repeated. The CSMA/CD protocol is used by local area networks that conform to the IEEE 802.3 standard defined by the Institute of Electrical and Electronics Engineers. Such networks are often described as Ethernet LANs.

Another popular media access protocol, called token ring, is intended for local area networks with ring topologies. A special signal called a token circulates around the network when all nodes are idle. A node wishing to transmit information to another node must obtain a free token as it passes. When transmission is completed, the token is released for other users. The token ring protocol is used by local area networks that conform to the IEEE 802.5 standard. The IBM Token Ring LAN is an example of such a network. Various nonstandard media access protocols are utilized by other local area networks.

Media access protocols aside, a given local area network can be connected to other local area networks or to wide area communication facilities. A microprocessor-controlled device called a "bridge" is used to interconnect two local area networks. It permits communication between nodes on different LANs, in effect creating one logical network from multiple physical implementations. A device called a "gateway" provides a connection between a local area network and a wide area network for purposes of communicating with external computers, typically on a timesharing basis. A reference librarian working at a LAN node in an academic or public library, for example, may want to search an online catalog operated by a neighboring library or obtain access to an online information service or bibliographic utility. Similarly, a corporate or government librarian in a branch office location may need to access a proprietary data base of research information maintained by a mainframe computer installed in a distant headquarters facility.

SUMMARY

The terms *batch* and *real time* denote modes of data processing. In a batch processing system, there is a gap in time between the occurrence of a transaction or other event and the computer's processing of information about that event. Batch processing systems are typically characterized by the offline collection of data for mass input at prescheduled intervals, the straightforward processing of data stored on magnetic tape, and the production of printed or COM-generated reports. These reports reflect the condition of a particular application as of the last schedule processing. They cannot reflect transactions or other events occurring since that time. In real time systems, information about transactions or other events is entered and processed at the time the events occur. The data maintained by such systems are always up-to-date. They are typically stored on magnetic disk drives or other direct-access devices for reference by online terminals.

While data are processed in the batch or real time mode, computer specialists are increasingly concerned with the development of interactive systems in which a computer prompts and guides a user in the performance of various information-processing tasks. Well-designed interactive programs are simple to use, forgive user errors, and allow the user to control the pace of interaction.

While interactive programs provide an intellectual interface between the computer and the user, online terminals serve as the required physical interface. An online terminal is a device that allows users to transmit data to, and receive data from, a computer or other information-processing machine. Terminals designed for interactive applications can be categorized by the complexity of their electronic circuitry, their output capabilities, the nature of their components, or their communication characteristics. With respect to their electronic circuitry, terminals can be categorized as dumb, smart, or intelligent. Dumb terminals derive all of their information-processing capabilities from the computer with which they are communicating.

Smart terminals are essentially enhanced versions of nonprogrammable dumb terminals. Intelligent terminals are actually programmable microcomputers that can also function as terminals. With reference to their output capabilities, terminals can be categorized as teleprinters or video display devices, the latter relying primarily on CRT technology. In terms of their components, terminals can be configured with a keyboard for interactive communication, without a keyboard for receive-only operation, or with a recording device for the preparation of data before interaction with a host computer. Most available terminals support ASCII asynchronous communication capabilities, which are compatible with a wide variety of computer systems. Bisynchronous, 3270-type terminals are specifically designed for communication with IBM and plug-compatible mainframes.

Regardless of the mode in which it is processed or the type of terminal used to access it, information stored on disks or tapes must be organized in a structured format. In terms of physical location, data are stored on a given device, such as a disk drive or tape unit, in a physical container called a "volume," which is, in the case of disks, divided into cylinders or tracks. The unit of data that can be read or recorded in a single operation is called a "physical record." In terms of logical structure, information is typically organized into files. The files may contain data, text, or images. Data files usually consist of one or more logical records which may be subdivided into fields. The loading of this logical structure onto a computer's physical storage devices and media is accomplished by an operating system or other system software in a manner that is largely transparent to the user. Various methods can be used to arrange stored records. In a sequentially organized file, for example, logical records are ordered by a designated key field. Where multiple retrieval parameters are used, various indexing techniques may be employed.

In many data processing applications, individual data files are specifically designed to meet the requirements of a particular application program—an approach that often results in redundant data, wasted storage space, high storage costs, and other problems. As an alternative, the data base approach replaces separate files with an integrated accumulation of computer-processable information organized in a manner that can address a variety of application requirements. Among its advantages, the integration of separate files eliminates redundancy, reduces storage costs, and improves the accuracy and integrity of data. The implementation of an integrated data base is accomplished through a set of programs called a data base management system (DBMS). Such programs are available for computers of all types and sizes. Some data base management systems feature special nonprocedural query languages—sometimes called "fourth-generation languages"—that simplify application development and permit information retrieval without formal programming.

Centralized computing facilities have often been criticized for failing to respond satisfactorily to the information processing requirements of remote users. Since the mid-1970s, many organizations have adopted distributed data processing systems that are designed to place computing power and information resources closer to the end user. A distributed system is an integrated configuration of computers that are used in combination to perform the work of a given application. Distributed systems can be organized along horizontal or hierarchical lines. Typically, the data bases which these systems process are distributed as well. In the partitioned approach to data base distribution, selected data are stored at specific sites in a distributed system. In the replicated approach, all data are stored at all sites.

The individual computers and terminals in a distributed processing system constitute nodes that are connected by communication facilities to form a computer network. Computer networks vary in their organization structure, geographic spans, and the types of communication facilities they use. Wide-area networks (WANs) may utilize a combination of leased telephone lines, fiber optics, terrestrial microwave, satellite microwave, and other high-speed linkages that permit long-distance communication. Local area networks (LANs), which have a narrowly circumscribed geographic span, may utilize twisted-pair wiring, coaxial cable, or fiber optics as communication links. Non-wire-based linkages are also possible. Local area networks have proven especially popular in microcomputer installations. Among their advantages, local area networks permit the sharing of hardware resources and information. Library automation systems and related information products are increasingly available in LAN versions.

ADDITIONAL READING

ALDEN, D., et al. "Keyboard Design and Operation: A Review of the Major Issues." *Human Factors* 14 (3): 275–93 (1972).

BARNETT, R. *Packet Switched Networks: Theory and Practice.* New York: Halsted Press, 1988.

BERNSTEIN, A., and LEWIS, P. *Concurrency in Programming and Database Systems.* Boston: Jones and Bartlett, 1993.

BERSON, A. *Client-Server Architecture.* New York: McGraw-Hill, 1992.

BEYNON-DAVIES, P. *Relational Database Systems: A Pragmatic Approach.* Boston: BSP Professional Books, 1991.

BLACK, U. *Data Communications and Distributed Networks.* Englewood Cliffs, N.J.: Prentice Hall, 1987.

BREWSTER, R. *Communication Systems and Computer Networks.* New York: Halsted Press, 1989.

BROWN, A. *Database Support for Software Engineering.* New York: Wiley, 1989.

CLARK, M. *Networks and Telecommunications: Design and Operation.* New York: Wiley, 1991.

DATE, C. *An Introduction to Database Systems.* Reading, Mass.: Addison-Wesley, 1987.

———. *Relational Database Writings, 1989–1991.* Reading, Mass.: Addison-Wesley, 1992.

DAVIES, D. *Security for Computer Networks: An Introduction to Data Security in Teleprocessing and Electronic Funds Transfer.* New York: Wiley, 1989.

DEMPSEY, L. *Libraries, Networks, and OSI: A Review with a Report on North American Developments.* Westport, Conn.: Meckler Corporation, 1992.

FINKELSTEIN, C. *An Introduction to Information Engineering: From Strategic Planning to Information Systems.* Reading, Mass.: Addison-Wesley, 1989.

FORTIER, P. *Handbook of LAN Technology.* New York: McGraw-Hill, Intertext Publications, 1989.

FREEMAN, W. *The Right of Privacy in the Computer Age.* New York: Quorum Books, 1987.

GESSFORD, J. *How to Build Business-Wide Databases.* New York: Wiley, 1991.

GORMAN, M. *Database Management Systems: Understanding and Database Technology.* Wellesley, Mass.: QED Information Sciences, 1991.

GUNTON, T. *Infrastructure: Building a Framework for Corporate Information Handling.* New York: Prentice Hall, 1989.

HELD, G. *Data and Computer Communications: Terms, Definitions, and Abbreviations.* New York: Wiley, 1989.

HENSHALL, J., and SHAW, S. *OSI Explained: End-to-End Computer Communication Standards.* New York: Halsted Press, 1988.

HINGE, K. *Electronic Data Interchange: From Understanding to Implementation.* New York: American Management Association, 1988.

INMON, W. *Database Machines and Decision Support Systems: Third Wave Processing.* Wellesley, Mass.: QED Information Sciences, 1991.

JORDAN, L., and CHURCHILL, B. *Communications and Networking for the IBM PC and Compatibles.* New York: Brady Books, 1990.

KIBIRIGE, H. *Local Area Networks in Information Management.* New York: Greenwood Press, 1989.

KROL, E. *The Whole Internet User's Guide and Catalog.* Sebastopol, Calif.: O'Reilly and Associates, 1992.

LAQUEY, T. *The Internet Companion: A Beginner's Guide to Global Networking.* Reading, Mass.: Addison-Wesley, 1993.

LEIGH, W., and PAZ, N. "The Use of SQL and Second Generation Database Management Systems for Data Processing and Information Retrieval in Libraries." *Information Technology and Libraries* 8 (4): 400–407 (1989).

LINOWES, D. *Privacy in America: Is Your Private Life in the Public Eye?* Urbana: University of Illinois Press, 1989.

MACKINNON, D., et al. *An Introduction to Open Systems Interconnection.* New York: Computer Science Press, 1990.

MARKS, K., and NIELSEN, S. *Local Area Networks in Libraries.* Westport, Conn.: Meckler Corporation, 1991.

MARTIN, J. *Principles of Data Communication.* Englewood Cliffs, N.J.: Prentice Hall, 1988.

———. *Telecommunications and the Computer.* Englewood Cliffs, N.J.: Prentice Hall, 1990.

MEYER, N., and BONE, M. *The Information Edge.* Homewood, Ill.: Dow Jones-Irwin, 1989.

MINOLI, D. *Telecommunications Technology Handbook.* Boston: Artech House, 1991.

MODELL, M. *Data Analysis, Data Modeling, and Classification.* New York: McGraw-Hill, 1992.

NAUGLE, M. *Local Area Networking.* New York: McGraw-Hill, 1991.

PARKER, D. *Computer Crime: Criminal Justice Resource Manual.* Washington, D.C.: U.S. Department of Justice, 1989.

PARKER, M., et al. *Information Strategy and Economics: Linking Information Systems Strategy to Business Performance.* Englewood Cliffs, N.J.: Prentice Hall, 1989.

REISS, L., and DOLAN, E. *Using Computers: Managing Change.* Cincinnati: South-Western Publishing, 1989.

RHODES, P. *LAN Operations: A Guide to Daily Management.* Reading, Mass.: Addison-Wesley, 1991.

ROSS, F. "Overview of FDDI: The Fiber Distributed Data Interface." *IEEE Journal on Selected Areas in Communications* 7 (7): 1043–51 (1989).

ROTHSTEIN, M., and ROSNER, B. *The Professional's Guide to Database Systems Project Management*. New York: Wiley, 1990.

RUBIN, M. *Private Rights, Public Wrongs: The Computer and Personal Privacy*. Norwood, N.J.: Ables Publishing, 1988.

SAFFADY, W. "Local Area Networks: A Survey of the Technology." *Library Technology Reports* 26 (1): 5–125 (1990).

SCHATT, S. *Linking LANs: A Micro Manager's Guide*. Blue Ridge Summit, Penn.: Windcrest, 1991.

SCHUTZER, D. *Business Decisions with Computers: New Trends in Technology*. New York: Van Nostrand Reinhold, 1991.

SCHWEITZER, J. *Computers, Business, and Security: The New Role for Security*. Boston: Butterworths, 1987.

SHANNON, C., and WEAVER, W. *The Mathematical Theory of Communication*. Urbana: University of Illinois Press, 1949.

SMOUTS, M. *Packet Switching Evolution from Narrowband to Broadband*. Boston: Artech House, 1991.

STAIR, H., and POWERS, J. *Megabit Data Communications: A Guide for Professionals*. Englewood Cliffs, N.J.: Prentice Hall, 1990.

STALLINGS, W. *Handbook of Computer-Communications Standards*. New York: Macmillan, 1987.

———. *Local Networks*. New York: Macmillan, 1990.

STRASSMAN, P. *Business Value of Computers*. New Canaan, Conn.: Economic Information Press, 1990.

TENNANT, R., et al. *Crossing the Internet Threshold: An Instructional Handbook*. Berkeley, Calif.: Library Solutions Press, 1993.

TRAVIS, D. *Effective Color Displays: Theory and Practice*. San Diego: Academic Press, 1991.

ULLMAN, J. *Principles of Database Systems*. Potomac, Md.: Computer Science Press, 1980.

WEIZENBAUM, J. *Computer Power and Human Reason: From Judgement to Calculation*. San Francisco: W.H. Freeman, 1976.

WESTIN, A., ed. *Information Technology in a Democracy*. Cambridge, Mass.: Harvard University Press, 1971.

WRIGHT, K. *Workstations and Local Area Networks for Librarians*. Chicago: American Library Association, 1990.

Automated Office Systems and Related Technologies

While data processing in general—and library automation in particular—has been dominated by the computer hardware and software concepts discussed in preceding chapters, a broader view of automated information processing includes word processing, document reproduction technologies, video-based information systems, and such electronic message transmission systems as facsimile, telex, computer-based messaging, and voice mail. These technologies, and the equipment in which they are embodied, are often collectively characterized as automated office systems because they are widely applied to the creation, storage, retrieval, reproduction, and dissemination of information in an office environment. Although several of the technologies discussed in this chapter have been commercially available for at least half a century, their popularity and utilization have increased dramatically since the 1980s, when widely acknowledged concerns about the productivity of the rapidly growing office workforce brought them to prominence.

From the mid-1970s through the early 1980s, the developed nations of North America and Western Europe experienced both a marked decline in historical patterns of productivity improvement and a significant shift in workforce composition. Some economists and other observers, seeing a causal relationship between the two trends, attributed declining productivity to the increasing migration of workers from highly automated, relatively productive manufacturing jobs to managerial and clerical white collar positions in offices, where much work was being performed manually or with rather primitive mechanical devices, such as typewriters.

Viewing this situation with alarm, many information specialists contended that a more pervasive application of technology would significantly increase the productivity of the rapidly growing white collar workforce, just as intensified automation previously improved the productivity of factory and farm workers. Although computers had been used to automate office operations since the 1960s, data processing applications through the late 1970s were largely limited to such routine transaction-oriented operations as payroll processing, accounts payable, and accounts receivable. Seeking greater productivity, many government agencies, corporations, and other organizations significantly expanded their automation activities in the early to mid-1980s, broadening the range of their computer operations and applying other technologies to information-processing tasks that computers could not successfully address. By the late 1980s, many office activities had been successfully automated. Today, the value of technology as an indispensable workplace component is widely recognized, and most of the technologies and equipment described in this chapter are routinely encountered in a variety of work environments.

Automated office systems likewise play an increasingly important role in libraries. With a large percentage of professional and clerical employees, library work environments are overwhelmingly white collar in character and include a significant office component. At a time when increased operating costs are accompanied by significant budgetary retrenchments, productivity improvements are essential to the continued delivery of library services. With proper planning, the technologies described in this chapter can prove useful in a broad range of library operations.

WORD PROCESSING

Since its introduction in the mid-1970s, the phrase "word processing" has intentionally conveyed the impression that conventional data processing has emphasized numbers to the exclusion of the textual information, or words, which form the content of a widely varied group of documents, ranging from ordinary business correspondence and reports to published books and articles. In the broadest sense, word processing encompasses a group of concepts, technologies, and methodologies that facilitate the preparation and production of such textual documents. In keeping with this broad definition, a fully and ideally configured word processing system includes equipment for the creation, storage, retrieval, and dissemination of textual information. Typically, however, the phrase is used in a narrower sense to denote the application of technology to the production of typewritten documents. This narrower definition reflects word processing's origins in the German term *textverarbeitung*—literally, the making of text.

Dictation Systems

Word processing technology is embodied in two different types of products: dictation systems and text-editing systems. The latter product category, discussed in a later section, has attracted so much attention that word processing is usually equated with text editing. While dictation systems have long been utilized in a wide range of general business applications, librarians have been slow to incorporate them into their established work patterns, and there is virtually no recent literature on their selection and use in library applications. This is especially unfortunate because dictation systems are primarily designed to enhance the productivity of professional workers. The following discussion surveys the advantages of dictation systems and describes equipment configurations, features, and functions of relevance for library automation.

In a fully configured word processing installation, document production begins with the conversion of the thoughts of a person called a "word originator" to a form suitable for transcription by a typist. In library applications, the word originator may be an administrator composing correspondence, a cataloger preparing bibliographic descriptions, an archivist inventorying newly accessioned records, or an information specialist preparing a literature review. Assuming that the word originator lacks typing skills, the required conversion of thoughts to words can be accomplished in three ways: by writing them in longhand; by dictating them to a stenographer; or by dictating them to a voice recording machine. While all methods have their advantages, they differ significantly in the type and amount of labor involved.

With longhand writing, special equipment, training, and working conditions are unnecessary. Longhand writing can be performed almost anywhere—in an office, at home, while traveling. Secretarial assistance is not required. The longhand method is especially well suited to such library work as the drafting of bibliographies containing esoteric terminology or foreign language citations. Assuming legible handwriting, the transcribing typist should experience little difficulty with unusual spellings or punctuation. Longhand writing is likewise well suited to the composition of multipage literature analyses, administrative reports, and similar long documents where reference to previously written passages is essential. Although secretarial involvement is not required, longhand writing can consume much of the word originator's workday.

Because the salaries of librarians/word originators are higher than those of clerical support personnel, the cost of document creation can often be reduced by having the word originators dictate to stenographers. When the word originator is properly prepared, shorthand dictation can prove two to three times faster than longhand writing. In most cases, the resulting savings in the word originator's time will offset the cost of clerical involvement. In addition, immediate interaction between the word originator and stenographer can help clarify ambiguous terminology, spelling, or punctuation, thus simplifying eventual transcription by a typist. Usually, the typing must be performed by the stenographer to whom the document was dictated, since most stenographers find it difficult to decipher shorthand written by others. Some flexibility in the assignment of work to clerical personnel must consequently be relinquished. As a further limitation, many libraries are unable to hire stenographers and, when available, their shorthand skills usually earn them higher salaries than conventional secretaries earn.

The speed advantages of voice dictation can be retained, however, through the use of recording equipment. In many cases, document creation costs can be reduced as well. Because dictation to a machine can occur at a faster rate than dictation to a stenographer, the word originator's involvement in document creation is minimized. A stenographer's presence is not required—an important consideration for libraries with a low ratio of clerical to professional employees and in applications, such as cataloging, where many word originators may be involved and the typical unit of work (a bibliographic description) is relatively short. Given the availability of portable recorders, dictation technology can be used effectively by traveling library administrators, by literature searchers extracting citations from indexes and abstracting journals, and by archivists and manuscript librarians who must inventory records in crowded storage areas. The absence of stenographic involvement in dictation results in a significant reduction in the clerical costs associated with document creation. As an additional advantage that simplifies the hiring of clerical personnel, training in shorthand is not required. Clerical productivity is likewise improved because typing or other work need not be interrupted to take dictation.

Turning from advantages to equipment configurations, a dictation system consists of two basic components: a recorder and a transcriber. While several companies offer equipment that records digitized voice signals, the most common recorder is a desktop device that captures spoken words as an analog signal on a magnetic tape cassette. All available recorders also offer some playback capability to allow the word originator to review previously recorded material. When dictation is completed, the recording medium is physically removed from the recorder and taken to a typist who inserts it into a transcriber, a device that converts the recorded signals to audible sounds for playback through a speaker or earphones. While dual-purpose devices suitable for recording and transcription are available, the typical transcriber is a less expensive, single-purpose unit designed to play back previously recorded media.

In addition to the basic operations familiar to users of mass market cassette recorders, most dictation systems incorporate features that facilitate the work of word originators and typists. As an example, the recorder's microphones usually filter out background sounds, thus permitting dictation in noisy work environments. Some models employ voice-operated relay technology in which the recording mechanism is activated only when the word originator is actually speaking, thus eliminating tape-wasting gaps during periods of thought or other pauses. Word originators can employ various mechanisms, including paper index strips and electronic coding, to mark the locations of special instructions or priority documents within a cassette.

Some transcribers are equipped with variable speed controls that allow the typist to adjust the playback rate to match typing speed without excessive voice distortion. Following pauses for typing, most transcribers can be set to repeat a few previously played words before playing new material. Several vendors offer multifunctional "voice processing" products that combine dictation and telephone equipment in a single unit. In addition to recording dictation, such devices can store telephone numbers, perform automatic dialing, send prerecorded messages, and function as telephone answering machines.

Although a desktop recorder with a separate transcriber is the most widely encountered dictation system configuration, certain library applications may be better served by other types of recording and transcribing equipment. Portable recorders, for example, are handheld devices designed to extend the utility of dictation systems to work environments where desktop units are impractical. They typically record communications on magnetic tape cassettes which can be replayed on a compatible transcriber. Portable recorders often serve as an auxiliary recording unit in a desktop recorder/transcriber configuration. Special microcassettes are sometimes used to decrease the recorder's size, although some portable units will accept the familiar standard-sized cassette used in consumer audio products.

As an alternative to portable and desktop units with self-contained recording capabilities, centralized dictation systems are accessed by simple microphones or ordinary telephones wired to a centrally located recorder/transcriber to which one or more typists are likewise connected by earphones. As new communications are dictated, previously recorded material is being transcribed. Analog centralized systems can accommodate several dozen to more than 100 hours of voice recording using automatic cassette changers. The most advanced centralized systems, however, employ digital recording techniques to store communications on magnetic disks for rapid, direct access by transcriptionists. While they are more expensive than analog devices, digital recorders are more versatile. They permit lengthy insertions in previously dictated material, use special codes to identify instructions pertaining to particular communications, and allow operators to easily transcribe communications out of their recorded sequence, thereby accommodating priority jobs.

Whether they employ digital or analog recording techniques, many centralized dictation systems are microcomputer-controlled. Using a video display terminal, a word processing supervisor can determine the status and estimated completion time of particular jobs, expedite the typing of priority material, and equitably allocate work to individual typists. Such systems are encountered in large word processing centers in corporations, government agencies, hospitals, and other work environments. Libraries affiliated with such organizations may be able to use them for their own document production applications.

Automated Text Editing

Dictation systems facilitate the conversion of a word originator's thoughts to a spoken form suitable for transcription. Until voice-driven printers are developed, the transcription process will continue to require typewriting or a similar form of keystroking. The typewriter was one of the first business machines to be used for library work, and typewritten documents remain important communication media in library administration, technical services, and information services. Library systems analysts, like their counterparts in corporations and government agencies, have long recognized that diminished productivity and consequently increased expenses are the inevitable result of some obvious shortcomings inherent in conventional typing.

As an often-cited example, repetitive text—such as the information contained in an acknowledgement letter sent to job applicants—must be manually retyped to produce additional typewritten originals, with the possibility of errors occurring in the retyping. Whether multiple originals are involved or not, typing errors are inevitable. When they occur, the usual methods of correction—erasure, overlaying with opaque material, or starting over—interrupt keystroking, take considerable time, and sometimes deface documents. As perhaps the most significant shortcoming of conventional typing, entire documents must be retyped to accommodate even minor revisions and format changes. Bibliographies, for example, must be completely retyped to insert a single additional entry in alphabetical sequence. Similarly, the contents of catalog cards cannot be conveniently reformatted to produce a list of newly cataloged materials.

As work methods analysts point out, a clerk who ostensibly types 60 words per minute may actually produce finished work at less than 25 percent of that rate when all retyping and error correction routines are considered. Automated text-editing systems—or, as they are more commonly called, "word processors"—improve typing productivity by recording keystrokes in machine-readable form on magnetic media before producing human-readable paper documents. Once recorded in this manner, the text of a document can be easily edited (corrected, altered, moved, deleted, or otherwise manipulated) without extensive retyping. Errors are easily corrected by overtyping. Global change capabilities can correct all occurrences of a given error with a single command. Line lengths are automatically adjusted to accommodate margin changes. To enhance the appearance of printed output, the operator can justify or otherwise control the contour of a page's right margin. Once the machine-readable version has been corrected or revised to the operator's satisfaction, it is dispatched to a printer which produces a presumably perfect paper copy. The machine-readable version, typically recorded on a magnetic disk, can be retained for later editing or other uses.

Certain text-editing capabilities are particularly useful for commonly encountered library tasks. An academic librarian responsible for assembling and updating a collection of college catalogs may prepare periodic mass mailings to be sent to registrars or other information officers. The text of each mailed request will usually vary slightly, if at all. The inside address and salutation will be different and selected sentences in the body of the letter may request information about specific academic programs, but the bulk of each letter will be identical. Such document production tasks are increasingly common as public and other libraries extend their activities to include job information centers, community referral programs, and similar services. Conventional document creation methodologies may approach such applications through a combination of photoduplication and original typing. In addition to requiring considerable handling, the resulting letter will have an impersonal, unimpressive appearance, which may fail to gain the attention of the intended recipient.

Consequently, additional labor will have to be expended on follow-up mailings.

Most text-editing systems offer document assembly capabilities which greatly simplify the creation of such nearly identical typewritten communications. While the specific approach varies from system to system, prerecorded text—such as the body of a letter to be used in a mass mailing—is automatically merged at printing time with prerecorded variable data, such as the names and addresses of recipients. As an attractive feature, some systems combine document assembly with a sort/select capability that automatically selects specified names or other text from a prestored list for merging with the body of a letter or other document. If desired, the list can be sorted into a specified sequence prior to printing. From the standpoint of clerical productivity in library applications, document assembly addresses one of the most severe limitations of conventional typewriting: the inability to use previously typed text to create multiple output products.

Historically, automated text-editing operations have been implemented in two ways: (1) as dedicated systems composed of equipment and programs designed specifically and exclusively for word processing, and (2) as software packages designed for execution on general-purpose computers of various types and sizes. Dedicated word processors dominated word processing implementations from the late 1960s through the early 1980s. The earliest models were specially designed typewriters that captured keystrokes on magnetic tape or magnetic-coated cards. Video display systems based on computer rather than typewriter technology became available in the mid-1970s. Self-contained systems, designed for standalone operation, were preprogrammed microcomputers equipped with a keyboard-send-receive (KSR) video terminal for text entry and editing, a receive-only (RO) printer for hardcopy output, and a floppy disk drive for text storage. Such devices were widely installed through the mid-1980s. For the most part, those installations have been supplanted by general-purpose microcomputers configured with prewritten word processing software packages, as discussed below. The few available models are principally marketed as typewriter replacements for consumer use rather than business installations.

During the mid-1980s, some government agencies, corporations, and other organizations replaced their standalone word processors with multifunctional, mainframe or minicomputer-based office systems that combined word processing with other capabilities, such as electronic mail and data management. Examples included the All-In-1 system from Digital Equipment Corporation, the Wang Office from Wang Laboratories, the IBM Professional Office System (PROFS), Officepower from ICL, and the Comprehensive Electronic Office (CEO) from Data General. As centralized, multiterminal configurations, such systems offered significant advantages, including peripheral sharing and cooperative document preparation. Variously described as office automation systems or integrated office systems, they are widely installed and remain available for sale. Increasingly, they incorporate microcomputers as intelligent terminals and can exchange documents produced by popular microcomputer-based word processing packages.

While multifunctional, integrated office systems offer attractive capabilities, microcomputers equipped with word processing software packages far outnumber other word processing methodologies. Compared to special-purpose word processors and integrated office systems, microcomputer-based products are less expensive and easier to implement—an important consideration for libraries with budgetary constraints and limited technical expertise. The earliest microcomputer-based word processing programs gave little indication of the product group's future potential, however. Introduced in the early 1980s, they were difficult to use and lacked essential text-editing capabilities; but a decade of refinement has yielded a variety of excellent products that can successfully address a broad range of document preparation requirements. Improvements in computer hardware have similarly enhanced the effectiveness of microcomputer-based word processing. Laser printers, for example, can generate high-quality paper output with varied typographic characteristics. High-capacity hard disk drives simplify text storage. Local area networks, as described in chapter 3, permit shared access to documents and peripheral devices.

Some microcomputer-based word processing programs are designed for first-time users who want a useful array of text editing and document formatting functions, but whose principal concerns are simplicity and ease of operation. Such programs are particularly well suited to managerial and professional workers with straightforward, occasional typing requirements. A more sophisticated group of full-featured word processing software packages is clearly designed for high-volume corporate and institutional applications requiring a wide range of editing and formatting capabilities, although they may also be used by managerial and professional workers. Assuming an appropriate printing device, such programs can produce attractively formatted documents in multiple type fonts and sizes. Text can be printed in multiple columns with borders, dividing lines, or other ornamentation. Some word processing programs can combine text with digitized illustrations, photographs, or other graphics generated by document scanners or transferred from other programs.

In addition to elaborate editing and formatting capabilities, full-featured word processing programs typically incorporate spelling verification, an electronic thesaurus, mailing list management, and other special features. Programs that automatically number footnotes and print them at the bottoms of appropriate pages are of particular interest to librarians responsible for the preparation of scholarly documents. Some word processing programs also include indexing modules that will automatically generate indexes and tables of contents from marked text segments or typed phrases.

Electronic Typewriters

While word processing technology can address a library's most sophisticated document production requirements, typewriters remain useful for certain purposes, such as the preparation of envelopes or multipart business forms. With word processing programs, considerable trial and error may be required to print information in the correct position within a form. As additional constraints, some printers cannot conveniently accommodate envelopes, and nonimpact devices, such as laser printers, cannot produce carbon copies.

Electronic typewriters offer the familiarity and relative simplicity of typewriting, while supporting error correction, repetitive typing, and other capabilities that can expedite straightforward typing tasks. Electronic typewriters are microprocessor-controlled devices. Their enhanced typing capabilities are derived from programs that are stored in read-only memories. Random-access memory circuits provide storage for a small amount of typed text.

Electronic typewriters are particularly appealing to clerical personnel who are uncomfortable with computers. They represent a significant improvement in functionality and convenience when compared to conventional typewriters, but they do not approach the text-editing and document formatting capabilities of even the simplest computer-based word processors. Most models feature a single-line liquid crystal display that simplifies the detection and correction of typing errors before they are recorded on paper. Most electronic typewriters can perform automatic centering and decimal alignment. A given model may support a variety of horizontal character spacings, and store frequently used phrases in random-access memory for rapid recall. Some models include spelling verification programs that use an internally stored dictionary to check individual words as they are typed. An alarm sounds when a possible misspelling is detected. Some electronic typewriters can be optionally equipped with a floppy disk drive. Such configurations, however, can cost as much or more than some microcomputer-based word processing systems.

DOCUMENT IMAGING TECHNOLOGIES

A document imaging system is an integrated configuration of hardware and/or software components that produces pictorial copies (images) of book pages, journal articles, technical reports, office records, and other documents for storage, retrieval, dissemination, or other purposes. This broad definition encompasses technologies and devices with widely varying characteristics and capabilities. Familiar examples of document imaging products include photocopiers, which make full-size or near-size reproductions of documents, and micrographic systems, which record source documents as miniaturized images on microfilm, microfiche, or other microforms. Such widely encountered imaging devices typically employ photographic technologies for document recording. An increasingly popular group of electronic document imaging systems uses scanners to store documents in computer-processable electronic formats on magnetic or optical media.

Micrographics

Micrographics is a specialized field of information processing that is concerned with the making and use of microforms—photographic information carriers that contain images, properly called "microimages," that are reduced to an extent requiring magnification to be read. Among specific types of microforms, 35mm microfilm is usually wound on plastic reels in 100-foot lengths. It is widely encountered in library applications involving newspapers, manuscripts, and other research materials. Sixteen-millimeter microfilm, which can likewise be wound on reels or loaded into self-threading cartridges, is routinely used to record office documents as well as some research materials, particularly in corporate and government libraries.

Microfiche are flat sheets of film on which document images are recorded in a grid pattern of rows and columns. The most common size of microfiche measures 105mm wide by 148mm high. With capacities ranging from 60 to more than 400 images, microfiche are used for technical reports, computer printouts, serial publications, and various other documents. Microfilm jackets are transparent acetate or polyester carriers which feature sleeves or channels for the insertion of strips of 16mm or 35mm microfilm cut from rolls. They have been used by some libraries to store vertical file materials and other collections that require the periodic addition of new documents. Aperture cards are tabulating-size cards that contain a hole or aperture designed to contain one frame of 35mm microfilm. The microform of choice for engineering drawings, maps, and other large documents, aperture cards are sometimes encountered in technical libraries which store such materials.

Regardless of type, microforms can be created in either of two ways: (1) source document microfilming uses specially designed cameras equipped with reducing lenses to record paper documents as miniaturized images; (2) as discussed in chapter 1, computer-output microfilm (COM) technology permits the direct recording of computer-processed, machine-readable information on microfilm or microfiche without first creating paper documents. In either case, a microfilm camera or a COM recorder produces latent (potentially visible) images that must be developed to become usable. This development is usually performed by a separate machine called a "microfilm processor." Most source document cameras employ silver gelatin microfilm, which requires development by liquid chemicals. A thermally processed microfilm, which is conveniently developed by heat without chemicals, is principally encountered in COM recording. A processed microform is usually reproduced by a duplicator to create one or more working copies. Following duplication, camera-original microforms are usually placed in a secure, environmentally controlled storage location; when properly processed and stored, silver gelatin microfilms will remain stable for hundreds of years. Working copies, intended for reference or research, can be displayed by magnifying devices called "microform readers." When hardcopies are required, reader/printers can produce paper enlargements of displayed images. When a high volume of printing activity is required, enlarger/printers can make high-speed paper prints

Reader/printers, a popular type of micrographics equipment in library installations, can display enlarged microimages and print paper copies on demand. (Courtesy: Canon)

of all or specified microimages from a roll of microfilm, sheet of microfiche, or stack of aperture cards.

Source document microfilming, the focus of this discussion, is a well-established technology that has been routinely and successfully utilized in business applications since the 1920s. Library applications date from the same period, when several American research libraries began using microfilm cameras to reproduce research materials contained in European libraries and archives. Since that time, microforms have been used by libraries of all types and sizes for collection development, to preserve the content of newspapers and other ephemeral materials, as an alternative to binding for serial backfiles, and to reduce storage space requirements for library materials.

Although some larger libraries have established microfilming facilities for in-house recording of source documents, most library microform collections contain materials purchased from third parties called "micropublishers." Broadly defined, micropublishing is the publication of information in multiple microform copies for sale or distribution. The term encompasses original micropublications, which contain information published for the first time in any form, and retrospective micropublications, which contain material previously published in paper form. The earliest micropublishers, active from 1930 to about 1960, followed the lead of library-administered microfilming projects in emphasizing research materials from foreign repositories as well as doctoral dissertations and similar specialized documents of narrow subject interest. Their projects involved original micropublishing of archives and manuscripts, as well as retrospective micropublishing of rare books. With the rapid expansion of higher education during the 1960s, however, a number of micropublishers began offering specially selected library core collections consisting of microform versions of important out-of-print monographs essential for students' term papers and recommended readings. At about the same time, micropublished versions of annual volumes of newspapers and serials became widely available.

Micropublications play such an important role in library installations that library administrators and collection development specialists have emphasized them to the virtual exclusion of other aspects of micrographics. While many libraries own microform readers and reader/printers, budgetary constraints and a lack of technical expertise have limited the implementation of in-house microform production facilities. Compared to their business counterparts, few libraries own microfilm cameras, even though such devices can prove very useful for such tasks as filming technical reports and laboratory notebooks in industrial libraries, preserving local newspapers in public libraries, and storing manuscripts and vertical file materials in historical societies and special collections.

Although some microfilm cameras and related production equipment are expensive to purchase and complex to operate, the micrographics industry does offer simpler, less costly products. Sometimes described as small-office-microfilm (SOM) systems, these products are designed for operation by clerical personnel with a modest amount of training in an office rather than a laboratory environment. SOM equipment can thus be viewed as the micrographics counterpart of small computer systems. The potential SOM market is extensive and includes a sizable library component. At the time of this writing, SOM products included desktop microfilm cameras, integrated camera/processors which expose and develop microfilm images in one continuous operation, desktop microfiche duplicators, and high-quality microfiche readers and reader/printers.

While SOM products extend the potential range of micrographics to include those libraries that cannot afford or effectively utilize complex systems, other products will appeal most strongly to libraries interested in upgrading their existing microform production facilities. Widespread business interest in so-called paperless information systems has led to important developments in micrographics technology that are of potential significance for library applications. Through the mid-1970s, micrographics equipment relied heavily on mechanical components. Since that time, however, manufacturers have emphasized "intelligent" micrographics products that incorporate microprocessors, read-only memories, and other electronic components to enhance versatility and reliability. Newer cameras, for example, can record document images on microfilm or microfiche in a variety of formats and reductions. Similarly, microprocessor-controlled retrieval units can be programmed to automatically display or print specified sequences of frames from within a given microform. Self-contained camera/

processors, as noted above, expose and develop microimages in a single, continuous series of work steps. As a convenience, they eliminate plumbing requirements and use specially packaged chemicals to simplify supply replenishment.

Much of the attention given to micrographics as a document storage alternative has emphasized the so-called computer/micrographics interface —a phrase that denotes the combined use of computer and micrographics technologies to address information processing requirements that cannot be as effectively accommodated by either technology alone. Computer-output microfilm (COM) is the most common manifestation of the computer/micrographics interface. As described in chapter 1, it offers a compact alternative to paper output for computer-generated reports. Computer-input microfilm (CIM), a second combination of computer and micrographics technologies, is actually a variant form of optical character recognition. A CIM device is a special-purpose OCR system that converts the information content of microfilm images to character-coded, computer-processible text. When used with COM, CIM would theoretically permit the printing of information onto, and subsequent reentry of information from, microforms, thereby making microfilm an economical, high-density alternative to magnetic tape and other media for offline storage of computer-processible data subject to future reprocessing. In actuality, however, such implementations have been impeded by the limited commercial availability of CIM products. At the time of this writing, the technology's future remained uncertain.

A third aspect of the computer/micrographics interface, computer-assisted retrieval (CAR), makes straightforward use of the unique advantages of computer and micrographics technologies. CAR systems use computers and magnetic disk storage to establish, maintain, and search an online index keyed to document images recorded on microforms. In a typical retrieval operation, the index is searched to determine the existence and microform locations of document images that satisfy specified retrieval parameters. In a library application involving technical reports, for example, the index may be searched by combinations of author, subject, or other categories of information. In this respect, the CAR concept resembles the data base management systems discussed in chapter 3, the critical difference being that retrieved index information directs the operator to specific frames in a separate file of microforms. When a designated microform is obtained from that file, it is loaded into a special retrieval unit which locates and displays desired frames. Paper enlargements can be printed for reference purposes.

CAR systems combine the space savings, media stability, and other advantages of microforms with the ability of computers to rapidly manipulate index data. Although CAR technology is widely promoted in corporate and government installations, it has its roots in library applications. The idea of automated microform retrieval for research documents was first discussed in the 1940s. Basic concepts were developed during the 1950s and 1960s, when a number of experimental microfilm-based systems were implemented for the storage and retrieval of scientific and technical documentation. The most famous of these experiments,

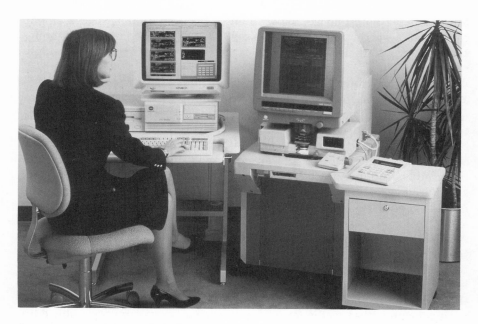

Computer-assisted retrieval (CAR) systems use computers to index document images that are recorded on microfilm or other microforms. In some CAR installations, like the one depicted here, microimages are digitized for display, printing, or transmission. (Courtesy: Minolta)

implemented as part of Project Intrex at the Massachusetts Institute of Technology, was designed to provide scientists with rapid, automated retrieval of technical publications stored on microfiche. In the early 1970s, the first turnkey CAR systems—consisting of integrated configurations of micrographics equipment, computer hardware, and prewritten data management software—were introduced. Today, a number of companies offer a variety of CAR products with flexible document retrieval capabilities. CAR implementations can be based on conventional data base management software packages, adapted for document indexing and microform retrieval, or on CAR-specific document indexing and retrieval programs that are available for various types of computers. While mainframe and minicomputer-based implementations can prove expensive, microcomputer software packages have proven particularly effective in extending the range and affordability of CAR technology.

Electronic Document Imaging

Unlike CAR systems, which employ a combination of computer and photographic technologies, electronic document imaging systems provide a completely computer-based approach to document storage and retrieval. Broadly defined, an electronic document imaging system is a combination of hardware and software that records documents as computer-processible digitized images. The systems described in this section are specifically designed for document retrieval and dissemination, usually as a high-performance alternative to paper-filing methodologies or micrographics technology. From the hardware standpoint, a basic electronic document imaging configuration includes a central processor, which may be a microcomputer, a Unix-based workstation, a minicomputer, or a mainframe; one or more scanners for conversion of paper documents to digitized images; one or more video monitors for data and image display, with keyboards for data entry and retrieval; one or more laser printers for hardcopy output; an appropriate group of computer storage peripherals; and cabling or some type of computer network to interconnect the various system components.

The characteristics of document scanners (document digitizers) as image-oriented input devices were described in chapter 1. Depending on the volume of documents to be stored and the required retrieval speed, the digitized document images generated by such scanners may be recorded on magnetic disks, magnetic tape, or optical disks. In most implementations, optical disks provide the most appropriate combination of high storage capacity and direct-access capabilities for rapid retrieval. Consequently, such systems may be described as optical filing systems. As previously described, write-once and rewritable optical disks are removable media encapsulated in plastic cartridges; autochangers can provide unattended, nearline access within several seconds to very large quantities of information. Fixed magnetic disk drives offer superior online retrieval performance but may lack sufficient capacity for high-volume applications. Certain varieties of magnetic tapes offer sufficient capacity for many electronic document imaging applications, but their retrieval speed is limited by serial access characteristics.

As with CAR systems, a computer-maintained data base serves as an index to recorded images. The data base is typically stored on a fixed magnetic disk drive. It contains one record for each indexable document stored by the system. An indexable document consists of one or more pages recorded as one or more electronic images. Each data base record contains fields that correspond to index categories specified by an application designer. Index data entry, file maintenance, and retrieval operations are supported by data base management software. Retrieval operations begin with a data base search to determine the existence and media addresses of electronic document images that satisfy specified retrieval parameters. Potentially relevant index records associated with particular document images are displayed on a video monitor for operator perusal. A field in each index record identifies the particular medium on which its associated image is recorded. If a desired image is stored on an online medium, such as a hard disk, it can be retrieved and displayed on operator command. Removable media, such as optical disk cartridges or magnetic tapes, must be obtained from their storage locations and mounted in an appropriate peripheral device for online access; autochangers, as previously noted, can eliminate manual media handling. Once a given medium is mounted, the data base management program locates the desired image and displays it for operator examination. Most systems also permit hardcopy production via laser printers.

Electronic document imaging implementations can yield significant benefits. Improved retrieval capability when compared to paper-based document management methodologies is perhaps the most frequently cited motive. While specific retrieval characteristics and capabilities depend on the software employed by a given system, data base searches and their associated image retrieval operations will usually prove more convenient and much faster to perform than browsing through paper files or library shelves. Most electronic document imaging systems can also perform complex searches involving combinations of fields and truncated search terms. Such searches may be difficult or impossible to perform in conventional paper-based filing or classification systems. Electronic document imaging systems can further improve retrieval by delivering needed documents quickly and conveniently to requesters. In conventional library or filing room installations, physical proximity to documents is a precondition for access and use. Electronic document imaging systems, in contrast, permit online access to index records and document images by remote users in a local or wide area computer network. Depending on the hardware and software configuration, retrieved document images can be routed through an electronic messaging system or faxed to designated locations.

Shelving or filing newly received books, reports, or other documents; removing them when requested for reference purposes; and reshelving or refiling them following retrieval activity are essential but time-consuming operations in libraries and other paper-based document repositories. They are also error-prone activities; misfiling is a common reason for loss of valuable documents, and considerable time and effort may be wasted in searches for misfiled or incorrectly shelved materials. Additional complications are posed by documents that have been removed from library shelves or files for reference or other purposes; such documents must be tracked to determine their locations in the event they are needed and to ensure that they are returned to the library in a timely manner following use. Even when extensive precautions are taken, documents removed from a library for reference purposes may be misplaced, stolen, or damaged by accident or through malicious intent. Frequently, reference documents are also subject to cumulative wear and tear, which may impair their utility.

Electronic document imaging systems simplify file maintenance by eliminating filing, refiling, and the potential for misfiling. Scanning and indexing replace shelving and filing for newly received items. In many electronic document imaging implementations, documents are converted to electronic images in the order of their arrival at a scanning station. Time-consuming sorting procedures are eliminated. The media locations of specific document images are system assigned; as previously noted, access is obtained through data base records which serve as an index to stored images. File integrity is likewise enhanced. Once documents are recorded as digitized images on optical or magnetic media, their sequence is fixed. Removal or misfiling of individual pages is impossible. Because electronic images are not removed from storage media for reference pur-

Electronic document imaging systems display digitized images on bit-mapped video monitors. (Courtesy: IBM Corporation)

poses, circulation control and other document tracking requirements are eliminated; instead, copies of images are transferred electronically to retrieval workstations. The document images themselves are unaffected by reference activity; unlike paper records, they cannot be damaged by use, stolen, or misplaced.

Automated workflow capabilities are among the most widely publicized and dramatically effective characteristics of electronic document imaging systems. In acquisitions and other transaction-oriented library applications, documents are often routed among designated employees in a formally defined sequence in order to obtain approvals, perform designated operations, or otherwise complete specific activities. Each employee adds information to or extracts information from a given document, then passes it on to the next person in the predefined routing path. Depending on employee proximity and the urgency with which particular operations must be completed, documents may be hand-carried from person to person; alternatively, interdepartmental mail or other physical delivery methodologies may be employed. Both approaches are time-consuming and subject to delays. Unless routing procedures are closely monitored, documents may be misplaced or allowed to languish in the in-baskets of designated recipients. Operations that must await the arrival of documents cannot proceed.

Automated workflow can address these problems. Under program control, electronic images of essential documents can be routed from one workstation to another over a local area network or other data communications facility. The workflow program defines the routing procedure and monitors each document's progress. Such automated workflow implementations can ensure that documents will be processed in the correct sequence; they also increase the likelihood that specific operations will be performed in a timely, accurate manner.

As a further advantage, electronic document images can significantly reduce storage space requirements for a given quantity of books, journals, reports, or other documents, thereby freeing a significant percentage of available floor space for other purposes. While space savings are rarely the sole justification for an electronic document imaging implementation, they can be an important secondary motive. Depending on media size, recording density, and other system characteristics discussed in subsequent chapters, an optical disk cartridge can store tens of thousands to hundreds of thousands of document images. Multicartridge autochangers can provide unattended, nearline access to millions of pages. In this respect, electronic document imaging systems compare favorably with micrographics technology; some optical disk cartridges, for example, can store the equivalent of dozens of rolls of microfilm or hundreds of microfiche.

Electronic document imaging systems can be custom-designed for particular applications, purchased as preconfigured turnkey combinations of hardware and software, or implemented as prewritten software packages on a library's own computer equipment. Customized electronic document imaging implementations are tailored to particular applications by contractors called "systems integrators." They are often based on specifications, requirements statements, and expectations delineated in requests for proposals (RFPs) or similar documents. Alternatively, the systems integrator may consult with the customer to determine required document imaging capabilities; requirements analysis and the preparation of system specifications are among the services offered by most systems integrators. Whether specifications are developed independently or with the systems integrator's assistance, the integrator obtains or develops hardware and software components appropriate to the specifications. The first electronic document imaging system in the United States was implemented in the mid-1980s by a systems integrator for the Library of Congress. Since that time, customized systems have been installed in diverse information management environments, including banks, pharmaceutical companies, government agencies, military bases, engineering organizations, and nuclear power plants.

As their most obvious disadvantage, customized electronic document systems can be time-consuming and prohibitively expensive to develop and implement. As a faster, less expensive (but not necessarily inexpen-

Electronic document imaging components include scanners, optical disk drives, and laser printers. (Courtesy: Minolta)

sive) alternative, turnkey electronic document imaging systems consist of preselected hardware and prewritten software components that are offered for sale as a bundled package ready for straightforward implementation and operation by nontechnical personnel. Complicated setup routines and software modifications are not required. Ideally, the customer installs the system and begins scanning documents, entering index data, recording document images, and performing retrieval operations. Training is limited to instruction in specific system operations. Turnkey electronic document imaging systems may be microcomputer- or minicomputer-based. The computer and its associated peripheral devices are included in the bundled configuration, as is document indexing and retrieval software.

An interesting and rapidly growing group of electronic document imaging systems consists of prewritten software packages that are marketed for use with specific hardware components that the customer must furnish. Such packages—which are increasingly available for various types of computers—support document digitization, data base creation, document imaging recording, data base searching, document image display, and other imaging operations. As with all purchased software, the computer configuration must meet minimum requirements for random-access memory, disk storage, and system software. The software developer provides a list of compatible document scanners, storage peripherals, video displays, laser printers, and other hardware components. In some cases, the software vendor also sells hardware, but customers are free to purchase designated equipment components at the best price from any source they choose. Sometimes described as "shrink-wrapped" imaging solutions, such software-based implementations take the mystery out of electronic document imaging and treat it, in effect, like word processing, spreadsheet processing, and other applications that are designed to automate widely encountered business tasks.

In an alternative approach to software-based implementations, electronic document imaging capabilities can be added to existing data base management systems, electronic mail systems, workgroup programs, and other software products. When such programs and applications are augmented by the incorporation of document images, they are said to be "image-enabled." In a library's acquisitions department, for example, a data base of order information may provide online access to most of the information needed to respond to inquiries about deliveries and payments, but some inquiries may require examination of purchase orders, invoices, or other source documents. In such cases, the required documents must be obtained from office files or other storage locations—a procedure that can prove time-consuming and labor-intensive. To facilitate responses to inquiries, images of the required documents can be added to the data base. Depending on the implementation, a data base record might incorporate a document image as a field type, the image being treated as a binary large object (BLOB). Alternatively, data base records may be linked to document images stored in separate files. In either case, data base searches are followed by the rapid, online retrieval of document images pertaining to specific data base records.

Copiers and Duplicators

The term *reprographics* is often used to denote the field of information processing that is concerned with technologies and equipment for document reproduction. Given this broad definition, the micrographics and electronic document imaging systems described above can be considered specialized facets of reprographics, but the term is usually applied more narrowly to photocopying and duplicating equipment that makes paper copies of paper documents. The difference between a copier and a duplicator is difficult to delineate precisely. Traditionally, a copier has been defined as a machine that is designed to make one or several copies of a given document, while a duplicator offers faster multicopy speeds and is better suited to applications requiring 10 or more copies of a given document. For high-volume applications, some duplicators can sustain speeds exceeding one copy per second. The traditional distinction between copiers and duplicators may not be observed in product specifications, however, and it is often ignored in practice; many libraries use copiers for duplicating and duplicators for copying.

While most of the attention given to library automation is properly focused on computers as the most powerful, versatile, and complex of available information processing machines, a strong case could be made for copiers and duplicators as historically the most important category of automated equipment in library applications. Every year, libraries make millions of copies to meet administrative needs and to provide users with more convenient access to journal articles, reports, portions of books, and other materials. Conventional and coin-operated copiers are ubiquitous and indispensable devices in libraries of all types and sizes, and the extent and potential impact of library copying activity have been major factors in revision of copyright legislation.

Despite their obvious and continuing importance, copiers and duplicators are sometimes cited as examples of "mature" product groups that are unlikely to experience significant growth or change. The xerographic (plain-paper) variant of the electrostatic process, the dominant photocopying technology, has completely supplanted coated-paper processes in office installations and offers a viable alternative to offset duplication in certain high-volume applications. No competing reprographic technologies are on the horizon, and, apart from improvements in the performance of specific machines, it is difficult to envision how the currently high level of xerographic copy quality can be significantly improved; in some cases, copies are of better quality than the originals from which they were made.

Although photocopying technology has not changed radically since the introduction of xerography and its subsequent refinement during the 1960s and 1970s, copying and duplicating equipment continues to acquire new operating capabilities and convenient features. Operating under the control of integral microprocessors and programs stored in read-only memories, copiers and duplicators use flat-panel video displays to prompt operators and provide diagnostic information. Shortened paper paths and increased use of electronic components have significantly improved reliability and reduced equipment size. Many models support such special features as job interruption and recovery, two-sided copying, variable reduction and enlargement, automatic erasure of dark borders, margin shifting, and multiple paper trays with automatic selection of copy size.

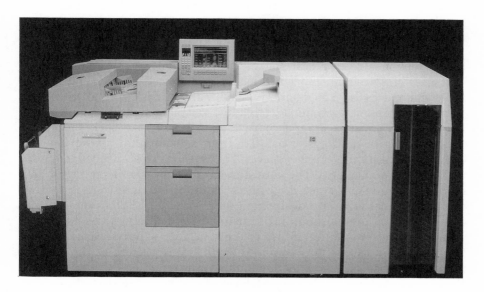

High-speed photocopiers can be configured with automatic page feeders, sorters, staplers, and other accessories. (Courtesy: Eastman Kodak)

Standard or optional attachments permit automatic feeding of documents, automatic sorting of multiple copies of multipage documents, and automatic stapling of copy sets. The newest copiers and duplicators employ digital imaging techniques that facilitate image editing and other manipulations; where documents contain proprietary or confidential information, for example, such machines can suppress reproduction of specific portions of a page. Color copiers, the subject of several innovative product developments since the late 1980s, can prove useful in various library applications.

From the standpoint of computer systems, the most important development in photocopying technology has been the development of multipurpose xerographic devices that can operate as both conventional copiers and laser printers. Such devices are sometimes described as "intelligent" copiers. Some models can also operate as document scanners or fax machines.

ELECTRONIC MAIL AND MESSAGE SYSTEMS

The phrase "electronic mail and message systems" (EMMS) encompasses a group of technologies that permit the electronic transmission of messages between compatible devices. As its name suggests, electronic mail provides a high-speed alternative to the physical delivery of messages by conventional mail service or private courier. In the broadest sense, voice communications by telephone can be considered a form of electronic mail and message system, but the scope of this group of automated office products is usually limited to those systems that transmit written messages generated by handwriting, typewriters, word processing programs, or any of the several special terminals described later in this section. As a notable exception, voice mail systems support noninteractive spoken communications.

Introduced in the early 1980s, voice mail systems allow users of touch-tone telephones to transmit spoken messages to designated recipients. The messages are transmitted to recipients indirectly, via a central computer that stores them on magnetic disks or optical disks as digitized audio signals. At some later time, a designated recipient will use a touch-tone telephone to enter command codes to recall and play back the stored messages. Voice mail systems differ from conventional answering machines in several important respects. The messages are encoded in digital rather than analog form. They are stored on disks rather than tapes; disk storage, as previously noted, permits rapid, direct access. As a further distinction, messages are designated for a specific recipient and are not accessible to others without authorization. Depending on the particular system employed and the nature of the message, a spoken response may be made, the message may be saved for future reference, or the original message can be forwarded, with comments or instructions, to a third party. Voice mail systems are a variant form of the computer-based message systems described later in this section. They have been implemented by many corporations, government agencies, and other organizations on in-house computer systems. Alternatively, some telephone companies offer voice-mail services.

Facsimile

Systems designed for the electronic transmission of written messages can be divided into two groups: those that transmit images of documents bearing messages, and those that transmit the content of a message as a sequence of encoded characters. Facsimile, also known as telefacsimile or simply fax, is the oldest of the image-oriented message transmission technologies. In a facsimile system, an encoded image of a document is transmitted electronically from one location to another, where it is reconstructed as a paper copy or facsimile, hence the name.

Facsimile's potential for library applications is obvious. It can be used to transmit library documents ranging from purchase orders and claiming notices for missing issues of periodicals to copies of journal articles, technical reports, and even entire books. From the mid-1960s through the early 1970s, a number of academic and public libraries experimented with facsimile transmission, primarily as a high-speed document delivery alternative in interlibrary loan applications. Those experiments were not successful; participating libraries reported significant problems with output quality, transmission time, equipment reliability, and compatibility. Over the past decade, however, facsimile technology has changed dramatically. Output quality is now acceptable for most library documents. As discussed below, transmission speed and reliability have improved, and compatibility problems have been resolved. In addition, drastic reductions in equipment costs and the availability of facsimile components for computer installations have made the technology more affordable.

As with other electronic mail and message technologies, a facsimile system is an integrated configuration of equipment and communication facilities designed for the transmission of information-bearing signals between two points. In most cases the transmission medium is an ordinary, voice-grade telephone line to which a facsimile machine is connected by means of a modem, although facsimile signals can also be transmitted by terrestrial microwave carriers, satellites, coaxial cable, or other communication facilities. The signal itself originates at a source terminal called a "facsimile transmitter," which combines the attributes of a document scanner and a communication device. The document being scanned, which is called the "subject copy," may contain textual or graphic information. Although facsimile transmitters for bound volumes have been developed, most commercially available devices feature a pass-through document feeder that can only accept individual sheets of paper. Some models can accept computer-printout-size (11-by-14-inch) or ledger-size (11-by-17-inch) pages, although documents larger than letter-size may be automatically reduced prior to transmission.

Like the document scanners described in chapter 1, a facsimile transmitter divides a subject copy into a grid of picture elements, or pixels, each of which is analyzed for its light-reflectance characteristics. The tonal values of successively encountered pixels are transmitted, in encoded form, over telephone lines or other communication links to a receiving device, which produces a printed facsimile of the subject copy. A facsimile implementation can thus be viewed as a kind of remote copying system in which the platen is located at one end of a telephone line and the out-tray is located at the other. Depending on the receiver's characteristics, the facsimile copy may be printed on plain or coated paper.

The earliest machines used analog coding techniques and required as long as six minutes to transmit a letter-size page. Digital facsimile systems, introduced in the early 1970s, used image compression techniques to achieve subminute transmission speeds but were incompatible with their analog counterparts. As a further complication, the analog and digital machines of different manufacturers were often incompatible with one another. These incompatibilities impeded the acceptance and implementation of facsimile systems, despite general acknowledgement that the technology satisfied a widely encountered need for rapid delivery of time-sensitive documents.

Beginning in the late 1970s, the Committee on International Telephony and Telegraphy (CCITT), the organization responsible for the development of worldwide telecommunication standards, addressed this problem by issuing standards for four groups of facsimile devices. CCITT Group I and Group II standards applied to analog facsimile equipment, which is now obsolete. Group III facsimile devices, which employ digital encoding, have dominated the technology since the 1980s. As noted above, they utilize image compression to achieve subminute transmission speeds over ordinary switched telephone lines. Depending on communication conditions, a letter-size page can be transmitted in less than 15 seconds. Group III facsimile devices are equipped with step-down modems which operate at a maximum rate of 9,600 bits per second. Conforming to CCITT specifications, however, such modems continuously monitor telephone line conditions and will automatically decrease the transmission rate to 7,200, 4,800, or 2,400 bits per second, should interference or other telecommunication problems be detected. Transmission speed is also affected by the characteristics of subject copies. The highest degree of image compression is obtained with documents that have wide margins and open spacing between lines. Densely printed documents, which are not as readily compressed, require longer to transmit. The Group IV facsimile standard likewise employs digital encoding and image compression but is intended for high-volume transmission of documents over leased rather than switched telephone lines.

In most cases, a facsimile transmitter and receiver are configured together as a dual-purpose device called a "facsimile transceiver," or simply a "fax machine." New models make extensive use of microprocessors and other electronic circuitry to simplify work steps and improve reliability. For improved management and control of electronic message traffic, many models can produce activity logs which list all transmissions and receptions, including such information as starting time, elapsed transmission time, and a remote terminal identifier. Unattended reception is a standard feature with all available fax machines. To eliminate confusion associated with documents received at night or during other periods of unattended operation, some machines will stamp copies with the date and time of reception. Some models feature an automatic dialer for speed dialing during the day and unattended transmission during evening or nighttime hours, when long-distance telephone rates are lower. A few Group III fax machines can also operate in the Group I and Group II modes for communication with older analog devices. Librarians should be aware, however, that Group I and Group II products have not been manufactured for many years, and their installed base has dwindled to the point where communication with them is rarely required.

Considerable recent attention has been given to the relationship between facsimile and computer technologies. Some Group III facsimile transceivers are equipped with an industry-standard RS-232C interface, which permits attachment to an external computer system, allowing them to operate as input peripherals for document digitization. As an increasingly popular alternative to single-purpose facsimile transceivers, a document scanner can be linked to a computer equipped with a fax modem and software. The scanner generates digitized document images, which are converted by the fax modem and software for transmission over a telephone line to a Group III facsimile machine or to another computer equipped with a Group III-compatible fax modem. The fax modem can also receive communications for local printing. A printer with graphic output capabilities is required for that purpose.

While microcomputer products have been most widely publicized, fax modems and software are available for computers of various types and sizes. In some local area networks, fax modems and software are implemented on one network node, which functions as a fax server for multiple workstations with occasional document transmission requirements. As an attractive feature, most fax modems and software support store-and-forward operations, in which digitized images generated by document scanners are recorded on magnetic disks or other media for transmission at a designated time. As a convenient capability, fax modems can convert word processing files, spreadsheet files, and other computer-processible information to a form suitable for facsimile transmission, thereby eliminating the need to print them as paper documents for scanning. For terminal-to-computer communication, most fax modems can also operate as conventional data modems.

Character-oriented Message Systems

Facsimile signals, as described above, encode the light-reflectance characteristics of successively encountered pixels within a subject copy. Character-oriented message systems, in contrast, transmit information as a sequence of individually encoded characters, in the manner of the computer terminals described in chapter 3. Most character-oriented message systems employ keyboard send-receive (KSR) terminals or microcomputers for message preparation. This is the case, for example, with telex—a long-established, character-oriented message transmission technology that has been utilized by libraries for more than a quarter century. As originally conceived, the telex communication network supported message transmission between specially designed terminals. The original telex terminal was an electromechanical teletypewriter with limited typographic characteristics, an unusual three-row keyboard, and minimal message transmission capabilities. Some devices were equipped with a paper tape punch for offline preparation of messages prior to transmission. As a more convenient alternative, software packages now permit the preparation of telex messages by microcomputers. Typically, microcomputer-originated messages are sent to an intermediary carrier, such as AT&T EasyLink Services or GRAPHNET, which routes them to a designated telex address. Some online information services, such as CompuServe and DELPHI, will also route messages to designated telex terminals.

While newer technologies offer faster and more varied message transmission capabilities, the telex network provides exceptional geographic coverage, particularly where international message transmission is required. Even in countries with primitive telecommunication infrastructures, libraries, businesses, and other organizations can usually be reached by telex. In the simplest telex configuration, a message, such as an interlibrary loan request, is key-entered at a terminal for transmission over a network of telegraph-grade lines to a designated compatible receiver, which prints it onto paper. Message reception does not require an operator in attendance.

Like other character-oriented transmission devices, the originating telex terminal converts an operator's keystrokes into a coded sequence of bits representing the individual characters that constitute a message. Often criticized as an old-fashioned, telegraph-derivative technology, telex transmits messages at 50 bits per second (66 words per minute) using the CCITT No. 2 code, sometimes known as the Baudot code. The Teletypewriter Exchange (TWX), a similar telegraph-derivative service that supported terminal-to-terminal message transmission within North America, was discontinued in 1991. Through the mid-1980s, TWX was utilized by libraries for transmission of interlibrary loan requests. It has been supplanted by more convenient messaging and interlibrary loan systems described in later chapters. Except for its continued utility in international communications, telex would have shared its fate.

Like facsimile machines, telex technology is designed to deliver messages to designated terminals. As such, it is well suited to time-sensitive communications which would lose their value if subject to the delays inherent in conventional mail delivery. Such messages must often be conveyed in written form, making the use of voice communication inappropriate. They do not require interaction or an immediate recipient response, apart from a simple acknowledgment of successful transmission. Interlibrary loan requests are an obvious category of messages having such characteristics. While computers may be used in such message transmission systems, their role is largely limited to the routing of messages between terminals.

In another approach to character-oriented message transmission, however, computers play a more significant role as intermediaries which accept messages, notify recipients, and store messages for varying periods of time as directed by the sender and/or recipient. Variously called computer-based message systems, electronic mail systems—or simply "e-mail" systems—they are actually software packages designed to operate on timeshared mainframes or minicomputers, or on microcomputers linked in local area networks. Unlike the telex service discussed above, computer-based message systems transmit messages to specified persons rather than designated terminals. Recipients can receive messages at any compatible terminal, regardless of location. Also in contrast to telex service, computer-based message systems are used less for transmission of time-sensitive messages than as alternatives to conventional memoranda, telephone conversations, and other traditional modes of communication when interaction or an immediate response is not required or necessarily desired. They have proven particularly popular as a means of facilitating communication in workgroup computing implementations which support the activities of project teams, committees, or other groups involved in cooperative work activities.

In the typical implementation, a user working at an online terminal directs the computer's operating system to make a message input program available. The program then prompts the user for the addressee's name or identification number, the subject of the message, and then the text itself. Most computer-based message systems provide a simple but effective text-editing subsystem for typing, error correction, and revisions. Alternatively, the text of the message may be prepared by a word processing program and imported by the message input program. In either case, the computer passively accepts the text without regard to its content or format, and stores the message on a magnetic disk or other direct-access storage medium, in a location that can be viewed as the recipient's "electronic mailbox."

When the designated recipient next signs onto the computer, he or she will be notified of the existence of any transmitted messages. With most systems, the recipient can scan the messages by having a list of their dates, senders, and subjects printed or displayed at a terminal. Alternatively, the entire text of any or all messages can be printed or displayed. Most systems likewise offer a range of message disposition options. Messages can, for example, be deleted once read, stored for later reexamination, filed under designated subject headings, or forwarded to other parties for further action.

Computer-based message systems have been in widespread use since the late 1970s. One of the earliest and most famous examples was developed to facilitate communication among members of the research community within the U.S. Department of Defense. Similar systems were subsequently developed by other government agencies and corporations. Today, software packages for computer-based messaging are available from dozens of companies for computers of all types and sizes. As an alternative to in-house implementations, a number of computer service bureaus, timeshared information services, and telecommunications companies offer computer-based message services. Examples include the CompuServe electronic mail service, the Dialmail electronic mail subsystem supported by the DIALOG Information Service, and the On-Tyme electronic mail system offered by Tymnet. The Internet, as discussed in chapter 3, links computer-based messaging capabilities implemented on many computers, allowing librarians to conveniently communicate with professional colleagues in other institutions.

In a variant form of computer-based message system called "computer conferencing," three or more persons can communicate with one another through terminals. In the simplest computer conferencing configurations, one participant sends a message to multiple recipients for comments. Individual responses are appended to the original message and can be reviewed by other participants. These, in turn, may provoke responses which are themselves made available for review and comment. The result is a computer-stored dialogue that can be reviewed, in whole or in part, by all authorized persons.

As is true of conventional computer-based message systems, computer conferencing removes barriers of time and geography, allowing individuals to participate at their own pace without the interruptions and contention that often characterize conventional meetings and conference telephone calls. As a further advantage, a transcript of the interaction is automatically created and can be stored for later retrieval and reference. As discussed in this context, computer conferencing is one of several attempts to use technology to eliminate unnecessary travel by facilitating communication among participants in a group endeavor. The elimination of time-wasting travel is likewise a goal of the videoconferencing systems described later in this chapter.

VIDEO-BASED INFORMATION SYSTEMS

Many libraries use video technology to record and display visual information. Video cameras and videocassette recorders are commonplace devices in libraries of all types and sizes. In communities with cable television, some public libraries have established video studio facilities, which produce programs for broadcast over public access channels. On a less ambitious scale, many public libraries submit information about their hours, services, or special events for display on "electronic bulletin boards" operated by some cable television franchises. In addition, libraries of all types maintain collections of prerecorded video material ranging from industrial training courses to commercial motion pictures. Since the mid-1980s, a number of public and academic libraries have circulated prerecorded videocassettes and videodisks.

But while these library activities emphasize the relationship between video technology and television systems, the scope of video technology encompasses a wide range of products and services, some of which are potentially significant for library information processing. In particular, increasingly close links are being established between video technology and computers. The earliest microcomputers, for example, utilized television receivers as display devices. Several companies currently offer adapter boards that permit the display of full-motion television images, in a separate window, on a computer video monitor. Many cable television services feature one or more "cabletext" channels which continuously display news headlines, weather forecasts, sports results, and other computer-generated textual information. In some areas, the coaxial cables that deliver television signals to homes are also used by businesses for high-speed data transmission between computer installations. Several libraries have similarly explored the use of cable television systems as a link between home television receivers and an online catalog.

As a related development, the design of new video equipment is increasingly influenced by computer technology. Television receivers, for example, now routinely incorporate microprocessors and other electronic circuitry. So-called digital televisions and videocassette recorders use internal computers to refine and enhance received signals prior to display, simultaneously display multiple images, and support a variety of other special effects and features. Component television systems resemble computers in their emphasis on a central tuner/controller that can support a video monitor, audio speakers, a videocassette recorder, a videodisk player, and other peripheral devices.

Videotext Services

The term *videotext* has been defined in several potentially confusing ways. It sometimes denotes a computer-based information service that is intended for consumer markets. According to that definition, which is principally utilized in the United States, the online information services offered by CompuServe and Prodigy are considered videotext services. Descriptions of such services often employ the variant spelling "videotex." This discussion, however, will adopt a definition that relates videotext to its European origins. In Europe, videotext services combine video and data base technologies to disseminate combinations of computer-generated textual and graphic information to modified television receivers or other relatively inexpensive terminals. Unlike ordinary television systems, the textual information is of primary significance, and the visual material plays a complementary or, in some cases, decorative role. Although animation is possible, videotext information typically consists of preformatted still frames dealing with specific topics. While some business-oriented systems have been implemented, most videotext systems offer consumer or personal services information of general interest and utility.

Typical videotext data bases emphasize news stories, weather forecasts, traffic reports, and sports results; financial information, including business news, stock market activity reports, and commodity prices; and such household information as grocery prices, recipes, postal rates, theater schedules, real estate listings, airline and train schedules, gardening tips, horoscopes, and descriptions of cultural events and local tourist attractions. Information providers include government agencies, nonprofit organizations, and businesses. In some cases, entire frames are devoted to product advertisements. Alternatively, a brief advertiser's logo or message may appear in the top or bottom margin of a frame that contains news or other information. Thus, in the manner of commercial television, a brewery may sponsor frames containing sports reports or a pharmaceutical company may sponsor frames containing health news.

Since their introduction in the early 1970s, videotext systems have been divided into two categories—teletext and viewdata—which are differentiated by the information dissemination methodology they employ. Teletext systems, sometimes called "broadcast videotext," utilize an otherwise unused portion of conventional television signals to transmit digitally coded information over the air or through cable services. Borrowing terminology from the publishing industry, teletext information is usually formatted as a "magazine" composed of a predetermined number of pages or frames that are continuously broadcast on a recirculating basis. Teletext subscribers are equipped with specially modified television receivers. After consulting a table-of-contents frame, the subscriber selects a desired information frame and enters its number into a keypad that operates with a television receiver equipped with a teletext decoder. The indicated frame is captured by the decoder as it is rebroadcast and is stored in the decoder's internal memory, from which it is displayed on the television screen. To achieve a reasonable retrieval time, most teletext magazines contain about 100 information frames.

Viewdata systems, like their teletext counterparts, present information that is formatted into frames, but the frames are maintained as a computerized data base on magnetic disks or other direct-access storage devices, where they await retrieval commands issued by user terminals that are connected to the data base by telephone lines. The simplest terminal is a television receiver equipped with a viewdata decoder, typewriter-like keyboard, and modem. Viewdata systems resemble conventional timesharing computer services, although the information they offer is a distinctively packaged combination of text and graphics. The size of a viewdata data base is limited only by the amount of available online storage, and systems that offer several hundred thousand frames have been implemented. Compared to viewdata technology, teletext systems are simpler, both conceptually and technically. They require no special telecommunications or computer facilities, but their interactive facilities are limited to the selection of desired pages from a recirculating collection of frames. With viewdata systems, the use of telephone lines permits interactive communication.

Given their computer-like attributes, viewdata systems can address a broader range of information processing applications than their teletext counterparts. For example, they can be expanded to offer conventional computing services, electronic message transmission, home banking, and home shopping. While teletext does not permit such expanded services, the two technologies do not necessarily compete with each other. A teletext system may serve as a simple precursor to viewdata in areas where videotext services are being introduced. Alternatively, the two services can coexist, teletext being used for news headlines or other rapidly changing information while viewdata serves users with more varied and detailed retrieval requirements.

In marked contrast to other innovations in information processing technology, most of which have originated in the United States or Japan, videotext, as previously noted, is a European development. The existing body of knowledge and assumptions about videotext is largely based on experience with systems that operate in European countries, especially the United Kingdom, where videotext experiments date from the 1970s. British teletext systems have been implemented as a logical extension of other broadcasting activities—a kind of "printed radio." They provide alternative treatment of topics covered by conventional broadcasting services. Compared to radio and television, teletext can immediately report news stories, weather forecasts, sports results, and similar developments that other broadcasting methodologies must usually delay until regularly scheduled intervals. As a further advantage over conventional broadcasting techniques, teletext viewers can select pages of interest and examine them at their leisure in any sequence. In this respect, teletext differs from the cabletext services mentioned above; such services display information frames in a predefined sequence.

In France, videotext systems were implemented as part of a government-sponsored plan to expand the country's computer and telecommunications industries, with the specific intention of developing technology for export. The German Bildschirmtext viewdata system is sponsored and operated by the national postal and telecommunications agency. Similar videotext services have been implemented, on an experimental or operational basis, in other European countries, including the Netherlands, Denmark, Sweden, Norway, and Austria. In Japan, the Character and Pattern Telephone Access Information Network (CAPTAIN) is a videotext system developed by Nippon Telegraph and Telephone. In Canada, videotext experiments have been conducted in several cities by the Canadian Broadcasting Corporation, local telephone companies, and other organizations.

The implementation of videotext systems in the United States has been impeded by important differences in the organization of American and European telecommunication activities. In Europe, where telecommunications and broadcasting services are largely nationalized, videotext research and implementations are subsidized by national governments. In some cases, as in the United Kingdom, videotext has been viewed as a means of stimulating telephone usage, which will correspondingly increase government revenues. Often, videotext implementations are adjuncts to social policies that are designed to stimulate education and culture, assist minorities and handicapped persons, and generally provide beneficial services to a nation's residents. In the United States, however, technological innovations are initiated as private enterprises which must be profitable. Although numerous videotext experiments have been implemented by broadcasting and communication companies since the 1970s, they have failed to confirm the technology's commercial viability.

In an American videotext experiment of considerable interest to libraries, the Channel 2000 Project, jointly sponsored by the Online Computer Library Center (OCLC) and Bank One, provided a viewdata service to several hundred households in Columbus, Ohio. As with European videotext services, the participants' television receivers were modified with decoders and keypads. A series of index screens guided the user in the identification and selection of information. The Channel 2000 Project emphasized reference and educational information. Available data bases included the catalog of the Public Library of Columbus and Franklin County, the full text of the *Academic American Encyclopedia,* a public information service, a community calendar compiled by the local chamber of commerce, and mathematical and reading programs prepared by Ohio State University.

Reinforcing concerns about the questionable profit potential of videotext technology, only 17 percent of Channel 2000 participants indicated that they would be willing to pay $10 to $15 per month for the service. When asked to indicate the type of videotext services for which they would be willing to pay $3 per month in a hypothetical system, participants listed home security, in-home computing, video games, library services, catalog shopping, a system that contacts a doctor, adult self-education, a video encyclopedia, household energy control, and an electronic bill payment system, in that order. Approximately 80 percent of the participants indicated a moderate to high probability that they would spend $15 per month for their six most desired services.

While videotext was originally conceived as a consumer-oriented technology for publicly available information services, some of the most interesting and successful implementations involve closed user groups. Such systems are used by corporations, government agencies, universities, hotels, convention centers, banks, and other organizations to display news bulletins, daily activity listings, schedules of community events, telephone directories, mass transit schedules, and other information. With their menu-oriented retrieval approach, videotext systems can prove easier to use and require less elaborate training and documentation than conventional computer-based information systems.

Videodiscs and Related Media

The analog optical videodisc is one of several platter-shaped media designed for the storage of conventional television images and accompanying audio signals. Introduced in 1978, the analog optical videodisc was the first commercially available optical storage medium. While products that permit direct recording of television images are available, the most widely encountered group of analog optical videodiscs consists of read-only media that contain prerecorded information. They are produced by mastering and replication techniques in special production facilities where program material is transferred from videotape, motion picture film, or other media to a photosensitive master disk. The master is used to create one or more intermediates from which individual plastic copies are produced. CD-ROM discs, as discussed elsewhere in this book, are manufactured in a similar manner, but analog optical videodiscs should not be confused with CD-ROM or with the read/write optical disks described in chapter 1. While such media employ optical storage technologies, the information they contain is encoded in digital rather than analog form.

Optical videodisks are read by special players equipped with lasers. The player is connected to a video or television receiver. (Courtesy: Pioneer)

Analog optical videodiscs must be further distinguished from such nonoptical videodiscs as the RCA Capacitance Electronic Disk (CED), which was discontinued in the 1980s, and the Video High Density (VHD) videodisc system, which was never marketed in the United States.

The most commonly encountered type of analog optical videodisk is variously called a "laserdisc," a "laser videodisc," a "LaserVision disc," or simply an "LV disc." It features a platter-shaped plastic substrate with a reflective metal layer and protective coating. Within the reflective layer, recorded information is represented by microscopic pits of varying sizes and spacings. A 12-inch analog optical videodisc—the original and most popular size—can store 54,000 still video images or 60 minutes of continuous, full-motion video accompanied by stereo audio signals on each of two sides. Videodiscs are also available in an eight-inch size, which can store 24,000 still images or 13.5 minutes of continuous full-motion video plus stereo audio per side. Both sizes of videodiscs are read by specially designed players that display the recorded images on a television receiver or video monitor. The most versatile models can retrieve and display specified video frames in as little as three seconds. Designed to operate under computer control, they support still-frame displays with sound, variable playback speeds, and seamless branching between images. Integral character generators can overlay video signals with one or more lines of text in various fonts, sizes, and colors.

Originally developed and promoted as a high-performance alternative to videotape for feature films and other entertainment programming, analog optical videodisc systems could not compete with videocassette recorders in the consumer market for which they were originally intended. They are, however, the information storage media of choice for interactive training, computer-assisted instruction (CAI), and other applications involving full-motion video images. Analog optical videodiscs are well suited to nonlinear applications in which the user controls the sequence in which specific information will be displayed. Operating under computer control, interactive videodisc implementations utilize branching techniques to display appropriate program segments in response to commands or data entered at a keyboard or other input device. In a self-paced instruction application, for example, specific video segments may be repeated if an operator's responses to computer-displayed questions do not indicate mastery of particular topics. Alternatively, correct answers may initiate the display of video segments dealing with more detailed and difficult material. Such nonlinear programming relies heavily on freeze-frame, slow motion, random frame access, and other visual effects and search capabilities supported by videodisc players.

U.S. government agencies, particularly the military, utilize videodiscs as an interactive alternative to conventional motion picture films and printed materials in a variety of training and recruitment applications. Some corporations likewise employ them for product-specific training. The substantial advantages of self-paced learning with minimal supervision have made the analog optical videodisc a popular medium for interactive continuing education programs designed for physicians and other professionals. Recognizing the potential of medical markets, several organizations have also produced analog optical videodiscs for patient education. Among other popular interactive applications, analog optical videodiscs are employed in point-of-purchase customer information systems and tourist orientation systems. Implemented as kiosk-type workstations, such systems have been widely installed in retail outlets, convention centers, hotels, and other public places.

With its high storage capacity and excellent image retrieval capabilities, the analog optical videodisc is also a useful publishing medium for visual data bases—an application that is of considerable interest to librarians, archivists, museum curators, and others responsible for large collections of photographs and other pictorial documents. Well-publicized examples of such applications include the Videodisc Catalogue produced by the National Gallery of Art and the videodisc edition of photographs from the collections of the National Air and Space Museum. Because they store video images that conform to prevailing broadcast television standards, analog optical videodiscs do not provide sufficient resolution for the consistently legible reproduction of the textual information contained in most typewritten or printed documents. With television broadcast standards used in North America, each video image is composed of 525 scan lines; images that conform to European broadcast standards contain 625 scan lines. In contrast, the electronic document imaging systems described above routinely provide 2,000 scan lines per letter-size page, and some devices record twice that number.

Several companies have introduced videodisc formats that combine analog-coded images with digitally coded, computer-processible information. With the Philips LV-ROM format, for example, each video image is accompanied by up to six kilobytes of digital data. The storage capacity of a 12-inch LV-ROM platter is 54,000 images plus 324 megabytes of data. Philips employed the LV-ROM format for the Domesday Book Project, which it implemented for the British Broadcasting Company and the United Kingdom Department of Trade and Industry. Designed as an educational resource and a reference tool, the Domesday Book is an archive of political, economic, social, and cultural events in the United Kingdom in the late twentieth century. The LV-ROM discs contain photographs, maps, and full-motion video segments. Digital data are used for textual and statistical information. Similar analog and digital storage capabilities are supported by the LD-ROM format developed by Pioneer Electronics. A 12-inch LD-ROM disc can store 54,000 video images plus up to 540 megabytes of data, the same amount as a CD-ROM disc.

The LV-ROM and LD-ROM formats are designed to address the widely publicized but vaguely defined field of multimedia computing, which combines computer-processible information with visual and audio components to create innovative information presentations that are not possible with conventional data processing methodologies. While CD-ROM, as discussed elsewhere in this book, can be utilized in multimedia applications, it cannot accommodate full-motion video images. Compact Disc-Interactive (CD-I) is a widely publicized multimedia format. Intended principally for consumer applications with education as a possible secondary market, CD-I products combine computer-processible data, character-coded text, graphic images, and audio signals. Unlike CD-ROM, which is a computer peripheral technology, CD-I discs are played by a self-contained device that must be connected to a television set or video monitor for visual output and to a stereo system for audio output. CD-I supports full-motion video images in a limited way; to date, however, CD-I implementations have relied on computer-generated animation for moving images.

Perhaps the most widely discussed alternative to analog optical videodiscs is Digital Video Interactive (DVI), a multimedia technology that uses proprietary data compression algorithms to store one hour of full-motion video images on a 4.75-inch compact disc. DVI images, which are encoded in digital rather than analog form, are drastically compressed for storage; in the absence of image compression, the limited surface area of a 4.75-inch compact disc can only accommodate a few minutes of full-motion video. DVI systems can combine full-motion video images with text, graphics, and stereo audio signals. DVI implementations are based on customized video, audio, and computer components intended for installation in an IBM-compatible microcomputer equipped with a color monitor and a CD-ROM drive. DVI components and prototype applications have been demonstrated at various professional meetings and on other occasions since the late 1980s. DVI adapter boards, software, and developers' kits are currently available. At the time of this writing, commercial implementations of DVI technology were just being introduced.

Videoconferencing

As their name suggests, videoconferencing systems utilize video and audio technology to conduct interactive meetings between geographically separated groups of people. As such, videoconferencing is a form of tele-conferencing. The latter is a generic term that denotes the combined use of telecommunications and electronic technologies as an alternative to in-person meetings. Other forms of teleconferencing include audioconfer-encing, which uses the familiar conference telephone call to establish a voice link between three or more people, and computer teleconferencing, a variant form of electronic message system described earlier in this chapter. As applied to videoconferencing, the term *meeting* encompasses a broad spectrum of group activities ranging from small planning sessions involving a few people to product introductions, press conferences, and educational presentations with hundreds of participants. Regardless of a meeting's size and scope, an emphasis on interactive communication among participants distinguishes videoconferencing from the mere tele-vising or video recording of such presentations.

First implemented in video telephone products, full-motion, two-way videoconferencing is the most interesting, sophisticated, and fully inter-active form of videoconferencing. Requiring special studio facilities equipped with voice-activated cameras, multiple video monitors, micro-phones, and related equipment, it provides both video and audio coverage of all participants and offers the most realistic approximation of in-person meetings. Two-way, full-motion videoconferencing is best suited to plan-ning sessions, project review meetings, or other small conferences involv-ing two geographically distant groups, each consisting of five to 10 people. In a typical two-way videoconferencing facility, participants sit on one side of a specially designed conference table, facing a group of video monitors that display participants at a remote site. Wall-mounted video cameras transmit close-up and overview images of conference participants. Addi-tional cameras may be dedicated to the display of chalkboards, flip charts, projected visuals, and similar graphic materials. Some videoconferencing studios also provide electronic stylus systems, which can transmit in-formation written on a sensitized surface, the most widely publicized example being a touch-sensitive device that resembles a conventional chalkboard. Support equipment may include telephone lines for private voice communication, computer terminals for electronic message trans-mission, videocassette recorders, and fax machines for document trans-mission and reception. In most cases, satellite communication facilities link the two videoconferencing sites.

One-way, full-motion videoconferencing with two-way audio capabilities provides a simpler and less expensive alternative to two-way systems. It is well suited to large group meetings involving a televised presentation by a single speaker or a panel of participants, followed by questions from an audience located at one or more geographically distant sites. Particu-larly useful for educational sessions, stockholder meetings, product intro-ductions, and other special events, one-way videoconferences must be carefully planned and formally produced. The specially equipped meeting rooms used for two-way videoconferencing are replaced by a conventional television studio that is connected to remote viewing sites by satellite communication facilities. The viewing sites are sometimes described as

Videoconferencing combines voice and image transmission to permit communication between groups of geographically scattered persons. Videoconferencing requires specially designed audiovisual equipment and facilities.

"downlinks." Audiences may be seated in small rooms or large auditoriums. Projection television systems may be used for large-screen display, and floor microphones are provided for questions from the audience, which are transmitted to the main site via telephone lines. The audience sites are not televised; participants at the main site can hear questions from audience members, but they cannot see the audience.

As an economical alternative to full-motion, one- and two-way videoconferencing systems, nonmotion videoconferencing transmits still video images over conventional telephone lines. The images, which are transmitted in a freeze-frame format, may depict a speaker, panel members, or prepared visuals. Replacement frames are transmitted at predetermined intervals. The geographically distant meeting sites are connected by a two-way audio link.

Audiographic conferencing, another form of nonmotion videoconferencing, combines two-way audio with devices such as special video projectors, electronic stylus systems, and remotely activated slide projectors that can transmit graphic images. Intended primarily for business strategy meetings, project review sessions, or other small group interactions, audiographic conferencing relies heavily on prepared visuals and documents. No attempt is made to transmit images of moving subjects. Audiographic conferencing can consequently be viewed as either a simplified type of videoconferencing or an enhanced form of audioconferencing.

High-definition Television

The definition, or amount of detail, in television visible in a video image is determined by the number of scan lines that form the image. As noted above, prevailing broadcast television standards specify video images that consist of 525 or 625 scan lines. The 525-line standard, developed by the National Television Systems Committee (NTSC), is utilized in North America, Japan, the Caribbean, much of Latin America, Saudi Arabia, and a few other parts of the world. The 625-line Phase Alternation Line (PAL) standard is used in the United Kingdom, West Germany, some other Western European countries, and parts of South America, Asia, and Africa. The Sequential Couleur a Memoire (SECAM) standard, which likewise specifies 625 lines per video image, is employed in France, Russia, other former Soviet republics, and parts of the Middle East.

As futurists and other critics frequently point out, NTSC, PAL, and SECAM were developed in the 1940s when television was just emerging. There has been considerable recent interest in new television formats that would take advantage of the significant technological advances that have occurred since that time. Such new formats are collectively described as high-definition television (HDTV). Employing 800 to 1,200 scan lines, they provide noticeably sharper images than those of existing television systems. High-definition images approach motion picture quality in their presentation of detail. As a further advantage with broad information processing implications, a video format offering such high definition is suitable for sophisticated computer graphic applications and for the display of textual information, including images of typewritten or printed documents.

Prototype HDTV systems have been demonstrated since the 1970s. An operational Japanese system—developed by NHK, the Japanese Broadcasting Company—supports video images with 1,125 scan lines. HDTV television receivers have been commercially available in Japan since the late 1980s, but they remain very expensive. Most are installed in department stores and other public locations to give the technology visibility. In addition to displaying sharper images than their conventional counterparts, HDTV television receivers feature wider screens that approximate the width-to-height ratio of motion picture screens. Videocassette recorders and videodisc players that support the NHK HDTV format have also been developed.

Like conventional television, the Japanese HDTV system employs analog coding methodologies. Several U.S. companies have developed prototype HDTV systems that are based on digital technologies. The Federal Communications Commission has specified digital coding as a requirement for any HDTV standard that it approves for the United States. Because high-definition television signals contain more information than conventional television signals, they require a much greater allocation of bandwidth within the television broadcast spectrum. A single HDTV channel would require a bandwidth equivalent to five conventional television channels. As their principal advantage, digital HDTV systems permit image compression for more efficient utilization of available broadcasting facilities.

SUMMARY

As a group, the automated office systems and other products described in this chapter are designed to improve the productivity of white collar workers by automating, and presumably facilitating, a variety of information-processing tasks. Since the library workforce is overwhelmingly white collar in character and includes a significant office component, such systems are of potentially great importance.

Word processing denotes a group of concepts, technologies, and techniques designed to simplify the production of typewritten and other textual documents. In its broadest sense, it encompasses dictation systems and automated text-editing systems. As an alternative to longhand drafting or the use of a stenographer, dictation equipment can facilitate the conversion of thoughts to a form suitable for transcription by a typist. Available equipment configurations range from inexpensive desktop units to complex centralized systems which feature digitized voice recording and operate under computer control. Portable recorders are available for use outside of conventional office settings.

Automated text-editing systems are often called "word processors." They are designed to simplify typing tasks by creating a machine-readable version of a textual document from which a printed copy can be produced. The machine-readable version, which is usually recorded on magnetic media, can be modified or otherwise processed to create successive drafts or multiple copies of typewritten documents. Since the 1970s, word processors have been available in a variety of configurations, ranging from automated, typewriter-like devices to elaborate multiworkstation systems that permit file sharing and cooperative document preparation. Since the mid-1980s, microcomputer software packages have increasingly dominated word processing implementations. They have virtually replaced the standalone, special-purpose word processors that dominated office installations in the 1970s and early 1980s.

As an alternative to paper and machine-readable storage, micrographics technology offers compact storage, simplified handling, and other advantages. While libraries have used microforms since the 1920s, they have tended to purchase them from micropublishers rather than create them in-house. Although relatively few libraries have established microform production facilities, a variety of source document cameras are available for operation by nontechnical personnel. Much recent attention has been given to the interrelationship of computer and micrographics technologies. Computer-output microfilm (COM), discussed in chapter 1, uses microforms as alternatives to paper for the production and distribution of computer-generated reports. Computer-input microfilm (CIM) is a variant form of optical character recognition. Computer-assisted retrieval (CAR) systems combine the space-saving advantages of microforms for documents storage with the ability of computers to rapidly manipulate index data.

Electronic document imaging systems offer a completely computerized approach to document storage and retrieval. Designed as an alternative to paper filing systems and micrographics technology, they utilize scanners to convert documents to digitized images suitable for computer storage. In most cases, the images are recorded on high-capacity optical disks. Index information is stored on magnetic disks, in the manner of CAR systems. Retrieved images can be displayed on video monitors or printed on paper. Some electronic document imaging systems incorporate optical disk autochangers, which provide convenient, unattended access to many document images.

Copiers and duplicators, long commonplace and important in library applications, are increasingly incorporating features and accessories that enhance flexibility and improve operator productivity. Examples include two-sided copying, image reduction and enlargement, automatic page sorting, automatic document feeding, and automatic stapling. Some companies offer multifunctional devices that can operate as copiers, computer printers, or fax machines.

Electronic mail and message systems offer a high-speed alternative to conventional mail service or other physical message-delivery methodologies. One of the oldest forms of electronic mail, facsimile technology, uses telephone lines or other communication facilities to transmit an image of a document to a remote location where it is reconstructed as a paper copy. In recent years, facsimile equipment has improved considerably in reliability, output quality, speed of transmission, and compatibility. The most widely encountered group of facsimile devices conforms to CCITT Group III standards. Depending on document characteristics and other factors, they can transmit a letter-size page in as little as 15 seconds.

While fax machines transmit images of documents, the telex network transmits typed messages composed of encoded characters. In libraries, telex terminals have been used for the transmission of interlibrary loan requests. Increasingly, however, they have been replaced by computer-based message systems which use a computer as an intermediary for the temporary storage of messages transmitted between individuals or organizations. A variant form of computer-based message system, called "computer teleconferencing," allows users to send messages to multiple recipients for comment, with each recipient having access to all responses.

A group of automated office systems employs video technology, alone or in combination with computers. Videotext systems deliver information to specially modified television receivers. Teletext and viewdata, the two forms of videotext, use broadcast and telephone line transmission, respectively. Teletext and viewdata systems have been implemented in European countries, Canada, and Japan, where they are often funded by government subsidies. In the United States, videotext systems have been implemented on an experimental basis with limited success. Uncertainty about their profitability as private-sector ventures has limited their availability. While one such experiment, conducted by OCLC, gave participants access to a library catalog, most have emphasized consumer-oriented information and recreational material.

Analog optical videodiscs are the most important storage medium in interactive training applications involving full-motion video information. Most analog optical videodiscs are read-only media. Although their limited resolution capabilities cannot support the legible reproduction of textual documents, analog optical videodiscs can store photographs, illustrations, and other visual materials encountered in library picture collections. Several companies offer videodisc formats that combine analog images with digitally coded, computer-processible information. Full-motion video images are also supported by several other storage media, including CD-I and DVI.

Videoconferencing combines voice and image transmission to permit communication between two or more groups of people in geographically scattered locations. Two-way videoconferencing, the most complex form, requires special studio facilities linked by satellites. One-way video conferencing with two-way audio capabilities is especially well suited to educational sessions and other large-group presentations. Less expensive, nonmotion videoconferencing systems are also available.

High-definition television (HDTV) provides video images that are significantly sharper and more detailed than those supported by conventional television technology. HDTV technology also offers potential for computer graphic applications and electronic image storage.

ADDITIONAL READING

ALBER, A. *Videotex/Teletext: Principles and Practices.* New York: McGraw-Hill, 1985.

ANDOLSEN, B. *Good Work at the Video Display Terminal: A Feminist Ethical Analysis of Changes in Clerical Work.* Knoxville: University of Tennessee Press, 1989.

ATKIN, B., ed. *Intelligent Buildings: Applications of IT and Building Automation to High Technology Construction Projects.* New York: Halsted, 1988.

AUMENTE, J. *New Electronic Pathways: Videotex, Teletext, and Online Databases.* Newbury Park, Calif.: Sage Publications, 1987.

BAETZ, M. *The Human Imperative: Planning for People in the Electronic Office.* Homewood, Ill.: Dow Jones-Irwin, 1985.

BATE, J. *Management Guide to Office Automation.* London: Collins, 1987.

Boss, R. "Imaging for Libraries and Information Centers." *Library Technology Reports* 28 (6): 639–723 (1992).

Bowman, H., and Christoffersen, M., eds. *Relaunching Videotex*. Boston: Kluwer Academic Publishers, 1992.

Bush, V. "As We May Think." *Atlantic Monthly* 176 (6): 101–18 (1945).

Casady, M. *Word / Information Processing: A Systems Approach*. Cincinnati: South-Western Publishing, 1989.

Cinnamon, B. *Optical Disk Document Storage and Retrieval Systems*. Silver Spring, Md.: Association for Information and Image Management, 1988.

Cushman, W. "Reading from Microfiche, a VDT, and the Printed Page: Subjective Fatigue and Performance." *Human Factors* 28 (1): 65–72 (1986).

D'Alleyrand, M. *Image Storage and Retrieval Systems*. New York: McGraw-Hill, 1989.

Durand, P. "The Public Service Potential of Videotext and Teletext." *Telecommunications Policy* 7 (1): 149–62 (1983).

Fallik, F. *Managing Organizational Change: Human Factors and Automation*. Philadelphia: Taylor and Francis, 1988.

Fischer, B. *Office Systems Integration: A Decision-Maker's Guide to Systems Planning and Implementation*. New York: Quorum Books, 1987.

Freeman, C., et al. *Support Staff Procedures in the Electronic Office*. Reston, Va.: Reston Publishing, 1986.

Galitz, W. *Handbook of Screen Format Design*. Wellesley, Mass.: QED Information Sciences, 1989.

Garson, B. *The Electronic Sweatshop: How Computers Are Transforming the Office of the Future into the Factory of the Past*. New York: Simon and Schuster, 1988.

Gibson, C., et al. *The Information Imperative: Managing the Impact of Information Technology on Businesses and People*. Lexington, Mass.: Lexington Books, 1987.

Gibson, H., and Rademacher, R. *Automated Office Systems*. New York: Holt, Rinehart, and Winston, 1987.

Goldfield, R. *Training in the Automated Office: A Decision-Maker's Guide to Systems Planning and Implementation*. New York: Quorum Books, 1987.

Grandjean, E., et al. "VDT Workstation Design: Preferred Settings and Their Effect." *Human Factors* 25 (1): 161–75 (1983).

Gropper, G. *Text Displays: Analysis and Systematic Design*. Englewood Cliffs, N.J.: Educational Technology Publications, 1991.

Harwin, R., and Haynes, C. *Healthy Computing: Risks and Remedies Every Computer User Needs to Know*. New York: American Management Association, 1992.

Haynes, C. *Portable Computing: Work on the Go*. New York: AMACOM, 1991.

Hurly, P., et al. *The Videotex and Teletext Handbook: Home and Office Communications Using Microcomputers and Terminals*. Philadelphia: Harper and Row, 1985.

Irving, R., and Higgins, C. *Office Information Systems: Management Issues and Methods*. New York: Wiley, 1991.

Isailovic, J. *Videodisc and Optical Memory Systems*. Englewood Cliffs, N.J.: Prentice Hall, 1985.

Jacobi, P. *Straight Talk about Videoconferencing*. New York: Prentice Hall, 1986.

Johansen, R. *Groupware: Computer Support for Business Teams*. New York: Free Press, 1988.

Kendrick, J. *Understanding Productivity: An Introduction to the Dynamics of Productivity Change*. Baltimore: Johns Hopkins Press, 1977.

Khoshafian, S., et al. *Intelligent Offices: Object-Oriented Multi-Media Information Management in Client / Server Architectures*. New York: Wiley, 1992.

Kleinschrod, W. *Critical Issues in Office Automation*. New York: McGraw-Hill, 1986.

Kleinschrod, W., et al. *Word / Information Processing Administration and Office Automation*. Indianapolis: Bobbs-Merrill, 1983.

KUPSCH, J., and RHODES, R. *Automated Office Systems.* Boston: PWS-Kent Publishing, 1989.

LAMBERT, S., and STALLIS, J., eds. *CD-I and Interactive Videodisc Technology.* Indianapolis: Bobbs-Merrill, 1987.

MANSFIELD, E. *Technological Change.* New York: Norton, 1971.

MOTHERSOLE, P., and WHITE, N. *Broadcast Data Systems: Teletext and RDS.* Boston: Butterworths, 1990.

MOURANT, R., et al. "Visual Fatigue and Cathode Ray Display Terminals." *Human Factors* 23 (4): 529–40 (1981).

NEWMAN, W. *Designing Integrated Systems for the Office Environment.* New York: McGraw-Hill, 1987.

NORA, S., and MINC, A. *The Computerization of Society.* Cambridge, Mass.: MIT Press, 1980.

OVERHAGE, C., and REINTJES, J. "Project Intrex: A General Review." *Information Storage and Retrieval* 10 (2): 157–88 (1974).

PORAT, M. "Global Implications of the Information Society." *Journal of Communications* 28 (1): 70–80 (1978).

SAFFADY, W. *Electronic Document Imaging Systems: Design, Evaluation, and Implementation.* Westport, Conn.: Meckler Corporation, 1993.

———. *Micrographic Systems.* Silver Spring, Md.: Association for Information and Image Management, 1990.

———. *Optical Disks vs. Micrographics.* Westport, Conn.: Meckler Corporation, 1993.

SMITH, R. *The Wired Nation.* New York: Harper and Row, 1972.

STRASSMAN, P. *Information Payoff: The Transformation of Work in the Electronic Age.* New York: Free Press, 1985.

THIERAUF, R. *Image Processing Systems in Business: A Guide for MIS Professionals and End Users.* New York: Quorum Books, 1992.

TUROFF, M., and HILTZ, R. *The Network Nation: Human Communications via Computer.* Reading, Mass.: Addison-Wesley, 1978.

TYDEMAN, J., and LIPINSKI, H. *Teletext and Videotext in the United States: Market Potential, Technology, and Public Policy Issues.* New York: McGraw-Hill, 1982.

WILLIAMS, T. *Computers, Work, and Health: A Socio-Technical Approach.* New York: Taylor and Francis, 1989.

Part Two

Library Operations

5

Automated Circulation Control

With the exception of archives, manuscript libraries, rare book collections, and other special repositories, the circulation of books and other materials is an important part of the mission of most libraries. People who visit a public, academic, school, corporate, or government library expect to be able to borrow materials for use in their homes or offices for predetermined periods of time—assuming, of course, that they qualify as authorized borrowers. Circulation control activities consequently address an important facet of a library's mission. Their principal purpose is to maintain records about the withdrawal of specific books or other library materials. Circulation records protect a library's investment in its collections by fixing the responsibility and date for the return of borrowed items. In addition, circulation records contain information about the use of library materials which, when extracted and properly analyzed, constitutes a valuable aid to collection development.

In manual implementations, a library's master circulation file usually consists of paper cards or slips, each of which contains information about a particular circulation transaction. The specific information content of these paper records may include a brief description of the item (the author, title, and call number, for example), its due date, and the borrower's identification number, name, and perhaps address. This master file reflects the library material in circulation at a given moment. It is typically arranged in a manner that reflects the library's need to obtain information about the status of a given item. In many public libraries, for example, cards are filed by due date for simplified identification and reprocessing of overdue items. In academic and special libraries, where it is often necessary to recall a given circulating item before the expiration of its loan period, the card file may be arranged by call number or author/title. In such applications, special edge-notched cards may be used to identify overdue items.

In addition to a master circulation file, most libraries also maintain records about authorized borrowers. Such records, which may be maintained on cards or as sheet-form rosters, usually include some combination of the following information for each borrower: name, identification number, address, telephone number, registration and card expiration dates, privilege category (such as adult or juvenile in a public library, faculty member or student in an academic library), and the name of the issuing branch or library (in a multibranch or multilibrary system). Additional files may be created to meet special circulation requirements. Some libraries, for example, maintain lists of delinquent borrowers or of circulating items to be held for specified persons on their return. Likewise, some libraries maintain circulation cards for returned items in a historical transaction file that is used for statistical analysis. Many scientific, technical, and business libraries maintain records of borrower interests which can be matched against newly acquired items. This approach to library service, sometimes described as the selective dissemination of information (SDI), is often considered a facet of reference service, but it can also be viewed as a form of anticipatory circulation.

Since the 1930s, libraries have sought, and more or less successfully applied, various automated alternatives to the manual recordkeeping practices described above. This chapter reviews automated circulation control systems in terms of both their historical development and the current state of the art. Following accepted systems analysis practice, the chapter opens with a review of the problems inherent in manual circulation control and of some automated alternatives that do not involve computers. The discussion of computerized circulation systems begins with a review of batch and real time approaches, continuing and expanding a topic introduced in chapter 3. The final, and most important, section of the chapter deals with prewritten software packages and preconfigured turnkey systems, the currently dominant approaches to computerized circulation control.

THE DEVELOPMENT OF AUTOMATED CIRCULATION

Circulation control is one of the most widely automated library operations. It is often the first activity that libraries consider automating, possibly because library circulation control systems bear an obvious resemblance to inventory management, retail charge-card operations, and other transaction processing systems that are widely encountered and have been successfully automated in general business applications. While specific circulation policies and procedures may be subject to considerable local variation, the major component of circulation control—the check-out/check-in procedure—is typically performed in a straightforward manner that is relatively easily understood by computer systems analysts lacking formal library training. As library users, many systems analysts have experienced circulation activity firsthand and are at least broadly familiar with its purpose and nature.

In addition, the bibliographic data required for circulation control are often less extensive and complex than those required to automate such activities as cataloging and acquisitions. As a result, data conversion costs and software development time may be substantially reduced. Certain hardware requirements associated with circulation control may likewise prove simpler to accommodate than those encountered in the automation of other library operations. Less auxiliary storage is usually required when compared to applications involving greater amounts of bibliographic data, for example, and hardcopy output requirements can usually be satisfied by relatively inexpensive dot matrix printers or low-speed line printers. Typewriter-quality output is seldom required.

Problems of Circulation Control

Although these characteristics of the circulation activity may simplify the development and implementation of automated alternatives, library interest in automated circulation is in large part based on a long-standing recognition of certain problems inherent in manual circulation control. Specifically, the recordkeeping operations associated with manual circulation systems are characteristically labor-intensive. They involve such time-consuming work routines as the filing of single- or multiple-copy book cards, the checking of card files to determine the circulation status of specific items, the identification of overdue items with the subsequent preparation of borrower notices, and the computation of fines. Assuming, for example, an average of just one minute of work time associated with the filing, removal, and other handling of each card in a master circulation file, then a library with an annual circulation of 200,000 items must expend almost 3,500 hours in file maintenance each year. At a labor rate of $6 per hour, including fringe benefits, the annual cost of file maintenance will approach $21,000. In many public and academic libraries, this required labor commitment is increased by a high volume of circulation activity, long hours of service, and, in the case of multibranch libraries, multiple service points.

As a further complication, most circulation control operations are clerical rather than professional in nature. Their routine character contributes to errors in filing and related recordkeeping tasks, as well as to low employee motivation and high staff turnover, with its associated retraining costs. Academic libraries, for example, often employ students as part-time circulation clerks, paying them lower hourly wages than would be required for full-time clerical personnel. Such students rarely find the job sufficiently challenging to maintain their interest. As a consequence, they may make errors or require considerable supervision, which, in turn, increases total system costs.

Errors and staff turnover aside, the scope of manual circulation systems is necessarily limited to activities directly related to the charging and discharging of library materials. In most cases, accurate circulation statistics—which are essential to the informed management of collection development activities in a period of reduced acquisitions budgets—are very difficult or impossible to derive. Properly prepared and presented, circulation statistics can assist bibliographers and other librarians in determining when additional copies of a given item are required and in identifying portions of a library's collection that are infrequently utilized and may consequently warrant a reevaluation of prevailing selection policies. Given the high prices libraries must pay for books and other materials, the ability to avoid inappropriate purchases is of obvious importance.

As a further constraint, there is typically little or no relationship between a manual circulation system's card or paper files and a library's catalog or other records that contain much of the same bibliographic information. Thus, a user who consults a library's catalog for the call number of a specified book cannot immediately determine the item's circulation status. Finally, from the service standpoint, manual circulation systems place much of the work load on the borrower, who must fill out charge slips or cards. This inconvenience, combined with long waiting times attributable to the slowness of the manual check-out procedure, can lead to user dissatisfaction.

These problems are not unique to library circulation control but are, in fact, characteristic of many business applications involving the maintenance and control of large document files. Such applications are widely encountered in insurance companies, hospitals and medical clinics, personnel departments within corporations and government agencies, registrars' offices in colleges and universities, law offices, police departments, and other paper-intensive work environments. Given the similarities between circulation control and much business data processing, it is not surprising that computerization is often viewed as a potentially effective alternative to the problems of manual systems.

Although computerized circulation systems are the subject of this chapter, there are other alternatives to manual circulation control. These alternatives employ photographic rather than electronic technologies. Compared to computer-based systems, they are outdated in concept, employ low-performance components, and offer limited functionality. Some small and medium-size public libraries, for example, have utilized photographic charging systems in which a book identification card, a borrower identification card, and date information pertaining to successive circulation transactions are recorded on microfilm using a specially designed camera. Following filming, the book identification card and a transaction slip are inserted into the pocket of the circulation book. The microfilmed documents, arranged by transaction number, provide the full record for each circulation transaction, thus eliminating the manual filing and other handling of charge cards.

But because the information on microfilm is in transaction number sequence, additional manual work routines are required. Presumably, transaction records are grouped on film by the due date of borrowed items. As items are returned to the library, the transaction slips are removed from their book pockets and filed in numeric sequence. At some specified time following the due date, this file must be examined, missing transaction numbers identified, and the appropriate microfilm reels consulted, using a reader, to determine borrowers' names and addresses. This information is then used to recall overdue items. While a microfilm reader/printer can be used to automatically generate copies of transaction-related documents and a preprinted form letter can be sent to delinquent borrowers, envelopes must still be addressed manually.

To reduce the required labor commitment, some libraries have developed computer-processible transaction card systems that permit full or partial automation of this recall procedure. In terms of performance, such combined photocharging/computer systems share most of the limitations of the batch processing circulation systems previously described in chapter 3. In addition to the necessity of manually identifying overdue items, photocharging systems provide no convenient means of determining the circulation status of a given item for purposes of recalling it before the due date. This limitation makes them unsuitable for use by many academic and special libraries.

While photocharging systems represent only a modest deviation from manual circulation control procedures, more radical departures have been suggested and, for the most part, dismissed. Few library administrators would, for example, accept the idea of abandoning circulation control in favor of an honor system in which borrowers assume personal responsibility for returning books after some specified period of time. Even if most borrowed materials were returned on time or eventually, such a circulation method leaves a library with little or no information about the status and use of its collection at a given point in time.

A somewhat less radical, but still striking, departure from conventional circulation control involves the substitution of duplication for circulation. In a paper delivered at the 1962 convention of the National Microfilm Association, Laurence Heilprin first outlined the concept of a duplicating library in which an inviolate collection of books and other materials, in full-size or microform, would be duplicated on demand and distributed to library users as an alternative to circulation. Recipients would be free to keep the copies or dispose of them. The cost of duplication would presumably be defrayed by the elimination of circulation-related expenses associated with record keeping, the recall of overdue materials, and the replacement of nonreturned items. In addition, since they are not removed from the library, materials are continuously available, and multiple-copy purchases can consequently be minimized.

Unfortunately, the relative economics of a wholesale conversion from circulation to duplication have never been fully explored. In addition, the requirements of prevailing copyright legislation may either render the duplicating approach impractical or increase its cost and complexity significantly. Although it is probably not a viable alternative for all library applications, the duplicating concept has been selectively adopted for certain types of library materials. It is, for example, the prevailing method of providing journal articles through interlibrary loan. Similarly, some libraries employ duplication as an alternative to the circulation of microfiche. Rather than circulating the library's master fiche, the requester is given a diazo or vesicular microfiche copy for personal use and disposition. A number of low-cost desktop microfiche duplicators are available for this purpose. In the case of microfiche report collections produced by the Educational Resources Information Clearinghouses (ERIC), the National Technical Information Service (NTIS), and other government agencies, there is no copyright impediment to such duplication. Copyright restrictions may, however, apply to the duplication of microforms purchased from commercial micropublishers.

In the broadest sense, the widespread availability of coin-operated copiers in libraries probably constitutes the most common and effectively implemented manifestation of duplication as an alternative to circulation. A would-be borrower who is not interested in an entire book or serial publication can copy relevant sections. The user, of course, pays for the copies made, but in many libraries the total cost of the copier operation is not recovered through such charges. Presumably, those libraries that subsidize coin-operated copier operations are doing so to encourage their use and to achieve a corresponding reduction in circulation-related costs.

Custom-developed Computerized Systems

Although the photocharging and duplicating systems described above have been successfully applied in certain library situations, only computer-oriented systems offer wide-ranging alternatives to the problems of manual circulation control. Perhaps more than any other library activity, the historical development of automated circulation control has reflected changes in the state of the art in data processing technology. Through the mid-1970s, most automated circulation control systems were custom-developed for a single library or library system. As early as the 1930s and extending into the 1960s, a number of libraries used punched cards in combination with sorters, collators, and other "unit record" equipment as an alternative to manual record keeping. Tabulating cards punched with information about books, borrowers, and due dates could be sorted, for example, to select overdue items or to identify all books on loan to a given person.

Such "precomputer" data processing systems, several of which were developed for academic libraries by methods and procedures analysts and operations research specialists, were typically based on inventory control models used in business. With the introduction of computers for business applications in the mid-1960s, a number of libraries developed computerized circulation control systems based on batch processing techniques. Such systems were typically implemented on a computer located in a data processing center operated by a university, municipality, or corporation with which the library was affiliated. While some of these batch processing systems remain in use, they are now mainly of interest for their limitations and impact on the design of subsequent systems.

The general characteristics of batch processing circulation systems were introduced in chapter 3. As described there, keypunch or key-to-tape devices are used to convert information about individual check-out and check-in transactions to the machine-readable, computer-processible form required for the automatic charging and discharging of library materials. Machine-readable records pertaining to successive circulation transactions are batched for processing at predetermined intervals by an institutional or corporate computing center. The computer processing itself consists of the updating of a master circulation file that is usually contained on one or more reels of magnetic tape. The specific contents of this file vary somewhat from system to system. Typically, they contain one logical record for each book or other circulating item in the library's collection. Individual fields within each record might include an accession number, author's name, title, imprint or additional bibliographic information, call number, copy number, borrower's identification number, and the due date. Records within the master circulation file are usually arranged in accession number sequence. With the earliest computerized circulation control systems, the master circulation file was typically created by keypunching, or otherwise keystroking, bibliographic and other data about the library's circulating collection, as described in chapter 1. Other approaches to data conversion are discussed later in this chapter.

In addition to the master circulation file, computerized circulation control systems also require a file of borrower information. This file, which in batch processing systems is usually maintained on magnetic tape, includes one record for each authorized borrower. Like the manual card file or roster described earlier, each borrower's record consists of such fields as identification number, name, address, telephone, privilege category, registration date, and expiration date. On the tape itself, borrower records are usually arranged in identification number order.

Although the specific work steps involved in individual batch processing systems may vary, the sequence of operations previously described in chapter 3 is typical:

1. Punched cards or other input records reflecting circulation transactions are sorted into the same sequence as the master circulation file.
2. Individual input records are then read by a computer program, which determines the accession number of the circulating item and locates its record within the master circulation file.
3. If the circulation transaction is a check-out, the borrower's number and due dates are added to the master record in fields provided for that purpose. If the transaction reflects the return of an item, the previously recorded charging information is erased.
4. When all circulation transactions have been processed, one or more lists are printed.
5. At predetermined intervals, the master circulation file and borrower's information files are further processed in order, for example, to identify overdue items, produce recall notices, derive and report circulation statistics, or print special lists of delinquent borrowers or of circulating items placed on hold.

While batch processing circulation systems can eliminate the maintenance of paper files and the time-consuming preparation of overdue and recall notices associated with manual circulation control, they are limited in several potentially important respects. With all batch processing systems, there is a gap in time between the occurrence of a transaction and the computer's processing and reporting of information about that transaction. Thus, the printed lists produced by a batch processing circulation control system necessarily reflect the status of a library's circulating collection at the time when the last batch of transaction records was taken from the library to the computer site for processing. Some of the information contained in such lists will necessarily be invalidated by circulation transactions occurring after a given batch was removed for processing.

As a further limitation, batch processing circulation control systems cannot effectively accommodate the "hold" function in which a library user requests that a given item be identified and reserved for him or her on its return from circulation. To implement the hold function, a separate card file or list must be maintained and manually consulted for each returned item. Alternatively, some libraries place a note or other hold indicator in the item's shelf position, thus alerting the shelving clerk that the item should be returned to the circulation desk. A similar limitation prevails in the identification of delinquent borrowers. As with holds, the library must maintain a card file or list and consult it manually at each check-out transaction.

While some batch processing circulation control systems may remain in operation, they reflect the state of the art in computer technology as it existed in the 1960s and early 1970s. By the mid-1970s, computer systems specialists had begun to concentrate on the development of online, real time systems. In a real time circulation system, check-out and check-in transactions are processed as they occur. Because the master circulation file is updated immediately, it always reflects the current status of a library's circulating collection. The hardware and software requirements of real time systems necessarily differ markedly from those encountered in batch processing implementations. The recording of information about circulation transactions takes place at online terminals rather than at offline keypunch machines. Similar terminals are used to inquire about the circulation status of given items. Most printed listings are consequently eliminated, although fine notices, recall notices, and other documents must still be produced in the batch mode. Rather than being stored offline on magnetic tape, the master circulation file is maintained on magnetic disks or other direct-access storage media for continuous, online availability.

During the 1970s, several libraries implemented custom-developed real time circulation control systems. Widely publicized examples have included the Library Computer System (LCS), developed at Ohio State University and subsequently replicated at the State University of New York at Albany and the University of Illinois; the Bell Laboratories Library Real-Time Loan (BELLREL) system; and a self-service, charge-out system developed by Northwestern University. Such real time systems successfully addressed the previously discussed limitations of batch processing. Specifically, real time systems do not suffer from the inaccuracy inherent in batch processing. Because the master circulation file is updated as transactions occur rather than at some later time, up-to-the-minute information about the circulation status of a given item can be obtained. Similarly, computer-processible files of items on hold and of delinquent borrowers can be automatically checked as items are charged or discharged. In addition, the implementation of an online, real time circulation system provides the potential for interfacing with other library systems, such as a computer-maintained catalog or computer-based acquisitions system, which may also operate in real time.

PREWRITTEN SOFTWARE AND TURNKEY SYSTEMS

Through the mid-1970s, computerized circulation control systems, whether operating in the batch or real time mode, were developed and implemented on a customized basis for a particular library. Following a detailed systems analysis, equipment was selected and programs written to meet the specific needs of a given application. As might be expected, the most interesting and innovative systems were developed by large academic, public, and corporate libraries which had access to institutional computing resources and technical expertise. For the typical medium- to large-size library, however, the computing facilities required to develop a customized circulation control system were too often unavailable. In most organizations, access to computing resources is allocated according to preestablished priorities, and the library's requirements are sometimes given inadequate consideration.

Even when a library is able to obtain computer time and terminal equipment—or perhaps purchase its own minicomputer or microcomputer system—problems of software development can prove significant. In computing applications generally, it is the absence of suitable software that constitutes the most formidable obstacle to automation. Comparatively few libraries have resident systems analysts or programmers. Institutional computing centers allocate software support personnel in much the same manner as hardware resources. In many cases, there is a long waiting list to consult a systems analyst or programmer/analyst, and, once begun, customized software development is a slow, labor-intensive, and error-prone activity.

While computerized circulation systems are still being custom-developed for individual libraries, a number of vendors offer generalized, preformulated approaches to the computerization of circulation control. These approaches, which eliminate the need for customized system development and speed the implementation process, have dominated automated circulation control since the mid-1970s. They can be divided into two related groups: (1) prewritten circulation control software intended for execution on a computer system operated by or for a given library, and (2) turnkey systems, consisting of preconfigured combinations of hardware and software marketed as self-contained products.

Introduced in the early 1970s, the earliest prewritten circulation software packages and turnkey circulation systems were single-purpose products designed specifically and exclusively for circulation control. During the 1980s, such single-purpose implementations were supplanted by "integrated" turnkey systems and software packages, which combine circulation control with other capabilities. Strictly defined, an integrated system utilizes a single bibliographic data base to support multiple library operations. In actual practice, however, the term encompasses a variety of multifunctional products, some of which employ multiple data bases to support different tasks. In addition to circulation control, the most complete integrated system implementations include interrelated application modules for cataloging, online catalog access by library users and/or staff, acquisitions, and serials control, perhaps supplemented by materials booking, a community bulletin board system, and electronic message transmission. In some cases, circulation control is a standard integrated system component that may be implemented alone or in conjunction with other functions. In others, circulation control is an optional application module that must be purchased separately.

Whether implemented as single-purpose products or as integrated system components, prewritten circulation software packages and turnkey systems recognize that certain aspects of circulation control can be automated in more or less the same way, regardless of their specific library setting, although most vendors do provide some ability to accommodate local requirements. Both approaches offer several significant advantages over custom-developed circulation control systems. Most significantly, prewritten software and turnkey systems can be implemented far more quickly than customized installations, where software development may require months or perhaps years to complete. Speed of implementation is an especially important consideration in applications where automation of the circulation activity will result in a cost reduction. In such applications, the sooner the automated system is operational, the sooner the library begins saving money.

Similarly, prewritten software packages and turnkey systems minimize or eliminate requirements for local software expertise. Libraries acquiring such products do not need to hire programming staff or take programming courses. In fact, customer programming is specifically prohibited by most vendors. Because the system design is predetermined, user training is limited to operational considerations. As a distinctive advantage of turnkey systems, procurement-related tasks are greatly simplified by the provision of a preconfigured combination of hardware and software components specifically designed to work together. With a single source for central processing equipment and peripheral devices, the necessity of dealing with multiple hardware vendors is eliminated, as are potential problems of equipment compatibility. It is likewise easier to fix maintenance responsibility for the system's various components. When equipment and software are procured from multiple sources, individual vendors may work harder to evade maintenance responsibility than to repair malfunctioning components.

Hardware Characteristics

All prewritten circulation control programs are designed for specific computer and operating system configurations. While prewritten circulation software packages are available for computers of all types and sizes, medium-size and larger public and academic libraries have typically relied on mainframe- and minicomputer-based products. Turnkey combinations of hardware and software are invariably minicomputer-based. Most vendors rely on such popular minicomputer platforms as the VAX product line from Digital Equipment Corporation and the HP 3000 Series from Hewlett-Packard. Microcomputer-based circulation control programs have proven particularly popular with small public, school, and special libraries. As a group, such products have benefited from a decade of functional enhancements plus the progressively greater information processing capabilities offered by increasingly powerful microcomputers. Most microcomputer-based circulation control programs are available in single-workstation and local area network versions; the latter offer a potentially economical alternative to minicomputer configurations for medium-size libraries. In the future, as discussed in chapter 1, microcomputer-based circulation control may offer a mainframe alternative for larger libraries interested in downsizing.

Regardless of the type of central processor employed, all available prewritten circulation control software packages and turnkey systems are designed to operate with online input and output devices. The function of the input devices is to convert information about individual circulation transactions to the machine-readable form required by the central processor. Although the earliest custom-developed circulation systems followed conventional data processing practice in using keyboard-oriented input devices, prewritten circulation control programs and turnkey systems invariably use some form of optical recognition technology to eliminate keystroking and consequently simplify data entry. As discussed in chapter 1, optical recognition devices use light to determine the data content of input records. Once identified, the data are encoded and, depending on the particular device, transmitted directly to a computer or recorded locally on magnetic media. In circulation control applications, barcode label recognition is the most common form of optical recognition.

In barcode label recognition, a specially designed label, consisting of blank spaces alternating with vertical lines, is used to encode a numeric identifier. Specific label characteristics were described in chapter 1. Barcode labels are customarily affixed to circulating library materials and, in most cases, to borrowers' identification cards. They contain numeric information that is encoded by varying the widths of the vertical lines. Barcode labels may be ordered preprinted or produced by the library itself. In either case, specific numbered labels must be associated with machine-readable circulation control records for the particular items and borrower cards to which they are attached.

Barcode labels can be affixed to library materials and associated with data base records in various ways. A barcode label can be attached to an item, the data base record for that item retrieved, and the label number scanned into the barcode field with the record. The data base record is then saved and the book shelved. Alternatively, duplicate labels can be affixed to library materials and their shelflist cards. When the shelflist is converted, the barcode label for each title is scanned into the record from the shelflist card. Another popular method involves "smart" barcode labels which include preprinted call numbers, titles, or other identifiers for library materials. Smart barcodes are produced from a library's data base and must be attached to the materials for which they are intended. Smart barcodes are typically printed in shelflist sequence to simplify the labeling of items. Regardless of the method employed, the barcoding of a library's collection is a time-consuming procedure that can take weeks or months to complete.

Various types of barcodes are available. Most formats encode 14 to 16 digits. In a typical implementation, the first digit is used to distinguish book labels from patron labels. The next several digits identify the library in a multilibrary installation, and the remainder identify the item or patron. A check digit, used for error detection, is often appended. Regardless of the labeling method utilized, each circulation control software package and turnkey system is designed to accept barcode labels in a particular format, and different formats cannot be intermixed in a given installation. Incompatibility of barcodes can pose problems and necessitate relabeling by libraries that switch from one circulation control system to another.

In the simplest and least expensive input equipment configuration, a specially designed scanning wand, containing a light source and a photocell, is manually passed over the barcoded label. This scanning wand, which is often called a "light pen," determines the label's character content by analyzing its light-reflectance properties. The light pen, which is a handheld device resembling a small flashlight, is usually attached to a conventional keyboard-send-receive video terminal. This configuration is sometimes described as a composite terminal. Alternatively, the light pen can be configured with a calculator-style keypad and single-line display as a special-purpose terminal. For offline operations such as bookmobile use or shelf inventorying, portable light pen terminals can store data in internal memory or on magnetic media for later transmission to a central processor. As an alternative to conventional light pens, most circulation control systems can be equipped with a laser scanner which is somewhat faster than a light pen device and eliminates the potential for wear resulting from passing a light pen over a label. In some cases, the laser scanner is configured with an auxiliary cash-register-style printer for the production of date due slips.

Though not as common as barcodes, some prewritten software packages and turnkey systems can be configured for use with OCR labels. As discussed in chapter 1, optical character recognition uses reflected light to determine the character content of input documents. Unlike systems designed to read barcodes, OCR devices accept input in the form of alphabetic characters, numeric digits, punctuation marks, and other symbols. The input is consequently both machine-readable and human-readable. The characters are normally imprinted on a specially designed label in a type font, such as OCR-A or OCR-B, that is optimized for machine recognition. The labels are usually read by a handheld wand that is similar to the light pen used with barcode. The wand OCR is attached to a keyboard-send-receive terminal.

As in any computer configuration, the function of the output devices used in circulation control systems is to convert the results of computer processing to human-readable form. As noted above, the scanners that read barcodes or OCR labels are attached to keyboard-send-receive terminals. Virtually identical to the video display devices discussed in chapter 3, their function is to perform various online inquiries which determine the status of given items or borrowers. The typical circulation control system includes one or more video terminals, each capable of displaying data in the familiar pattern of 24 lines containing up to 80 characters each. To highlight information and to alert the operator to unusual conditions, these terminals are capable of a variety of visual effects, including blinking fields and reverse video displays.

To print patron notices and reports, all circulation control systems include one or more paper output devices. For the production of date due slips, fine receipts, and similar items, most equipment configurations include one or more printers. As previously noted, some systems also support barcode printing equipment.

The final hardware element in a typical circulation system configuration, auxiliary storage retains item and borrower information in machine-readable form until it is required by the central processor. As online, real time systems, prewritten circulation software packages and turnkey systems utilize fixed magnetic disk drives as their principal storage peripherals. The amount of disk storage required in a given installation will depend on such factors as the number of circulating items in a library's data base, the amount of information stored for each item, the number of registered borrowers, the volume of circulation transactions, the specific data base management methodologies employed, and the number and nature of the indexes that support record retrieval. In addition to storing item and borrower records, a circulation control system must include sufficient disk space for system and application software. Disk space is usually expandable in varied increments up to some predetermined limit. In some cases, a library begins with sufficient disk storage to accommodate present and short-term expansion requirements, then acquires additional disk drives as storage requirements increase. Some libraries, however, initially purchase enough disk storage for five or more years of collection growth.

As discussed in chapter 1, fixed magnetic disk drives are vulnerable to various malfunctions, which can lead to loss of recorded data. To minimize the impact of such damage, circulation and borrower records must be periodically copied onto other media. To provide backup for disk files and as a means of entering machine-readable data obtained from bibliographic utilities and other sources to be discussed in chapter 6, most mainframe- and minicomputer-based circulation control systems support one or more nine-track magnetic tape drives. Microcomputer-based systems typically use magnetic tape cartridges or, in some cases, floppy disks for backup purposes.

Circulation Data Files

Regardless of capacity or backup method, the fixed magnetic disk drives described in the preceding section provide online storage for circulation data files and their associated indexes. As previously indicated, all computerized circulation control systems maintain files of machine-readable data pertaining to a library's circulating collection and its borrowers. Collection-related information includes both bibliographic and copy data. As its name suggests, a bibliographic data file contains bibliographic information—such as a main entry, title, imprint, and physical description—for each title in a library's circulating collection, although some libraries also include records for noncirculating items. Bibliographic data files usually contain one record for each title, regardless of the number of copies in the library's collection. An item data file—sometimes called a holdings file— contains records pertaining to the individual copies of specific titles that the library owns. Such item records—which may include copy numbers, barcode numbers, and copy locations—are essential to the circulation activity, since a library circulates copies rather than bibliographic entities. With some microcomputer-based circulation software packages, bibliographic and copy data are merged in a single file. In most mainframe- and minicomputer-based systems, however, they are maintained separately to eliminate redundant data and enhance processing efficiency. In such cases, the two files are linked by pointer fields.

The structure and content of bibliographic data files have been widely discussed at professional meetings and in library literature. Some circulation systems store bibliographic records in a manner that conforms to the MARC format, a standard format for the interchange of bibliographic data which is discussed more fully in chapter 6. Although the complex combination of data fields associated with full MARC-format records is seldom required for circulation control itself, the MARC format is widely utilized by integrated library systems which support circulation control as one of several application modules, although system-specific variations are widely encountered.

Some prewritten circulation control software packages and turnkey systems, for example, support the MARC record format strictly and exclusively, although they may permit the entry of brief bibliographic records that can later be upgraded to the full MARC format. Other systems allow modifications or extensions to MARC records. In some cases, a library can specify the MARC format components to be included in bibliographic records. Alternatively, it may be able to add fields for materials—such as proprietary technical reports, vertical file literature, software, games, puzzles, and even audiovisual equipment—that are included in a library's circulating collection but are not covered by MARC formats.

Following a practice established by the earliest vendors of turnkey circulation control products, some prewritten software packages and turnkey systems support the MARC format as well as a briefer format which requires less disk space. Other systems accept input in the MARC format but convert records to a proprietary format for internal storage and processing. While the MARC format is strongly preferred in academic and public library installations, brief bibliographic records are sometimes utilized in circulation control systems implemented by corporate, government, and school libraries. Typically, such implementations involve a subset of MARC bibliographic fields, accompanied by such special user-specified fields as security classification and access authorization codes.

Subject to product-specific variations, a circulation control system's item data file will usually include some combination of the following information for each copy in a library's holdings: the barcode numbers or other item identifiers noted above, loan period, data entered into the data file, local call number, normal location or branch, temporary location or branch, media type, original price, replacement cost, circulation status, the date of last circulation activity, borrower's identifier, and due date. Copy data are often stored in fixed-length fields, which are usually less complex than the variable-length fields associated with bibliographic records.

While specific file structures and content will necessarily vary from product to product, all prewritten circulation software packages and turnkey systems support a borrower file which contains one machine-readable record for each authorized library user. In public libraries serving medium-size and larger cities, this file may contain 100,000 or more records. Academic, school, and special libraries, in contrast, usually have smaller clienteles.

File size aside, common data fields include the borrower's name, address, and telephone number; the date registered, expiration date, and date of last circulation activity; the borrower's category (such as faculty member, graduate student, or undergraduate student in an academic library, adult or juvenile in a public library); the borrower's card number, social security number, or other identifier; the name of the issuing library in a multilibrary system; an indication of delinquency status with a reason for delinquency; a count of the number of items in circulation; and a message field for several lines of text. Several systems also provide optional data fields for personal and demographic information that supports statistical analysis of circulation activity for particular types of library users. Typical examples include age group, occupation, and primary language.

While most of the data elements enumerated above are straightforward, slight variations can have an impact on system convenience and performance. To accommodate students' campus and home addresses, for example, circulation control systems that are suitable for academic libraries usually permit multiple values for those fields. Systems intended for corporate and government libraries may similarly provide fields for office and home addresses and telephone numbers. Several systems maintain a count of the number of lost books, claimed returns, and similar problems associated with individual borrowers.

As a potentially significant constraint, most circulation control systems store borrower identification numbers in proprietary internal formats that consist of prescribed combinations of digits and prefixes. To avoid the issuing of new borrower cards when an existing computerized circulation control system is replaced with the product of a different vendor, libraries should determine whether the replacement system can convert existing borrower numbers into the required internal format. Most systems also support the use of social security numbers as primary or alternate borrower identifiers, thereby permitting the input or updating of borrower files from registrars' records, payroll records, voter registration records, tax rolls, or other machine-readable data sources. As an additional advantage, social security numbers are often memorized by library users, most of whom will not have memorized their library-assigned borrower numbers.

Regardless of their nature and specific content, bibliographic, item, and borrower files can be established in either of two ways: (1) in advance of circulating any items, or (2) as individual items are circulated for the first time. Libraries have generally favored the former alternative, in which required circulation control information is converted to machine-readable form in advance of system operation, but such implementations sometimes prove impractical or economically impossible. For a public library that weeds its collection extensively on a regular schedule, for example, conversion in advance of system operation may not prove cost-effective for some older items subject to removal from the shelves. In such situations, the conversion of items at the time they are first circulated following system installation may prove more practical.

This technique, sometimes described as "conversion on the fly," can be used for bibliographic, copy, and borrower records. As an inconvenience, it extends the time required to complete circulation transactions for items and borrowers not already in the system. This problem is, however, self-limiting as more and more data are converted to machine-readable form. It should further be noted that file creation in advance of system operation and conversion on the fly are not necessarily mutually exclusive alternatives. In some applications, they can be profitably employed in combination to reduce data entry time and cost.

Whether established in advance of, or following, system installation, the creation of machine-readable bibliographic, item, and borrower data files is the library's responsibility. As described in chapter 1, direct key-to-disk data entry can be used to convert the required information from a library shelflist, borrower rosters, or other paper records, but such data entry procedures are time-consuming and labor-intensive. As an example, a relatively small bibliographic file containing 100,000 records averaging just 300 characters each would require 30 million keystrokes for initial data entry, plus an additional 30 million verification keystrokes. At a data entry rate of 7,000 keystrokes per hour, file creation and verification will require 8,570 person-hours. If data entry operators are paid $8 per hour including fringe benefits, the estimated labor cost to establish the bibliographic file is $68,560.

For reasons discussed in chapter 1, it is unlikely that optical character recognition (OCR) can be effectively used for data conversion in most circulation control applications. As an alternative to key entry, however, most prewritten circulation software packages and turnkey systems provide some mechanism for establishing bibliographic and borrower files from machine-readable data obtained from external sources. Some libraries, for example, have machine-readable files utilized by a previously implemented computerized circulation control system. Alternatively, a library may purchase machine-readable bibliographic records from another library with a similar collection. More commonly, most prewritten circulation control programs and turnkey systems can accept machine-readable data obtained from one or more of the bibliographic utilities or CD-ROM cataloging systems discussed in chapter 6. Such data may be purchased on magnetic media or transferred to the circulation control system through an online interface. Some vendors of circulation control software and turnkey systems support their installations with data entry and record conversion services. Such services are also offered by other companies.

The transfer of machine-readable records from registrars' tapes, personnel records, or other external sources can minimize the time and labor required to create borrower files in academic, school, and special libraries. Although special conversion software must be created to convert transferred records to the format required by the circulation system, the cost of required programming usually compares favorably with the cost of keystroking labor required for original data entry. In most cases, vendors of prewritten circulation control programs and turnkey systems will develop such conversion programs for a negotiated price. Rather than loading borrower records from external sources, some public libraries reregister all of their borrowers at the time an automated circulation system is installed, thereby purging their files of obsolete records.

System Capabilities

Although their computer hardware is often the focal point of library attention, circulation control systems derive their performance characteristics and capabilities from the application programs which accomplish specified circulation-related tasks. While the specific manner in which their capabilities are implemented will necessarily vary, all prewritten circulation control software packages and turnkey systems provide programs that support three broad types of operations: charging and discharging, online file inquiries, and offline report production.

With the earliest circulation control programs and turnkey systems, libraries were forced to accept predetermined loan periods, borrower categories, and other operating parameters. Newer products, however, provide flexible support for a broad range of circulation requirements encountered in libraries of all types and sizes. Unlike earlier systems, which contained rigidly coded procedures to control charging, discharging, and related activities, all newer products are highly parameterized—that is, they allow the library to specify the conditions under which items will be circulated, file inquiries made, and reports produced. Rather than being written into programs, particular operating parameters are selected by libraries from a range of possibilities. The resulting flexibility broadens the range of applications that a given system can address and is particularly important in installations where a single prewritten software package or turnkey system will be shared by multiple libraries with different circulation policies.

With some prewritten circulation programs and turnkey systems, operating parameters are established by vendor representatives during a preinstallation "profiling" session. Alternatively, the system may include a programmable module that allows libraries to define or change their own operating parameters. In most cases, individual libraries can specify loan periods, restrictions applicable to specific types of borrowers, overdue policies, and fines procedures. In multibranch or consortium installations, these parameters need not be uniform. As an example, each library can define the number of days that items will be loaned to, and renewed for, particular types of borrowers. It can differentiate fine rates by borrower type, specify fines immunity for particular groups of borrowers, grant a specified number of grace days before fines are incurred, and specify the number of overdue notices that different classes of borrowers will receive. Libraries can also impose limits on the amount of fines that given types of borrowers can incur before circulation privileges are revoked. If desired, borrower privileges can be limited to specific branches or libraries within a system.

Different loan and renewal periods can likewise be specified for various types of library materials. Some systems permit renewal periods that differ from the original loan period. Addressing a commonly encountered academic library requirement, most prewritten circulation software packages and turnkey systems can charge out items until the end of a semester or another fixed date. If desired, this option can be limited to specific types of borrowers—faculty members and graduate students, for example—or to particular types of library materials. Fine rates can also vary by borrower or item type. To ensure that holidays are not used in fines computation and that due dates do not fall on holidays, most prewritten circulation software packages and turnkey systems allow the library to specify dates on which it will be closed. Addressing the common practice among special libraries of maintaining selected items in the work areas where they are most frequently utilized, some systems can accommodate permanent loans to desk or laboratory locations rather than to individuals. For chargeback purposes, such systems may also link the use of specific items to individual departments or cost centers within a corporation or government agency.

As discussed earlier in this chapter, all prewritten software packages and turnkey systems execute circulation transactions in real time—that is, all item and borrower records are immediately updated as materials are charged out or checked in. If circulation control is implemented as one application module in a multifunctional integrated system, it is usually accorded the highest priority for execution, so that charging and discharging will be performed before catalog searches or other operations. Charging procedures are typically straightforward. After entering a command to put the circulation control system in the charge-out mode, an operator scans the barcode or OCR labels on the borrower's identification card and on individual items. In most cases, the borrower's identification number is scanned once, regardless of the number of items being checked out. Where barcode or OCR labels are absent or damaged, item and borrower identifiers can be key-entered. Such key entry may also be used for telephone renewals.

As item and borrower identifiers are entered, most circulation control programs automatically check for exceptional conditions that will temporarily or permanently block a charge-out transaction. Such exceptional conditions include borrowers with overdue items or outstanding fines, borrowers who have exceeded the library's predefined charge-out limit, borrowers who are using an identification card reported lost or stolen, and items that are being held for another library user, are already checked out to another borrower, or are not part of the library's circulation collection. Some prewritten software packages and turnkey systems automatically block circulation transactions where a borrower's circulation privileges will expire before an item's due date. Most systems distinguish between "soft" blocks, which can be overridden by a circulation clerk or other authorized person, and "hard" blocks, which require the correction of exceptional conditions before the circulation transaction can be completed.

With most prewritten circulation control software packages and turn-key systems, check-in is a repeating transaction that is initiated by a command followed by the scanning of item identifiers. The check-in command, which may be activated by a labeled function key on a circulation terminal, is usually entered once for multiple items. During the check-in procedure, most systems will detect such exceptional conditions as items that are on hold for other borrowers, items that were never properly charged out, and items returned to the wrong location. To reflect the in-house use of library materials in statistical reports, some systems permit the discharging of items removed from shelves but never checked out. As a useful capability for libraries where long reshelving delays are common, at least one turnkey circulation system will check items in to a book cart or other temporary location so they can be located while awaiting shelving.

When overdue items are checked in, most systems will calculate fines for immediate collection. If overdue items are dropped in book bins, or the borrower is otherwise unavailable or unable to pay the fine, it is typically added to his or her record. With most systems, a library can specify the amount of fines that borrowers can incur before circulation privileges are revoked. A few systems support amnesty days, when all fines for overdue items are forgiven.

To facilitate the completion of specific transactions, all prewritten circulation control programs and turnkey systems support the online retrieval and display of bibliographic and item records by barcode numbers, call numbers, special search codes based on a specified group of characters derived from author and title fields, or other unique identifiers. Where circulation control is implemented as an integrated system component, bibliographic records are usually retrievable by author, title, and subject headings. As discussed in the next chapter, integrated systems may also offer flexible keyword searching capabilities. Once desired bibliographic records are identified, their associated item records can also be displayed.

With most circulation control programs and turnkey systems, borrower records can be accessed by a library card number, a social security number, or a full or partial name. While the content of displayed records will vary from system to system, it often combines borrower data with information derived from the bibliographic and copy records with which borrower records are linked during the charge-out activity. As an example, some prewritten circulation control programs and turnkey systems respond to borrower file queries with a basic display that includes the borrower's name, address, telephone number, home library (in a multilibrary installation), the date borrowing privileges were granted, and the date of last circulation activity. After examining this information, an operator can request a more detailed, second-level display that includes the specific items the borrower has charged out, any items the borrower has requested, an indication of overdue items or other delinquency status, and a comments field.

The effective management of holds, recalls, and reserves is one of the features that most clearly distinguishes real time circulation control systems from the batch-oriented implementations described in chapter 3. As used in this context, a hold causes an item in circulation to be trapped on its return and held for a specified borrower. It is a passive request. The borrower waits for the desired item to be returned, although he or she must usually specify a cancellation date after which the item will no longer be required. A recall, in contrast, is an active request that changes the due date for a circulating item in order to obtain its immediate return. Reserves are items that are subject to special circulating conditions.

Most prewritten circulation control software packages and turnkey systems support the placement of holds at the bibliographic level—that is, on all copies of a specified title—or on a specific copy only. Bibliographic-level requests will trap the first available copy of a specified title involved in any circulation transaction. In multisite installations, copy-level requests are usually made by borrowers who do not want to travel to another library or branch location to obtain an item. Recalls are usually placed at the copy level and backed up with holds at the title level. Where multiple requests are received for a given item, most systems maintain a hold queue. In most cases, the requesting date determines a borrower's position in the queue, although circulation personnel may be able to prioritize requests.

To preserve response time for online operations, most prewritten software packages and turnkey systems print circulation reports and notices at night or during other off-peak hours. Some systems provide a selection of preconfigured operational and statistical reports suitable for a wide range of library requirements. Others support a general-purpose report-writing program that the library can utilize to generate the reports it requires. A few systems combine preconfigured and custom-generated reports.

Regardless of their production methodology, useful examples of operational reports include borrower rosters with identification numbers, addresses, phone numbers, and similar data; lists of borrower records added or changed since a specified date; lists of borrowers with excessive overdue items, fines, or other delinquencies; lists of borrowers with outstanding bills; lists of borrowers with more than a specified number of items in circulation; lists of items being held for specified borrowers; lists of items on hold in call number or title sequence; lists of exceptional items on hold, including lost, missing, or long overdue items; lists of items with hold queues longer than a specified number of names; lists of requesters, with phone numbers, for items on hold; lists of fine receipts by workstation location; and lists of overdue items for shelf searching prior to the printing and mailing of borrower notices. A special group of operational reports supports inventory control activities. Examples include lists of lost or missing items arranged by call number, material type, or other parameters; lists of items withdrawn from the library's collection since a specified date; lists of delinquent items claimed to be returned; and lists of unsatisfied holds since a specified date.

Statistical reports provide information that is useful for knowledgeable collection development as well as for the management of the circulation activity itself. Perhaps the most important example provides circulation totals by specified call number groups. It may be produced monthly, quarterly, or at other specified time intervals. For comparison purposes, such reports often provide statistics for the same period during the preceding year. Other useful statistical reports summarize circulation activity by borrower category or the type of library material; present total charge-out, check-in, and holds activity for specified time periods; and indicate workstation activity by day, week, month, or other time periods.

All circulation control software packages and turnkey systems can generate recall notices, overdue notices, fine notices, and similar borrower notices, as well as bills for lost items. They are usually printed on letter-size paper with the borrower's address formatted for compatibility with window-size envelopes, although some systems can also print notices on postcards. Notices may be sorted by zip code prior to printing.

Designed specifically for academic and school libraries, reserve room capabilities maintain circulation records linked to courses and instructors. Reserve room materials are subject to special, usually short, loan periods. Circulation periods for reserve materials are customarily measured in hours or even minutes, although most systems will permit overnight circulation if the allowable charge-out period extends beyond the library's closing time. Most systems will print lists of items on reserve for particular courses. Some systems can also print lists of charge-out activity arranged by course number and item.

SUMMARY

Library interest in automated circulation control is in large part based on a long-standing awareness of the problems inherent in manual circulation systems. These problems include labor-intensive and time-consuming recordkeeping requirements, inaccuracy, high personnel turnover, an inability to generate statistics about circulation activity, and the lack of an interface between circulation files and other library files which contain much the same bibliographic data. Alternatives to manual circulation control are not limited to computer-based systems but include photocharging systems and the substitution of duplication for circulation. Neither of these alternatives, however, addresses the broad spectrum of circulation control requirements. Their use is consequently restricted to certain types of library applications.

Perhaps more than any library application, the historical development of automated circulation control has reflected changes in the state of the art in computer technology. Systems implemented between the early 1960s and the early 1970s used batch processing techniques. Such systems were limited by the inaccuracy inherent in all batch processing systems, as well as by an inability to conveniently block circulation by delinquent borrowers or to identify items to be held for specific patrons. During the mid-1970s, those limitations were successfully addressed by custom-developed real time circulation control systems developed by larger libraries and library systems.

Most libraries, however, lack access to the computing resources required to implement a real time circulation control system on a custom-developed basis. The requirements of such libraries can usually be satisfactorily addressed by prewritten circulation control software and turnkey circulation control systems. Prewritten circulation control software consists of one or more application programs intended for execution on computer equipment operated by or for a given library. Turnkey systems provide an integrated configuration of preselected hardware and prewritten software. Compared to customized system development, prewritten circulation software and turnkey systems offer the significant advantages of rapid implementation, simplified procurement, and elimination of requirements for in-house software expertise.

All prewritten circulation control programs and turnkey systems are designed for real time operation with online input and output devices. To simplify the entry of information pertaining to circulation transactions, most systems employ barcode recognition, although optical character recognition has also been utilized. Both methodologies feature special labels affixed to circulating items and borrower identification cards. The labels are read by handheld wands or laser scanners. The typical system also includes printers for the production of patron notices and reports. Circulation data are maintained on fixed magnetic disk drives for convenient online availability, with backup copies on other media.

Whether custom-developed or implemented as preconfigured products, all computerized circulation control systems must maintain files of machine-readable information about circulating materials and their borrowers. Such files are usually established in advance of system operation, although some installations utilize "conversion on the fly" to create machine-readable records as items are charged out. Most vendors support interfaces to one or more bibliographic utilities, CD-ROM products, or other cataloging systems or services as a means of reducing the keystroking required for data entry. Machine-readable borrower records can sometimes be obtained from registrars' offices, personnel offices, or other sources.

All prewritten circulation software packages and turnkey systems support the charging and discharging of library materials, online file inquiries about the status of circulating items and borrowers, and offline report production. In most cases, circulation control programs are parameterized to allow the library to specify the conditions under which items will be circulated, file inquiries made, and reports produced. In multilibrary installations, such flexibility preserves local autonomy without disrupting system operation.

ADDITIONAL READING

AAGAARD, J. "An Interactive Computer-based Circulation System: Design and Development." *Journal of Library Automation* 5 (1): 3–11 (1972).

AAGAARD, J., and FURLONG, E. "Automating Reserve Activities at Northwestern University." *College and Research Libraries News* 51 (2): 98–101 (1990).

ALABI, G. "A Cost Comparison of Manual and Automated Circulation Systems in University Libraries: The Case of Ibadan University Library." *Information Processing and Management* 21 (6): 525–33 (1985).

ARMSTRONG, P. "Automated Circulation for the Small Public Library." *Canadian Library Journal* 41 (6): 334–37 (1984).

BERTLAND, L. "Circulation Analysis as a Tool for Collection Development." *School Library Media Quarterly* 19 (2): 90–97 (1991).

BLOOMBERG, M. *Introduction to Public Services for Library Technicians.* Littleton, Colo.: Libraries Unlimited, 1985.

BLUH, P. "Barcoding a Library Collection." *Law Library Journal* 82 (4): 727–36 (1990).

BOYKIN, J. "Library Automation, 1970–1990: From the Few to the Many." *Library Administration and Management* 5 (1): 10–15 (1991).

BRITTEN, W., and WEBSTER, J. "Comparing Characteristics of Highly Circulated Titles for Demand-driven Collection Development." *College and Research Libraries* 53 (3): 239–48 (1992).

BUCK, D. "Bringing up an Automated Circulation System: Staffing Needs." *Wilson Library Bulletin* 60 (7): 28–31 (1986).

DEKLERK, A. "Barcoding a Collection: Why, When, and How." *Library Resources and Technical Services* 25 (1): 111–24 (1981).

FAYEN, E. "Automated Circulation Systems for Large Libraries." *Library Technology Reports* 22 (4): 385–469 (1986).

FRANCIS, S. "Management Problems Arising from the Introduction of Automation." *Electronic Library* 2 (1): 25–29 (1984).

GATTEN, J. "Bar Coding Projects: Preparation and Execution." *Library Hi Tech* 8 (1): 21–27 (1990).

GAUDET, J. "Automating the Circulation Services of a Small Library." *Library Resources and Technical Services* 31 (3): 249–55 (1987).

GUPTA, K. "Computer Library Services: Automated Circulation Control in the USA." *International Forum on Information and Documentation* 14 (4): 24–30 (1989).

HEISE, G. "Barriers to Cooperative Computerized Circulation Systems in Public Libraries." *Resource Sharing and Information Networks* 3 (1): 83–99 (1985).

ISKANDERANI, A., and ANWAR, M. "Automated Bilingual Circulation System Using PC Local Area Networks." *Information Services and Use* 12 (2): 141–56 (1992).

KELLY, G. "Printing Barcode Labels with a Laser Printer." *Computers in Libraries* 11 (4): 43–46 (1991).

KOEN, C. "Another Use for the Library Computer: The Study of Circulation Statistics." *South African Journal of Library and Information Science* 56 (2): 131–37 (1988).

KOHL, D. *Circulation, Interlibrary Loan, Patron Use, and Maintenance: A Handbook for Library Management.* Santa Barbara, Calif.: ABC-Clio, 1986.

LEE, D., et al. "Using an On-line Comprehensive Library Management System in Collection Development." *Collection Management* 14 (3): 61–73 (1991).

LEE, H. "Trends in Automation in American Libraries: Ohio University's Experiences." *Journal of Educational Media and Library Sciences* 27 (1): 1–23 (1989).

LOGAN, S. "The Ohio State University's Library Control System: From Circulation to Subject Access and Authority Control." *Library Trends* 35 (4): 539–54 (1987).

LOGSDON, L. "Bookmobile Online Circulation via Cellular Telephone." *Computers in Libraries* 10 (4): 17–18 (1990).

MACKEY, K. "Automating Overdues in a Non-automated Library: The Hypercard Solution." *College and Research Libraries News* 50 (1): 23–27 (1989).

MATTHEWS, J. *Choosing an Automated Library System: A Planning Guide.* Chicago: American Library Association, 1980.

———. "Microcomputer Circulation Control Systems: An Assessment." *Library Technology Reports* 22 (1): 9–152 (1986).

MATTHEWS, J., and HEGARTY, K., eds. *Automated Circulation: An Examination of Choices.* Chicago: American Library Association, 1984.

MATTHEWS, J., et al. "Microcomputer-based Library Systems: An Assessment." *Library Technology Reports* 26 (2–3): 131–444 (1990).

MILLER, G., and COLERIDGE, F. "Conceptual Model for Circulation Control Systems." *Journal of the American Society for Information Science* 28 (2): 196–205 (1977).

MOSLEY, I. "Cost Effectiveness Analysis of the Automation of a Circulation System." *Journal of Library Automation* 10 (3): 240–54 (1977).

RICHARDSON, I. "Circulation System Development at Lancaster University Library: Experiments with Downsizing and Fault Tolerance." *Vine* (85): 8–10 (1991).

SCHLUMPF, P. "A Matrix Model of Circulation Control." *Information Processing and Management* 27 (5): 551–58 (1991).

SKAPURA, R. "Automating the Small Library." *Technical Services Quarterly* 7 (3): 45–56 (1990).

SMITH, T., and VITUCCI, V. "The Circulation Control Facility at the Library of Congress." *Information Technology and Libraries* 8 (1): 75–79 (1989).

SPALDING, H., et al. "Behind Bars in the Library: Northwestern University's Bar Code Project." *Information Technology and Libraries* 6 (3): 185–89 (1987).

STEEN, D. "Computerizing Circulation Systems." *Ontario Library Review* 65 (1): 4–27 (1981).

STEPHENS, I. "Getting More out of Call Numbers: Displaying Holdings, Locations, and Circulation Status." *Cataloging and Classification Quarterly* 13 (3): 97–102 (1991).

THOMPSON, V. "Training for Automated Circulation Systems: The New Zealand Experience." *Library Management* 13 (2): 4–44 (1991).

THORSEN, A. "The Economics of Automated Circulation." In *Proceedings of the 1976 Clinic on Library Applications of Data Processing: The Economics of Library Automation.* Urbana: University of Illinois Graduate School of Library Science, 1977.

Automated Cataloging

$\mathbf{A}$s with circulation control, librarians have long been interested in automated alternatives to manual cataloging systems. Automated cataloging experiments involving such precomputer equipment as card sorters and paper-tape typewriters date from the 1940s. Computers were first applied to the production of catalog cards and book catalogs in the early 1960s. In 1963, for example, the Yale University Medical Library began using computers to print catalog card sets from bibliographic data recorded on punched cards. In the same year, the University of Toronto began a project involving the computerized production of book catalogs for five new universities in Ontario. Through the late 1960s, a number of similar computer applications were reported by academic, public, school, and special libraries. Computer-based systems for the printing of catalog cards were developed by libraries in such diverse organizations as the U.S. Navy Bureau of Ships, the Philip Morris Company, Indiana University, the Albuquerque Public Schools, and the Nassau County (New York) Public Library System. Similarly, computers were used—often with considerable difficulty—to produce book-form catalogs at Florida Atlantic University, Washington University School of Medicine, Stanford University, the Widener Library of Harvard College (the famous Widener shelflists project), Boeing Aircraft, and Baltimore County Public Library.

As is the case with automated circulation control, the operational characteristics and limitations of these early cataloging systems reflected the prevailing state of the art in computer technology. Batch processing was used exclusively, with bibliographic data being input via punched cards and stored on magnetic tape. But unlike circulation control—which is characterized by relatively straightforward, easily understood work steps that are analogous in many respects to those found in business transaction processing—the automation of cataloging is a complex undertaking involving potentially large files composed of bibliographic records with complicated structures. Data conversion, storage, and printing requirements are likewise complicated. While the requirements of library circulation control systems can often be analyzed by persons with a general business background, the effective analysis and design of cataloging systems require extensive familiarity with bibliographic activities and, in some cases, professional library training.

To some extent, the difficulties of developing and implementing automated cataloging systems are increased by the multifaceted nature of the cataloging activity itself. Cataloging systems, whether manual or automated, encompass two interrelated activities: descriptive cataloging and the production of library catalogs. This chapter reviews the problems associated with conventional manual approaches to both activities and examines various automated alternatives.

COMPUTERS AND DESCRIPTIVE CATALOGING

The purpose of descriptive cataloging is to produce informative bibliographic and physical descriptions of library materials in sufficient detail to permit the conclusive identification of a given item and to differentiate it from other, possibly similar items. In most academic and larger public libraries, where the library catalog is considered a bibliographic tool as well as a finding list, descriptive cataloging is performed according to the detailed set of instructions embodied in the Anglo-American Cataloging Rules, the second edition of which is the latest in a 125-year series of efforts to standardize cataloging practices in American libraries. Smaller public libraries, school libraries, and many corporate libraries may follow locally developed cataloging practices that are presumably better suited to their collections and clienteles.

Regardless of their source, rules for descriptive cataloging specify the choice and form of the names or other terms under which a given item will be entered in a library catalog or other bibliographic product, the words or phrases to be used in describing an item, and the order in which the descriptive elements are to be recorded. In most libraries, the description of an item also includes subject headings and a classification number. The end product of descriptive cataloging is a series of entries for inclusion in a library's catalog, which may be in a card, book, or online format.

Apart from any particular physical representation of catalogs, librarians have long recognized the problems associated with manual approaches to descriptive cataloging. As an intellectual activity requiring considerable decision making, descriptive cataloging is time-consuming. Many libraries consequently experience cataloging backlogs which impede the flow of materials into circulating and reference collections, thereby preventing library catalogs from representing those collections fully and accurately. In some research libraries, for example, materials of presumably limited interest may be placed in offsite storage facilities with only an abbreviated catalog record being created. In most libraries, conventional descriptive cataloging is not even considered for individual titles in large microform sets, even though such titles often significantly augment a library's resources in particular subject areas, and the failure to catalog them may impair their usefulness. Analytic cataloging, involving the making of additional catalog entries for individual contributions within edited works or the individual chapters of monographs, is rarely done. As a labor-intensive activity requiring special training and sometimes considerable experience, descriptive cataloging can prove expensive, so much so that the cost of cataloging a given item may approach or even exceed the value of the item itself. Consequently, many libraries do not catalog paperbound books, low-cost government publications, or other relatively inexpensive items. Similarly, the cost of cataloging can make a library reluctant to accept gifts and bequests.

In an attempt to simplify decision making, save time, and reduce the costs associated with descriptive cataloging, libraries have historically relied on a practice called "cataloging with copy," in which published library catalogs and bibliographies are searched for descriptive cataloging information prepared by other libraries. The various published catalogs of the Library of Congress, especially the *National Union Catalog,* are among the most widely consulted sources of such cataloging copy. The purchase of printed cards from the Library of Congress, book jobbers, or other sources is a variant form of cataloging with copy. While cataloging with copy is generally faster and less costly than original cataloging, the time-consuming and labor-intensive work steps characteristic of manual cataloging systems are not entirely eliminated. Many libraries, for example, modify cataloging copy to conform to local practices regarding the choice and form of main and added entries. Unless printed cards are ordered, the library must type or otherwise prepare entries for inclusion in the catalog. Even when printed cards are used, some combination of typing and copying is usually required to prepare complete card sets.

The MARC Program

In the early 1960s, librarians became increasingly aware that descriptive cataloging might be simplified if cataloging copy could be obtained in machine-readable, computer-processable form. The Library of Congress, as the nation's primary source of cataloging copy, commissioned several studies of the potential and problems inherent in the development of such an alternative bibliographic product. Those studies, which indicated the feasibility and potential advantages of recording LC cataloging data in machine-readable form, were discussed at a series of conferences in 1965 and 1966. The outcome of those conferences was the MARC (Machine Readable Cataloging) Pilot Project.

Funded by the Council on Library Resources, the MARC Pilot Project established a format, now known as the MARC I format, for recording bibliographic data in machine-readable form. From November 1966 through June 1968, it distributed some 50,000 machine-readable cataloging records in that format to 16 participating libraries. The records, which were distributed weekly on magnetic tapes that came to be known as MARC tapes, contained descriptive cataloging data which also appeared in human-readable form in LC printed catalogs and cards. Participating libraries used MARC tapes, together with their institutional computers and locally developed software, to produce catalog cards, book catalogs, and specialized bibliographic listings.

While the MARC Pilot Project allowed participating libraries to experiment with the manipulation of machine-readable cataloging records, the MARC I format required revision before the Library of Congress and other libraries could develop extensive programs based on the interchange of bibliographic data in machine-readable form. Those revisions are embodied in the MARC II communications format. Introduced in 1967, the MARC II format is designed to facilitate the exchange of bibliographic data about all types of materials by a wide range of libraries using varied computer equipment and software. The MARC II format—now simply termed the USMARC or LC MARC format—is described in detail in various publications of the Library of Congress and will be summarized here only briefly.

The MARC II format specifies a basic structure for machine-readable bibliographic records that consists of three components:

1. A leader, composed of fixed-length fields, provides information about the length, type, and bibliographic level of the ensuing record. Record types are designated by codes that identify the record as a printed book, manuscript, microform, map, music, or other entity. Codes for bibliographic level indicate whether the work is a self-contained monograph, part of a series, a serial publication, an analytic component within a larger bibliographic work, or a collection of manuscripts, pamphlets, or other items cataloged as a single unit.
2. A record directory indicates the locations of specific variable fields within each record. It is analogous to the table of contents of a book. Each record directory entry consists of a content designator, or tag, which identifies the variable field within the record; an indication of the length of the variable field; and the position of the first character within the record. The record directory facilitates the retrieval of selected fields from within a MARC record.
3. The variable fields within each MARC record contain bibliographic data accompanied by numeric labels called "tags," which reflect the content of the fields and any subfields into which they may have been divided.

Logically related groups of MARC tags are assigned to specific types of bibliographic data. The "100" tag, for example, denotes a personal name as main entry; the "110" tag is used for a corporate name as main entry, while the "111" tag denotes a conference or meeting name as main entry. Similarly, the "400" tag denotes a series statement that consists of a personal name; the "410" tag is used for a series statement that consists of a corporate name; while the "411" tag identifies a series statement that consists of a conference or meeting name. The "600" tag identifies a personal name as a subject added entry; the "610" tag denotes a corporate name as a subject added entry; while the "611" tag is used for a conference or meeting name as a subject added entry. The "650" tag identifies one of the most common data elements, a topical heading as a subject added entry, while the "651" tag is used for a geographic name as a subject added entry. Subfields associated with specific tags are identified by letter designations. For the "245" tag, for example, subfield code "a" identifies a short title or title proper, while subfield code "b" identifies the remainder of the title.

The MARC II record structure has been adopted by the American National Standards Institute (ANSI) and the International Standardization Organization (ISO). These organizations have not, however, standardized the content designators and subfield codes that identify the elements within records or rules for the creation of the data content of the records themselves. Bibliographic record formats developed by other organizations have widely adopted the MARC II record structure, although they may differ in the content of their variable fields and in the specific tags used as content designators. This is the case, for example, with the MARC records created by such organizations as the Institute of Electrical Engineers, the European Association of Scientific Information Dissemination Centers (EUSIDIC), and the Educational Resources Information Clearinghouses (ERIC).

Considerable variation in content designators is also characteristic of MARC formats developed by national libraries in Canada, Great Britain, France, Germany, Italy, Australia, Denmark, Sweden, Norway, Japan, and the Latin American countries. The Canadian MARC (CANMARC) format, for example, uses more content designators than are permitted by the Library of Congress, and the UK MARC and French INTERMARC formats permit a wider range of content designators than the Canadian format does. To facilitate the international exchange of bibliographic data in machine-readable form, the International Federation of Library Associations (IFLA) has endorsed a UNIMARC format that standardizes content designators at a level of specificity lower than that being used by various national systems, thereby allowing libraries and other organizations to translate UNIMARC records into their own national MARC formats.

In the United States, the Library of Congress has developed MARC formats for various types of library materials, including books, serials, maps, visual materials, archives and manuscripts, musical scores, and computer files. USMARC formats have also been developed for authorities —that is, names, subjects, and uniform title headings—and for holdings information. The MARC Distribution Services unit of the Library of Congress commenced operation on a subscription basis in 1969, with magnetic tapes containing MARC records being distributed weekly. The scope of the MARC program, which was initially limited to English-language monographs, has gradually broadened to include all monographs written in languages using roman scripts, and nonmonographic materials regardless of language. Cataloging-in-publication (CIP) data was added to the MARC program in 1971.

The LC MARC data base, the name given to the accumulation of machine-readable cataloging records produced and distributed by the Library of Congress, is usually subdivided by the types of materials being cataloged. At the time of this writing, the MARC Distribution Services unit offered MARC records in the following categories:

1. As noted above, the English-language books segment of the LC MARC data base dates from the inception of the MARC program. Cataloging records for books written in French, German, Spanish, Portuguese, Italian, Dutch, and other languages employing roman alphabets were added in stages between 1973 and 1977. Romanized records for books written in Cyrillic, Greek, Arabic, Hebrew, Yiddish, Persian, Chinese, Japanese, Korean, and Southeast Asian languages were added between 1979 and 1985. At the time of this writing, the Books All segment of the LC MARC data base contained approximately four million bibliographic records for monographs cataloged by the Library of Congress, including cataloging-in-publication (CIP) data and minimal-level cataloging (MLC) records. It also contained records contributed by participants in the National Coordinated Cataloging Program (NCCP), which authorizes selected research libraries to create national-level bibliographic records for inclusion in the LC MARC data base. Each year, approximately 550,000 new records are added to the Books All segment of the LC MARC data base. The Library of Congress also offers a Books English subset of the LC MARC data base. As its name suggests, it contains cataloging records for English-language monographs published in the United States and elsewhere. At the time of this writing, the Books English subset contained approximately 2.25 million bibliographic records and was growing at a rate of 225,000 records per year.

2. As an alternative to the widely criticized practice of romanization, the LC MARC data base also includes vernacular cataloging records for books published in certain languages. The Books All segment of the LC MARC data base contains romanized records for Chinese, Japanese, and Korean (CJK) monographs cataloged between 1983 and 1985. CJK cataloging records issued by the Library of Congress since that time are distributed separately, in both vernacular and romanized form, as the Books CJK segment of the LC MARC data base. At the time of this writing, it contained approximately 220,000 cataloging records and was growing by about 30,000 records per year. The Books Hebrew segment of the LC MARC data base contains vernacular and romanized records for Hebrew and Yiddish monographs cataloged by the Library of Congress since 1989. At the time of this writing, it contained approximately 12,000 records. About 3,000 records are added annually. Romanized Hebrew and Yiddish cataloging records for the period 1983 through 1988 are included in the Books All segment. A Books Arabic segment of the LC MARC data base, which will include vernacular cataloging records in Arabic and related languages, has been announced for future availability. Romanized Arabic cataloging records have been included in the Books All segment since 1983.

3. Cataloging records for serial publications in languages that utilize roman alphabets, as well as romanized versions of serial publications in other languages, were added to the LC MARC data base in 1973. Cataloging records for newspapers were added to the data base in 1975. The Library of Congress also distributes cataloging records authenticated by

the Cooperative Online Serials (CONSER) program, which is discussed in chapter 8. At the time of this writing, the Serials segment of the LC MARC data base contained approximately 900,000 bibliographic records. It is growing at an approximate rate of 175,000 records per year. The Library of Congress has announced a Serials CJK segment for future availability. It will include vernacular and romanized data for Chinese, Japanese, and Korean serials records.

4. LC MARC cataloging records for cartographic materials—including single- and multisheet maps, map sets, and serially issued maps—date from 1973. Materials in nonroman languages are romanized for cataloging purposes. At the time of this writing, the Maps segment of the LC MARC data base contained approximately 155,000 bibliographic records. Approximately 15,000 records are added annually.

5. The Library of Congress has distributed cataloging records for music—including printed and manuscript musical scores, as well as musical and nonmusical sound recordings—since 1984. Materials in nonroman languages are cataloged in romanized form. At the time of this writing, the Music segment of the LC MARC data base contained approximately 100,000 bibliographic records. It is growing at an approximate rate of 20,000 records per year.

6. The Visual Materials segment of the LC MARC data base includes cataloging records for films, film strips, video recordings, transparencies, media kits, and other graphic materials cataloged by the Library of Congress or cooperatively cataloged with other agencies. The oldest records date from 1972. Materials in nonroman languages are cataloged in romanized form. Since 1992, current cataloging has been limited to motion picture/video recordings and to pictorial materials retained for LC collections. At the time of this writing, the Visual Materials segment of the LC MARC data base contained approximately 110,000 bibliographic records. Approximately 4,000 records are added to the data base annually.

7. The Computer Files segment of the LC MARC data base contains cataloging records for machine-readable data files and computer software. At the time of this writing, it contained approximately 1,000 bibliographic records. About 300 records are added annually.

LC cataloging records for monographs are distributed weekly. Cataloging records for serials, maps, music, visual materials, and CJK books are distributed every four weeks. Cataloging records for computer files and Hebrew books are distributed quarterly.

The MARC Distribution Services unit also distributes cataloging records produced by organizations other than the Library of Congress. The GPO Cataloging file, for example, contains bibliographic records produced by the U.S. Government Printing Office and published in the *Monthly Catalog of United States Government Publications*. Covering monographs, serials, maps, and visual materials, GPO cataloging records have been distributed on LC MARC tapes with monthly updates since 1976. At the time of this writing, the GPO Cataloging file contained approximately 420,000 bibliographic records. Approximately 35,000 records are added each year.

The MARC Distribution Services unit also offers cataloging records produced by several other national libraries. The Books Canada file, for example, contains cataloging records produced by the National Library of Canada for monographs pertaining to Canada or bearing Canadian imprints. The records, which date from 1975, are received by the Library of Congress in the CANMARC format and are converted to the USMARC format prior to distribution. The British National Bibliography (BNB) file contains cataloging records produced by the British Library for books and first issues of serials published in the United Kingdom. The records are chiefly for English-language imprints. The British Library's cataloging-in-publication records are also included. The BNB file is produced in the UK MARC format. It is converted to the USMARC format by the Library of Congress prior to distribution. The Australia/New Zealand file contains cataloging records produced by the national libraries of those countries. At the time of this writing, the Library of Congress had announced future plans to distribute cataloging records produced by the Bibliotheque Nationale, Deutsche Bibliothek, and the National Diet Library of Japan.

Like most machine-readable bibliographic data bases, MARC tapes are prospective in that they emphasize items cataloged since the inception of the MARC program. Several projects have, however, extended the scope of MARC data retrospectively. The RECON Pilot Project, funded by the Council on Library Resources in 1969, provided an initial exploration of the feasibility of retrospective conversion. While the project converted some 58,000 titles identified by a study of the most frequently ordered printed catalog cards, its most important technical achievement was the refinement of automatic format recognition (AFR) techniques for the simplified creation of MARC records. When conventional conversion techniques are used, content designators are manually assigned to each variable field by catalogers or technical assistants before input. With automatic format recognition, however, computer programs are used to recognize the variable fields in a given MARC record and assign appropriate content designators to them. While the potential for error still necessitates proofreading by human editors, some keystroking is saved through the elimination of content designators from the input data. The International Standard Bibliographic Description (ISBD), which uses specified combinations of punctuation symbols to separate the various elements in a catalog record, was developed in part to facilitate the use of automatic format recognition techniques, especially where foreign language records are involved.

To avoid possible confusion, it is important to distinguish automatic format recognition from optical character recognition (OCR). As discussed earlier, OCR is a method of converting human-readable information to the machine-readable form required for computer processing. Automatic-format recognition is a computer processing technique that requires the prior conversion of data to machine-readable form. Such conversion may be accomplished by means of OCR, but for reasons discussed in chapter 1, keystroking methodologies are more often used. Ideally, retrospective conversion of cataloging records to the MARC format might be accomplished by using an OCR reader to input data from existing catalog cards to an automatic format recognition. Such capabilities are not, however, within the current state of the art in data entry technology.

Following the RECON Pilot Project, which ended in 1971, a number of libraries participated in a conference to explore the interchange of machine-readable bibliographic data at which the possibility of sharing locally converted MARC records was discussed. The Cooperative MARC (COMARC) project was the outcome of that discussion. Funded by the Council on Library Resources in 1974, it represented a further attempt to extend the MARC data base retrospectively. As participating libraries converted cataloging records from the *National Union Catalog,* LC printed cards, or other LC cataloging copy to machine-readable form, they transmitted them in the MARC II format to the Library of Congress, where they were reprocessed as required and made available through the MARC Distribution Service, just as non-LC cataloging appears in the *National Union Catalog.* COMARC project participants included the Washington State Library, the University of Chicago, Northwestern University, Cornell University, Yale University, the University of Illinois, the University of Tennessee, the University of Wisconsin, the Boston Theological Institute, and the 3M Company. The project ended in 1978.

While the RECON and COMARC projects resulted in the addition of some older cataloging records to the MARC data base, the most ambitious MARC retrospective conversion project was undertaken by a private firm, the Carrollton Press, which was subsequently acquired by Utlas International. Begun in 1980, the REMARC (Retrospective MARC) project includes over five million records cataloged by the Library of Congress from 1897 through the inception of the MARC program. (English-language works are included through 1968; works in other languages are included up to the time they entered the MARC program.) All REMARC records observe the MARC II format, with nonroman languages being transliterated.

MARC-derivative Products

At the inception of the MARC program it was felt that, in the manner of the *National Union Catalog* and LC printed cards, libraries would acquire MARC tapes for use in locally developed cataloging systems implemented on their own computing equipment. It was further assumed that libraries would develop, purchase, or otherwise obtain their own programs to print catalog cards or book catalogs, perform bibliographic searching, or accomplish other tasks. The Library of Congress itself has offered no software for the processing of MARC data beyond the few programs distributed to participants in the original MARC Pilot Project. As a result, the earliest applications of MARC tapes were primarily developed by a relatively small number of large research libraries and public library systems with access to the computer hardware, programming resources, and funds required for systems analysis and software development.

From 1969 through the mid-1970s, data bases composed of MARC tapes, supplemented by the local input of additional catalog records, were used to print catalog cards, book catalogs, and other bibliographic products at such institutions as the New York Public Library, Stanford University, Rice University, the University of California, the California State Library, the Orange County Public Library, the Hennepin County Public Library, Trinity University in San Antonio, and the University of Guelph in Ontario. The Library of Congress itself makes extensive use of MARC data for various purposes, including the production of book catalogs and catalog cards. As an alternative to acquiring and processing MARC tapes, however, libraries of all types and sizes obtain access to MARC data through products and services developed by publishers, computer system developers, timesharing services, and other intermediaries. Among the earliest examples of such MARC-derivative products were computer-output microfilm (COM) publications designed to provide libraries with timely and varied access to Library of Congress cataloging data in support of bibliographic verification, cataloging with copy, and related activities.

Librarians have long complained that the distribution delays and limited number of access points associated with the publication and distribution of the *National Union Catalog* and other LC printed catalogs seriously impair their utility. Conventionally printed issues of the NUC typically arrived in libraries several weeks after their cover date. Because the catalog records they contain are only accessible by main entry, considerable familiarity with LC cataloging practices is required to use them effectively. Addressing these problems, the Library of Congress replaced the conventionally printed NUC with a COM-generated microfiche version, produced from the MARC data base, in 1983. Each annual issue of the main *National Union Catalog*—called the *National Union Catalog: Books*—occupies about 350 fiche. Issued monthly, it subsumes its discontinued hardcopy predecessor, as well as LC Books: Subjects and the Chinese Cooperative Catalog. Entries, consisting of complete cataloging records in the traditional main entry format, are arranged on fiche by an LC-assigned registry number. The user consults main entry, title, series, and subject indexes to determine the registry numbers associated with particular bibliographic items. The index entries contain brief bibliographic data—including publisher, date, and LC class number—that may satisfy some information requirements and eliminate the two-step retrieval procedure. A similar arrangement is employed by the *National Union Catalog: Audiovisual Materials, National Union Catalog: Cartographic Materials,* and other COM-generated NUC catalogs for nonbook materials. Bibliographic entries contained in the various NUC micropublications are supplemented by listings included in the COM-generated version of the *National Union Catalog: Register of Additional Locations.*

While it provides more varied access to bibliographic data than its conventional printed predecessor, the COM-generated version of the NUC retains the printed edition's monthly publication frequency. Combining the production speed of COM-generated micropublication with economical first-class mailing permitted by the compactness of microforms, MARC-FICHE—produced by MARC Applied Research, a division of the Library Corporation—is a weekly publication that gives subscribing libraries access to Library of Congress cataloging data within a few days of the distribution of MARC tapes. Primary coverage includes LC MARC cataloging since 1967, COMARC contributed cataloging, cataloging records for Canadiana contributed by the National Library of Canada, and cataloging records for 90,000 additional 20th century imprints not included in the MARC data base. As with the COM-generated NUC, entries conform to the traditional main entry format and are recorded in random-order sequence on fiche. Access to desired cataloging data is obtained through indexes to main entry/title, LC card number, LC class number, and International Standard Book Number. The indexes themselves are on COM-generated fiche and cumulate quarterly. Weekly index updates cumulate weekly between quarters. Other indexes are optionally available.

Books in English (BIE) is produced by the British Library from a combination of the LC MARC and UK MARC data bases. BIE is a bimonthly alphabetical author/title list of English-language books cataloged by the Library of Congress or the British Library. It thus approximates the scope of H.W. Wilson's *Cumulative Book Index* but, like the *National Union Catalog,* its entries contain full cataloging data. Originally published on ultrafiche for maximum compactness, BIE has since been converted to conventional COM-generated fiche. Information is current through the month preceding publication. Each entry gives full cataloging data, including LC and Dewey class numbers, LC card numbers, added entries, and subject headings. As an unusual feature, successive issues cumulate continuously and contain all cataloging records published since the beginning of the current year. Various cumulations are available for earlier years.

The *WLN Resource Directory* is a COM-generated microfiche bibliography of cataloging records for items held by participants in the Western Library Network (WLN). As such, it is a printed subset of WLN's online data base, which is described later in this chapter. Published annually, it contains cataloging records for approximately three million items. As an unusual feature, it supplements cataloging copy from the LC MARC data base with bibliographic records contributed by WLN participants. Entries are alphabetized by author, title, and subject. Entries in the title section contain complete cataloging information. The author and subject sections contain briefer bibliographic descriptions.

While the COM-generated micropublications described above are essentially printed reports produced by batch processing of MARC tapes, several online search services—including Dialog and Wilsonline—provide timeshared access to the LC MARC data base. The Dialog implementation corresponds to the Books All segment of the LC MARC data base. It includes cataloging records for both English- and foreign-language monographs. As discussed in chapter 7, Dialog supports a very broad range of retrieval capabilities. LC MARC records can be searched for the occurrence of any word or word root. Alternatively, retrieval operations can be restricted to specific fields, including author, title, subject, series, publisher, publication date, LC card number, International Standard Book Number, language, and intellectual level. Searches can likewise be limited to fiction or nonfiction titles. Boolean operators and proximity commands can be used to create complex retrieval specifications. Retrieved records can be displayed with MARC tags. By special arrangement, Dialog will supply specified LC MARC records on magnetic tape. It should be noted that several other Dialog data bases include some MARC-format records for monographs. Examples include the MEDLINE data base, produced by the National Library of Medicine, and the AGRICOLA data base, produced by the National Agricultural Library. Dialog also provides online access to the REMARC data base described above.

Wilsonline divides its implementation of the LC MARC data base into separate data files for English- and foreign-language titles. In both cases, coverage begins with 1977, thus excluding LC MARC records created from 1968 through 1976. Unlike the Dialog implementation, which is limited to monographic publications, Wilsonline's LC MARC files include cataloging records for serials, maps, visual materials, sound recordings, and music. As with Dialog, power retrieval capabilities are supported. Retrieved records can be displayed with MARC tags or in a catalog card format. Among other computer-based information services, the Canadian On-Line Enquiry (CAN/OLE) search service provides online access to CANMARC records produced by the National Library of Canada, but access is limited to Canadian libraries. Operated by the Bibliographic Services Division of the British Library, the Blaise-Line search service offers online access to the UK MARC data base, the machine-readable counterpart of the British National Bibliography, and AVMARC, the computer-processible version of the British Catalogue of Audiovisual Materials.

CD-ROM Cataloging Systems

Although the MARC-derivative products and services described to this point succeed in providing more timely and varied access to Library of Congress cataloging copy than has been possible with conventional printed sources, they do not include a catalog production component. With MARC-FICHE, Books in English, and the COM-generated versions of the NUC, individual catalog records must be transcribed onto cards using typewriters or word processors. Alternatively, they can be entered into a locally maintained computer data base by means of key-to-disk terminals or other input devices. In either case, considerable manual labor is required. Similar limitations apply to records retrieved from the MARC data bases supported by Dialog, Wilsonline, and other online search services. While microcomputers might conceivably be used to download such records, some customized programming or other extensive data manipulations will be required to produce finished sets of catalog cards or to prepare such records for input to circulation control, catalog access, or other local systems.

These limitations are addressed by cataloging support products based on Compact Disc-Read Only Memory (CD-ROM) technology. As previously described in chapter 1, CD-ROM is a high-capacity, read-only optical disk format that is principally intended for data base publishing and distribution. CD-ROM cataloging support products provide data bases of bibliographic records on compact discs that are distributed to customer sites for processing by software operating on locally installed microcomputers. BiblioFile, the first CD-ROM cataloging support system and one of the earliest CD-ROM information products of any type, was introduced by the Library Corporation in 1985. Conceptually similar systems include Laser-Quest from General Research Corporation, SuperCat from Gaylord Information Systems, CD-CATSS from Utlas, CAT CD450 from OCLC, LaserCat from WLN, Precision One from Brodart, and Alliance Plus from Follett Software. The Library of Congress introduced CDMARC Bibliographic, a CD-ROM implementation of the LC MARC data base, in 1991. The Library of Congress also offers CD-ROM editions of its Name Authority File and Subject Authority File.

While they differ in details, CD-ROM cataloging support systems feature similar capabilities and operating procedures. Designed for both current cataloging activities and retrospective conversion projects, they typically include all or part of the LC MARC data base—supplemented, in some cases, by cataloging records from other sources—on one or more compact discs. BiblioFile, for example, divides the LC MARC data base into English- and foreign-language subsets. It also offers separate discs that contain CANMARC records, GPO records, and cataloging for audiovisual materials. OCLC's CAT CD450 system, Utlas's CD-CATSS system, and WLN's LaserCat system include records contributed by subscribers to those bibliographic utilities, which are described later in this chapter. A BiblioFile option provides cataloging records contributed by school and public libraries or academic and research libraries. LaserQuest similarly includes cataloging records obtained from General Research Corporation's customers. Some CD-ROM cataloging support products offer features for specific audiences. Follett Software's Alliance Plus system, for example, includes Sears and LC children's subject headings in cataloging records. BiblioFile likewise offers cataloging records with Sears subject headings. Brodart's Precision One Disc includes a selection of one million LC MARC records for titles considered appropriate for school and public libraries.

Regardless of data base scope, cataloging records are generally stored on CD-ROM discs in the full USMARC formats associated with specific types of library materials. Menu-driven software permits the retrieval of bibliographic records by various parameters. With BiblioFile, for example, browsable indexes provide access to cataloging records by main entry, title, LC card number, International Standard Book Number, and International Standard Serial Number. Data base searches can be narrowed by publication date and type of material. WLN's LaserCat system supports an even broader range of retrieval parameters, including keyword searching of author, title, and subject fields. Specific retrieval capabilities aside, software permits the modification of cataloging copy for conformity with local practices, retention of the modified records in machine-readable form for input to an online catalog or circulation control system, and printing of catalog card sets and labels. Input of original cataloging records, via specially designed data entry templates appropriate to the various US MARC formats, is also supported.

CD-ROM cataloging support systems offer a potentially useful and cost-effective alternative to the online, timeshared cataloging services, such as those offered by the bibliographic utilities described in the next section. With most timeshared services, customers pay for cataloging products and services as they use them. Transaction charges are incurred, for example, each time a bibliographic record is accessed or whenever output products are ordered. CD-ROM users, in contrast, pay a fixed annual subscription fee that permits unlimited data base and software usage without additional transaction charges. CD-ROM cataloging systems will consequently prove particularly attractive in high-volume current cataloging operations or retrospective conversion projects where a low unit cost per cataloging transaction can be achieved.

Such comparisons assume, of course, that the data bases provided by CD-ROM cataloging support systems contain bibliographic records appropriate to the items being cataloged by a given library. As a potentially significant limitation, CD-ROM systems typically provide fewer cataloging records than the bibliographic utilities described below. Most rely heavily or exclusively on the LC MARC data base, which may be segmented or offered as a series of separately priced subsets. With BiblioFile and SuperCat, for example, the LC MARC data base is subdivided into English- and foreign-language segments for which separate subscriptions are required. BiblioFile likewise requires separate subscriptions to the CANMARC data base and contributed cataloging discs. As CD-ROM cataloging products developed by bibliographic utilities, the OCLC CAT CD450, Utlas CD-CATSS, and WLN LaserCat systems include many cataloging records from non-LC sources, but each CD-ROM data base is a subset of its timeshared counterpart. The CAT CD450 system, for example, contains less than one-fifth of the records in the OCLC Online Union Catalog. Because CD-ROM data bases are typically updated at monthly or quarterly intervals, they may not contain full cataloging records for a library's most recently acquired items. In contrast, the data bases maintained by bibliographic utilities and other timesharing services are updated at more frequent intervals through subscriptions to resource files, and continuously by participants' original cataloging activity.

BIBLIOGRAPHIC UTILITIES

Although the products and services discussed in the preceding section can provide timely and varied access to Library of Congress cataloging copy, they are all limited in some important respect. COM-generated, MARC-derivative micropublications and the online MARC data bases supported by timesharing search services are useful in bibliographic verification or the retrieval of cataloging copy, but they lack a catalog production component. Their scope is, for the most part, limited to machine-readable cataloging data generated by the Library of Congress; with few exceptions, they do not provide information about the holdings of specific libraries. Books in English incorporates UK MARC as well as LC cataloging copy, but like MARCFICHE, it lacks a catalog production component. While CD-ROM cataloging support systems incorporate data entry and record editing capabilities, most are self-contained products that do not provide the library holdings information commonly associated with a union catalog. Book jobbers and retrospective conversion companies maintain large data bases derived from both MARC and non-MARC sources, but they cannot be accessed online in an interactive manner, and they do not provide holdings information.

These limitations are addressed, and largely overcome, by the shared cataloging services offered by the bibliographic utilities—organizations that maintain large bibliographic data bases and offer various products and services to subscribers who access them on an online, timesharing basis. The data bases maintained by most bibliographic utilities are essentially online union catalogs. As described below, the bibliographic utilities acquire cataloging records in machine-readable form from the Library of Congress and other subscription sources. Their data bases also include cataloging records contributed by participating libraries. In either case, the records contain two kinds of information: (1) descriptive cataloging and classification data, typically in the USMARC format appropriate to the item being cataloged, and (2) holdings information for libraries that have added specific items to their collections.

The earliest bibliographic utilities were organized in the 1970s to support technical processing operations through cooperative cataloging and computer-assisted card production. While they have steadily expanded their activities since that time, their continued emphasis on cooperative cataloging and technical services most clearly distinguishes them from other online information services that provide timeshared access to bibliographic records. Dialog and Wilsonline, as previously noted, provide online access to the LC MARC data base, but neither of those vendors supports the entry of original cataloging data, record editing, card production, or other services associated with technical processing operations. Their LC MARC implementations are principally intended for general bibliographic searching and other reference and research applications. As a further point of contrast, the contents of data bases maintained by the bibliographic utilities are largely monographic in character. Serials, where included, are treated as entire issues or volumes. As discussed in chapter 7, most of the data bases offered by online search services contain records pertaining to individual journal articles.

As computer-based cataloging resources, bibliographic utilities principally compete with the CD-ROM systems described in the preceding section. Because they are larger and updated more frequently than their CD-ROM counterparts, the data bases maintained by bibliographic utilities can presumably satisfy a greater percentage of a given library's copy cataloging requirements, thereby minimizing time-consuming and expensive original cataloging activity. As computer-based service organizations, bibliographic utilities also offer capabilities appropriate to resource sharing, acquisitions, and other library operations that are not addressed by CD-ROM systems. Because the cataloging records maintained by bibliographic utilities include library holdings symbols as well as bibliographic data, they can support interlibrary loan activities. Such capabilities may give bibliographic utilities a functional advantage over CD-ROM systems in certain library situations.

OCLC

While there has been much discussion of cooperative relationships among them, the various bibliographic utilities operate separate and, to some extent, competing services which differ from one another in data base size and composition, the number and nature of their subscribers, and the types of services offered. Measured by the number of participating libraries, the Online Computer Library Center (OCLC) is the largest bibliographic utility. It was incorporated in 1967 as the Ohio College Library Center, a not-for-profit organization intended to function as a computerized regional processing center for academic libraries in Ohio. Operating from headquarters in Columbus, OCLC implemented an offline catalog card production system in 1970, using a data base of LC MARC records. An online system for shared cataloging became operational in 1971 and was employed by 54 academic libraries by the end of that year. It established the pattern followed by other bibliographic utilities in providing timeshared access to an online data base consisting of LC MARC records plus original cataloging contributed by member libraries.

In 1972, OCLC participation was extended to nonacademic libraries in Ohio. Interstate operations were initiated with the installation of several terminals in Pennsylvania libraries in late 1972. In 1973, OCLC abandoned its regional orientation and opened its membership to libraries outside of Ohio, setting the stage for a rapid expansion of its customer base. OCLC's membership list had grown to 2,400 libraries by 1980, at which time OCLC served customers in all 50 states. The organization's national—and, since the late 1980s, increasingly international—orientation has been reflected in two name changes: to OCLC, Incorporated, in 1977, and to the Online Computer Library Center in 1981.

OCLC is a general-purpose bibliographic utility. Participation is open to libraries of all types and sizes, regardless of geographic location. OCLC recognizes two principal membership categories: (1) online cataloging members agree to use the OCLC online system for all of their current cataloging activity and to contribute original cataloging records and holdings information to the OCLC data base; (2) tapeloading members do a portion of their current cataloging online and contribute the remainder of their current cataloging via magnetic tape for inclusion in the online data base. Tapeloading membership is designed for libraries that utilize a different bibliographic utility, a CD-ROM product, or another methodology for part of their current cataloging activity.

At the time of this writing, OCLC had approximately 5,000 active participating libraries; directly or indirectly, it served more than twice that number of institutions through group access capabilities, serials union lists, and other products and services. A Group Access Capability (GAC), for example, permits local and regional use of the OCLC online system by nonmember libraries that are part of consortia or other preformed groups. GAC participants can access brief bibliographic records and holdings information for libraries within their consortia.

While independent participation is possible, OCLC encourages North American libraries to become members through regional networks which operate as its authorized agents. Such regional networks, and their service areas, include the AMIGOS Bibliographic Council (Arizona, Arkansas, Oklahoma, New Mexico, and Texas with additional members in Kansas, Louisiana, and Nevada); the Bibliographic Center for Research (Colorado, Idaho, Iowa, Kansas, Montana, Nevada, Utah, and Wyoming); CAPCON (District of Columbia, Maryland, Virginia); the Federal Library and Information Center Committee, FEDLINK (U.S. government libraries); ILLINET (Illinois); INCOLSA (Indiana); the Michigan Library Consortium (Michigan); MINITEX Library Information Network (Minnesota, North Dakota, South Dakota); Missouri Library Network Corporation (Missouri); NEBASE (Nebraska); NELINET (Connecticut, Massachusetts, Maine, New Hampshire, Rhode Island, Vermont); OHIONET (Ohio); PACNET (Alaska, California, Hawaii, Idaho, Montana, Oregon, Washington); PALINET (Delaware, District of Columbia, Maryland, eastern Pennsylvania); PRLC (western Pennsylvania, West Virginia); SOLINET (Alabama, Florida, Georgia, Kentucky, Louisiana, Mississippi, North Carolina, Puerto Rico, South Carolina, Tennessee, Virginia, Virgin Islands); SUNY/OCLC (New York); Utlas International (Canada); and WILS (Wisconsin). As a group, the regional networks help member libraries install OCLC equipment and implement OCLC operations. They provide system documentation in the form of operators' manuals, equipment selection aids, newsletters, and similar written communications; conduct training courses; collect fees for OCLC usage; and generally serve as liaison agencies between OCLC and member libraries.

The OCLC Europe office—located in Birmingham, England—serves libraries in the United Kingdom, continental Europe, the Middle East, and Africa. OCLC participation by European libraries ranges from full online contributing membership to applications involving a single OCLC service, such as retrospective conversion or interlibrary loan. The OCLC Asia Pacific Services office—located at OCLC headquarters in Ohio—covers libraries in Asia, the Pacific Rim, and Latin America. In the Asia/Pacific region, OCLC also markets its products and services through selected local distributors. OCLC cataloging users in the Asia/Pacific region include the National Library of Australia, the University of Western Australia, the National Library of New Zealand, the National Central Library in Taiwan, the National Taiwan University, Hong Kong University of Science and Technology, and more than two dozen Japanese libraries.

OCLC's online cataloging service operates on computers located in Dublin, Ohio. Members use locally installed workstations to access the system via leased or dial-up telephone lines, as well as through value-added carriers. Most installations employ IBM-compatible microcomputers, purchased from OCLC or other sources, as workstations, although conventional terminals are also supported. A specially equipped, microcomputer-based workstation is required for cataloging CJK records in vernacular scripts.

As a group, the bibliographic utilities provide online access to large data bases of cataloging records that support descriptive cataloging, subject cataloging, classification, preorder bibliographic verification, interlibrary loan, and other library operations. The OCLC data base is termed the

Online Union Catalog because it includes information about participants' holdings. At the time of this writing, it contained approximately 30 million cataloging records and 390 million location symbols. Approximately 85 percent of the OCLC data base consists of cataloging records for books.

As previously noted, the OCLC Online Union Catalog incorporates files of cataloging records purchased on magnetic tape from subscription services, plus cataloging records contributed by participating libraries. The LC MARC data base is the largest single-source component in the Online Union Catalog. At regular intervals, OCLC loads magnetic tapes containing the most recently issued LC MARC records for books, serials, maps, musical scores, sound recordings, visual materials, and computer files. For the first several years of operation, LC MARC records constituted the major portion of the OCLC Online Union Catalog. By 1973, however, cataloging contributed by OCLC members represented almost half of the online records. The ratio of contributed records to those obtained from subscription sources has increased steadily and significantly since that time, as participating libraries have contributed cataloging records for older imprints and other items not included on LC MARC tapes. At the time of this writing, contributed cataloging accounted for more than 83 percent of the records in the Online Union Catalog and approximately 87 percent of the 40,000 new bibliographic records added to the OCLC data base each week.

The dramatic growth of the contributed cataloging portion of the Online Union Catalog is in large part attributable to the previously discussed broadening of OCLC's customer base during the 1970s, as well as to retrospective conversion projects undertaken by OCLC participants to support the implementation of local library automation systems. As their principal contribution to the Online Union Catalog, such retrospective conversion projects have added cataloging records for older imprints that predate the LC MARC program and the inception of OCLC's online cataloging system.

To catalog an item, an OCLC user first searches the Online Union Catalog for appropriate cataloging copy. Since its inception, OCLC has supported the retrieval of cataloging records by numeric identifiers and derived search keys. The former permit searches by Library of Congress Card Number (LCCN), International Standard Book Number (ISBN), International Standard Serial Number (ISSN), CODEN, government document number, music publisher's number, and OCLC control number. Search procedures are straightforward. To retrieve a record by Library of Congress Card Number, for example, an OCLC workstation operator simply enters that number. Because the numeric identifiers listed above are often unique to specific bibliographic records, they will yield the fastest retrieval results and are consequently preferred where appropriate.

Derived search keys permit searches by personal or corporate author (whether in main or added entries), title, or a combination of author and title. Derived search keys are based on specified combinations of characters from individual words in a desired name and/or title. An author search key, for example, is composed of the first four or fewer characters of the author's surname, the first three or fewer characters of the author's first name, and, where applicable, the author's middle initial. Thus, the derived author search key for George V. Higgins would be "higg,geo,v"—the individual segments being entered in lowercase, separated by commas. Search keys for corporate authors are constructed in much the same way, although the OCLC search system includes a stoplist of commonly encountered words in corporate authors' names. Such words can be omitted when deriving search keys, thereby limiting the retrieval of irrelevant records.

Similar rules apply to the formulation of title and combined author/title search keys. The search key for a given title consists of the first three or fewer characters of the first word in the title, the first two or fewer characters in each of the next two words, and the first character of the fourth word. Initial articles are ignored. Thus, the key for a title search for James M. Cain's *The Postman Always Rings Twice* would be "pos,al,ri,t." The key for combined author/title searches consists of the first four or fewer characters of the author's surname and the first four or fewer characters of the first nonarticle word in the title. For the above example, the author/title search key would be "cain, post." While such parameters as the LCCN and ISBN are unique and usually retrieve just one record, the derived keys for author, title, and combined author/title searches are not necessarily unique; they often retrieve multiple, irrelevant records along with the desired items. Considerable numbers of records may be retrieved, for example, in author/title searches where truncation results in search keys of a common form, such as "john,hist."

Derived search keys are reasonably effective for technical processing, but general reference and other public services applications require a broader range of retrieval capabilities. Other bibliographic utilities permit the direct entry of author names and titles, singly or in combination. They also support a broader range of retrieval parameters, as well as search statements that contain multiple retrieval parameters linked by Boolean operators.

The PRISM service, which was implemented by OCLC in 1990 as a replacement for its original search system, introduced several useful retrieval enhancements. In particular, it provides two new retrieval techniques: combined key searches and title browsing. The former permits search statements containing two retrieval parameters, excluding the OCLC control number, linked by the Boolean AND operator. Combined key searching based on derived author and derived title keys can be used, for example, in situations where an author/title derived key would retrieve too many records. Title browsing capability, a feature of many online public catalog access systems described later in this chapter, is based on entries in the title and uniform title fields of bibliographic records. Users can enter up to 60 characters from a desired title. The appropriate section of an alphabetized title list is then displayed for operator browsing and selection of specific cataloging records.

While combined record searching and title browsing can facilitate the identification of bibliographic records for technical processing, they cannot satisfy the diverse retrieval requirements of reference and research applications. Librarians interested in subject searching, more complete Boolean capabilities, or other retrieval operations involving the OCLC Online Union Catalog must utilize EPIC or First Search services, described in chapter 7.

Where one data base record is retrieved by a given search, it is displayed in the full MARC format with labeled fields. Multiple records are initially displayed in abbreviated form for operator review and selection of those for which a full MARC display is desired. Displayed cataloging copy can be modified to meet a given library's requirements by moving, adding, deleting, or otherwise editing the contents of individual fields. Local holdings information is also added to the record. Modifications to data base records are reflected in catalog cards and other output products ordered by member libraries. The original records themselves are not changed, and participants' modifications are not retained online. In theory, then, the OCLC Online Union Catalog should contain just one cataloging record for each edition obtained from subscription sources or contributed by participants. Some duplication, however, inevitably results from mechanical problems, such as typographical errors during data entry, and intellectual factors, such as variations in descriptive cataloging practices and difficulties in distinguishing different printings and editions of a given title. Over the years, OCLC has undertaken several initiatives to detect and eliminate such duplicate records.

As previously discussed, online and tapeloading general members agree to use OCLC for all of their cataloging activity. Where previously entered cataloging copy for a given book or other item is not retrieved by a data base search, a general member must perform original cataloging, thereby contributing a new record to the Online Union Catalog. Original cataloging records are input in the MARC format, using displayed workforms that consist of labeled fields with adjacent blank spaces for data entry. Contributed cataloging records can be immediately entered into the OCLC Online Union Catalog or routed to a temporary "save" file pending review by the contributing library.

Member-contributed cataloging creates data base records that will be used by other OCLC participants. Contributed records remain in the data base until they are superceded by Library of Congress cataloging. Where LC copy and a previously entered member record vary in the choice or form of main entry, both records are maintained. Because the appropriateness of cataloging copy decisively influences the effectiveness of a shared cataloging system in which only one version of a record is available online, OCLC participants have been much concerned about the quality of member-contributed cataloging records. OCLC has established cataloging standards based on MARC formats and Library of Congress practice. Level I standards cover original cataloging in the full MARC format. K-level cataloging standards omit some data elements found in full MARC records. While OCLC's cataloging system software does not review member-contributed records for correctness, it does perform data validation routines to prevent the entry of inappropriate data elements in specific fields. Under the Enhance program, which was established in

1983, OCLC authorizes certain libraries to correct and replace unacceptable cataloging records contributed by other participants. Selected for inclusion in the program on the basis of their high-quality cataloging, Enhance libraries receive training in OCLC enhancement policies and procedures. Enhance participants include approximately 100 institutions of various types and sizes.

To improve cataloging quality by facilitating the selection of standardized headings, OCLC offers online access to the Library of Congress Name Authority File and Library of Congress Subject Authority File. Both files are implemented as search-only information resources. The LC Subject Authority File is updated weekly via magnetic tapes received from the Library of Congress. The LC Name Authority File is updated daily by the Library of Congress through the Linked Systems Project, which transmits new authority records electronically to OCLC.

Once an original cataloging record is entered or modifications to an existing data base record are completed, an OCLC workstation operator can order printed card sets which will be produced offline according to the individual specifications or "profile" prepared when the ordering library became an OCLC participant. These cards, and other output products, reflect modifications that a library makes to individual cataloging records. The data base records themselves, as previously noted, are unaffected by such changes.

OCLC can print catalog cards in a wide range of formats. In addition to main entry and other bibliographic information, printed cards can include call numbers from any classification system printed in various card locations; added entries and subject headings; general, local, and contents notes; and location, medium, and size designations. The cards can be delivered to the ordering library in sets or sorted alphabetically or by call number.

As libraries convert from card to computer-processible catalogs, the number of cards printed offline by OCLC has declined significantly. As an alternative or complement to printed cards, libraries with local automation systems can order machine-readable copies of their cataloging records on magnetic tapes through the OCLC-MARC Subscription Service. Tapes produced by the OCLC-MARC Subscription Service can be used to update data bases maintained by local automated systems or to produce the CD-ROM or computer-output-microfilm catalogs described later in this chapter. To support the initial implementation of local systems, OCLC can generate magnetic tapes containing part or all of the cataloging records produced by a particular library since the inception of its OCLC activity or for another specified time period. Multi-institution tapes are available, provided that appropriate permissions are obtained.

RLIN

The Research Libraries Information Network (RLIN) is a bibliographic utility and online information retrieval system operated by the Research Libraries Group (RLG). RLIN was established in 1978 as an outgrowth of BALLOTS, a library automation program developed by Stanford University. BALLOTS—an acronym for Bibliographic Automation of Large Library Operations using a Time Sharing System—was ambitiously conceived as an integrated information processing system in which shared bibliographic and other data files would support both technical processing operations and information retrieval activities. The latter component of the BALLOTS program was an outgrowth of the Stanford Physics Information Retrieval System (SPIRES), an interactive online retrieval system developed in 1967. A prototype BALLOTS implementation, introduced in 1969, was followed by a production system for the Stanford University Libraries in 1972. In 1976, BALLOTS became available as a shared cataloging service to other California libraries. At that time, it was widely regarded as a potential West Coast alternative to OCLC.

BALLOTS' destiny was significantly altered in 1978 when it was selected by the Research Libraries Group as the system with the greatest potential for meeting its requirements for automated bibliographic control. RLG was founded in 1974 by Harvard, Columbia, Yale, and the New York Public Library as a resource-sharing consortium. One of the group's original goals was the establishment of a computer-based bibliographic processing system, and it initially experimented with an online link to the Library of Congress. When the decision was made to adopt BALLOTS as its bibliographic utility, Harvard withdrew from RLG and was replaced by Stanford, which became the utility's host institution.

Although they were developed for—and are specifically designed to serve—large or specialized research libraries, RLIN's services are comparable to those offered by the other general-purpose bibliographic utilities discussed in this chapter. Available to libraries of all types and sizes in the United States and elsewhere, RLIN has two broad categories of participants: RLG members and non-RLG libraries. RLG membership is open to research libraries, archives, museums, historical agencies, scholarly societies, or other not-for-profit institutions with educational, cultural, or scientific missions. Two categories of membership are distinguished: general members are institutions that serve a clientele of more than 5,000 faculty, researchers, students, professionals, or others; special members are institutions that serve 5,000 or fewer users. At the time of this writing, RLG had more than 50 general members and more than 70 special members. Participation in RLIN is not a requirement for RLG members in either category, although most members use RLIN to support some activities.

RLIN distinguishes techical processing customers, who have full access to the system's cataloging support and related capabilities, from search service users, who are limited to the retrieval of data base records for reference and research purposes. At the time of this writing, RLIN had approximately 250 technical processing customers and more than 1,000 search-only accounts. The latter are available to individuals as well as institutions.

RLIN's computer facilities, which are located at Stanford University, can be accessed through various telecommunication facilities. Leased-line access, via RLG's private packet-switched network, is required for interactive cataloging support and other technical processing applications. Dial access, which provides read-only access to the RLIN data base, is appropriate for individual researchers as well as for reference desk installations in those libraries that utilize leased lines to access RLIN for cataloging support. The RLIN system can be reached by direct local or long-distance dialing, through SprintNet, or via the Internet in organizations where such access is available.

As cataloging workstations, RLIN supports IBM-compatible microcomputers equipped with terminal emulation software supplied by RLG. In its standard version, the terminal emulation program supports bibliographic processing using roman script only. An extended version permits bibliographic processing in any script, including nonroman scripts, supported by the microcomputer hardware in use. RLIN was the first bibliographic utility to support the cataloging and retrieval of bibliographic records in Chinese, Japanese, and Korean (CJK) vernacular scripts. It requires a specially equipped, multiscript workstation. RLIN added Cyrillic-language capabilities in 1986, followed by Hebrew in 1988 and Arabic in 1991. RLIN's Cyrillic cataloging capability supports the Russian, Belorussian, Bulgarian, Macedonian, Serbian, and Ukrainian languages. RLIN's Hebrew cataloging capability supports ancient and modern Hebrew as well as Yiddish. RLIN's Arabic script capability supports a Pan-Arabic character set that is appropriate for Farsi, Urdu, and Ottoman Turkish.

The principal components of the RLIN data base, the so-called central bibliographic files, form an online union catalog of library materials held by the utility's participants. Like their counterparts supported by other bibliographic utilities, RLIN's central bibliographic files contain records from two broad sources: subscription source files and cataloging contributed by participating libraries. RLIN, like other bibliographic utilities discussed in this chapter, obtains cataloging records for books, serials, maps, sound recordings, music, and visual materials from the Library of Congress. The Library of Congress itself uses the RLIN system for online entry of MARC cataloging records in Chinese, Japanese, Korean, Hebrew, and Arabic scripts. RLIN also loads U.S. Government Printing Office (GPO) cataloging records; CANMARC records produced by the National Library of Canada for Canadian imprints and books about Canada; BNB MARC records produced by the British Library for books about the United Kingdom or bearing United Kingdom imprints; and CATLINE records for biomedical materials cataloged by the National Library of Medicine.

Unlike the OCLC Online Union Catalog, which maintains all bibliographic records in a single repository, RLIN's central bibliographic files are divided, by type of library material, into eight segments. The Books file accounts for approximately 90 percent of the cataloging records in the central bibliographic files. Other files contain cataloging records for serials, musical scores, sound recordings, visual materials, maps, machine-readable data, and archives and manuscripts. At the time of this writing, the central bibliographic files contained approximately 58 million cataloging records. That total makes RLIN the largest bibliographic utility, but, unlike the OCLC Online Union Catalog, the central bibliographic files store duplicate and variant records for the same titles and editions cataloged by different libraries. Measured by the number of unique editions, the central bibliographic files contain fewer cataloging records than the OCLC Online Union Catalog. Among its advantages, the storage of duplicate and variant records gives RLIN participants a broader range of choices for copy cataloging. It also simplifies interlibrary loan transactions by providing online access to exact holdings information, including local call numbers, contributed by RLIN participants.

Contributed records, which are based on the original cataloging activities of participating libraries, account for about 85 percent of the cataloging records in the RLIN data base. Most RLIN participants use online data entry to contribute bibliographic records that reflect their current cataloging activities, although they are not required to do so. Records produced by retrospective conversion projects or transferred from other systems, such as OCLC, are typically loaded from magnetic tapes. During the 1980s, such tapeloading operations dramatically expanded the RLIN data base as new RLG members and others added their holdings to the central bibliographic files.

Given RLIN's role as a bibliographic utility for research libraries, it is not surprising that its central bibliographic files contain contributed cataloging records that reflect the highly specialized, often distinctive materials held by its participants. Such materials include publications in a wide variety of foreign languages, as well as many rare books. Since the early 1980s, RLG has devoted considerable attention to the bibliographic control of library materials in specific subject areas, such as East Asian studies and art and architecture. In early 1993, the RLIN data base contained more than one million CJK records contributed by the Library of Congress and other participants. The RLIN data base also contains the largest collection of bibliographic records in Middle Eastern languages. Among the bibliographic utilities, RLIN has most actively encouraged the entry of information about archival and manuscript collections. Its involvement with such materials dates from 1983, when RLG established an Archives and Manuscripts Task Force to promote the development of a national data base of primary source materials. To accommodate the requirements of archives and manuscript repositories, the RLIN system permits the repeated modification of a bibliographic record as an individual collection progresses through various stages of processing. It should be noted, however, that the data bases maintained by other bibliographic utilities also contain cataloging records for distinctive and important research materials. The OCLC Online Union Catalog, for example, contains many cataloging records contributed by special collections departments in participating libraries.

The RLIN system's sophisticated information retrieval component supports bibliographic verification, copy cataloging, literature searches, interlibrary loan, and other library operations. To retrieve a cataloging record, an RLIN user must specify the particular file to be searched. Records can be retrieved by various numeric and textual parameters. The former include an RLIN control, Library of Congress Card Number, International Standard Book Number, International Standard Serial Number, U.S. government document number, GPO Monthly Catalog number, CODEN for scientific and technical journals, publisher's number of music, and Library of Congress, Dewey Decimal, or National Library of Medicine classification number.

RLIN's extensive textual retrieval capabilities can locate cataloging records by personal, corporate, and conference names; titles; and subjects. Personal name indexes can be used to retrieve cataloging records that contain names in main and added entries, including authors, editors, illustrators, and compilers. The indexes apply to all bibliographic files. Names can be entered in normal or inverted order. The searcher can specify an exact or partial form of a personal name to be matches. Corporate and conference name indexes permit searches for words or phrases contained in the indicated headings. The RLIN title and subject indexes similarly support retrieval by words and phrases for records in all bibliographic files. Phrase searches can match specified character strings at the beginning of a subject heading or within subject heading subdivisions. Local indexes permit searches for a library's own records. A call number index, for example, will search for records containing a particular locally assigned call number. In the Archives and Manuscripts Control file, it will search for records containing a specified record group number. Other local indexes permit searches for records containing local purchase order numbers, status indicators, words or phrases in donor names, or other identifiers.

Regardless of the particular search parameters employed, RLIN's retrieval procedures are straightforward and should be easily mastered by librarians familiar with other online information services. Unlike OCLC, with its derived retrieval keys, RLIN users enter field names and search terms directly. Thus, a command of the form "find pn patricia highsmith" will initiate a search of the personal name index for records where the indicated name appears as a main or added entry. As this example indicates, field names are typically abbreviated and an "equals" sign between the field name and search argument is assumed. Search terms can be truncated to compensate for uncertain spelling or to retrieve all field values with a common root. To further enhance retrieval flexibility, the Boolean AND, OR, and NOT operators can be used to combine multiple search specifications.

As previously noted, the RLIN system maintains duplicate and variant records for the same edition of a title cataloged by multiple participants. Originally, RLIN stored each library's cataloging records in separate files. To minimize redundancy and save space, the system now clusters records that pertain to the same edition of a given title. Within a cluster, a record with the fullest level of cataloging, as outlined later in this report, is designated a primary cluster member. When a cataloging record for a given edition is retrieved, the displayed bibliographic information is taken from the primary cluster member. Holdings symbols for other libraries that have cataloged the indicated edition are listed alphabetically. An operator can request a full MARC display for any record in a cluster.

Retrieved records can be modified to meet local requirements by adding, moving, or deleting data elements. All changes made to existing records enter a deferred queue file, which is processed at night. The system assigns a unique control number; adds a copy of the record, incorporating all modifications plus an identifier for the contributing library, to the central bibliographic files; and updates the appropriate indexes. The cataloging record on which the modified record was based is unaffected by any changes made to it by RLIN customers. Once entered in the central bibliographic files, a contributed cataloging record is available to other RLIN participants. Newly entered records are accessible, with limited indexing, by searching the deferred queue file. A given record will remain in the central bibliographic file until it is deleted by the library that contributed it.

If a data base search fails to identify an appropriate cataloging record, the RLIN workstation operator can place the system in the original cataloging mode. The operator indicates the desired MARC input format, and the system responds by displaying an appropriate workform. RLG standards for original cataloging are based on the Anglo-American Cataloging Rules, as interpreted by the Library of Congress; LC practice for name and subject headings; and the MARC II communications format. RLIN recognizes three levels of detail for original cataloging: (1) full-level original cataloging, which is based on National Level Bibliographic Record standards delineated for the various MARC formats with authority control for name and subject headings; (2) minimal or base-level original cataloging, which employs the MARC format but omits some fields associated with full-level records; and (3) briefer cataloging records, which do not conform to RLIN cataloging standards.

To encourage libraries to conform to RLIN's cataloging standards, input charges are waived for original cataloging records contributed in the full-level format. Input charges for nonstandard cataloging records are twice as high as those for base-level records. Original cataloging is not reviewed by RLIN staff members prior to inclusion in the appropriate bibliographic file. RLIN participants may augment or correct cataloging errors detected in their own records, but they are not authorized to correct or change records contributed by others. Since the RLIN data base makes all modified versions of cataloging records available to all participants, formal error detection procedures are less important than they are in the OCLC Online Union Catalog, which maintains just one copy of a cataloging record.

To facilitate cataloging decisions, RLIN provides online, search-only access to the Library of Congress Name Authority and Subject Authority files. Authority records can be retrieved by a variety of parameters, including personal names, subject words, subject subdivisions, and words or phrases in corporate names, conference names, and titles. LC subject authority records can also be retrieved by similarly phrased groups of headings.

Once an original cataloging record is entered or modifications to an existing data base record are completed, an RLIN workstation operator can order catalog card sets to be printed offline according to specifications prepared when the ordering library became an RLIN participant. Like other bibliographic utilities, RLIN can print catalog cards in a wide range of formats. RLIN participants can have their online records converted to

MARC-format magnetic tapes suitable for input to a local library automation system or for the production of book-form or CD-ROM catalogs. The RLIN system can also generate various types of printed reports for customers.

In addition to its operation as a bibliographic utility for technical processing, RLIN provides online access to certain subject-oriented data bases that support reference and research activities. Examples include the Avery On-Line Index, which covers architecture periodicals; the Art and Architecture Thesaurus, an authority file produced by the Art History Information Program of the J. Paul Getty Trust; the SCIPIO (Sales Catalog Index Project Input Online) data base, which contains records for art auction catalogs held by art libraries and museums; the Research-In-Progress (RIP) data base, which contains brief descriptions of recently funded art research projects plus pre-publication information from various humanities journals; the Eighteenth-Century Short Title Catalog (ESTC), which contains bibliographic records for books, broadsides, and other works published in Great Britain and its colonies between 1701 and 1800; and the RLG Conspectus data base, which contains information about RLG members' collections in various subject fields. RLIN's CitaDel service, which was introduced in 1992, provides online access to popular and scholarly bibliographic data bases, some of which are also offered by online information services described in chapter 7.

Utlas

The Utlas bibliographic utility is an outgrowth of library automation activities at the University of Toronto. Utlas traces its history to 1963, when the University of Toronto began examining the potential of computers for library operations. In the mid- to late 1960s, the university participated in the Ontario New Universities Library Project (ONULP), which resulted in a computer-produced book catalog. In the late 1960s, the library established a systems department, established a dedicated computer facility, and began to convert its bibliographic records to machine-readable form.

From its inception, the systems department was charged with responsibility for developing automated systems and services for the library community in general. In 1971, the department was reorganized as a separate administrative unit and renamed as the University of Toronto Library Automation System. The new unit was popularly identified by the uppercase, acronymic designation UTLAS. It introduced an online cataloging support system in 1973, initially to serve public and academic libraries in Ontario and Quebec. In the mid-1970s, Utlas broadened its focus to include other Canadian libraries; in 1980, the Rochester Institute of Technology became the first Utlas participant in the United States.

In 1977, Utlas was removed from the library and made an ancillary enterprise of the University of Toronto. It has experienced several organizational and ownership changes since that time. In 1983, Utlas was incorporated as an Ontario company wholly owned by the University of Toronto. In early 1985, Utlas was acquired by the International Thomson organization, a Canadian-based multinational company with broad interests in publishing and information services enterprises. It was renamed Utlas International Canada; the uppercase form of the name, which was retained for a time in some product literature, was eventually dropped. In late 1992, Utlas was acquired by ISM Information Systems Management Corporation, Canada's largest computer service bureau.

Utlas's bibliographic utility offering is called CATSS, an acronym for Cataloging Support System. Like competing services, it provides time-shared access to a large data base of bibliographic records. Unlike OCLC, Utlas is not a membership organization; libraries become Utlas customers by signing a computer services contract. As a for-profit company, Utlas markets its services to libraries of all types and sizes. At the time of this writing, it had contracts with more than 600 institutions representing more than 2,500 libraries. Approximately 90 percent of Utlas's customers are Canadian libraries.

The Maruzen Company Limited, a Tokyo-based publisher and bookseller, has been Utlas's representative in Japan since 1981. While its initial offerings were based on Utlas's North American data base and catalog access software, a Japanese-language implementation of the Utlas bibliographic utility was introduced in 1987. Called Japan CATSS, it is based on the Japan MARC format and the Japan Industrial Standard character set. The Japan CATSS data base contains more than one million bibliographic records from the National Diet Library in Tokyo, plus CJK records distributed by the Library of Congress. At the time of this writing, about 60 Japanese libraries were using either Japan CATSS or Utlas's North American CATSS data base for cataloging support. Under an experimental program, the University of Toronto library has been using the Japan CATSS system to place electronic orders for Japanese-language books with Maruzen, thereby simplifying the preparation of orders in Japanese vernacular script.

Chinese CATSS, a Chinese-language implementation of the Utlas bibliographic utility, was installed in 1989 at the National Central Library in Taiwan. At the time of this writing, it was being used by 15 libraries, including the National Central Library. The Chinese CATSS implementation is based on the Chinese MARC format and supports a larger repertoire of characters than its North American and Japanese counterparts. A Korean implementation of the CATSS data base was introduced in 1992. The Asian replications of CATSS support user messages and system prompts in five languages: English, French, Chinese, Japanese, and Korean.

The North American CATSS data base resides on computers located in Toronto. Libraries in metropolitan Toronto can access Utlas through a local telephone call. Utlas operates a private, packet-switched data communications network for Canadian libraries in high-usage areas, including Ottawa, Montreal, and Edmonton. Canadian libraries in other locations can access Utlas through Datapac, Telecom Canada's value-added network. U.S. libraries can access Utlas through Sprintnet. Japanese customers use a direct cable link to access the Japan CATSS data base, which resides on the same computers as the conventional CATSS data base. The Chinese CATSS data base is installed on computers located in Taiwan. The Korean CATSS system operates on computers located in Seoul. To effectively serve its geographically dispersed clientele, Utlas has supported a wide variety of terminals since its inception. The CATSS data base can be accessed by any library equipped with an ASCII asynchronous terminal or appropriately configured microcomputer. For the CJK character sets supported by the Asian replications of CATSS, Utlas uses microcomputers from the countries concerned.

The CATSS system is a collection of programs and data that support descriptive cataloging, subject cataloging, classification, preorder bibliographic verification, reference service, interlibrary loan, and other library operations. The counterpart of the OCLC Online Union Catalog, the CATSS data base forms the core of Utlas's operation as a bibliographic utility. It provides online access to a very large collection of cataloging records derived from subscription sources and contributed by participating libraries. The CATSS data base incorporates an impressive group of resource files, including the LC MARC data base; the CATLINE data base, produced by the National Library of Medicine; several Canadian cataloging resources, including the CANMARC data base from the National Library of Canada, the MARC Québeçoise data base from the Bibliothèque Nationale du Québec, and the CIHM data base from the Canadian Institute for Historical Microreproductions; the BNB MARC data base, produced by the British Library; the INTERMARC data base, produced by the Bibliothèque Nationale; cataloging data bases produced by the national libraries of Australia and New Zealand; cataloging records for religious books created by the American Theological Library Association; and the REMARC data base, which contains cataloging records from the shelflist of the Library of Congress prior to the inception of the MARC program.

At the time of this writing, the complete CATSS data base, including both source files and contributed cataloging, contained more than 50 million bibliographic records. Measured by the number of records available online, Utlas is second only to RLIN among bibliographic utilities. As with RLIN, the size of the CATSS data base is increased by the separate storage of duplicate and variant cataloging records derived from or contributed by individual libraries. In terms of unique records, it is smaller than the OCLC Online Union Catalog. The distinctive characteristics of the contributed cataloging segment of a given bibliographic utility's data base are determined by the number and nature of its customers. Given its history and sizable Canadian customer base, Utlas offers the best online resource for cataloging records pertaining to Canadian imprints, works about Canada, and specialized materials held by Canadian government, corporate, technical, and academic libraries.

Utlas offers powerful and flexible retrieval capabilities that are equally well suited to cataloging and reference operations. English- and French-language interfaces are provided. The CATSS data base can be searched by precise or browsable parameters. The former include such numeric identifiers as the Library of Congress Card Number, International Standard Book Number, International Standard Serial Number, National Library of

Medicine citation number, government documents control number, Canadiana number assigned by the National Library of Canada, BNQ number assigned by the Bibliothèque Nationale Québeçoise, British National Bibliography number, French National Bibliography number, and OCLC control number. Browsable searches retrieve exact or nearest matching records from alphabetically arranged indexes of authors (including personal, corporate, and conference names), titles, series, and subjects. Utlas users can also search a general index. As an interesting feature that offers flexible retrieval capabilities for users familiar with the MARC format, search statements can specify values to be matched in any field within a MARC record.

Whether precise or browsable retrieval parameters are utilized, Utlas's search procedures are straightforward. The operator simply enters a field name and search argument when the system prompts for an access key or other retrieval command. The field name may be abbreviated. Thus, a command of the form "AU/highsmith patricia" will retrieve cataloging records for all books or other works written by Patricia Highsmith, while "L/83-7164" will search for the cataloging record associated with the indicated Library of Congress Card Number. Upper- and lowercase characters can be utilized interchangeably in search statements. Punctuation and diacritics are omitted. Leading articles are omitted in title searches.

Utlas offers various capabilities for broadening or narrowing search statements. Any browsable retrieval parameter can be truncated for root word or partial name searches involving a minimum of six characters. Utlas also supports a single-character wildcard symbol in search arguments. Boolean operators can be used to link multiple search specifications in a single retrieval command. Utlas supports keyword searches but only in the second stage of a Boolean retrieval operation.

As previously noted, Utlas stores individual participants' modifications to cataloging records. The CATSS data base may consequently contain several or many cataloging records for a given item, each of the records differing only slightly from one another, if they differ at all. Cataloging records from the LC MARC data base or other source files do not take precedence over, or replace, contributed cataloging records as they do in the OCLC Online Union Catalog. When multiple cataloging records are retrieved, they are sorted in a manner specified in a user profile established at the time a library becomes an Utlas customer. Records from the library's preferred cataloging sources are at the top of the sorted list. Individual entries contain brief author and title information, and indicate the library that produced the cataloging record, the level of cataloging, and the format of the item. If the list contains an appropriate record, it can be displayed and edited—by moving, changing, deleting, or otherwise modifying individual field values—to meet local cataloging requirements. The library's customer profile determines whether a full record or selected fields are displayed for editing purposes.

If a data base search fails to identify an appropriate cataloging record, the operator activates the original cataloging mode. The system displays MARC content designators as prompts for the entry of individual data elements of a new cataloging record. Utlas participants can create full MARC or skeletal cataloging records; the latter are often created for items that are on order. Utlas does not impose minimum cataloging standards, nor does it provide formal mechanisms for reporting, detecting, and correcting errors in contributed cataloging records. Since the CATSS data base stores multiple versions of cataloging records and makes the various versions available to all participants, formal error detection procedures are less important than they are for those bibliographic utilities that maintain just one copy of a cataloging record. At the time of this writing, however, Utlas was planning a significant restructuring of its data base. For customers who maintain their principal data base on the CATSS system, Utlas will continue the current practice of maintaining copies of modified cataloging records online. For customers who maintain an online catalog on a local system and do not use CATSS for that purpose, Utlas will retain holdings information but not modified cataloging records.

Utlas offers flexible, interactive authority control capabilities. When the authority control option is selected, Utlas software automatically creates linkages between a library's bibliographic records and headings in specified authority files. The linkages ensure that the most current forms of headings are contained in bibliographic records, regardless of when the records were entered. Utlas provides online access to several authority files, including the Library of Congress Name Authority File and Subject Authority File, Library of Congress children's subject headings, the CAN-MARC Name Authority File from the National Library of Canada, Medical Subject Headings (MeSH) from the National Library of Medicine, and the Répertoire de Vedettes Matière File, a partial translation of the Library of Congress Subject Authority File prepared by Laval University. Utlas participants can also create their own authority records to reflect local cataloging practices.

Like other bibliographic utilities, Utlas can print catalog card sets in a variety of formats. In addition to main entry and other bibliographic information, catalog cards can include class numbers from any classification system printed in various card locations; added entries and subject headings; general, local, and contents notes; and location, medium, and size designations. Cards can be ordered in sets for single catalogs, in streams for multiple catalogs, or as single shelflist cards. Libraries with local automation systems can order machine-readable copies of their cataloging or authority records on magnetic tapes in a variety of MARC formats. For IBM-compatible microcomputers, Utlas offers a software package that permits downloading of bibliographic records from the CATSS data base. Utlas also offers book catalogs and keyword indexes, either printed on paper or COM-generated on microfilm or microfiche. Such catalogs may employ dictionary or divided arrangements and may be based on records selected by language, publishing medium, or other parameters.

WLN

The Western Library Network (WLN) is a general-purpose bibliographic utility offering online cataloging support and related services. Originally known as the Washington Library Network, WLN was formed in the early 1970s to support resource sharing activities by libraries in the state of Washington. Its first project, a batch-processed union catalog produced in 1972, was followed by the implementation of an online cataloging system. An early system version, introduced in 1975, became fully operational in 1977.

The WLN online system initially served 10 Washington libraries, but it quickly attracted subscribers elsewhere in the Pacific Northwest. Its customer base, which totaled about 100 libraries in the early 1980s, had more than tripled by the end of the decade. To more accurately identify its client base, the Washington Library Network changed its name to the Western Library Network in 1985. At the time of this writing, WLN had more than 750 subscribers, approximately 40 percent of which were in the state of Washington. Of the remainder, the largest concentration is located in Oregon, Idaho, Montana, Alaska, California, Arizona, and British Columbia. Through the late 1980s, WLN was a regional bibliographic utility. While its many interesting capabilities gave it national visibility, it restricted the service area for its online system to libraries in western North America, particularly the Pacific Northwest. That geographic restriction has since been removed.

WLN's organizational structure has changed several times since its inception. It originally operated as a division of the Washington State Library. In 1990, WLN became a private, not-for-profit corporation. Participation is open to libraries of all types and sizes. Its membership policy differentiates two broad types of participants: those who add records to the WLN data base and those who do not. Contributing online members access the WLN data base via online workstations. They agree to contribute original cataloging records and holdings information for new acquisitions not included in the data base, to add holdings information for all new acquisitions for which data base records already exist, to keep previously entered holdings information up to date, and to provide interlibrary loan for nonrestricted items from their collections. Contributing offline members contribute holdings to the WLN data base on magnetic tape; by using LaserCat, WLN's CD-ROM cataloging system; or through other batch input methodologies. They do not have access to the WLN data base online. Union list members add original cataloging and serials holdings information to the WLN data base for purposes of participating in a union list. Search-only members can access the WLN data base for reference, bibliographic verification, interlibrary loan, or other purposes but are not obligated to contribute original cataloging records or holdings information. At the time of this writing, approximately 400 online and offline members were contributing cataloging records and holdings information to the WLN data base.

The WLN online system operates on computer equipment located at Washington State University in Pullman. Participating libraries can access the WLN data base through leased or dial-up telephone lines. The WLN workstation is an IBM-compatible microcomputer, which can be purchased from WLN or other sources. WLN provides terminal emulation software to leased-line users.

Like its counterpart in other bibliographic utilities, the WLN data base is an online union catalog. It contains bibliographic records plus information about participants' holdings. At the time of this writing, the WLN data base contained approximately 8.5 million bibliographic records derived from the LC MARC data base, other subscription files, and member-contributed cataloging.

As one of its most important and attractive features, the WLN computer system supports a powerful and flexible group of online retrieval capabilities that are well suited to technical services and public services applications. By using online workstations, WLN participants can retrieve cataloging records by various combinations of the following numeric parameters: WLN internal sequence number, WLN record ID number, International Standard Book Number, International Standard Serial Number, Library of Congress Card Number, and publisher's number for music. Cataloging records can also be retrieved by keywords in titles; exact, keyword, or truncated personal, corporate, and conference names used in main or added entries; exact, keyword, or truncated series; keywords in untraced series; exact, keyword, or truncated subject headings; exact, keyword, or truncated uniform titles used in main or added entries; and keywords in contents notes. WLN's retrieval software also permits forward and backward browsing of cataloging records by title in alphabetical sequence.

Search statements consist of a command, a field name, and a data value to be matched. Field names can be abbreviated. Thus, a statement of the form "find i 0444877657" will locate a cataloging record for the book identified by the indicated International Standard Book Number. Similarly, a search command of the form "find t management" will retrieve cataloging records containing the word "management" in the title field. Search terms can be truncated after three characters. Boolean operators can be used to construct complex retrieval specifications.

To catalog a specific book or other item, a WLN participant uses one of the retrieval parameters outlined in the preceding section to search the data base for an appropriate bibliographic record, which may have been loaded from a subscription source file or contributed by a participating library. If existing cataloging copy is available, it can be displayed in the full MARC format for editing; the WLN operator can move, delete, change, or otherwise modify individual field values to meet local cataloging requirements. The library's call number and any related location indicators are added to the record as holdings information that is stored in a separate file that is linked to bibliographic records. To facilitate interlibrary loan, the online display of holdings symbols includes local call numbers and other location indicators.

If a data base search fails to identify an appropriate cataloging record, contributing online members must perform original cataloging and add the record to the WLN data base. As with other bibliographic utilities, data entry is simplified by displayed workforms appropriate to the type of material being cataloged. All WLN contributing online members agree to accept the latest versions of the Anglo-American Cataloging Rules; the Standard Bibliographic Description; Library of Congress name, series, and subject authorities; and the full USMARC data entry format. The WLN system has several features that promote input quality. The online CHECK command checks all headings in a cataloging record against authority files to determine whether they are authorized forms. WLN provides online access to Library of Congress authority records. The online INSERT command allows the user to search and select a heading from an authority file for automatic insertion into a cataloging record.

As a distinctive feature of WLN input procedures, all contributed cataloging records—as well as records received from external subscription services—are subject to a series of formal and selective computer and human reviews. Such reviews are designed to maintain a high-quality data base with consistent descriptive cataloging, appropriate headings, and accurately applied MARC content designators. Computer programs examine each record for inappropriate content designators, suspicious subfield codes, and other potential problems. Programs also match name, subject, and series headings against authority records. If a heading matches an unauthorized form—that is, one that contains a "see" reference to a single authorized heading—it is automatically changed to the authorized form before the cataloging record is added to the data base. If such a change cannot be made—as would be the case with "see" references that point to two or more authorized headings—the cataloging record is returned to the originating library with explanatory messages.

Cataloging records contributed by WLN participants enter a working file for review by WLN staff members. While the utility's original intention was to review all records prior to inclusion in the data base, its staff is not large enough to perform such reviews in a manner compatible with timely data base updates. Comprehensive reviews are limited to cataloging records contributed by new subscribers. Records contributed by other libraries may be reviewed selectively, depending on the quality of the library's cataloging. Any library can request the review of a specific cataloging record. If a problem is suspected, the record can be routed back to the originating library with a message indicating the appropriate corrective action. Cataloging records received from the Library of Congress and other subscription services are automatically matched against the WLN data base. Such records are generally added to the data base without review unless they will replace records that have been used by one or more WLN participants and the machine matching was inconclusive.

WLN can print catalog cards and labels according to library-prepared profiles that specify card quantities, call number types and formats, and subject heading sources. Printed cards can contain LC or Dewey Decimal classification numbers. WLN also offers special call number treatments for biography, fiction, and juvenile materials. Libraries can create multiple profiles to address the varying requirements of different branches or special collections. WLN participants can also obtain machine-readable cataloging records on magnetic tapes or diskettes for input to local library automation systems. Other output products include CD-ROM catalogs, COM catalogs, paper book-form catalogs, printed bibliographies, and shelf-list reports.

Other Utilities

Although they are not as widely publicized as OCLC, RLIN, Utlas, and WLN, several other companies and organizations offer cataloging support services typically associated with bibliographic utilities. Examples include the AGILE III system from Auto-Graphics Incorporated, Brodart's Interactive Access System, and Open DRANET from Data Research Associates.

The AGILE III system is the latest version of a bibliographic utility developed in the late 1970s and formally introduced in 1981. Like other utilities, it offers online access to subscription files and contributed cataloging. Its largest and most important subscription resource is the LC MARC data base. It also provides a data base of cataloging records prepared by Auto-Graphics itself for pre-1968 imprints not included in the LC MARC data base. The Auto-Graphics data base contains approximately half a million cataloging records for books in various languages, plus additional records for serials, musical scores, sound recordings, visual materials, and maps.

Because it has fewer participants than the bibliographic utilities described above, AGILE III provides a much smaller collection of contributed cataloging records. Contributed cataloging records are stored in separate participants' files that are individually searchable. AGILE III users have the option of storing their cataloging records in shared or private files. If the shared file option is selected, a library's cataloging records are available on a reciprocal basis to other AGILE III participants. Cataloging records stored in private files are not accessible to other participants, but libraries that select the private file option cannot access other participants' files.

AGILE III stores all records in the MARC format. It supports a flexible and convenient group of online retrieval capabilities that are well suited to cataloging support and resource sharing applications. To retrieve cataloging copy for a given item, an operator must specify data base segments to be searched and the sequence in which searches will be performed. As an example, a participant's own segment of the data base may be searched first, followed by the LC MARC file, followed by other libraries' files—assuming, as discussed above, that they are shared files. Once a search path is specified, cataloging records can be retrieved by various parameters, including author, title, subject, internal accession number, Library of Congress Card Number, International Standard Book Number, International Standard Serial Number, and publisher's number for music.

Numeric search procedures are straightforward. To initiate a search, the user types the identifier for the desired numeric parameter and enters the appropriate value. To conduct an author or title search, an operator types the author's name, surname first, or up to 59 characters of the title in a term entry window. Subject searching is optionally available. Searches can be qualified by publication date, record type, language, and keywords.

If an appropriate cataloging record is located, it is copied into a temporary working file. During this transfer procedure, the AGILE III system eliminates data elements, such as local call numbers, that are specific to the source from which the record was derived. The working file copy is then displayed for editing—by moving, changing, deleting, or otherwise modifying individual field values—to meet local cataloging requirements. When editing is completed, the system assigns a unique accession number. Batch processing routines will later add the new record to the user's segment of the AGILE III data base. The cataloging record on which the edited record was based is unaffected by any changes made to it. Once entered in a shared file, the modified cataloging record is available to other AGILE III participants. Newly entered records are indexed prior to inclusion in the data base and are immediately searchable. A record will remain in a given library's segment of the data base until it is deleted by the library that entered it.

If a data base search fails to identify an appropriate cataloging record, the AGILE III operator places the system in the original cataloging mode by selecting the New Input option from the main menu, and contributes a new cataloging record to the data base. If the contributing library is a shared file participant, the new record will be accessible to other AGILE III customers. In the original cataloging mode, the user specifies a format (book, serial, map, etc.) for the item to be cataloged, and AGILE III displays a data entry workform appropriate to that format. Unlike OCLC and WLN, Auto-Graphics does not require that participants use the AGILE III system for all of their cataloging activity, although it is presumably advantageous for them to do so.

For both original and copy cataloging, AGILE III automatically validates MARC tags, indicators, and subfield codes for each field in which data are entered or modified. The system displays a warning message if errors are detected, and will not store the incorrect record unless the user specifically overrides the validation. AGILE III does not impose minimum cataloging standards, however, nor does it provide formal mechanisms for reporting, detecting, and correcting cataloging errors.

In addition to maintaining cataloging records, the AGILE III system can store a library's name and subject authority records in the MARC format. As an unusual feature of particular interest to public libraries, AGILE III users can create information and referral (I&R) records describing government agencies, professional associations, and other organizations that provide community services of interest to a given library's clientele. Typically, a separate record is created for each community service program. Records can be retrieved by internal control number, agency name, and program name. Subject retrieval is optionally available.

The AGILE III system supports local printing of catalog cards. Libraries can also obtain cataloging records in the MARC format on magnetic tape. Auto-Graphics can also produce COM catalogs, printed bibliographies, and other output products to address specific library requirements.

The Interactive Access System (IAS) is a bibliographic utility operated by the Brodart Automation division of the Brodart Company, a well-known supplier of library materials and services. Brodart uses the Interactive Access System for its own cataloging and retrospective conversion services. It has offered it to libraries as an online cataloging support service since 1982. As a general-purpose bibliographic utility, the Interactive

Access System is available to libraries of all types and sizes, regardless of geographic location. At the time of this writing, it was being used for online cataloging by a number of public libraries, school library systems, and academic libraries.

The IAS data base combines cataloging records from subscription sources with those contributed by participants. The LC MARC data base is the largest subscription resource. IAS also offers the Brodart MARC data base, which contains more than 2.5 million cataloging records created by Brodart's Books Division and by retrospective conversion projects undertaken by Brodart Automation for specific customers. It is divided into separate segments for print and nonprint materials.

Like AGILE III, the Interactive Access System stores individual participants' cataloging records—including original cataloging as well as modified versions of cataloging records created by others—in separate, individually identifiable and searchable segments of the IAS data base. IAS participants have access to cataloging records created by other participants unless a given library specifically prohibits such access. When libraries become IAS participants, they obtain access to the LC MARC and Brodart MARC segments of the data base plus their choice of data files created by other IAS participants. The Interactive Access System stores all cataloging records in the MARC format.

To locate cataloging copy for a particular item, an IAS operator completes a displayed workform which lists searchable fields with adjacent blank spaces for the entry of data values to be matched. The IAS data base can be searched by various combinations of the following parameters: Library of Congress Card Number, International Standard Book Number, International Standard Serial Number, internal control number, personal or corporate author, title, and subject. As a potentially useful feature that is supported by some public access catalog programs, the Interactive Access System supports anyword searches based on any number of words from author, title, and subject fields, up to a maximum of 150 characters. All IAS searches employ keyword concepts. Partial titles can be entered in any word sequence. The Boolean AND operator is implied when two or more words are included in a retrieval specification. For Boolean OR searches, words can be enclosed in parentheses.

The IAS system searches a library's own data file first to confirm that the library has not already cataloged the item in question. Failing to locate an appropriate record, the system will then search other files in a sequence specified in a profile created when a library becomes an IAS participant. A retrieved cataloging record is copied into the user's working file. A Brodart Access Number is assigned, and the record is displayed with MARC tags for review and editing to meet local requirements. Displayed records can be modified by deleting or typing over existing characters. The original cataloging record is unaffected by such changes. While any field within a bibliographic record can be modified, the Interactive Access System can restrict the editing capabilities of specific users to designated fields. In a multibranch or consortium installation where cataloging is performed by a central staff, for example, individual libraries' modifications might be limited to holdings fields within data base records. Specific editing privileges are determined by passwords. When cataloging a subsequent edition of a previously cataloged item, a library can make a copy of the existing record in its own data file and edit the copy.

If an appropriate bibliographic record cannot be located in IAS source files, the workstation operator activates the original cataloging mode. The system displays a formatted screen that includes commonly utilized fields from within MARC records. Other fields can be added as needed. When entry of catalog data is completed, the record is added to the library's data file. Brodart does not require participants to contribute original cataloging records to the IAS data base, but most libraries will find the system simpler and easier to use than conventional cataloging methodologies. IAS participants can delete records from their data files at any time. Brodart does not impose minimum cataloging standards on IAS participants, nor does it provide formal mechanisms for reporting, detecting, and correcting cataloging errors.

Catalog cards can be printed locally. IAS participants can obtain cataloging records in the USMARC or OCLC MARC format on magnetic tape for entry into local automation systems or for other purposes. Brodart can also generate printed book catalogs, subject bibliographies, COM catalogs, and CD-ROM catalogs to customer specifications.

Open DRANET is a bibliographic utility operated by Data Research Associates (DRA), a leading supplier of minicomputer-based integrated library systems that support public catalog access, circulation control, and other operations. Open DRANET is an outgrowth of DRANET, a computer service established in 1980 as an online cataloging utility for customers of DRA's library automation systems. Over time, DRANET incorporated additional information resources, including subject-oriented data bases that contain citations to journal articles and other publications. In 1992, the DRANET service became available to all libraries, whether or not they utilize DRA as their automation vendor. It was renamed Open DRANET to reflect its broadened availability.

As its principal cataloging resource, Open DRANET provides online access to the LC MARC data base. Data bases produced by other libraries are accessible by individual arrangements with those institutions. Cataloging records can be retrieved by author, title, original record control number, call number, Library of Congress Card Number, International Standard Book Number, and International Standard Serial Number. Search specifications indicate the field to be searched and a character string to be matched. Thus, a command of the form "T=STRANGERS ON A TRAIN" will retrieve cataloging records for books of that title. For author searches, the last names are entered first. To be matched correctly, numeric search keys must be entered in the exact manner in which they appear within the cataloging records. Any search key can be truncated.

Retrieved records can be edited, augmented, or otherwise modified to meet local requirements. If a cataloging record is retrieved from the LC MARC data base or another library's data base, it is copied for editing purposes into the participant's own data base, which resides on a local automation system. The original cataloging record is unaffected by such copying or editing operations. When editing is completed, the record is saved in the participant's local data base, and a control number is assigned to it. As an unusual and potentially useful capability, an Open DRANET participant can overlay a record from another data base onto a record for the same title in its own data base. Participants can specify fields to be retained during the overlay procedure.

To facilitate cataloging operations, Open DRANET provides online access to the Library of Congress Name Authority File and Subject Authority File. As a useful feature, a verification command can be used to compare headings in cataloging records to those in a specified authority file.

The foregoing discussion has emphasized U.S. and Canadian bibliographic utilities, some of which are available internationally. Similar bibliographic utilities and cooperative cataloging systems have been implemented by national libraries and other organizations in Europe and the Pacific Rim. Examples include the British Library's BLAISE-LINE service, the Australian Bibliographic Network (ABN), and the Dutch Project for Integrated Catalogue Automation (PICA).

COMPUTER-BASED CATALOG PRODUCTION

The automation of descriptive cataloging addresses only one part of the cataloging activity. Libraries are also interested in automated approaches to the production, maintenance, and use of their catalogs. While some of the computer-based descriptive cataloging systems and services described in the preceding sections include a catalog production component, many of them were originally developed to print catalog cards. Although all bibliographic utilities offer subscribers the option of ordering machine-readable cataloging records on magnetic tape, their card production activities remain substantial. At OCLC, where card production is sometimes regarded as an interim output activity pending the development of automated catalogs by member libraries, several million cards are printed each year.

The Problem of Card Catalogs

Librarians have long recognized the many problems associated with the production, maintenance, and use of card catalogs. Writing in the 1940s, Fremont Rider pointed out the substantial amounts of space consumed by the card catalogs of research libraries. Today, at a time of high construction costs and greatly diminished capital funds for new library buildings, the efficient use of available floor space remains an important concern among libraries of all sizes and types. Card catalogs also require expensive cabinets. A frequently cited 1969 study by R&D Consultants found that the typical 60-drawer card catalog cabinet contains 43,200 cards when filled to 60 percent of capacity. At the time this chapter was written, such a cabinet cost several thousand dollars. Assuming an average of six cards per title, the catalog of a library with a monograph collection of 100,000 titles would occupy more than $30,000 worth of cabinets. Assuming a new acquisitions rate of 10,000 titles per year, more than $6,000 would have to be spent every two years for additional cabinets. Additional expenditures will be required for work tables customarily provided in the card catalog area.

As previously noted, card catalog cabinets and related furnishings can require considerable space. Assuming an average of 20 square feet for each cabinet and its required adjacent aisle and work space, the card catalog for a collection of 100,000 titles will occupy approximately 280 square feet of contiguous floor space, a portion of which might be put to other uses were the catalog converted to a more compact format. At a rate of 10,000 new titles per year, an additional 30 square feet will be required to accommodate annual catalog growth. If the collection is not weeded, the size of the catalog will double in 10 years.

While the floor space and furnishings required to maintain card catalogs can entail substantial expenses, the labor required to establish and maintain card catalogs is even more costly. Such labor involves the creation of the cards themselves, whether ordered in printed form or generated internally; the sorting and interfiling of new cards; and the removal, modification, and refiling of existing cards. Similar labor must be expended in the production and maintenance of guide cards, cross-reference cards, and authority files. Of these tasks, the creation of catalog cards has been directly affected by the automated systems described in preceding sections; computer-produced cards can be ordered from bibliographic utilities, printed locally by CD-ROM cataloging support systems, or purchased from book jobbers. Alternatively, most word processing programs offer text-editing capabilities suitable for the automated production of catalog card sets. Such word processing systems can be used in conjunction with MARCFICHE or other MARC-derivative, COM-generated bibliographic products described earlier in this chapter.

Utilization of a bibliographic utility or self-contained card production system does nothing, however, for other aspects of catalog maintenance. While cards may be printed automatically, they must still be filed manually. Assuming that a library assistant can file an average of one card per minute, then the annual acquisition of 10,000 titles will necessitate the filing of 60,000 cards at an expenditure of 1,000 hours, or one-half of a person-year. In many libraries, this expenditure is doubled by the use of additional labor to check newly filed cards for correct placement before their permanent inclusion in the catalog. In some cases, the lack of sufficient labor for catalog maintenance results in considerable delays in the filing of newly produced records. Consequently, some cards never enter the catalog. As an example, libraries that acquire micropublished collections consisting of multiple titles are often unable to allocate the labor required for the filing of the printed catalog cards that may accompany such collections.

Similar substantial costs are incurred in the removal of previously filed cards as collections are weeded, location information is added to or deleted from union catalogs, or existing file headings are modified to conform to revised cataloging practices. The cost of such heading modifications gained considerable prominence when the Anglo-American Cataloging Rules were revised. A study by the Library of Congress indicated that full implementation of the provisions of AACR2 would necessitate changes in at least 37 percent of the form of headings then in use by LC and that the changes would require modification of at least 49 percent of LC catalog cards. High as they are, such percentages do not reflect the impact of revised rules for corporate authorship which would necessitate additional card modifications reflecting changes in the choice of headings. Presumably, comparable modifications would be required in other libraries, each modification involving the removal and refiling of the affected cards. As a further source of potential expenditures to those libraries desiring to make their cataloging practices conform to those of the Library of Congress, LC closed its card catalog in favor of a computer-based system in 1981. As several librarians have pointed out, the Library of Congress has in the past been constrained in changing headings by the inconvenience inherent in having to manually modify its own card catalog. Since such constraints no longer apply, LC catalogers will presumably be inclined to make more heading changes in the future.

The expense of file maintenance aside, card catalogs offer only limited performance and convenience, both for library users and for libraries themselves. Except where telephone inquiries are accepted, a user must visit a library to consult its catalog, even though time might potentially be saved if users could determine in advance whether a given item is in the library's holdings. Ideally, a university library's catalog should be readily accessible to faculty members in individual departments; a technical library's catalog should be available in user work areas; and a public library's catalog might be consulted in schools, stores, and even homes. Unfortunately, the cost of production, floor space, cabinets, and file maintenance discussed above prevent the replication of all or portions of conventional card catalogs. The necessity of maintaining a union catalog in a system headquarters or other centralized location is especially constraining in multibranch libraries and library systems. In such cases, library users are denied convenient access to information about system-wide holdings. In addition, the time and cost of resource sharing may be significantly increased by the necessity of routing all interlibrary loan requests to the central union catalog where library locations can alone be determined. If the union catalog were conveniently accessible in individual libraries, the holding library could be determined and contacted directly by the borrowing institution.

Additional limitations make card catalogs inconvenient for library users. As an example, individual cards cannot be removed from the catalog for photocopying. The user must, instead, take notes, usually while standing at work tables. Although many libraries consider the card catalog an important local bibliographic resource rather than a mere location device, they rarely provide a comfortable work setting for its prolonged use. Critics of card catalogs further point out the limited number of access points they provide, noting, for example, that users cannot retrieve books by title keywords and that searches involving the logical coordination of several headings cannot be conveniently performed. While there is no intellectual impediment to the making of additional catalog cards for title keywords or other parameters, such a practice would significantly increase the size of the catalog, compounding the space consumption and file maintenance problems noted above. Expense aside, the logical coordination of headings cannot be conveniently implemented with card-form catalogs.

As a further shortcoming, card catalogs are vulnerable to intentional or inadvertent damage or destruction. Individual cards are subject to wear and tear in daily use, and the entire card catalog or substantial portions of it can be destroyed by fire or vandalism. Because the card catalog is a unique and vital operating record which if damaged or destroyed would seriously impair a library's ability to function, a protective microfilming program may need to be initiated to produce a backup copy. In addition, older catalog cards that are in poor condition must be periodically replaced, thus increasing maintenance costs.

Retrospective Conversion

Presumably, some or all of the problems discussed in the preceding section could be minimized or eliminated by the replacement of card catalogs with the computer-based book-form or online catalogs described later in this chapter. The implementation of such catalogs requires, however, the conversion of a library's catalog records to machine-readable, computer-processible form. Such conversion can be relatively easily accomplished for cataloging records pertaining to recent or ongoing acquisitions. As previously noted, libraries subscribing to one of the bibliographic utilities can order archival magnetic tapes containing machine-readable records for the items they have cataloged since becoming subscribers. Depending on the particular bibliographic utility used, archival tapes may be available on a quarterly, monthly, or more frequent basis. Libraries using CD-ROM cataloging support products also create machine-readable versions of cataloging records. As an additional source of machine-readable cataloging data, libraries that purchase books and other materials through jobbers can often obtain magnetic tapes containing machine-readable records that reflect their acquisitions for a specified period of time. Some book jobbers maintain machine-readable data bases of MARC records supplemented by local cataloging which can be used for this purpose.

Thus, many libraries can readily obtain machine-readable versions of records acquired and cataloged since the mid-1970s or, in some cases, earlier. For the implementation of book-form or online catalogs, these machine-readable records can be used as input to a local computer system, although software must usually be developed to convert them to a format appropriate to local use. The retrospective conversion of older catalog records, however, presents more serious problems. Unfortunately, variations in typography and quality prevent the use of optical character recognition (OCR) to convert the information content of existing catalog cards to machine-readable form. Existing catalog records can, of course, be converted by direct data entry—that is, keystroking—but that is a conversion technique of last resort. The preferred retrospective conversion method involves the use of abbreviated keystroking to search for and obtain machine-readable copies of cataloging records from existing resource data bases.

While some libraries may purchase or otherwise acquire the machine-readable catalog of a comparable library against which their own holdings will be matched, the data bases offered by bibliographic utilities and CD-ROM cataloging support products are the most important and widely used sources of cataloging copy for retrospective conversion. Although the LC MARC resource records maintained by all bibliographic utilities and CD-ROM products primarily pertain to post-1968 imprints, they do include some earlier titles converted through the previously discussed RECON project and COMARC program, as well as occasional pre-1968 imprints acquired and cataloged by the Library of Congress since the inception of the MARC Distribution Service. More importantly, cataloging contributed by subscribers of bibliographic utilities includes many records for older imprints entered by libraries that either have recently acquired and cataloged those items or had previously contributed them as part of their own retrospective conversion projects. As a previously noted advantage, the Utlas data base incorporates REMARC records, which are an excellent resource for retrospective conversion.

The use of bibliographic utilities and CD-ROM cataloging support products for retrospective conversion involves straightforward work steps. A bibliographic data base is searched to obtain cataloging copy for each record in a library's shelflist or card catalog. To simplify input and speed response, records are typically searched by LC card number or another unique identifier. If an appropriate bibliographic record is retrieved, it can be edited to conform to local cataloging practice, and—in the case of bibliographic utilities—the library's holdings symbol is added to it. Records processed in this manner can be ordered from a bibliographic utility in machine-readable form on magnetic tape. With CD-ROM cataloging support products, the records are transferred from the CD-ROM data base to a hard disk drive from which they may later be copied onto tapes or diskettes. To eliminate the need for magnetic tape or diskette preparation, several vendors of automated catalog access and circulation control systems have developed interfaces that permit the direct transfer of records retrieved from bibliographic utilities and CD-ROM data bases.

The retrieval and modification of existing resource records, while still time-consuming and labor-intensive, will prove faster and less expensive than full keystroking of the information content of a library's shelflist. It also results in a MARC-format record. Full keystroking of original cataloging records remains necessary, however, for items not found in data bases provided by bibliographic utilities or CD-ROM cataloging support products. In such cases, the library uses cataloging copy from its shelflist or card catalog as the basis for input. Items cataloged in this manner can likewise be ordered on magnetic tape or, in the case of CD-ROM products, captured on a hard disk drive for later transfer to a local catalog access or book catalog production system. Alternatively, MARC-format cataloging records retrieved from a CD-ROM data base can be transferred to floppy disks and sent to the CD-ROM system vendor for conversion to a magnetic tape suitable for input to a local library automation system.

Several bibliographic utilities offer products that permit the offline preparation of identifiers for records to be converted. As an example, OCLC's CAT ME Plus (Cataloging Micro Enhancer Plus) is a batch-oriented retrospective conversion program for OCLC M300 series workstations and other IBM-compatible microcomputers. Working from a shelflist or other card file, a CAT ME Plus user prepares diskettes that include a search key to identify the materials for which records are to be converted, accompanied by call numbers, holdings information, and other local data. Once prepared, the diskettes are shipped to OCLC's retrospective conversion unit, which retrieves the indicated MARC-format cataloging records from the Online Union Catalog, adds the library-supplied local information, and transfers the results to magnetic tape for delivery to the customer. CAT ME Plus can also upload modified records and original cataloging to the Online Union Catalog. Because it supports automatic log-on procedures at a time specified by the user, CAT ME Plus can be used for current cataloging and retrospective conversion during evening hours when OCLC's rates are lower and a library's cataloging department is either closed or operating with a small staff.

The WLN Recon System and RLIN BRCON 2 program are conceptually similar offerings. With the WLN Recon System, a library submits search keys to WLN on diskettes prepared by IBM-compatible or Apple microcomputers. The search key can include a Library of Congress Card Number, title, publisher, date, edition, WLN Record ID number, or other information, accompanied by a local call number. The search keys are matched against the WLN data base. When an exact match between a Recon search key and a cataloging record is detected, the library's call number and holdings symbol are added to the WLN data base and the record is transferred, in the full MARC format, to a magnetic tape. Printed edit lists are produced for unmatched items.

Using an IBM-compatible microcomputer and software provided by RLG, an RLIN BRCON 2 customer likewise creates brief search records that contain minimal bibliographic information plus call numbers and other holdings data for titles to be converted. The search records are captured on a diskette, which is mailed to RLG for matching against the RLIN data base; alternatively, the search records can be uploaded electronically to RLG. In either case, BRCON 2 search records that match a single source record in the RLIN data base generate new cataloging records based on the data provided. Customers can specify the cataloging level—full, basic, or unknown—required for an acceptable match, although the highest hit rate is obtained by accepting records cataloged at any level. Printed reports indicate records for which matches exist at lower cataloging levels, allowing libraries to resubmit the records and override the default cataloging requirements. If desired, BRCON 2 matches can be limited to records in roman or vernacular scripts.

Taking a different approach, the Utlas DisCon system combines batch-oriented retrospective conversion with CD-ROM cataloging support. A microcomputer-based workstation includes millions of abbreviated records from the MARC and REMARC data bases on CD-ROM discs. A library searches the data bases to locate items contained in its shelflist. Software supports retrieval by LC Card Number, title, series, and alternate titles. LC MARC records can also be searched by International Standard Book Number. Title searches can be qualified by author, edition, publisher, place of publication, or date. When a record is retrieved, a call number and other local data can be entered into displayed workforms. The record is then transferred to a diskette for mailing to Utlas, which will extract the corresponding complete MARC records from the CATSS data base, add local data from the diskettes, and ship them to the customer on magnetic tape. Brief identifying information and local data, extracted from shelflists or other library files, can be entered for items not located in the DisCon data base.

In addition to bibliographic utilities and CD-ROM products, machine-readable cataloging records can be obtained from book jobbers and other companies that specialize in retrospective conversion services. Examples include Auto-Graphics, Brodart, Baker and Taylor, General Research Corporation, Marcive Incorporated, and Inforonics. As described above, libraries typically supply lists of LC card numbers or other identifiers for desired records. These identifiers may be supplied on diskettes for batch processing against the vendor's data base; alternatively, a library may send its shelflist to the retrospective conversion company. In either case, the conversion company furnishes MARC format records on magnetic tape for input to mainframe and minicomputer-based library automation systems or on diskettes for input to microcomputer-based systems. In the latter case, most retrospective conversion companies can supply MARC records in the MicroLIF format, which is accepted by most microcomputer-based library automation systems.

While the use of bibliographic utilities or other sources of machine-readable data can facilitate retrospective conversion, a conversion project may prove too expensive for a given library. As a potential limitation, the retrospective conversion techniques described above are not invariably applicable to cataloging records created in nonroman character sets. Most existing data bases and local computer systems cannot accommodate such records without transliteration, a practice that librarians and users often find unacceptable or, at best, confusing. Given these constraints, some libraries that have implemented computer-based book-form or online catalogs have decided to "close" or "freeze" their card catalogs rather than convert existing records to machine-readable form.

As used in this context, closing theoretically means that no additional records will be entered into the card catalog after some predetermined date. In effect, a static, retrospective card catalog will coexist with a growing computer-based book-form or online catalog. For some libraries, the implementation of AACR2, with its revised rules for choice and form of headings, increased the attraction of closing an existing catalog, much of which would require modification if converted to machine-readable form. With the card catalog closed, the new rules could then be adopted for ongoing cataloging work.

In actual practice, however, the complexity of library activities and bibliographic records rarely permits the complete closing of a card catalog. The two most common catalog closing strategies, which are based on cataloging date and imprint date, are each limited in several important respects. In the former instance, all records for items cataloged after a predetermined date are entered into a library's computer-based catalog, regardless of the imprint date of the item. While this is probably the simplest closing strategy from the cataloging department's standpoint, open entries for serials, series, and multivolume sets must be removed before closing. In addition, users seeking older imprints must consult both the retrospective and current catalogs, as must the library staff when using the catalog for bibliographic verification and reference.

While a closing strategy based on imprint date may be more convenient for the library user, it does not permit a complete closing of a card catalog, since older imprints may be acquired and cataloged in the future. Records for such items must be added to the card catalog. If separate sets of rules are applied to the old and new catalogs, catalogers must be trained in both sets. A closing strategy based on imprint date does, however, permit the continued maintenance of open entries in the card catalog. An additional problem for research libraries is that neither of these closing strategies addresses the handling of records in nonroman languages. Although some computer systems can accommodate bibliographic records written in Cyrillic, Hebrew, Farsi, Arabic, and other nonroman alphabets, most cannot. Unless transliteration is acceptable, the card catalog must remain open for such records, as well as for those containing the ideographic symbols used in the Chinese, Japanese, and Korean languages.

Even when a card catalog is completely closed, a library must continue to maintain it. Cards will remain subject to wear and tear, necessitating some replacement activity. Similarly, heading changes will be required to maintain compatibility with a library's ongoing computer-based catalog. If separate cataloging rules are used for the two catalogs, some cross-references will be required.

Book-form Catalogs

Once cataloging data have been converted to machine-readable form, they can be stored on disks for online access or be batch-processed to produce book-form catalogs. Broadly defined, a book-form catalog consists of successive bibliographic records listed in a page format on paper or microforms. The specific content and appearance of individual entries will vary with application requirements. Book-form catalogs produced by research libraries, for example, typically provide full bibliographic records for main entries, the data being formatted in the familiar image of a catalog card. In contrast, the book-form catalog of a corporate library may consist of a simple register of abbreviated entries designed primarily as a finding list. In either case, book-form catalogs, like their card-form counterparts, may use either a dictionary or a divided arrangement.

Book-form catalogs were widely used by American libraries through the nineteenth century. During the early part of the twentieth century, however, they were largely displaced by card catalogs, which could be more quickly and easily updated. Because it cannot reflect items cataloged or weeded in the interval between printings, the book-form catalog of a changing collection is necessarily an incomplete bibliographic resource. Book-form catalogs are typically updated by periodic supplements which are themselves out of date by the time they reach the library user. Card catalogs, on the other hand, can be updated at any time by the insertion of cards for newly cataloged items or the removal of cards for items that have been removed from the library's collections. The renewed interest in book-form catalogs which characterized the late 1970s and early 1980s apparently reflected a willingness to sacrifice this immediate updatability for certain operational advantages not offered by card catalogs. Foremost among these is the ability to distribute copies of a book-form catalog to multiple locations, thereby permitting remote access to information about a given library's holdings and facilitating resource sharing. As a result, book-form union catalogs have proven especially popular with multi-branch libraries and library systems.

While book-form catalogs have been created by sequential card photography and other semi-automated techniques, computer-produced book-form catalogs were among the earliest examples of library automation. Computer preparation of book-form catalogs can lower production time and costs while eliminating the labor-intensive file maintenance routines associated with card catalogs. In addition, the storage of catalog records in machine-readable form can minimize or eliminate cabinet purchases and reduce floor space requirements, although the printed catalogs themselves and related processing and support equipment may require as much or more space than a card catalog in some installations. As a further advantage, computer-stored catalog records can be duplicated for protection against damage or destruction, and the existence of multiple copies of a book-form catalog affords additional vital records protection.

As with the other automated activities discussed in this book, computer production of a book-form catalog is accomplished by one or more application programs. These programs may be custom-developed by a library for its own use, acquired from another library, or adapted from prewritten software packages. Alternatively, several bibliographic utilities, various book jobbers, and other companies can produce book-form catalogs from machine-readable bibliographic data provided by a given library. Widely used since the 1960s, these services permit the implementation of book-form catalogs by libraries lacking the requisite in-house hardware and software resources. In most cases, they can accept input in the form of archival tapes produced by one or more of the bibliographic utilities.

From the data processing standpoint, book-form catalogs are essentially computer-generated reports that are produced by processing machine-readable bibliographic data in the batch mode. As such, they are analogous to the printed reports that support circulation control or other library activities. Depending on the amount of data involved and other application characteristics, book-form catalogs can be printed on paper or microforms. The suitability of the available paper printers for book catalog production depends on the number of records to be printed and the library's typographic and quality requirements. Where the number of records to be printed is small (perhaps several hundred pages or less) and output quality is a secondary consideration, simple dot matrix printers, installed at local workstations and operating at speeds of up to 250 characters per second, may be used. Such devices can often print accent marks, diacritics, and other symbols used in bibliographic data, but they do not produce fully formed, typewriter-quality characters. They are consequently most useful for the production of a few copies of brief finding lists or bibliographies of transient significance.

The chain-type line printers encountered in mainframe and minicomputer installations can operate at speeds ranging from several hundred to several thousand lines per minute, but their suitability for book catalog production is often limited by operational and aesthetic factors. Typical line printer output consists of 11-by-14-inch, fan-folded, edge-punched paper, which is subsequently bound between pressboard covers. Book-form catalogs printed and bound in this manner are unattractive, can be awkward to handle, and seldom prove durable in extensive use. While some line printers can be equipped with a print chain containing the special characters and symbols used in bibliographic data, their output quality does not approach that of laser printers discussed above. Although chain-type line printers produce fully formed characters, tonality is often uneven and lines may be imperfectly aligned. In addition, the use of an extended character set will significantly reduce printing speed.

As further constraint on output quality and speed, most chain-type line printers use carbon-interleaved paper in combination with repeated print runs to create multiple copies. Thus, 20 copies of a book-form catalog would most likely be produced by printing the job five times using four-ply paper or four times using five-ply paper. In either case, the resulting copies will not be of uniform quality, and the total printing time may be very long. At 500 lines per minute, for example, the printing of 20 copies of a 600-page catalog could take six hours or longer, with additional time required for the separating, binding, and distribution of individual copies. As an alternative noted above, photocopying or offset printing can be used to produce multiple copies from a master created by a line printer. While this technique produces copies of uniform quality, it requires considerable manual intervention.

Laser printers are preferred for applications requiring high quality and varied typographic capabilities. They print onto single sheets of letter-size bond paper rather than the fan-folded stock used by chain printers and dot matrix printers. With some devices, pages can be printed on both sides of a sheet of paper. Alternatively, type may be reduced to fit four or even six page-images on a double-sided sheet. Laser printers can intermix typefaces, sizes, and styles within a single page. Vertical and horizontal spacing can be adjusted to meet special application requirements. Desktop publishing programs, as described in chapter 2, provide flexible page layout capabilities. Because multiple copies are created by successive printer runs rather than with carbon paper, quality is uniform. Alternatively, multiple copies can be produced by photocopiers. Various hardcover and softcover binding techniques can be used to package individual copies for distribution.

Employed in in-house installations or through service bureaus, computer-based phototypesetting and photocomposition devices offer the highest output quality and greatest typographic versatility. Computer-driven phototypesetters are nonimpact printers that produce typeset text on photosensitive paper or film. While older models maintained a master matrix of type styles as photographic images on internally stored disks, drums, or strips, newer electronic phototypesetters generate individual characters from digitally stored definitions. In either case, the phototypesetter responds to computer-processed data and commands, printing the typeset text as continuous lines and paragraphs on long sheets of paper. With conventional phototypesetters, page layouts are manually created by cutting and pasting. A photocomposer is a more sophisticated phototypesetting device that performs page makeup automatically. With both phototypesetters and photocomposers, page layouts are usually converted to offset masters for printing. Individual copies must be bound between hard or soft covers before distribution.

As an alternative to paper, computer-output microfilm (COM) technology permits the printing of book-form catalogs in microform. As discussed in chapter 1, a COM recorder is a type of nonimpact computer printer that converts machine-readable data to microfilm or microfiche without creating an intervening paper copy. Depending on the reduction ratio selected, a conventional 100-foot roll of 16mm COM-generated microfilm may contain the equivalent of 1,800 or more pages of computer printouts, while a sheet of microfiche measuring 105mm by 148mm may contain 270 or more pages. The COM recorder, which typically operates at speeds exceeding two pages per second, produces the master microfilm or microfiche only. High-speed duplicators are used to produce the required number of distribution copies. Readers are required for the magnified display of COM-generated images. Reader/printers can be used to create paper copies for reference purposes.

While libraries have used COM for book-form catalog production and other technical services applications since the late 1960s, the widespread implementation of COM catalogs began in the mid-1970s and coincided with the previously noted revival of interest in book-form alternatives to the card catalog. A number of service bureaus, book jobbers, bibliographic utilities, and other vendors have developed software capable of producing COM catalogs from library-supplied, machine-readable bibliographic data, thereby eliminating the need for an in-house COM recorder and customized programming. Most of these vendors will accept archival tapes containing MARC format obtained from bibliographic utilities or other sources.

Compared to conventional paper-based book catalogs, COM catalogs offer several advantages, the most important being economy of production. Where 10 or more copies are required, COM production costs will often prove lower than those associated with catalogs produced by computer printers or phototypesetters, even when the cost of microform readers is considered. COM's production cost advantages are especially significant in applications requiring many copies of very long catalogs. In addition, COM catalogs are more durable and compact than paper copies, although the latter advantage is partially offset by the space required for display equipment. In terms of output characteristics, COM recorders offer typographic capabilities exceeding those of the typical line printer, but they cannot usually match the typographic and formatting versatility of laser printers or phototypesetters. Most COM recorders will produce highly legible uppercase and lowercase characters. Depending on the model, variations in type size and intensity may be possible, and some recorders can generate the accented characters and other special symbols used in bibliographic data. A few devices can produce Cyrillic, Hebrew, and other nonroman characters.

The implementation of COM catalogs has been accompanied by considerable concern about library users' acceptance of nonpaper media and their ability to operate the special equipment required to display images from microfilm or microfiche. Similar concerns have been expressed about the implementation of the online catalogs discussed in the next section. In the case of COM catalogs, most libraries have experienced favorable user reactions. As is the case with much information-processing technology, microforms are more common in offices than in libraries. As a result, many library users are accustomed to operating readers and reader/printers as part of their daily work responsibilities. Several vendors have introduced special devices for library applications. Featuring preprinted instructions and simple controls, they employ large reels of 16mm or 105mm microfilm, the latter containing several hundred uncut microfiche. In most cases, a library's entire catalog can be contained on a single reel, which remains inside the reader and need not be handled by the user.

Online Catalogs

While computer-produced book-form catalogs can successfully address the problems of remote access, labor-intensive maintenance, and possibly space consumption associated with conventional card catalogs, they suffer from an inherent limitation of all batch-processed output—they cannot accurately reflect the status of a changing collection. Book catalogs are normally updated through periodic supplements which are themselves limited in several important respects. From the reference standpoint, supplements are inconvenient because they necessitate multiple retrieval operations. In a typical application, a library might have a self-contained retrospective book-form catalog (or perhaps a closed card catalog) reflecting its collection up to a particular date, book-form supplements that cumulate annually, and monthly book-form updates that cumulate quarterly up to year's end. Even if the annual supplements are cumulated at regular intervals, many searches will still require the consultation of at least three catalog segments. As a further constraint, book-form catalogs cannot reflect items added to, or removed from, a library's collection during the interim between the printing of successive supplements, regardless of their frequency. In some applications, records for these items are maintained in a temporary card catalog, but this card catalog, however small, is subject to the problems and limitations previously discussed.

For most librarians seeking an alternative to card catalogs, computer-produced book-form catalogs represent a partially satisfactory solution to problems that can be more effectively addressed by online catalogs. Broadly defined, an online catalog is an organized, machine-readable accumulation of bibliographic records that are maintained on fixed magnetic disk drives or comparable direct-access computer storage devices for retrieval by library users and staff members working at interactive terminals or appropriately configured microcomputer workstations. If an online catalog is primarily intended for a library's clientele (as opposed to library staff), it may be described as a public access catalog (PAC) or an online public access catalog (OPAC). Such implementations are the focal point of this discussion.

When compared to card and book-form catalogs, online catalogs offer a number of potential advantages. As with computer-produced book-form catalogs, much of the labor-intensive file maintenance associated with card catalogs is eliminated, and—assuming an appropriate equipment configuration—remote access is possible. But unlike book-form catalogs, which must be distributed to remote locations in anticipation of reference, online catalogs can be accessed from any location by authorized persons equipped with compatible terminals. Thus, for example, a scientist or engineer working at a home terminal could consult the online catalogs of one or more technical libraries; similarly, university faculty members might access the online catalogs of academic libraries or special collections to determine the existence and locations of needed research materials. If online workstations are equipped with printers, customized bibliographies can be generated. Unlike batch-processed book-form catalogs, the updating of online catalogs is not dependent on periodic supplements. If desired, online catalogs can be updated in real time, with records being added or removed as items are cataloged or weeded. Alternatively, changes can be made in the batch mode on a daily or other periodic basis.

As an additional capability, online catalogs can support information retrieval operations which are not possible with card or book-form catalogs. As previously discussed, the expense of file maintenance and space requirements prevent the expansion of a card catalog's access points to include such additional parameters as title keywords. Book-form catalogs typically follow card catalog practice in this respect. With online catalogs, however, the implementation of additional access points may prove economically feasible, although additional system resources will be required. As a further potential advantage, online catalogs typically permit interactive searches involving the logical coordination of retrieval parameters. In this respect, they offer capabilities comparable to those of the online information services discussed in the next chapter.

Online catalogs can be implemented in various ways. Libraries that subscribe to certain bibliographic utilities, for example, already have a portion of their catalog records accessible online. As previously noted, RLIN, Utlas, AGILE III, and Brodart's Interactive Access System (IAS) store the changes that individual subscribers make to catalog records. OCLC and WLN include holding symbols which indicate whether a given title is held by a particular library, although they do not maintain local call numbers or location information online. RLIN, WLN, and Utlas offer powerful information retrieval capabilities that support keyword searching and the logical coordination of search parameters, as well as conventional author, title, and subject searches. It is thus possible that a subscribing library could use the data base of a bibliographic utility as its online catalog, subject to several important operational and economic limitations.

In terms of scope, for example, the online catalog would be limited to those records that a given library had cataloged as a subscriber of the bibliographic utility. Unless a retrospective conversion is undertaken, a card or book-form catalog must still be maintained for older records not in machine-readable form. In addition, an appropriate quantity of terminals, modems, and related communication facilities would be required to access the online catalog. If leased lines are utilized as communication links, the resulting fixed costs can prove substantial. Library users must be trained in the bibliographic utility's commands and search procedures. In the case of OCLC, for example, users must learn the special procedures associated with the derivation of search keys. Other bibliographic utilities use more conventional retrieval approaches which combine commands with the direct entry of search terms, but special training will still be required. As a further constraint for subscribers of the largest bibliographic utility, OCLC does not support subject searching; a local subject catalog must consequently be maintained in card or book form. Finally, libraries that rely on bibliographic utilities as their online catalogs will relinquish direct control over the management of downtime and response time.

In addition to the bibliographic utilities, various timesharing companies offer hardware, software, and other computer support that allow a library to establish and maintain an online catalog for access from interactive terminals. While many computer service bureaus offer generalized data base management systems which can be used for this purpose, several companies offer services that are specifically designed for bibliographic data. As an example, the online information services—including Dialog, Orbit, BRS, and others described in chapter 7—offer "private file" capabilities that allow customers to establish their own bibliographic or other data files for access through the same retrieval software used with publicly available data files. Such private files can be used to maintain a subscribing library's online catalog.

As an alternative to the timeshared hardware and software resources offered by the bibliographic utilities and computer services, online catalogs can be implemented on computer hardware operated by a library or its parent organization. Such locally implemented systems may employ custom-developed or prewritten software. As an example of the former approach, the Library of Congress Computerized Catalog provides online access to the LC MARC data base plus other items cataloged by the Library of Congress; LC, as previously noted, closed its card catalog in 1981. The computerized catalog is accessed through video display workstations, some of which are equipped with auxiliary printers for the creation of customized bibliographies. Searchable by author, title, and subject, the computerized catalog is one of several data files accessible through a custom-developed information retrieval program called SCORPIO (Subject Content Oriented Retriever for Processing Information Online). Other available data files include the Legislative Information Files, which provide information on legislation introduced in Congress since 1975; the Bibliographic Citation File, which lists articles, pamphlets, and other publications in the fields of public policy and current affairs; and the General Accounting Office Files, which provide abstracts of information dealing with various types of federal programs.

Several academic libraries have likewise implemented online catalogs based on custom-developed software. At Ohio State University, for example, online catalog access is offered as a subsystem within a custom-developed circulation control system. As with OCLC, author, title, and author/title searches are based on derived search keys rather than the direct entry of names or phrases. Subject heading searches are also permitted. Retrieved records can be displayed in abbreviated or full bibliographic form. Called the Library Computer System (LCS), the software developed by Ohio State has been installed in several other libraries. Other examples of online catalogs based on custom-developed software include the MELVYL system at the University of California, the LIAS system at Pennsylvania State University, the Catalog Access System at Mankato (Minn.) State University, the JEFFCAT system at Jefferson County Public Library in Colorado, the LSCAN system at the Dallas Public Library, the SULIRS system at Syracuse University, the Phoenix system at the University of New Brunswick, the Dartmouth Online Catalog at Dartmouth College, and the PaperChase system at Beth Israel Hospital (Boston).

As discussed in chapter 2, customized software development can address a library's special application characteristics but requires a substantial investment of resources. In most cases, the time and cost required to implement any computer system can be significantly reduced through the acquisition of appropriate prewritten software. As previously discussed, some general-purpose data base management systems may be suitable for this purpose. Such programs are widely available for computers of all types and sizes, although a considerable systems analysis and implementation effort may be required to adapt them to library requirements. Of greater significance for this discussion are data base management programs that are either designed specifically for, or are directly applicable to, bibliographic data.

As an example noted earlier in this chapter, the Western Library Network will license its software to libraries interested in using it for online catalog implementations or other applications. The TECHLIB Plus implementation of the famous BASIS Plus data management program similarly supports cataloging maintenance, online catalog access, and other library operations. Marketed by Information Dimensions, which was acquired by OCLC in 1993, versions of TECHLIB Plus are available for various mainframes and minicomputers. It is installed in many technical and industrial libraries. A number of special libraries have likewise implemented online catalogs using data base management programs such as INMAGIC from Inmagic Incorporated and the STAR system from Cuadra Associates. The MINISIS software package, produced by the International Development Research Centre and sold by Systemhouse, can be configured for catalog maintenance and online inquiry, as well as a variety of general records management applications. It has proven especially popular with academic and government libraries in developing countries.

Since the mid-1980s, online catalog implementations have been dominated by so-called integrated library systems, which combine data base management and catalog access capabilities with other operations. Broadly defined, an integrated library system is a computer-based product that automates multiple library operations. The conceptual advantages of integrated library systems have been widely discussed since the 1970s, and some customized systems were implemented during that decade. The earliest commercially available products, however, were introduced in the 1980s. They are variously marketed as prewritten software packages for installation and operation on customer-owned computers or as preconfigured, turnkey combinations of hardware and software. Some integrated library systems are augmented versions of products that were originally developed for a single application, such as circulation control; as noted in chapter 5, multifunctional integrated systems have largely replaced single-purpose circulation control products. Other integrated systems were developed with multifunctionality as a primary goal. In either case, the most complete implementations include application modules for cataloging, catalog access by library patrons and staff members, circulation control, acquisitions, and serials control, perhaps supplemented by materials booking for audiovisual media, electronic mail, and bulletin board capabilities. Most integrated library systems are built around core modules for cataloging and circulation control; subject to availability, other application modules can be acquired and implemented on an as-needed basis.

Mainframe- and minicomputer-based integrated systems are widely installed in medium-size and larger libraries. Mainframe-based products are typically sold as prewritten software for installation on a computer operated by a university, municipality, corporation, or other government agency with which a given library is affiliated. They are a popular choice for organizations that want to utilize existing computing facilities to automate library operations, thereby minimizing required investments in computer hardware. The NOTIS Library Management System, which evolved from library automation activities at Northwestern University, is the best-known library automation software package for IBM and plug-compatible mainframes. Other integrated library systems for IBM mainframes are offered by VTLS Incorporated and Extended Library Access

Solutions (ELiAS) N.V. of Leuven, Belgium. The latter company sells the DOBIS/LIBIS software package, which was developed by IBM itself. Library automation software from CARL Systems Incorporated runs on Tandem computers. The PALS system from Unisys Corporation runs on that company's mainframes.

Integrated library systems for Digital Equipment Corporation's popular VAX minicomputers are offered by Advanced Computer Concepts Incorporated, Centel Federal Systems, Comstow Information Services, Data Research Associates, Gaylord Information Systems, and the Georgetown University Medical Center Library, among others. Systems for Hewlett-Packard HP 3000 Series minicomputers are sold by VTLS and Data Research Associates. Companies such as Computer Management and Development Services, Far West Data Control, Gateway Software Corporation, National Computer System Incorporated, and United Systems Technology Incorporated offer library automation software for IBM AS/400 minicomputers. Library automation programs for computers that utilize the Unix operating system are offered by a growing number of companies. Examples include Advanced Computer Concepts, Carlyle Systems, Centel Federal Systems, Comstow Information Services, Dynix, Geac, IME Systems, Innovative Interfaces, Sirsi Corporation, and SOBECO Ernst & Young. As one of their principal advantages, Unix-based library automation programs are often compatible with hardware from various computer manufacturers, including Sun Microsystems, IBM, Digital Equipment Corporation, Hewlett-Packard, NCR, Sequent, and others.

Microcomputer-based integrated library systems are designed for smaller libraries. Their principal markets include school libraries, public libraries in villages and towns, four-year college libraries, community college libraries and learning centers, and special libraries in corporations, government agencies, professional associations, nonprofit organizations, law firms, hospitals, and medical clinics. As a market segment, small libraries are usually defined—however imprecisely—by collection size. The bibliographic data bases maintained by integrated library systems typically contain one record for each title in a library's collection. Some microcomputer-based systems impose limits on the number of records their data bases can accommodate—a maximum of 300,000 titles, for example. Alternatively, data base size may be limited by hardware characteristics, particularly the availability of fixed magnetic disk storage. Depending on the product, a microcomputer-based integrated library system will require one to three megabytes of disk space per 1,000 bibliographic records. Additional space will be required for program storage, working files, and borrower records if circulation control is implemented. Thus, a 500-megabyte fixed magnetic disk drive, a large size for a microcomputer installation, may store as few as 150,000 or as many as 450,000 bibliographic records, depending on the system.

With prices routinely exceeding several hundred thousand dollars for required hardware and software components, the cost of mainframe- and minicomputer-based implementations exceeds the entire multiyear budgets of many small libraries. To take advantage of mainframe- or minicomputer-based technology, small libraries must participate in consortia or other co-operative arrangements, pooling their limited financial resources with those of other institutions, thereby obtaining access to prewritten software or turnkey systems that would otherwise be unaffordable. A number of small libraries currently participate in such shared implementations. Often, the shared system is operated by a medium-size or larger library; small libraries obtain timeshared access through communication facilities and are charged for those system resources that they utilize. Recognizing that shared systems can promote the implementation of union catalogs, interlibrary loan proce-dures, and other resource-sharing tools, library funding agencies may provide grants and other financial support to encourage the participation of small libraries. For many small libraries, however, reliance on computing resources provided by another organization necessitates an unacceptable loss of local autonomy as well as potentially reduced flexibility in system implementa-tion. In shared implementations, decisions about hours of service, hardware upgrades, application modules to be added, and other aspects of system operation are strongly influenced by the requirements and preferences of the largest participants. A small library's viewpoint, while not necessarily ig-nored, may not be accorded equal weight.

Microcomputer-based integrated library systems offer an affordable, practical alternative to such shared system arrangements. Addressing the small library's financial constraints, they are much less expensive to purchase than their mainframe- and minicomputer-based counterparts. Equally important, they are designed for implementation and use by nontechnical personnel. Compared to larger organizations, small libraries are much less likely to have employees with computer expertise appro-priate to complicated system implementations. Technical expertise and programming capability are not required for successful implementation and operation of microcomputer-based integrated library systems, al-though familiarity with computer concepts and prior microcomputer ex-perience are unquestionably helpful.

Microcomputer-based integrated library systems are typically sold as prewritten software packages for implementation on customer-owned equipment. Most products are intended for IBM-compatible microcom-puters configured with designated peripheral devices. Examples include BiblioFile from the Library Corporation, BiblioTrac from Novara Soft-ware, Circulation/Catalog Plus from Follett Software, the Columbia Li-brary System from CTB/Columbia Computing Services, DavexPlus from Faxon Canada Limited, the Eloquent Librarian from Eloquent Systems Incorporated, the Manager Series and ULS Professional Series from Data Trek, MicroCAT from TKM Software Limited, MOLLI from Nichols Ad-vanced Technologies, the SydneyPlus Library Management System from International Library Systems, and Winnebago CIRC/CAT from Winne-bago Software Company. To reach the small library market, VTLS, Dynix, IME Systems, and other vendors of minicomputer-based integrated li-brary systems have added microcomputer-based implementations to their product lines. Companies that offer integrated library systems for Macintosh computers include COMPanion, Chancery Software Limited, and Winnebago Software Company.

A library may own the required microcomputer hardware or purchase it specifically for an integrated system implementation. Some vendors sell selected equipment components or, in rare instances, complete turnkey combinations of hardware and software, but libraries may be able to obtain required hardware at lower prices from other sources. School, academic, and public libraries, in particular, can usually purchase microcomputers and peripherals at attractive educational or municipal discounts. Most microcomputer-based integrated library systems are available in versions for local area networks. For medium-size libraries interested in "downsizing" as described in chapter 1, such products offer a potentially cost-effective alternative to minicomputer-based integrated library systems.

Among the most widely publicized approaches to online catalog implementations, a number of companies offer microcomputer-based public access catalog systems that employ CD-ROM technology to store bibliographic records. Examples include LePac from Brodart, the Impact system from Auto-Graphics, LaserGuide from General Research Corporation, Marcive/PAC from Marcive Incorporated, and The Intelligent Catalog from the Library Corporation. In such implementations, a library provides a machine-readable version of its catalog, typically consisting of MARC-format records on magnetic tapes obtained from bibliographic utilities or other sources. The CD-ROM catalog system vendor indexes and otherwise prepares the data base for conversion to one or more CD-ROM discs. As described in chapter 1, the CD-ROMs themselves are created by a mastering and replication process in specially designed production facilities. The library receives the required number of CD-ROM copies plus software for public catalog access. In many cases, a library's entire catalog, with its associated indexes, will fit on a single CD-ROM, thereby eliminating media handling. Such CD-ROM catalogs are increasingly implemented as high-performance replacements for book-form COM catalogs. They have proven especially popular for the distribution of union catalogs.

Whether implemented on mainframes, minicomputers, or microcomputers, public access catalogs must be designed for ease of use, often by a diverse clientele with little or no instruction. The best products feature one or more introductory screens that briefly explain the purpose of the system, describe the search functions and retrieval operations available to the user, give examples of the ways in which functions and operations can be invoked, and indicate how additional help can be obtained. To facilitate user orientation, some systems employ a uniform display format that places specified data elements in consistent, recognizable locations. As an example, the top of the screen may be reserved for titles and system messages, while the middle of the screen displays retrieved bibliographic data and the bottom portion includes instructions or input areas. Following a practice that is now commonplace in the implementation of interactive computer programs, most automated library systems provide online help screens that are available to the user at any point in a catalog search.

Such screens typically provide detailed information about specific functions or operations. Having consulted a help screen, the user can resume a search at the point of interruption. In some cases, the content of help screens is predetermined by the system vendor; in others, libraries can customize them to meet local requirements.

The sizable body of library literature on public access catalogs differentiates command-driven and menu-oriented systems. In command-driven implementations, a user enters a search string that specifies the field to be searched followed by a specific value to be matched in that field. Often, mnemonic field abbreviations—such as "A=", "T=", and "S="—are used for author, title, and subject searches. Because they permit the rapid, direct entry of search statements, command-driven catalog access systems are attractive to experienced users. While some command-driven systems provide excellent instruction screens with concise directions that enable novice users to begin searching quickly, others require some initial training for effective utilization. Menu-oriented systems are consequently preferred for inexperienced or occasional users.

As their name suggests, menu-oriented catalog access systems display lists of search commands and retrieval options for perusal and selection by the user, thereby eliminating the need to memorize a repertoire of available commands. The typical menu-oriented catalog access program displays a list of searchable fields, followed by additional lists and prompts for specific search parameters. Often, menus are combined with formatted screens that facilitate the entry of search parameters adjacent to appropriate field labels. Some microcomputer-based systems rely on pulldown menus and dialog boxes of the type associated with the graphical user interfaces described in chapter 2. While the distinction between command-oriented and menu-oriented systems is conceptually useful, some systems support both access methodologies. With menu-based systems, a command-driven "expert" mode is often supported; experienced users can enter commands to anticipate and circumvent certain menus and prompts. Similarly, most command-driven systems display occasional menus for operations that have multiple options associated with them.

Whether a command-oriented or menu-based user interface is employed, online public catalog access systems employ indexes to retrieve bibliographic records. Mirroring search capabilities traditionally associated with card catalogs, most systems maintain author, title, and subject indexes. Classification number indexes are essential if libraries are to discard their shelflists in favor of computerized records. Some online public catalog access systems also maintain indexes of corporate names, conference names, and series titles. Going beyond the capabilities of conventional card catalogs, many systems support searches by one or more unique record identifiers, such as a system control number, Library of Congress Card Number, International Standard Book Number, or International Standard Serial Number, although such capabilities will usually prove more appropriate for library staff members than for library users. Keyword searches based on titles, corporate names, and conference names are supported, with some variations, by many online public access catalog systems. Some systems support the retrieval of catalog records by publisher, publication date, country of publication, language of publication, and media type. Others allow previously entered searches to be limited by such parameters.

In addition to straightforward searches involving a single field value, most online public access catalog systems permit complex retrieval specifications that contain multiple field values linked by logical operators. Some systems support an "anyword" capability that will search all indexed fields for a specified value. A few online public access catalog systems permit proximity searches, searches for embedded character strings, wildcard searches, and other capabilities commonly associated with the online information services described in chapter 7, but such capabilities are seldom employed effectively by uninstructed users. Most online public catalog access systems support root-word searches based on right-truncation of search terms; the user enters the beginning portion of a field value, and the system retrieves all catalog records where the indicated field value begins with the specified character string.

Most online public access catalog systems will immediately display catalog records that correspond to a specified system control number, LCCN, ISBN, or other unique identifier. Record display procedures for author, title, subject, and keyword searches are more varied. Some systems initially respond to a search command with a count of the number of catalog records that satisfy the retrieval specification. If desired, the user can then enter one or more narrowing search statements. In other cases, however, the online public catalog access system responds to author, title, and subject retrieval specifications by displaying the appropriate alphabetical section of the relevant online index for the searcher's perusal. The display usually indicates the number of catalog records associated with each index entry. Where indexes are based on authority files, displayed entries may also include cross-references. Most systems support paging commands which permit index browsing.

Once suitable records are identified, the searcher can instruct the online public access catalog system to display them. Display formats often vary with the number of records retrieved by a given search. If only one record is retrieved, for example, most systems will display full bibliographic data as either a catalog card image or as a list of labeled fields and their associated values. Library staff members can often obtain a display in the full MARC format with content designators and subfield codes. If a search retrieves multiple records, they are initially displayed in a briefer format, usually as a number list of one- or two-line entries containing some combination of abbreviated author, title, imprint, and edition information. The searcher can then request full bibliographic displays for specific items. In integrated library system implementations that include a circulation control module, the searcher can also obtain a display of copy data, including branch locations, call numbers, and circulation status with due dates for items checked out.

SUMMARY

The automated systems discussed in this chapter address two interrelated facets of cataloging activity: descriptive cataloging, and the preparation and production of library catalogs. The automation of descriptive cataloging depends on the availability of cataloging copy in machine-readable form. In the late 1960s, the Library of Congress developed the MARC format for the communication of bibliographic data on magnetic tape and began distributing machine-readable cataloging copy. Other national libraries and library organizations have established similar programs. Several projects have attempted to extend the coverage of the MARC-format bibliographic records retrospectively to include cataloging data for library materials published before the MARC program. The most ambitious example is the REMARC data base from Utlas International.

While MARC tapes can be purchased from the Library of Congress for input to local computer systems, most libraries obtain access to MARC data through products and services offered by publishers, computer system developers, timesharing services, and other intermediaries. Among the earliest of these MARC-derivative products were computer-generated micropublications, such as MARCFICHE and Books in English, which provided more timely access to LC cataloging data than could be obtained through the conventionally printed *National Union Catalog*. The NUC was itself discontinued in favor of a COM implementation in the early 1980s. Several vendors offer online access to the LC MARC data base. Examples include the Dialog and Wilsonline information services. Since the mid-1980s, various companies have introduced microcomputer-based cataloging support systems which supply the LC MARC data base on CD-ROM discs, accompanied by information retrieval and card production software. As an alternative to the self-contained operation offered by such products, book jobbers and other vendors use MARC data bases to generate a variety of bibliographic products, including catalog cards and magnetic tapes, for library customers.

Bibliographic utilities are organizations that maintain large data bases of cataloging records which libraries can access on a timesharing basis. Examples include OCLC, RLIN, Utlas, WLN, the AGILE III system from Auto-Graphics, the Interactive Access System (IAS) from Brodart Automation, and Open DRANET from Data Research Associates. Participating libraries can retrieve cataloging copy from online terminals, modify it to meet local requirements, and order printed card sets or other bibliographic products. Local workstations are also used to input original cataloging for use by other subscribers. The bibliographic utilities differ from one another in data base size and composition, the number and nature of their subscribers, the specific cataloging and retrieval capabilities they support, and the types of services they offer.

The automation of descriptive cataloging addresses only one part of the cataloging activity. Libraries are also interested in automated approaches to the production, maintenance, and use of their catalogs. Since the 1970s, considerable attention has been given to the problems and limitations of conventional card catalogs. The most frequently cited problems include substantial space consumption; a requirement for expensive cabinets; labor-intensive and time-consuming file maintenance routines, which are intensified by changes in cataloging rules affecting the choice and form of entries; and limited convenience and retrieval capabilities.

Presumably, many of these problems can be minimized or eliminated by the replacement of card catalogs with computer-produced book-form catalogs or online catalogs. Such replacement, however, requires the conversion of a given library's catalog records to machine-readable, computer-processible form. Such conversion can be accomplished relatively easily for cataloging records pertaining to recent or ongoing acquisitions, but the retrospective conversion of older catalog records presents serious problems. The preferred retrospective conversion method involves the use of abbreviated keystroking to search for and obtain machine-readable copies of cataloging records from resource data bases maintained by bibliographic utilities or other organizations. Such techniques are time-consuming and can prove difficult to apply to cataloging records in nonroman character sets. As a result, a library that implements a computer-based catalog may decide to close or freeze its card catalog rather than convert existing records to machine-readable form.

Cataloging records in machine-readable form can be batch-processed to produce book-form catalogs, or stored in an online data base. A book-form catalog consists of successive bibliographic records listed in a page format on paper or microforms. Book-form catalogs can successfully address many of the limitations of card catalogs. File maintenance is automatically performed, copies can be distributed to remote users, and some space may even be saved. Book-form catalogs suffer, however, from an inherent limitation of all batch-processed output products: they cannot accurately reflect the status of a changing library collection, since they must be updated by supplements which are themselves out of date before they are printed. This limitation does not apply to online catalogs. Such catalogs are increasingly implemented as components of integrated library systems, which also support circulation control and other operations. Integrated library systems are offered by several dozen vendors for mainframe, minicomputer, and microcomputer implementations. Alternatively, library catalogs may be recorded on CD-ROM discs for online access through microcomputer-based workstations. In either case, online catalogs typically offer faster, more varied retrieval capabilities than their card or book-form counterparts.

ADDITIONAL READING

AVRAM, H. "International Standards for Interchange of Bibliographic Records in Machine-readable Form." *Library Resources and Technical Services* 20 (1): 25–35 (1976).

———. *MARC: Its History and Implications*. Washington, D.C.: Library of Congress, 1975.

BALLARD, T. "The Unfulfilled Promise of Resource Sharing." *American Libraries* 21 (10): 990–93 (1990).

BARRETT, B. "Hit Rates with the OCLC CD450 Cataloguing System: A Test with Recent, Academic Approval Books." *Cataloging and Classification Quarterly* 12 (2): 63–81 (1990).

BEARMAN, D. "Archives and Manuscript Control with Bibliographic Utilities: Challenges and Opportunities." *American Archivist* 52 (1): 26–39 (1952).

BEAUMONT, J. *Make Mine MARC: A Manual of MARC Practice for Libraries.* Westport, Conn.: Meckler Corporation, 1992.

———. "Retrospective Conversion on a Micro: Options for Libraries." *Library Software Review* 5 (4): 213–18 (1986).

BEISER, K., and NELSON, N. "CD-ROM Public Access Catalogs: An Assessment." *Library Technology Reports* 25 (2): 279–453 (1989).

BILLS, L., and HELGERSON, L. "User Interfaces for CD-ROM PACs." *Library Hi Tech* 6 (2): 73–113 (1988).

———. "CD-ROM Catalog Production Products." *Library Hi Tech* 7 (1): 67–92 (1989).

BOSS, R. "Integrating and Interfacing Library Systems." *Electronic Library* 3 (2): 124–31 (1985).

———. "Linked Systems and the Online Catalog: The Role of OSI." *Library Resources and Technical Services* 34 (2): 217–28 (1990).

———. "The Procurement of Library Automated Systems." *Library Technology Reports* 26 (5): 629–750 (1990).

———. "Retrospective Conversion: Investing in the Future." *Wilson Library Bulletin* 59 (2): 173–78, 238 (1984).

BOUCHER, V. "The Impact of OCLC on Interlibrary Loan in the United States." *Interlending and Document Supply* 15 (3): 74–79 (1987).

BROERIG, N. "Emergence of an Electronic Library: A Case Study of the Georgetown University Library Information System." *Science and Technology Libraries* 5 (1): 1–21 (1985).

BYRNE, D. *MARC Manual: Understanding and Using MARC Records.* Littleton, Colo.: Libraries Unlimited, 1991.

CAIN, J. "UTLAS Development with Japanese and Chinese Scripts." In *Automated Systems for Access to Multilingual and Multiscript Library Materials: Problems and Solutions.* IFLA Publication no. 38. New York: K.G. Saur, 1987, 163–84.

CAMPBELL, B. "Whither the White Knight: CD-ROM in Technical Services." *Database* 10 (4): 22–40 (1987).

CATHRO, W. "The Australian Bibliographic Network: A Survey of Its First Decade." *Australian Academic and Research Libraries* 22 (4): 37–52 (1991).

CHAO, D. "Cost Comparisons between Bibliographic Utilities and CD-ROM-based Cataloging Systems." *Library Hi Tech* 7 (3): 49–52 (1989).

CHRISMOND, L. "Quality Issues in Retrospective Conversion Projects." *Library Resources and Technical Services* 25 (1): 48–55 (1981).

CO, F. "Retrospective Conversion on CD-ROM: A Cost Analysis." *CD-ROM Librarian* 5 (1): 11–20 (1990).

COLGLAZIER, M. "A Book Catalog Produced from USMARC Records Using Bibliofile, Pro-Cite, Biblio-Link, and WordPerfect." *Information Technology and Libraries* 7 (4): 417–29 (1988).

COOPER, D. "The Computerization of East Asian Languages." *Library Software Review* 3 (2): 179–86 (1984).

COSTERS, L. "The New PICA Library Network." *Resource Sharing and Information Networks* 7 (1): 127–32 (1991).

COYNE, F., and MIFFLIN, I. "Shared Authority Control at the Western Library Network." *Library Resources and Technical Services* 34 (4): 493–503 (1990).

CRAWFORD, W. *MARC for Library Use: Understanding Integrated US MARC.* 2nd ed. Boston: G.K. Hall, 1989.

———. *Technical Standards: An Introduction for Librarians.* White Plains, N.Y.: Knowledge Industry Publications, 1986.

DeGennaro, R. "Integrated Online Library Systems: Perspectives, Perceptions, and Practicalities." *Library Journal* 110 (2): 37–40 (1985).

Dickson, J., and Zadner, P. "Authority Control and the Authority File: A Functional Evaluation of LCNAF on RLIN." *Cataloging and Classification Quarterly* 9 (3): 57–73 (1989).

Dowlin, K. "Maggie III: The Prototypical Library System." *Library Hi Tech* 4 (4): 105–19 (1986).

Dwyer, J. "The Effect of a Closed Catalog on Public Access." *Journal of Academic Librarianship* 5 (2): 132–41 (1979).

Elman, S. "Automation in East Asian Libraries in the United States: A Review and Assessment." *College and Research Libraries* 52 (6): 559–73 (1991).

Gorman, M. "The Online Catalog of the University of Illinois at Urbana-Champaign." *Information Technology and Libraries* 4 (4): 306–11 (1985).

Griffin, D. "Review of Cataloging at the Western Library Network." *Resource Sharing and Information Networks* 6 (1): 17–37 (1990).

Guenther, R. "The Development and Implementation of the USMARC Format for Classification Data." *Information Technology and Libraries* 11 (2): 120–31 (1992).

Hawks, C. "The Integrated Library System of the 1990s: The OhioLINK Experience." *Library Resources and Technical Services* 36 (1): 61–77 (1992).

Heller, P. "Remote Access: Its Impact on a College Library." *Electronic Library* 19 (5): 287–89 (1992).

Hildreth, C. "Library Networking in North America in the 1980s, Part 1: The Dream; The Realities." *Electronic Library* 5 (4): 22–28 (1987).

———. "Library Networking in North America in the 1980s, Part 2: The Response of Bibliographic Utilities to Local, Integrated Systems." *Electronic Library* 5 (5): 270–75 (1987).

———. *Online Public Access Catalogs: The User Interface.* Dublin, Ohio: Online Computer Library Center, 1982.

Hoadley, I. "The Future of Networks and OCLC." *Journal of Library Administration* 8 (3): 85–91 (1987).

Joy, A., and Keane, N. "CDMARC Subjects: The Library of Congress Subject Headings on CD-ROM." *CD-ROM Librarian* 4 (9): 36–45 (1989).

Kilgour, F. *Collected Papers of Frederick G. Kilgour.* Dublin, Ohio: Online Computer Library Center, 1984.

———. "The Economic Goal of Library Automation." *College and Research Libraries* 30 (3): 307–11 (1969).

Knox, A., and Miller, B. "Predicting the Number of Public Computer Terminals Needed for an Online Catalog: A Queuing Theory Approach." *Library Research* 2 (1): 95–100 (1980).

Lazinger, S. "Israel's Research Library Network: Background, Evolution, and Implications for Networking in a Small Country." *Information Technology and Libraries* 10 (4): 275–91 (1991).

Lewis, D. "Research on the Use of Online Catalogs and Its Implications for Library Practice." *Journal of Academic Librarianship* 13 (2): 152–56 (1987).

McCue, J., et al. "An Analysis of Cataloging Copy: Library of Congress vs. Selected RLIN Members." *Library Resources and Technical Services* 35 (1): 65–75 (1991).

Matthews, J. "Benchmark and Acceptance Tests: Why and When to Use Them." *Library Hi Tech* 4 (1): 43–50 (1986).

———. *The Impact of Online Catalogs.* New York: Neal-Schuman, 1986.

———. *Public Access to Online Catalogs.* New York: Neal-Schuman, 1985.

Michalko, J. "Costly Boundaries: Costs, New Technologies, and Bibliographic Utilities." *Technical Services Quarterly* 8 (1): 29–36 (1990).

Saffady, W. "Characteristics and Experiences of Integrated Library Systems Installations." *Library Technology Reports* 23 (5): 651–767 (1987).

――――. "The Cost of Automated Cataloging Support: An Analysis and Comparison of Selected Products and Services." *Library Technology Reports* 25 (4): 461–627 (1989).

――――. "The Bibliographic Utilities in 1993: A Survey of Cataloging Support and Other Services." *Library Technology Reports* 29 (1): 5–142 (1993).

TAYLOR, R. "Determining the Number of Online Terminals Needed to Meet Various Library Service Policies." *Information Technology and Libraries* 6 (3): 281–96 (1979).

TOLLE, J. *Public Access Terminals: Determining Quantity Requirements.* Dublin, Ohio: Online Computer Library Center, 1984.

TRUITT, M. "USMARC to UNIMARC/Authorities: A Qualitative Evaluation of US-MARC Data Elements." *Library Resources and Technical Services* 36 (1): 37–58 (1992).

7

Automated Reference Service

Broadly defined, the function of reference service is to help library users obtain access to required information. While such activities as circulation control and cataloging reflect the custodial and bibliographic aspects of librarianship, reference is a public service activity in which librarians function as professionally trained information specialists. Reference service is usually provided in response to a question or problem posed by a library user. Such questions range from simple inquiries about the locations of particular library facilities and resources to complex research requests requiring the retrieval and analysis of information in specialized subject disciplines. Much of the reference work for which librarians are specifically trained involves two types of transactions: (1) so-called ready reference questions requiring straightforward factual responses—for example, the population of a specified city, the quantity of a given product manufactured in a particular location during a specified time period, or the reported earnings of a particular corporation; and (2) literature searching—the preparation of bibliographies on specified topics.

Similar reference methodologies are employed in both types of transactions. A reference librarian first interviews an inquirer to clarify information requirements and determine the desired outcome. A reference strategy is then formulated, and appropriate books or other likely sources of the required information are identified. In some cases, the inquirer is merely directed to those sources and perhaps provided with instruction in their use. In others, the reference librarian actually performs the search, providing the inquirer with the requested information in the form of facts or bibliographic citations. Following the discussion and evaluation of these initial search results, additional searching, perhaps based on a modified reference strategy, may be undertaken. The process is repeated until satisfactory results are obtained or possible information sources are exhausted. This fuller type of reference service is common in technical and business libraries within corporations and government agencies where considerable staff time may be devoted to literature searching and other reference-related activities.

While the reference methodology described above is time-consuming, certain work steps—notably, the reference interview and the evaluation of search results—depend on interaction between persons and are not generally amenable to automation. Although some information retrieval systems allow users to type their reference inquiries in conventional paragraph form at terminals for automatic analysis by a computer program, such systems have typically been implemented in experimental applications involving relatively small, specialized collections of information sources. Neither their cost-effectiveness nor their viability in a broad range of library applications has been demonstrated. Although a few libraries have developed computer-based orientation and instruction programs that can assist users in locating specific physical facilities and identifying potentially relevant information resources, the most prevalent and effective approaches to the automation of reference service have concentrated on the search procedure itself—that is, the consultation of appropriate reference books and other information resources for facts and/or bibliographic citations.

As in the case of cataloging with copy, the availability of machine-readable reference sources is a precondition for computer-based reference service. The opening section of this chapter provides examples of machine-readable bibliographic and nonbibliographic data bases, indicating the specific subject disciplines that they primarily support. Subsequent sections discuss the ways in which libraries currently access and use those data bases, as well as some economic and operational implications of automated reference service.

MACHINE-READABLE REFERENCE SOURCES

Performed manually, literature searching—that is, the preparation of bibliographies on specified topics—relies heavily on printed indexing and abstracting journals, bibliographic lists, and other sources that facilitate subject or other access to monographs, periodical literature, technical reports, and other published and unpublished materials. These printed bibliographic sources are published by a variety of organizations, including government agencies, professional associations, and private companies. During the 1960s and early 1970s, many publishers of printed bibliographies and indexes attempted to simplify and reduce their production costs by using computer-based text-editing and phototypesetting techniques. Such techniques, which are now commonplace, require the conversion of bibliographic data to machine-readable form before a work is typeset and published. Thus, the earliest machine-readable bibliographic data bases were created as by-products of efficiencies in the production of printed copies.

Bibliographic Data Bases

The late 1960s and early 1970s were, coincidentally, characterized by an emerging interest in the application of computers to information storage and retrieval. Recognizing the value of machine-readable data to organizations interested in implementing automated information-processing systems, publishers of indexing and abstracting journals and bibliographies began selling machine-readable versions of their products in addition to, or in place of, their printed equivalents. These data were, and still are, offered to prospective purchasers on industry-standard reels of magnetic tape, together with descriptive information about their format. The MARC tapes discussed in the preceding chapter were among the earliest examples of such machine-readable bibliographic products.

Today, hundreds of printed indexing and abstracting journals and bibliographies are available in machine-readable versions, and a smaller but growing number of bibliographic products have been introduced specifically for use in computerized information retrieval systems. These machine-readable products are sometimes called "bibliographic data bases"; because of its prevalence in library literature, that usage will be followed in this chapter. As discussed in chapter 3, however, the term *data base* broadly denotes an integrated accumulation of computer-processible data organized in a manner suited to a wide range of applications. Following that definition, the bibliographic products discussed here are more accurately considered data files, which must usually be reorganized to meet specific application requirements. Thus, according to this usage, LC MARC records distributed on tape by the Library of Congress comprise a data file, while the OCLC Online Union Catalog, which incorporates those LC MARC records along with other cataloging information, is a data base that can be used for online searching, shared cataloging, card production, and other applications.

Some machine-readable bibliographic data bases are interdisciplinary in character and can consequently be viewed as the computer-processible counterparts of general reference sources. This is the case, for example, with the previously discussed LC MARC, BNB MARC, CANMARC, and REMARC data bases, which contain cataloging records pertaining to published materials regardless of field. Interdisciplinary scope likewise characterizes such news and current affairs data bases as the NATIONAL NEWSPAPER INDEX, NEWSEARCH, and MAGAZINE INDEX data bases produced by Information Access Company; the NEWSPAPER INDEX, produced by Bell and Howell; the MONITOR data base, produced by the Christian Science Monitor; and the CIS data base, which is the machine-readable counterpart of the *Index to Publications of the United States Congress* produced by Congressional Information Service, Incorporated. Other examples of interdisciplinary bibliographic data bases include the READER'S GUIDE TO PERIODICAL LITERATURE and BOOK REVIEW DIGEST data bases from H.W. Wilson; the machine-readable versions of *Books in Print,* produced by R.R. Bowker; BRITISH BOOKS IN PRINT, produced by J. Whitaker and Sons Limited; the COMPREHENSIVE DISSERTATION INDEX, produced by University Microfilms International; the CONFERENCE PAPERS INDEX, produced by Cambridge Scientific Abstracts; the MONTHLY CATALOG OF UNITED STATES GOVERNMENT PUBLICATIONS, produced by the U.S. Government Printing Office; and the BRITISH OFFICIAL PUBLICATIONS data base, produced by Chadwyck-Healey Limited. Produced by the International Translations Centre and the Centre National de la Recherche Scientifique, the WORLD TRANSLATIONS INDEX is a data base of translated works.

Like their printed counterparts, most machine-readable bibliographic data bases provide coverage of the literature of one or more specialized disciplines within the sciences, social sciences, or humanities. Since corporate and governmental technical libraries were among the earliest users of machine-readable bibliographic data bases, it is not surprising that the largest percentage of available data bases addresses the literature of science and technology. Some of these data bases provide coverage of multiple scientific and technical disciplines. This is the case, for example, with SCISEARCH, the machine-readable counterpart of the *Science Citation Index* and *Current Contents* publications of the Institute for Scientific Information; the NTIS data base, the machine-readable version of *Government Reports Announcements and Index,* published by the National Technical Information Service of the U.S. Department of Commerce; the PASCAL data base, the machine-readable counterpart of the *Bulletin Signalétique,* produced by the Centre de Documentation Scientifique et Technique; and the various patent data bases produced by such organizations as Derwent Publications, IFI/Plenum Data Company, the International Patent Documentation Center, Pergamon International, and Mead Data Central.

Data bases dealing with a single scientific or technical discipline are more numerous than general-purpose scientific information resources. Well-known examples include CA SEARCH, produced by Chemical Abstracts Service; BIOSIS PREVIEWS, produced by BIOSIS Incorporated as the machine-readable counterpart of *Biological Abstracts* and *Biological Abstracts/RRM;* the SPIN (Searchable Physics Information Notices) data base, produced by the American Institute of Physics; and the MATHSCI data base, produced by the American Mathematical Society. Geological and geographic literature is covered by the GEOREF data base, produced by the American Geological Society; the GEOARCHIVE data base, produced by Geosystems; the GEOBASE data base, produced by Geo Abstracts Limited; and the GEODE data base, produced by the French Bureau de Recherches Geologiques et Minieres. METEOROLOGICAL AND GEOASTROPHYSICAL ABSTRACTS, produced by the American Meteorological Society, covers the worldwide literature of those subjects and related topics.

Some highly specialized scientific disciplines are served by a surprising number of machine-readable bibliographic data bases. The literature of aquatic science and oceanography, for example, is covered by such data bases as AQUACULTURE, produced by the National Oceanic and Atmospheric Administration; AQUATIC SCIENCES AND FISHERIES ABSTRACTS, which corresponds to the printed Cambridge Scientific Abstracts publication of the same name; AQUALINE, produced by the Water Research Centre; WATER RESOURCES ABSTRACTS, produced by the U.S. Department of the Interior; the WATERNET data base, produced by the American Water Works Association; and the AFEE data base, produced by the Association Française pour l'Étude des Eaux.

The reference requirements of health science libraries are addressed by many bibliographic data bases, the most famous being MEDLINE, the machine-readable counterpart of three printed indexes produced by the National Library of Medicine: *Index Medicus,* the *Index to Dental Literature,* and the *International Nursing Index.* EMBASE is the machine-readable counterpart of the printed *Excerpta Medica.* Specialized aspects of medicine and health care management are covered by various data bases, including CANCERLIT and TOXLINE, produced by the National Library of Medicine; CLINICAL ABSTRACTS, produced by Medical Information Systems Reference and Index Services; BIOETHICS LINE, produced by Georgetown University; and RTEC, produced by the National Institute for Occupational Safety and Health. The RINGDOC data base, produced by Derwent Publications; INTERNATIONAL PHARMACEUTICAL ABSTRACTS, produced by the American Society of Hospital Pharmacists; and the PHARMACEUTICAL NEWS INDEX, produced by UMI/Data Courier, provide comprehensive coverage of pharmaceutical literature. Derwent's VETDOC data base covers the literature of veterinary medicine. The CURRENT BIOTECHNOLOGY ABSTRACTS data base, produced by the Royal Society of Chemistry, covers scientific and technical journals dealing with biotechnology. Data bases that cover the worldwide literature of agriculture, food science, and related subjects play a particularly important role in developing countries, where agricultural librarianship is an important area of professional practice. Examples of useful information resources include AGRICOLA, produced by the National Library of Agriculture; CAB ABSTRACTS, produced by the Commonwealth Agricultural Bureaux; AGREP, produced by the Commission of the European Communities; AGRIS, produced by the Food and Agriculture Organization of the United Nations; FOOD SCIENCE AND TECHNOLOGY ABSTRACTS (FSTA), produced by International Food Information Services; FAIREC, produced by the Institut de Recherches sur les Fruits et Agrumes; IALINE, produced by the Centre de Documentation des Industries Utilisatrices des Produits Agricoles; and FOODS ADLIBRA, produced by Komp Information Services. The PESTDOC data base, produced by Derwent Publications, covers the literature dealing with agricultural chemicals.

Excellent general coverage of the field of engineering is provided by two data bases: COMPENDEX PLUS, produced by Engineering Information Incorporated, as the machine-readable counterpart of the *Engineering Index;* and the INSPEC data base, which corresponds to three printed indexing and abstracting journals published by the Institution of Electrical Engineers: *Physics Abstracts, Electrical and Electronics Abstracts,* and *Computer and Control Abstracts.* Many engineering specialties are further served by one or more data bases. The APILIT and APIPAT data bases, produced by the American Petroleum Institute, cover the literature of petroleum engineering, as does the TULSA data base, produced by the

University of Tulsa as the machine-readable counterpart of the printed *Petroleum Abstracts*. As its name suggests, the CHEMICAL ENGINEER-ING ABSTRACTS data base, produced by the Royal Society of Chemistry, covers the literature of chemical engineering, as does the DECHEMA data base, produced by the Deutsche Gesellschaft für Chemisches Apparatewe-sen. The Royal Society of Chemistry also produces the ANALYTICAL AB-STRACTS data base, which indexes publications on analytical chemistry.

The literature of metallurgical engineering is covered by the META-DEX, WORLD ALUMINUM ABSTRACTS, and ENGINEERED MATE-RIALS ABSTRACTS data bases, produced by ASM International; the NONFERROUS METALS ABSTRACTS data base, produced by the Brit-ish Non-Ferrous Metals Technology Center; the ZINC, LEAD, AND CAD-MIUM ABSTRACTS data base, produced by the Zinc Development Association; and the BIIPAM CETIF data base, produced by the Centre Techniques des Industries de la Fonderie. The ISMEC data base, produced by Cambridge Scientific Abstracts, covers the literature of mechanical engineering. SAE ABSTRACTS, produced by the Society of Automotive Engineers, and the VWWW data base, produced by Volkswagenwerk AG, deal with the literature on self-propelled vehicles. Examples of other data bases that support literature searching in specialized engineering fields include the BHRA FLUID ENGINEERING data base, produced by the British Hydromechanics Research Association; SAFETY SCIENCE AB-STRACTS, produced by Cambridge Scientific Abstracts; RAPRA AB-STRACTS, produced by the Rubber and Plastics Research Association of Great Britain; SURFACE COATINGS ABSTRACTS, produced by the Paint Research Association of Great Britain; WELDASEARCH, produced by the Welding Institute; the WORLD TEXTILES data base, produced by the Shirley Institute; and the growing number of data bases dealing with the literature of energy conservation and environmental engineering: ENERGYLINE and ENVIROLINE, both produced by EIC/Intelligence Incorporated; POLLUTION ABSTRACTS, produced by Cambridge Sci-entific Abstracts; DOE ENERGY, produced by the U.S. Department of Energy; the APTIC data base, produced by the U.S. Environmental Pro-tection Agency; the ENVIRO data base, produced by the Ministere de l'Environment du Québec; the EDF-DOC data base, produced by the Direction des Études et des Recherches de l'Électricité de France; and the ENVIRONMENTAL BIBLIOGRAPHY data base, produced by the Envi-ronmental Studies Institute.

While the earliest bibliographic data bases emphasized the sciences and technology, coverage of the social sciences has expanded rapidly since the late 1970s. Combined coverage of the various social science disciplines is provided by the SOCIAL SCISEARCH data base, the machine-readable version of the *Social Science Citation Index*, published by the Institute for Scientific Information. ERIC—one of the oldest, best-known, and most widely utilized machine-readable bibliographic data bases—is the pri-mary information resource in the field of education, broadly interpreted to include such fields as library science. Produced by the Educational Resources Information Center of the U.S. Department of Education, the

ERIC data base is the machine-readable counterpart of two printed publications: the *Current Index to Journals in Education* and *Resources in Education.* As a supplement to ERIC, the EXCEPTIONAL CHILD EDUCATION RESOURCES (ECER) data base, produced by the Council for Exceptional Children, indexes the published and unpublished literature on gifted and handicapped children. The NICSEM/NIMIS data base, produced by the National Information Center for Special Educational Materials, covers media and devices for use with handicapped children, while the AV-ONLINE data base, produced by Access Innovations, provides comprehensive coverage of audiovisual materials for all educational applications. The AIM/ARM data base, produced by the Center for Vocational Education at Ohio State University, provides bibliographic coverage of the literature on technical and vocational education. The EUDISED data base is produced by the Documentation Centre for Education in Europe.

PSYCINFO is the primary bibliographic data base in the field of psychology. Produced by the American Psychological Association, it is the machine-readable counterpart of the printed *Psychological Abstracts.* Other bibliographic data bases of relevance to psychology include MENTAL HEALTH ABSTRACTS, produced by IFI/Plenum Data Company; the CHILD ABUSE AND NEGLECT data base, produced by the National Center on Child Abuse and Neglect; the FAMILY RESOURCES data base, produced by the National Council on Family Relations; and LANGUAGE AND LANGUAGE BEHAVIOR ABSTRACTS, produced by Sociological Abstracts, Incorporated, which also produces SOCIOLOGICAL ABSTRACTS, the primary bibliographic data base in sociology and related disciplines. Specialized facets of sociology, psychology, and related fields are covered by such data bases as PAIS INTERNATIONAL, produced by the Public Affairs Information Service; the POPULATION BIBLIOGRAPHY, produced by the University of North Carolina; the ASI data base, produced by Congressional Information Service as the machine-readable counterpart of the *American Statistics Index;* the NCJRS data base, produced by the National Criminal Justice Reference Service; and the CRIMINAL JUSTICE PERIODICALS INDEX, produced by University Microfilms International. Given the close relationship between psychology, sociology, and education, the data bases developed for any one of those fields will typically prove useful for the others.

In addition to the news and current affairs information sources discussed above, the literature of political science is covered by several data bases, including U.S. POLITICAL SCIENCE DOCUMENTS, produced by the NASA Industrial Applications Center at the University of Pittsburgh, and the WORLD AFFAIRS REPORT data base, produced by the California Institute of International Studies. Produced by the American Economic Association, the ECONOMIC LITERATURE INDEX data base corresponds to the index section of the quarterly *Journal of Economic Literature* and to the annual *Index of Economic Articles.* The ECONOMICS ABSTRACTS INTERNATIONAL data base, produced by Learned Information Limited, is the machine-readable counterpart of two printed indexes: *Economic Titles / Abstracts* and the *Key to Economic Science and Managerial Science.*

The rapidly growing interest in data bases that cover the literature of business is largely attributable to increased management emphasis on the utility of information in business decision making. General business literature is covered by several data bases, including ABI/INFORM, produced by UMI/Data Courier; the BUSINESS PERIODICALS INDEX from H.W. Wilson Company; the MANAGEMENT CONTENTS, TRADE AND INDUSTRY INDEX, and INDUSTRY DATA SOURCES data bases, produced by Information Access Company; the PTS PROMT and INFO-MAT INTERNATIONAL BUSINESS data bases, produced by Predicasts; and the CANADIAN BUSINESS AND CURRENT AFFAIRS data base, produced by MicroMedia Limited. Published literature dealing with specialized business activities is covered by such data bases as the ACCOUNTANTS INDEX, produced by the American Institute of Certified Public Accountants; the CHEMICAL BUSINESS NEWSBASE, produced by the Royal Society of Chemistry; CHEMICAL INDUSTRY NOTES, produced by Chemical Abstracts Service; INSURANCE ABSTRACTS, produced by University Microfilms International; the MATERIALS BUSINESS FILE, produced by ASM International; the P/E NEWS data base, produced by the American Petroleum Institute; the PHARMACEUTICAL AND HEALTHCARE INDUSTRY NEWS data base, produced by PJB Publications; the COMPUTER DATABASE, produced by Information Access Company; the AGRIBUSINESS USA data base, produced by Pioneer Hi-Bred International; and COFFEELINE, produced by the International Coffee Organization. ADTRACK, an interesting and unusual data base produced by Corporate Intelligence Incorporated, indexes advertisements printed in consumer magazines. It can prove useful to special libraries associated with advertising agencies, government regulatory agencies, and companies in consumer product industries.

An interesting group of machine-readable bibliographic data bases deals with one or more humanistic disciplines, although data base coverage of the humanities still lags well behind that of the sciences and social sciences. The ARTS AND HUMANITIES SEARCH data base, produced by the Institute for Scientific Information, is the machine-readable counterpart of the *Arts and Humanities Citation Index.* The FRANCIS data base, produced by the Centre de Documentation Sciences Humaines du CNRS, provides extensive coverage of European published literature in the humanities and social sciences. Published historical literature is indexed and abstracted in two data bases produced by ABC-CLIO, Incorporated: HISTORICAL ABSTRACTS covers world history from 1450 to the present, excluding publications dealing with the United States and Canada, which are covered in the AMERICA: HISTORY AND LIFE data base. Both data bases are available in printed versions under the same names.

ABC-CLIO also produces the ARTBIBLIOGRAPHIES MODERN data base, which provides coverage of monographs, periodicals, exhibition catalogs, and other publications dealing with art and design from 1800 to the present. The ART LITERATURE INTERNATIONAL data base, produced by the International Repertory of the Literature of Art, corresponds to the printed publication entitled *RILA*. The ARCHITECTURE DATABASE, produced by the British Architectural Library at the Royal Institute of British Architects, is the machine-readable counterpart of the *Architectural Periodicals Index*. The literature of music is covered by MUSIC LITERATURE INTERNATIONAL, also known as the RILM data base; it is produced by the City University of New York as the machine-readable version of the *Répertoire International de Littérature Musicale*. The MLA BIBLIOGRAPHY data base is the machine-readable version of the well-known printed bibliography produced by the Modern Language Association. The literature of philosophy and related fields, such as religion, is covered by the PHILOSOPHER'S INDEX, produced by the Philosophy Documentation Center at Bowling Green State University, and the RELIGION INDEX, produced by the American Theological Library Association.

As previously noted, the ERIC data base covers the literature of library and information science. The LISA data base, produced by Library Association Publishing, is the machine-readable counterpart of the printed *Library and Information Science Abstracts*. Produced by IFI/Plenum Data Company, the INFORMATION SCIENCE ABSTRACTS data base is the machine-readable counterpart of the printed publication of the same name, as is the LIBRARY LITERATURE data base produced by H.W. Wilson Company. Additional coverage of library activities in particular disciplines can often be found in the data bases for those disciplines. MEDLINE, for example, includes citations to publications about health sciences librarianship.

Nonbibliographic Data Bases

The machine-readable data bases described in the preceding section contain bibliographic citations and, in some cases, abstracts. While such data bases support computer-based literature searching, they are not directly useful in answering reference questions where the desired response is factual information rather than citations. Such reference applications are addressed by an increasing number of nonbibliographic data bases. Broadly defined, a nonbibliographic data base contains data other than citations to books, articles, or other library materials. In terms of their utility for library reference applications, nonbibliographic data bases can be divided into two broad groups: (1) textual data bases, which contain information equivalent to that found in such commonly used printed reference sources as encyclopedias, directories, and periodical publications; and (2) numeric data bases, which contain statistical, financial, or other quantitative information.

Of the two groups, textual data bases more closely resemble printed reference sources in concept, are easier to understand, and can be more readily assimilated into the broad spectrum of reference applications. In the 1960s, models of so-called libraries of the future predicted the online availability of computer-stored encyclopedias that could be accessed on demand through terminals. Today, the *Academic American Encyclopedia,* the *Encyclopaedia Brittanica, Everyman's Encyclopedia,* and other encyclopedias are available as machine-readable data bases accessible through the online search services discussed later in this chapter. Several encyclopedias are also available in CD-ROM editions. Among specialized encyclopedias available in machine-readable form, the KIRK-OTHMER data base, produced by Wiley Electronic Publishing, corresponds to the *Kirk-Othmer Encyclopedia of Chemical Technology.*

Directory-type data bases are among the most common nonbibliographic reference sources available in machine-readable form. Gale Research Company, for example, offers the ENCYCLOPEDIA OF ASSOCIATIONS data base, a machine-readable version of its popular printed publication. Machine-readable records for each professional and trade association include such basic descriptive information as address, phone number, and organization size, together with a summary of the association's scope and purpose. Gale also offers the BIOGRAPHY MASTER INDEX, a mixed bibliographic and nonbibliographic data base that serves as a master index to biographical information found in directories, dictionaries, and other published sources. Each machine-readable record includes birth and, where appropriate, death dates, together with citations to publications where published biographical information can be found. Other machine-readable sources of biographic information include the MARQUIS WHO'S WHO data base, produced by National Register Publishing Company; STANDARD AND POOR'S REGISTER-BIOGRAPHICAL, produced by Standard and Poor's Corporation; and AMERICAN MEN AND WOMEN OF SCIENCE, produced by R.R. Bowker.

The Foundation Center offers machine-readable versions of several of its popular printed directories. The FOUNDATION DIRECTORY data base, for example, provides descriptions of more than 25,000 grant-making foundations, while the FOUNDATION GRANTS INDEX data base contains information on grants awarded by more than 400 American philanthropic foundations. Produced by Oryx Press, the GRANTS data base contains information about more than 1,500 grant programs available through governmental and private sources. It is the machine-readable counterpart of the printed publication entitled *Grant Information System.*

Several data bases provide directory-type coverage—including name, address, and similar straightforward descriptive information—for specific industries or activities. As the machine-readable counterpart of a widely utilized business reference resource, the THOMAS REGISTER data base, produced by Thomas Publishing Company, contains information about U.S. manufacturers and their products. The various DUN'S ELECTRONIC YELLOW PAGES data bases, produced by Dun's Marketing Services, provide directory listings for manufacturers, construction agencies and contractors, and financial services companies. The DUN'S ELECTRONIC YELLOW PAGES—PROFESSIONALS DIRECTORY covers the fields of medicine, law, engineering, accounting, insurance, and real estate. The TRINET COMPANY and TRINET U.S. BUSINESS data bases, produced by Trinet Incorporated, provide address and marketing information about U.S. companies. The FINIS data base, produced by the Bank Marketing Association, contains information for financial services companies, including banks, credit unions, insurance companies, and brokers.

The FOREIGN TRADERS INDEX data base provides information about firms that represent U.S. exporters. Produced by the U.S. Department of Commerce, each record in the data base indicates the name of the firm, its size, names of its executive officers, and its areas of business activity. The TRADE OPPORTUNITIES data base, also produced by the Department of Commerce, provides information about export opportunities in the form of direct sales leads, overseas representation opportunities, and foreign government calls for tenders. The CATFAX data base, produced by Grey House Publishing, corresponds to the printed *Directory of Mail Order Catalogs*. Each record lists the name of a supplier, its address, the types of products offered, payment options, and frequency of catalog publication. The DMS CONTRACTORS data base, produced by DMS Incorporated, identifies companies involved in international defense and aerospace programs. The FROST AND SULLIVAN DM2 (Defense Market Measures System) data base contains information about U.S. government contracts, requests for proposals, and other procurement activities in such areas as aerospace, communications, data processing, transportation, medical instrumentation, navigation, and basic research.

The KOMPASS UK data base, produced by Information Services Limited as the machine-readable counterpart of various printed publications, provides directory, ownership, and management information about more than 100,000 companies in the United Kingdom. The ICC BRITISH COMPANY DIRECTORY data base, produced by ICC Information Group Limited, provides addresses and ownership information for all limited liability companies in the United Kingdom. The KEY BRITISH ENTERPRISES data base, produced by Dun and Bradstreet, provides similar directory-type information. The HOPPENSTEDT DIRECTORY OF GERMAN COMPANIES, produced by Hoppenstedt Wirtschaftsdatenbank, provides address and general business information about 35,000 German companies. Similar Hoppenstedt data bases are available for Austria and the Netherlands.

In the field of education, the EDUCATIONAL DIRECTORY data base, produced by Market Data Retrieval Incorporated, contains information about public and private schools, school districts, and public libraries in the United States. Each machine-readable record includes the school name, address, enrollment, and types of microcomputers in use, among other information. It can be used to obtain information about a specific school or as a data resource for researchers analyzing trends in American education. As a source of directory-type information about higher education, PETERSON'S COLLEGE DATABASE is the machine-readable counterpart of *Peterson's Guide to Four-Year Colleges* and *Peterson's Guide to Two-Year Colleges*. The GRADLINE data base is equivalent to *Peterson's Annual Survey of Graduate Education*. The AMERICAN LIBRARY DIRECTORY data base, produced by R.R. Bowker, corresponds to the printed publication of the same name.

A number of directory-type, nonbibliographic data bases contain information about chemical substances. Probably the best known examples are such Chemical Abstracts Service data bases as CHEMNAME, CHEMZERO, and CHEMSIS, which list CAS Registry numbers, molecular formulas, ring data, available synonyms, and other information on substances that have been named in documents appearing in *Chemical Abstracts* or the CA SEARCH data base, its machine-readable counterpart. Similarly, the TSCA CHEMICAL SUBSTANCES INVENTORY lists chemical substances in commercial use in the United States, giving their CAS Registry numbers, preferred names, synonyms, and molecular formulas. The PESTICIDE DATABANK, produced by the British Crop Protection Council and CAB International, provides directory-type information for fungicides, herbicides, insecticides, and other microbial agents and chemicals used in agricultural, veterinary, and public health applications. The HEILBRON data base, produced by Chapman and Hall Limited, identifies chemical substances by their derivative names, CAS Registry numbers, compound variants, molecular formulas, and other parameters. The MARTINDALE ONLINE data base, produced by the Pharmaceutical Society of Great Britain, provides information about drugs and medicine, including generic and proprietary names, CAS Registry numbers, physical and pharmaceutical properties, dosages, and contraindications. The MERCK INDEX data base, produced by Merck and Company, is the machine-readable version of a widely utilized guide to chemicals, drugs, and biologicals. The DRUG INFORMATION FULLTEXT data base, produced by the American Society of Hospital Pharmacists, is the machine-readable counterpart of two printed publications: the *American Hospital Formulary Service* and the *Handbook on Injectable Drugs*.

The growing number of directory-type data bases dealing with computer-related topics includes the BUYER'S GUIDE TO MICRO SOFTWARE, produced by Online Incorporated; the SOFTWARE DIRECTORY from Black Box Corporation; the BUSINESS SOFTWARE DATABASE, produced by Information Sources Incorporated; and the MICROCOMPUTER SOFTWARE GUIDE, produced by R.R. Bowker. The COMPUTER-READABLE DATABASES, produced by Gale Research Company, corresponds to the printed *Computer-Readable Databases: A Directory and Data Sourcebook*.

Numeric data bases, containing financial and statistical information, have been used for a number of years by businesses and government agencies as a means of analyzing demographic and market trends. Commonly cited and widely available examples include the CENDATA data base, produced by the U.S. Bureau of the Census, and the DONNELLEY DEMOGRAPHICS data base, produced by Donnelley Marketing Services. The latter information resource contains demographic estimates and projections for U.S. states, counties, municipalities, and zip code areas. Recently, the use of such data bases in conjunction with computer-generated graphics output has received considerable business attention. Library applications of numeric data bases are less common, although such data bases can play a useful role in specialized reference activities. Widely utilized in business libraries, the DISCLOSURE and DISCLOSURE/SPECTRUM OWNERSHIP data bases, produced by Disclosure Incorporated, contain financial and ownership information pertaining to publicly owned U.S. companies. The information is extracted from several sources, including reports that those companies must file with the Securities and Exchange Commission. Addressing the same applications, the COMPUSTAT data base, produced by Standard and Poor's Corporation, contains more detailed information and includes more historical information than DISCLOSURE. The VALUE LINE data base, produced by Value Line Incorporated, provides detailed financial information and projections for the approximately 1,700 companies that account for about 95 percent of stock trading volume in the United States. The EXSTAT data base, produced by Extel Group, provides financial data on 2,500 international corporations. The ICC BRITISH COMPANY FINANCIAL DATASHEETS data base, produced by ICC Information Group Limited, provides financial data for more than 160,000 British companies. The PTS ANNUAL REPORTS data base provides statistical and textual information abstracted from the annual reports of more than 4,000 publicly held U.S. and international companies, while the INVESTEXT data base, produced by Technical Data International, contains the complete texts of financial research reports prepared by leading investment banking firms.

Data bases that contain historical and predictive economic information are an increasingly common resource in corporate, banking, brokerage, government, and other libraries that support financial planning and econometric analysis. Examples of such data bases include CITIBASE, produced by Citibank; ECONBASE, produced by the WEFA Group; the CONSUMER PRICE INDEX (CPI) and PRODUCER PRICE INDEX (PPI) data bases, produced by the U.S. Bureau of Labor Statistics; the PTS U.S. FORECASTS, PTS U.S. TIME SERIES, and PTS INTERNATIONAL FORECASTS data bases, produced by Predicasts; the BI/DATA TIME SERIES, produced by Business International; the CONFERENCE BOARD DATA BANK, produced by the Conference Board; the CANSIM data base, produced by Statistics Canada and the Bank of Canada; the FLOW OF FUNDS and INTERNATIONAL FINANCIAL STATISTICS data bases, produced by the International Monetary Fund; the MAIN ECONOMIC INDICATORS data base, produced by the OECD; SITE II, a demographic data base produced by Data Resources Incorporated; the CURRENCY AND SHARE INDEX DATABANK, produced by the Financial Times; the FINANCIAL AND ECONOMIC DATABANK, produced by the Bank of England; the SPHINX data base, produced by the Institut National de la Statistique et des Études Économiques; and the CRONOS-EUROSTAT data base, produced by the Statistical Office of the European Communities. In addition to their obvious importance for corporate libraries that support business decision making and for academic libraries that support graduate business curricula and faculty research, such data bases will prove attractive to public libraries interested in developing fee-based information services for their local business communities.

ONLINE INFORMATION SERVICES

As previously indicated, libraries can purchase machine-readable bibliographic and nonbibliographic data bases on magnetic tape for processing on their own computers using custom-developed information retrieval software. During the late 1960s and early 1970s, a number of such computer-based literature searching systems were implemented to automate the production of comprehensive retrospective bibliographies and current awareness listings. In the typical application, a scientist or other researcher submitted a request for a literature search to a specially trained librarian or information specialist, who formulated an appropriate search strategy consisting of a combination of commands and search terms. These search requests were then keypunched and batched for processing against one or more data bases at prescheduled intervals, the computer producing printed lists of citations for each request. Subject to the limitations of offline, noninteractive data processing, these early computer-based systems simplified the performance of certain complex and/or comprehensive literature searches requiring the logical coordination of multiple search terms.

Custom-developed literature retrieval systems based on the acquisition of bibliographic data in machine-readable form were primarily implemented by large university, corporate, and government libraries, especially those serving researchers in scientific and technical disciplines. As with the acquisition of cataloging data on MARC tapes, most libraries lacked access to the computer resources and programming expertise necessary to take advantage of available machine-readable bibliographic data resources. During the 1960s and early 1970s, the needs of these libraries were addressed by fee-based search services operated by the producers of machine-readable data bases or by third parties such as university-based technical information centers. These services, like their in-house counterparts, customarily operated in the offline, batch-processing mode.

Taking the MEDLARS search service operated by the National Library of Medicine as an example, librarians in medical schools, hospitals, and other health service facilities first interviewed researchers locally in order to prepare a written statement of their information requirements to be mailed or otherwise transmitted to the National Library of Medicine. There, an information specialist analyzed the submitted statement and formulated a search strategy to be executed in a batch with other incoming search requests against the machine-readable MEDLARS data base. The results, consisting of a printout of retrieved citations, were mailed or otherwise delivered to the originating library for dissemination to the researcher who requested the search. As with in-house literature searching systems, this approach simplified and speeded the completion of lengthy and complex searches which are difficult and time-consuming to perform manually. In the absence of direct interaction between requesters and search specialists, however, such searches typically lacked precision—that is, some or even many of the retrieved citations proved irrelevant to the researchers' stated or implied information requirements.

Online Search Concepts

As discussed elsewhere in this book, developments in library automation have generally reflected trends in the broad field of data processing.

In the early 1970s, the data processing industry began to shift its emphasis from offline, batch-oriented computing to the development of online systems in which users process information on demand from remote terminals in a time-sharing environment. As applied to computer-based literature searching, this shift to online systems entails the maintenance of machine-readable bibliographic data bases on fixed magnetic disk drives for interactive searching by librarians working at local terminals. As with offline search systems, a requester's information requirements are first delineated and a search strategy, consisting of commands and search terms, formulated. But rather than being keypunched and batched for later input, the search strategy is entered at an online terminal, and an immediate indication of the number of presumably relevant citations is obtained. A few citations can then be displayed or printed for immediate examination, and the search strategy modified to improve precision. Once the appropriateness of the search strategy is confirmed, all or selected results can be displayed or printed. Alternatively, search results can be printed offline for later distribution to the requester.

A few government and corporate libraries have developed their own online search capabilities, using machine-readable bibliographic data bases created locally or purchased from publishers of printed indexing and abstracting services. Most libraries, however, obtain online, timeshared access to bibliographic and nonbibliographic data bases through fee-based information services. As outlined later in this chapter, such information services differ in the number and type of data bases offered, but they share a common operating methodology: they create, purchase, or otherwise obtain bibliographic and nonbibliographic data bases in machine-readable form, convert them to a format required for storage on their own computers, and allow libraries or other subscribers to perform various retrieval operations on the data using prewritten data base management software. Some services also offer private file capabilities which allow libraries or other customers to establish their own data bases for online access through the search service's prewritten software. As noted in chapter 6, such private file capabilities can be used for online catalog implementations.

Like the general-purpose data base management systems discussed in chapter 3, the bibliographic data base management systems implemented and operated by online information services feature nonprocedural query languages that allow users to initiate literature searches or other retrieval operations by entering a series of commands accompanied by specified retrieval parameters. Although they do require study and practice to use effectively, these query languages are easily learned and do not require the memorization of elaborate sets of rules and careful attention to the formulation of algorithms which characterize conventional procedural programming languages.

Taking the query language utilized by the popular Dialog Information Service as an example, most operations can be performed with a simple set of commands. Following the entry of passwords that identify the terminal user as a valid DIALOG subscriber, the BEGIN command, followed by the number of a desired data base, informs the DIALOG system that the user wants to begin retrieval operations in that data base. All DIALOG data bases are identified by numbers contained in a master list which is available in printed form or can be accessed online. Thus, a command of the form:

BEGIN 15

will initiate retrieval operations in the ABI/INFORM data base, which covers business publications. If desired, several data bases can be searched simultaneously, either by entering their identifying numbers or by selecting one of the preformed data base groups assembled by DIALOG for subject-oriented information retrieval. The GEOLOGY group, for example, includes the GEOARCHIVE, GEOREF, GEOBASE, NTIS, COMPENDEX PLUS, and PASCAL data bases.

Once a given data base has been selected, the EXPAND command, followed by a search term or phrase, enables the searcher to determine whether that term or phrase is listed in the master index for the active data base and, if so, how many times it appears in the data base's individual records. In effect, the EXPAND command causes the DIALOG system to print or display that section of the data base index where the indicated search term or phrase appears. In many cases, terms or phrases that are alphabetically adjacent to the indicated term may prove relevant to the search. The DIALOG system indexes every significant term that appears in any part of a record. With some data bases, the operation of the EXPAND command can be limited to the occurrence of the search term in a specific part of a record, such as the assigned subject headings or the title.

The EXPAND command is useful in identifying possible search terms or phrases. Specific retrieval operations are initiated by the SELECT commands. When followed by a search term or phrase, the SELECT command instructs the DIALOG system to establish a set of data base records indexed with the indicated term or phrase. Thus, the command:

SELECT VIDEO

will establish a set of records in which the term *video* appears. As with the EXPAND command, operation of the SELECT command can be restricted to a specific part of a record. As an interactive search system, DIALOG responds to each SELECT command by assigning a set or statement number to it, indicating the number of index entries for the specified search term or phrase and repeating the command itself for confirmation purposes. Thus, a response of the form:

1   408   VIDEO

indicates that the DIALOG system has identified a set of retrieved records that it will hereafter refer to as set number 1, that the set contains 408 records, and that the records contain the search term *video*.

While some literature searches or other information retrieval operations involve a single search term, many are based on combinations of several terms. In the DIALOG system, such retrieval requirements are met by using logical operators to combine the sets created by two or more SELECT commands. As an example, a search for citations on the use of video technology in medicine might be accomplished by the following sequence of search statements:

<pre>
SELECT VIDEO
   1   408   VIDEO
SELECT MEDICINE
   2   946   MEDICINE
SELECT S1 AND S2
   3   28   S1 AND S2
</pre>

The last SELECT command instructs the DIALOG system to apply the logical AND operation to citations contained in the sets created by the first two select commands. The results constitute a third set, which might later be combined with other sets.

Three logical operators are widely encountered in computer-based information retrieval systems: AND, OR, and NOT. These logical operators, which are also supported by some online public access catalog systems, are sometimes called Boolean operators. They are named for George Boole, a nineteenth-century mathematician who pioneered the application of mathematical concepts and algebraic symbols to the field of logic. In the example depicted above, the logical AND operator creates a third set from records which are members of both of two previously established sets— that is, those records that contain the terms *video* and *medicine*. In effect, the AND operation seeks the logical intersection of the two sets. Much of the power of computer-based reference service is derived from the use of the logical AND operator.

The logical OR operator takes two previously established sets and combines them into a third set. It thus establishes the logical union of two sets. In information retrieval applications, it can be used to group synonymous terms into a single set for search purposes. Hence, the sequence of search statements:

<pre>
SELECT VIDEO
   1   408   VIDEO
SELECT TELEVISION
   2   312   TELEVISION
SELECT S1 OR S2
   3   705   S1 OR S2
SELECT MEDICINE
   4   946   MEDICINE
SELECT S3 AND S4
   5   46   S3 AND S4
</pre>

combines the sets of records indexed with either the terms *video* or *television* into a third set that is then combined, using the AND operator, with the set of records indexed with the term *medicine*. The result is the retrieval of records indexed with both video and medicine or with both television and medicine.

Experienced DIALOG users can perform the same operation with a single command of the form:

SELECT (VIDEO OR TELEVISION) AND MEDICINE

In this example, the DIALOG system will perform the parenthesized operation first, responding to the command with a listing of search terms and set numbers:

408	VIDEO
312	TELEVISION
705	VIDEO OR TELEVISION
946	MEDICINE
46	(VIDEO OR TELEVISION) AND MEDICINE

If desired, the SELECT and EXPAND commands can be combined with a truncation operator to search for terms with common roots. Thus, a command of the form:

SELECT VIDEO?

will select records indexed with videos, videotape, videocassette, videodisc, videotext, and other singular and plural words that begin with the character string "video." Similarly, the SELECT command can combine with operators that specify the desired proximity of two search terms. Thus, a command of the form:

SELECT VIDEO (W) TERMINALS

will retrieve records that contain the word "video" immediately followed by the word "terminals." Other DIALOG commands permit the storage of specified command sequences for use in subsequent online sessions.

Records from specified sets can be displayed online in various formats. Alternatively, search results can be printed offline at DIALOG headquarters and mailed to the customer. Other online information services support similar retrieval capabilities, although the syntax and semantics of particular commands will necessarily vary from one service to another. For inexperienced or untrained users, some services feature menu-driven interfaces.

Multidisciplinary Services

Online information services can be divided in two broad groups: (1) multidisciplinary services that provide data base coverage of a varied range of subjects for a broad clientele; and (2) specialized services that provide access to one or more data bases relevant to a particular subject, academic discipline, profession, or activity. Multidisciplinary information services have traditionally dominated library reference applications. Such services acquire data bases from various publishers or other producers and make them available to libraries and other customers through a common software interface. While some data base producers have exclusive arrangements with particular online information services, there is considerable overlap among multidisciplinary services. Although no service exactly duplicates the offerings of any other, certain data bases are so widely available that, apart from cost differences, no multidisciplinary information service can base its competitive position on them. Examples include ABI/INFORM, BIOSIS, CA SEARCH, COMPENDEX PLUS, INSPEC, MANAGEMENT CONTENTS, MEDLINE, NTIS, and PSYCINFO. Instead, the various multidisciplinary data base services are largely distinguished by the breadth and depth of their offerings beyond this common core.

Measured by the number and variety of data bases it offers, DIALOG is the world's largest and most diverse multidisciplinary information service. Owned by Knight-Ridder, it provides online access to approximately 400 data bases and has long been the best choice for libraries seeking the broadest possible subject coverage from a single vendor. Its general reference and news information sources are excellent. As a further competitive advantage, DIALOG offers more data bases per subject area than any other multidisciplinary information service. While the expansion of other services has increased the amount of overlap, DIALOG remains the exclusive online source for many data bases.

Reflecting the historical development of online searching, the largest group of DIALOG data bases provides bibliographic coverage of scientific and technical subjects. The breadth and depth of DIALOG's offerings compare favorably with the specialized sci-tech and biomedical search services described later in this chapter. In addition to such major interdisciplinary scientific data bases as SCISEARCH and PASCAL, DIALOG supports chemistry research with at least 15 data bases. Biomedical researchers can draw on several dozen data bases, including an impressive group of pharmaceutical information resources. Bibliographic coverage of specific health problems is provided by such data bases as AIDSLINE, SMOKING AND HEALTH, and SPORT. DIALOG's patent information resources are extensive. It offers at least one data base for each engineering specialty, and some fields are covered by multiple information sources. Energy and environmental engineering, for example, are treated in no fewer than a dozen data bases.

DIALOG's business-oriented offerings include indexes to general business periodicals; specialized bibliographic coverage of particular industries, such as defense, finance, and insurance; business news data bases, which contain press releases and company reports; and a variety of non-bibliographic resources which provide numeric and directory-type information about specific companies and business activities. DIALOG's coverage of the social sciences and humanities, while less extensive than its offerings for science and business, compares favorably with that of other multidisciplinary search services. DIALOG provides at least one data base for each major subject discipline, and some fields are supported by extensive information resources. As an example, public affairs, current events, and international studies are covered by PAIS INTERNATIONAL, WORLD AFFAIRS REPORT, FACTS ON FILE, CURRENT DIGEST OF THE SOVIET PRESS, and the ARAB INFORMATION BANK, as well as various newswire and data bases.

The ORBIT and BRS information services have each changed ownership several times. At the time of this writing, they were both owned by Maxwell Online, although they operated as separate, complementary services. ORBIT, one of the oldest online information services, offers approximately 100 data bases. While it retains sufficient subject diversity to be categorized as a multidisciplinary service, ORBIT emphasizes scientific and technical information resources. It provides excellent bibliographic coverage of specialized scientific and engineering disciplines, particularly chemistry, earth science, environmental engineering, materials science, and patents and trademarks. Its exclusive offerings include the AQUALINE data base of water resources literature; the COLD data base, produced by the Cold Regions Research and Engineering Laboratory of the U.S. Army Corps of Engineers; the ENERGY BIBLIOGRAPHY, produced by the Texas A&M Library; GEOMECHANICS ABSTRACTS, produced by the Rock Mechanics Information Service; IMAGING ABSTRACTS from the Royal Photographic Society; the JAPIO data base from the Japan Patent Information Organization; the LITALERT listing of patent and trademark infringement suits, produced by Research Publications; and WORLD SURFACE COATINGS ABSTRACTS, produced by the Paint Research Association. For North American libraries, ORBIT is the most conveniently accessible, though not the exclusive, source for certain other sci-tech data bases; examples include RAPRA ABSTRACTS from Rapra Technology Limited, SAE GLOBAL MOBILITY data base from the Society of Automotive Engineers, and the ICONDA data base of construction and civil engineering literature.

While ORBIT is nominally multidisciplinary, its emphasis on scientific and technical data bases avoids direct competition with BRS, which offers broader subject coverage. With approximately 150 data bases online, BRS is a general-purpose information service, although heavy concentrations of data bases in selected subject areas—notably, health care and pharmacology—enable it to compete effectively with certain specialized information services. For the convenience of biomedical researchers, BRS offers separately packaged subsets of certain health-related data bases. Examples include MEDLINE REFERENCES ON AIDS and EMBASE DRUG INFORMATION; they contain information that can also be found in the full MEDLINE and EMBASE data bases, respectively. In addition, BRS offers several "superfiles," which combine multiple data bases that are typically implemented separately by other information services. The CAMBRIDGE SCIENTIFIC ABSTRACTS LIFE SCIENCES data base, for example, combines the LIFE SCIENCES COLLECTION, AQUATIC SCIENCES AND FISHERIES ABSTRACTS, OCEANIC ABSTRACTS, and POLLUTION ABSTRACTS. BRS's competitive position is further strengthened by its exclusive biomedical offerings, such as the MEDICAL AND PSYCHOLOGICAL PREVIEWS data base. Produced by BRS itself, it indexes 240 journals in clinical medicine and psychology within 10 days of their receipt and provides access to bibliographic citations weeks or months before they are indexed in MEDLINE, PSYCINFO, or other data bases.

BRS's business coverage, while less extensive than DIALOG's, is nonetheless useful. As an attractive adjunct to its health care offerings, BRS's social science coverage provides excellent support for social work research and professional practice with such data bases as SOCIAL PLANNING/POLICY AND DEVELOPMENT ABSTRACTS, INTERNATIONAL REVIEW OF PUBLICATIONS IN SOCIOLOGY, SOCIAL WORK ABSTRACTS, AGELINE, ABLEDATA, REHABDATA, and FAMILY RESOURCES. Education-oriented data bases include two BRS exclusives: RESOURCES IN VOCATIONAL EDUCATION and the ONTARIO EDUCATION RESOURCES INFORMATION SYSTEM.

Regardless of their competitive positions, DIALOG, ORBIT, BRS, and most other multidisciplinary information services provide access, through common software, to data bases produced by a wide variety of organizations. Although some multidisciplinary services produce certain data bases themselves, such proprietary information products comprise a very small percentage of their total offerings. The Wilsonline search service is a notable exception; it emphasizes data bases produced by the H.W. Wilson Company, a well-known publisher of printed indexes on a wide variety of topics. Introduced in 1987, Wilsonline is representative of the producer-operated information services that were widely discussed in the mid-1970s but which subsequently fell out of favor, perhaps because few information producers cover a sufficiently broad range of subjects to satisfy the requirements of a truly multidisciplinary service. Such early online search services as MEDLINE and the NEW YORK TIMES INFORMATION BANK provided access to the information of a single producer, but they could not be categorized as multidisciplinary and neither of them currently operates in its original form. As discussed later in this chapter, MEDLINE is just one of several data bases offered by the National Library of Medicine's search service, while the INFORMATION BANK has been incorporated into the NEXIS service offered by Mead Data Central.

While Wilsonline offers several non-Wilson data bases—including LC MARC, as discussed in chapter 6—its competitive position is based on Wilson-produced information resources, particularly the machine-readable counterparts of such well-known and widely used publications as the *Readers' Guide to Periodical Literature, Book Review Digest, Business Periodicals Index, Applied Science and Technology Index,* and *Library Literature.* At the time of this writing, Wilsonline offered approximately 25 data bases. Its broad subject coverage and attractive rates have proven popular with academic and public libraries where Wilson indexes are widely used and well-respected reference tools.

EPIC is a multidisciplinary information service established in 1990 by OCLC. FIRST SEARCH, an allied service intended expressly for end-user searching, features a menu-driven interface and provides online access to a subset of the EPIC data bases. The two services' most important data base is the OCLC Online Union Catalog, which was described in chapter 6. EPIC and FIRST SEARCH offer the only complete implementations of the Online Union Catalog which permit subject searching; the OCLC bibliographic utility, which emphasizes technical processing rather than reference service, limits retrieval to specified numeric parameters and specially constructed search keys based on authors' names and title words. Other EPIC and FIRST SEARCH offerings include such widely available data bases as BIOSIS, ERIC, GEOREF, and the GPO MONTHLY CATALOG.

Although DIALOG, BRS, ORBIT, and other U.S. search services are available and widely used in Canada, several organizations have developed multidisciplinary search services designed specifically for the Canadian market. Of these, the Canadian Online Enquiry (CAN/OLE) System bears the closest resemblance to U.S. search services. Developed and operated by the Canadian Institute for Scientific and Technical Information (CISTI), a division of National Research Council Canada, CAN/OLE is only available in Canada. Its search commands can be entered in either English or French, and all documentation is available in both languages.

While CAN/OLE, like ORBIT, emphasizes scientific and engineering information, its data base roster is sufficiently broad to warrant categorization as a multidisciplinary service. A medium-size information service with approximately 40 data bases online, its offerings include AQUATIC SCIENCES AND FISHERIES ABSTRACTS, BIOSIS PREVIEWS, CA SEARCH, COMPENDEX, GEOREF, INSPEC, METADEX, NTIS, SCISEARCH, and several other U.S. data bases that are widely available through other search services, although CAN/OLE's relatively low prices make it an attractive alternative to U.S. information services for Canadian libraries. Its most distinctive feature, however, is a group of data bases that draw on Canadian information resources, many of them produced by Canadian universities and government agencies. Examples include the ALBERTA OIL SANDS INDEX (AOSI), produced by the Alberta Research Council; the AQUAREF data base of aquatic science literature, produced by the Inland Waters Directorate of Environment Canada; the BOREAL data base of monographs, reports, and other documents cataloged by the Boreal Institute for Northern Studies at the University of Alberta; CANREG, a register of Canadian research in the social sciences, produced by the University of Western Ontario; IRCPBUS, a bibliographic data base produced by the Institute for Research in Construction; STATCAN, a data base of references to documents published by Statistics Canada; STATNORM, which provides access to current Canadian standards published by organizations that comprise the National Standards System; the ENVIRONMENT LIBRARIES AUTOMATED SYSTEM (ELIAS), a union catalog of the Environment Canada Library Network plus collections of Fisheries and Oceans Canada; NLCATBN, an online catalog of books, government publications, and other documents published in Canada or written by Canadians; and TRANSCAT, a data base of nonrestricted government publications and other documents dealing with transportation.

Measured by the number of data bases it offers, QL QUICKSEARCH is Canada's largest online information service. Operated by QL Systems Limited, it is difficult to categorize. With its excellent selection of Canadian legal, tax-related, and news-oriented information resources, QL QUICKSEARCH resembles the specialized legal information services discussed below, but it provides a sufficiently diverse group of other data bases to warrant inclusion in this discussion of multidisciplinary services. Its news and public affairs offerings include CANADIAN PRESS NEWS-TEX, the national wire service cooperative of Canadian newspapers; CANADA NEWSWIRE, which contains press releases from 5,000 sources; LA PRESSE CANADIENNE, the French-language newswire from the Canadian Press; BUSINESS INFORMATION WIRE, which contains Canadian, U.S., and European business news stories since 1987; the CANADIAN JOURNALISM DATABASE, an index to journalism periodicals and other information sources, produced by the Graduate School of Journalism at the University of Western Ontario; and the full texts of various newspapers published in Canada and the United Kingdom.

Other QL QUICKSEARCH data bases cover a variety of subjects. The FILM-VIDEO CANADIANA and FILM-VIDEO PRODUCERS AND DISTRIBUTORS data bases, produced by the National Film Board of Canada, contain bibliographic references and directory listings pertaining to the Canadian film and television industries. The CERTIFIED PRODUCTS DATABASE lists products that have been tested and certified for sale by the Canadian Standards Association. QL QUICKSEARCH offers the BOREAL NORTHERN TITLES data base, which is also accessible through the CAN/OLE search service; the YUKON BIBLIOGRAPHY; the ARCTIC SCIENCE AND TECHNOLOGY data base, produced by the University of Calgary; and the SCOTT POLAR RESEARCH INSTITUTE LIBRARY CATALOGUE. A limited group of technical information resources emphasizes environmental sciences and metallurgy.

The SDM search service, based in Montreal, emphasizes information of interest to French-speaking persons living and working in Quebec. While a few SDM data bases contain English-language records, the majority are French-language information resources produced in Quebec by SDM itself or by government agencies and other organizations. Examples include CHOIX, a bibliographic data base of monographic and serial publications on a variety of subjects; REPERE, an index to popular French-language periodicals distributed in Quebec; EDUQ, a data base of educational literature produced by the Quebec Ministry of Education; PUBLIQ, a data base of official publications of the Government of Quebec; DAVID, which contains bibliographic citations for audiovisual materials; PRODIL, a directory of software producers in Quebec; and HISCABEQ, which provides bibliographic coverage of Quebec and Canadian history. SDM is the exclusive online source for all of the data bases it offers.

The U.S. multidisciplinary information services described above are readily accessible to libraries and other customers outside of North America through international telecommunication facilities. To serve overseas users, DIALOG has sales offices or representatives in Europe, Japan, the Middle East, Latin America, Hong Kong, Korea, and Australia. Similarly, Maxwell Online has offices and representatives in Europe, Japan, Korea, and Australia. While U.S. information services account for a significant percentage of foreign online retrieval activity, a number of European government agencies, research organizations, and private companies have implemented online search services. Originally designed for the European market, these services have been available to U.S. and Canadian subscribers since the mid-1980s. Multidisciplinary in character, they combine commonly encountered U.S. data bases with European information resources that are otherwise unavailable in North America. While they cannot replace American search services, their extensive coverage of international information resources can effectively supplement familiar data bases in applications where exhaustivity or a particular regional focus is required. As such, the European search services are of greatest relevance to university libraries that support graduate programs in European area studies; to research-oriented organizations with an international emphasis; and to business and technical libraries in corporations with offices, research facilities, factories, subsidiaries, or investment interests in specific countries.

The DATA-STAR information service—which operates on computers located in Berne, Switzerland—was established by Radio Suisse in the early 1980s to serve continental Europe and the United Kingdom. It subsequently expanded its customer base to other countries, including the United States, through subsidiaries and authorized agents. It was acquired by Knight-Ridder, which also owns DIALOG, in 1993. DATA-STAR offers a combination of familiar U.S. data bases, plus an impressive array of European information resources, some of which are unique to the DATA-STAR search service. Biomedical information is perhaps DATA-STAR's strongest subject area. In addition to such widely available data bases as MEDLINE, EXCERPTA MEDICA, CANCERLIT, NURSING AND ALLIED HEALTH, and BIOSIS, DATA-STAR provides exclusive online access to various European health-related data bases. Examples include DHSS-DATA, a health services data base produced by the Department of Health and Social Security Library; DHSS-DHMT, a medical toxicology data base; the ALLIED AND ALTERNATIVE MEDICINE data base, produced by the British Library; the BRITISH MEDICAL ASSOCIATION PRESS CUTTINGS data base; the FORS data base, produced by the Home Office Forensic Science Service; and the IMMUNOCLONE data base, which contains information about cells of immunological interest. DATA-STAR's unique European pharmaceutical information resources include the PHARMLINE data base, produced by the Regional Drug Information Service at the National Health Services; the EUROPEAN PHARMACEUTICAL MARKET RESEARCH ASSOCIATION data base, produced by The Resource Group; the AERZTE ZEITUNG data base, which contains the full text of articles from the leading German medical newspaper; and the KOSMET data base, produced by the International Federation of the Societies of Cosmetic Chemists.

DATA-STAR's business offerings emphasize such European and international data bases as HOPPENSTEDT BENELUX, a guide to 78,000 companies in the Netherlands, Belgium, and Luxembourg; HOPPENSTEDT AUSTRIA, the online counterpart of the *Oesterreich 2000* directory; DDR COMPANIES, which provides directory-type profiles for businesses in the new German federal states; the FINN and COIN data bases, which provide financial information about German industrial and service companies; KOMPASS ISRAEL, a directory of Israeli companies; the GENERALE DE BANQUE, which covers banking and finance in Belgium and the European Communities; and TRADSTAT, a data base of international trade statistics. DATA-STAR also provides useful international coverage of general, financial, and industrial news sources. Its sci-tech data bases include several European information resources that are unavailable elsewhere. While many of DATA-STAR's data bases are in English, some require a knowledge of French or German for effective searching.

The European Space Agency-Information Retrieval Service (ESA-IRS) has offered online information services for two decades. Operating on computers located in Italy, it maintains national centers in most western European countries and has authorized agents and other business representatives in North America, Asia, Africa, and Latin America. With its historical emphasis on scientific and technical data bases, ESA-IRS most closely resembles ORBIT among the multidisciplinary search services. While it also offers information resources of interest for business and the social sciences, it lacks the breadth of coverage provided by DIALOG, BRS, and DATA-STAR. Its unusually strong offerings in aerospace engineering, building and construction, environmental science, materials science, and mechanical engineering draw heavily on European data bases, many of which are either unique to or most conveniently available from ESA-IRS. Examples include AFEE, a water resources data base produced by the Association Française pour l'Étude des Eaux; BIIPAM-CTIF, a metallurgical data base produced by the Centre de Recherches de Pont-à-Mousson; the BRIX/FLAIR data base, produced in the United Kingdom by the Building Research Station; CETIM, the machine-readable counterpart of *Technologies Mécaniques;* and MERLIN-TECH, an electrical and electronics engineering data base produced by Merlin Gerin in Grenoble, France.

The Questel information service—a subsidiary of Télésystemes, which is part of France Telecom Group—operates on computers located in Valbonne, France. Its subject coverage includes science and technology, health and safety, news, business, and the humanities. While it offers such well-known U.S. data bases as CA SEARCH and MEDLINE, Questel's competitive position is principally based on French and other European information resources, some of which are unique to Questel. Examples include ADHEMIX, a compendium of information about structural glues produced by Commissariat à l'Énergie Atomique; CIM, a data base of bibliographic references to publications on cements and hydraulic binders produced by the Centre d'Études et de Recherches de l'Industrie des Liants Hydrauliques; DAUGAZ, an international bibliography on gaseous fuels produced by Gaz de France; ECOMINE, a bibliographic data base on mining and minerals produced by the Bureau de Recherches Geologiques et Minières; the LOGOS data base of French government documents and official pronouncements produced by Direction de la Documentation Française; BELGI, a directory of Belgian companies produced by EURO DB; NORIANE data base of French and European standards produced by the Association Française de Normalisation; and several European patent and trademark data bases produced by the Institut National de la Propriété Industrielle and other organizations. For university libraries that support graduate programs in European studies, the FRANCIS data base, produced by the Centre de Documentation Sciences Humaines du CNRS, provides extensive bibliographic coverage of European publications in the humanities and social sciences since 1972. As a potential constraint, some Questel data bases require a knowledge of French for effective full-text searching. To facilitate searching by international subscribers, several of the service's French-language data bases include titles and/or descriptors in other languages, such as English and German. For domestic customers, Questel's implementation of MEDLINE includes French titles and descriptors.

The BLAISE-LINE search service is operated by the Bibliographic Services Division of the British Library, which produces the majority of BLAISE-LINE's data bases. BNB MARC, which was mentioned briefly in chapter 6 as the machine-readable counterpart of the *British National Bibliography,* contains cataloging records for British books and serial titles published since 1950. Other BLAISE-LINE data bases include BLISS, which contains the acquisitions of the British Library; BRITISH LIBRARY CATALOGUE PREVIEW, which contains entries generated by the British Library Catalogue Conversion Project; the REGISTER OF PRESERVATION MICROFORMS, which is produced by the British Library's National Preservation Office; the DOCUMENT SUPPLY CENTRE CATALOGUE, which lists monographs available through the British Library Document Supply Centre; and the online counterparts of the British Library's humanities, social sciences, science reference, and music catalogs. BLAISE-LINE offerings produced by other organizations include the WHITAKER data base of British books and English-language titles available for sale in the United Kingdom; the HMSO data base of items published by Her Majesty's Stationery Office; the NSDC data base of serials records produced by the United Kingdom National Serials Data Centre; and the ESTC and ISTC data bases, which are the online counterparts of the *Eighteenth Century Short Title Catalogue* and the *Incunable Short Title Catalogue,* respectively. BLAISE-LINE also offers the LC MARC data base.

PFDS ONLINE, which operates on computers located in the United Kingdom, offers business-oriented and semitechnical data bases of principal interest to corporate and research libraries. Its offerings are sufficiently diverse to warrant categorization as a multidisciplinary search service, although it certainly lacks the breadth and depth of the larger services described above. Among its strengths, PFDS ONLINE provides useful coverage of United Kingdom and European corporations with such data bases as DUNS EUROPEAN MARKETING ONLINE, which contains management and financial information about 1.8 million Western European companies; EUROPE'S LARGEST COMPANIES and SCANDINAVIA'S LARGEST COMPANIES, two directory data bases produced by ELC Limited; IRISH COMPANY PROFILES, which covers the 9,000 largest companies in the Republic of Ireland; and the TDS BUSINESS FILE, which contains marketing information for 800,000 U.K. businesses, produced by Telephone Database Services Limited. Its sci-tech coverage emphasizes business aspects of technology. Information about the chemicals industry, for example, is contained in the CHEMICAL AGE PROJECT FILE from Reed Telepublishing, the CHEMICAL PLANT and CHEMICAL TRADE STATISTICS data bases from Chemical Intelligence Services, and the CHEMICAL BUSINESS NEWSBASE from the Royal Society of Chemistry. Unusual PFDS ONLINE offerings include the WATERLOW LEGAL DATABASE, a directory of solicitors in the United Kingdom, and the ART SALES INDEX, which lists works of art sold at international auctions since 1970.

Various other European information services provide online access to data bases not readily available elsewhere. Such services offer a relatively small number of data bases, but their subject coverage is sufficiently broad to warrant categorization in the multidisciplinary group. The varied offerings of BERTELSMANN INFORMATIONSSERVICE GMBH, for example, include AERZTE ZEITUNG and PHARMA MARKETING SERVICE, two health care industry data bases; WER LIEFERT WAS (WHO SUPPLIES WHAT), a directory of German and Austrian vendors; FIRMEN-INFO-BANK, which contains financial information about 23,000 German companies; the PATOS series of European patent data bases; and MUNZINGER-LAENDERARCHIV, a data base of geographic information. The Belgian Information Dissemination Service (BELINDIS) is operated in Brussels by the Belgian Ministry of Economic Affairs. Its principal offerings are an interesting and unique group of legal and public affairs data bases produced in and pertaining to the Benelux countries. It also offers a small number of European technical data bases, including the INIS data base from the International Atomic Energy Agency. Several BELINDIS data bases provide information about library collections in Belgium. ANTILOPE, for example, is a union list of serials for university libraries, while the COLLECTIVE CATALOGUE OF BELGIUM lists monographs available in university and scientific libraries.

The ECHO search service was established by the Commission of the European Communities (CEC) in 1980. Operating on computers located in Luxembourg, it provides online, multilingual access to a small but unique group of data bases, several of which are produced by the CEC itself as online guides to information processing products, projects, and services available in Europe. One of these contains descriptive listings for European data bases, data base producers, online information services, CD-ROM information products, gateways, and information brokers. I/S DATACENTRALEN, a Danish search service, offers online access to CRONOS, a voluminous, broadly useful statistical data base derived from information provided by various national governments and international organizations, including the European Communities, UNESCO, and the International Monetary Fund. Several of I/S DATACENTRALEN's offerings deal with Scandinavian topics. The NCOM data base, for example, indexes Nordic publications pertaining to mass communications and social communications. The NORDISK ENERGI INDEKS is a data base of energy-related publications and projects in Nordic countries. LIST STAT is a bibliography of statistical publications held by libraries in Denmark, Finland, and Norway. ALIS is a catalog of monographic and serial holdings developed by the National Technological Library of Denmark. A Stockholm-based search service operated by AFFAERS DATA AB likewise provides online access to information created in or pertaining to Scandinavia. Examples include ELEXINFO, which contains the full text of export regulations for Scandinavian countries; NYHETSBYRAN DIREKT, a Swedish business and economic news data base; PARAD ONLINE, a directory of key personnel in Swedish companies; SVERIGES HANDELSKALENDER, a directory of 15,000 Swedish companies and sales representatives; and TIDNINGS-DATABASEN, which provides bibliographic coverage of Swedish business periodicals and newspapers.

News-oriented Services

Many of the multidisciplinary information services discussed in the preceding sections provide news and public affairs data bases as part of their varied offerings. The services described below are multidisciplinary in scope but specialize in news information. Several of them are outgrowths of newsroom automation projects, and they increasingly offer the full text of news items rather than mere citations or abstracts. Given the reference and research value of news information, their library significance is obvious. Used alone or in combination with news-oriented data bases offered by other search services, they combine rapid information retrieval with a breadth and depth of coverage that is difficult to achieve with conventional printed sources.

Breadth and depth of coverage, combined with the exclusive availability of valuable information resources, are important attributes of NEXIS, the most widely publicized and comprehensive news-oriented information service. Developed and operated by Mead Data Central, NEXIS offers an expanding group of data bases that provide access to the complete texts of major news sources, including newspapers, magazines, wire services, and newsletters. NEXIS data bases are arranged in groups called "libraries." The largest selection of online newspapers, most of which are online the day after their publication in print, is contained in the General News and Business Library. It includes major American newspapers, an excellent selection of regional and business newspapers, and a useful group of foreign newspapers. NEXIS's magazine files include such general news publications as *Time, Newsweek,* and *U.S. News and World Report;* business news magazines, including *Business Week, Dun's Review, The Economist, Forbes, Fortune,* and *Industry Week;* general-interest magazines like *People, Life, Money,* and *Sports Illustrated;* and publications that provide news coverage of special fields, such as *Legal Times, Chemical Week, Electronics, Microwave Systems News and Communications Technology, Oil and Gas Journal,* and *Public Relations Journal.*

Other NEXIS libraries incorporate publications pertaining to specific subjects, such as banking, computers and communications, energy, insurance, law, and marketing. The NEXIS People Library contains biographical information and selected stories about government officials and other newsmakers. An excellent selection of online wire services provides international coverage of political events, business developments, and sports. Of special interest to business and technical libraries, NEXIS's online collection of newsletters emphasizes financial and energy-oriented publications. Among unusual news information sources, NEXIS offers online access to transcripts from the BBC World Broadcasts, MacNeil/Lehrer NewsHour, ABC News, and Official Kremlin International News Broadcasts. NEXIS also offers selected bibliographic and directory-type data bases of business interest.

Like NEXIS, the VU/TEXT search service emphasizes online access to the full texts of newspapers and other news-related information resources, such as newswires and newsmagazines. It is operated by VU/TEXT Information Services, a subsidiary of Knight-Ridder, the same company that owns DIALOG. Some VU/TEXT newspaper data bases are also available on DIALOG, but VU/TEXT's news-oriented offerings are more extensive and the two services employ different retrieval software. VU/TEXT data bases include the complete texts of such major American newspapers as *USA Today, Christian Science Monitor, Washington Post, Los Angeles Times, Chicago Tribune, Boston Globe, Houston Post, Miami Herald,* and *Detroit Free Press.* It also provides extensive coverage of regional U.S. newspapers, including the *Anchorage Daily News, Fresno Bee, Fort Lauderdale News, Evansville Courier, Wichita Eagle, Lexington Herald-Leader, Buffalo News, Akron Beacon Journal,* and *Knoxville News Sentinel.* Other VU/TEXT offerings include news magazines, newswire data bases, and several business publications.

While its coverage is national, the DATATIMES information service is best known for online access to regional newspapers, particularly its extensive coverage of the southwestern United States. Examples include the *Arizona Daily Star, Arkansas Gazette, Baton Rouge State-Times, Daily Oklahoman, Tulsa Tribune, Dallas Morning News, Fort Worth Star-Telegram,* and *Houston Chronicle.* DATATIMES also offers newspapers from other areas, as well as several newswires. The DECISIONLINE search service provides summary news information prepared by the staff of *USA Today.* The summaries are organized into such topical categories as advertising, banking and the economy, business law, health, international issues, real estate, sports, technology, and travel. The user scrolls through displayed headlines for each category in order to select desired information.

Based in Toronto, INFO-GLOBE is the online search service of *The Globe and Mail.* It combines Canadian news-oriented data bases with general reference and business information resources. Its principal data base is THE GLOBE AND MAIL ON-LINE, which contains the full text of Canada's national newspaper. INFO-GLOBE's implementation of *The Globe and Mail* was the first online newspaper to include every article from each issue, and the first to be published in print and electronic versions on the same day. Other Canadian news data bases offered by INFO-GLOBE in full-text form include THE FINANCIAL TIMES OF CANADA; MACLEAN'S, a weekly Canadian newsmagazine; CANADA NEWSWIRE; and THE NORTHERN MINER, which covers the Canadian mining industry. Other INFO-GLOBE offerings include the CANADIAN NEWS INDEX, which contains citations to selected contents of major Canadian newspapers; the CANADIAN PERIODICALS INDEX ONLINE, which contains bibliographic citations from English- and French-language publications; CANADIAN WHO'S WHO ONLINE; and CORPORATE CANADA ON-LINE, which provides financial and management information about several thousand Canadian companies.

The DOW JONES NEWS/RETRIEVAL SERVICE provides online access to news information with a business emphasis. Its principal news data bases are the online counterparts of various Dow Jones publications, supplemented by additional information resources. The full text of *The Wall Street Journal* has been available online since January 1984, and *Barron's* is online since January 1987. DOW JONES NEWS/RETRIEVAL is the only search service that provides such extensive backfile coverage of those two publications. It is also the exclusive online source for the European edition of *The Wall Street Journal,* which provides more detailed coverage of European business news than its U.S. counterpart. The WIRES data base provides timely online access to various newswires, including the DOW JONES NEWS SERVICE, which contains company and industry news. It is updated within 90 seconds of the receipt of an item, and stories are maintained online for 90 days. Items can be retrieved by various combinations of specified fields. Queries initially yield a headline list, but the full text of stories is also available. Other online newswires include DOW JONES INTERNATIONAL NEWS; CAPITAL MARKET REPORT, which contains news about fixed-income and financial futures markets; and FEDERAL FILINGS, which covers significant Security and Exchange Commission and other regulatory filings.

The DOWQUEST data base provides full-text access to selected articles from 175 general and regional news and business publications. As its most distinctive feature, a DOWQUEST retrieval query is entered as an English-language question, which contains presumably relevant words, without regard to the search commands, field names, relational expressions, and Boolean operators employed by conventional retrieval software. The DOW JONES NEWS/RETRIEVAL SERVICE is obviously intended for corporations, government agencies, and other organizations that demand timely access to business news. During the 1980s, however, it was also marketed to consumers, and it continues to offer selected general-interest data bases for that audience. Examples include the ACADEMIC AMERICAN ENCYCLOPEDIA, MAGILL BOOK REVIEWS ONLINE, CINEMAN MOVIE REVIEWS, PETERSON'S COLLEGE SELECTION SERVICE, and online sports and weather reports. An online shopping service is also provided.

Operating on computers located in the United Kingdom, the FT PRO-FILE information service is operated by FT Information Online Limited, a part of the Financial Times Group. It combines international news and business-oriented information resources with a European emphasis. Its collection of online, full-text newspapers includes *The Financial Times,* which is available online on the day of print publication; *The Independent* (both daily and Sunday); *The Times* and *Sunday Times; The Daily Telegraph* and *Sunday Telegraph; The Guardian; The Observer; The Scotsman;* and *The European,* Europe's weekend newspaper. FT PROFILE also offers a good selection of newswire data bases and various European financial data bases.

TEXTLINE, an online information service operated by Reuters Historical Data Division, provides online access to newspapers, magazines, newswires, and other general and specialized information sources from many countries. Its competitive position is principally based on its comprehensive coverage of European and Asian newspapers. TEXTLINE offers online versions of more than 40 newspapers published in the United Kingdom, plus impressive coverage of French, German, Italian, Swiss, Spanish, Portuguese, Belgian, Dutch, Austrian, Swedish, Norwegian, Danish, and Finnish newspapers. Its Middle Eastern, Asian, and African offerings are likewise extensive. TEXTLINE also provides online access to brief summaries of articles from specialized, business-oriented magazines and newsletters, most of which are not indexed by other online search services. Among subject areas covered are banking and finance, insurance, real estate, marketing, advertising, engineering, electronics, and construction. As an adjunct to TEXTLINE, Reuters offers NEWSLINE, an international current awareness and news monitoring service that provides online access to summaries of headlines from selected European newspapers on the morning of the day of publication.

Addressing a useful group of publications that are widely encountered in business and technical libraries, the NEWSNET search service provides online access to the full text of hundreds of newsletters and related publications. The majority of NEWSNET's information resources appeal to narrowly focused audiences and cover recent developments in a specific industry or activity, such as aerospace business and technology, biotechnology, chemicals, defense information management, entertainment, finance, and telecommunications. NEWSNET also offers a useful group of international newswires.

The NIKKEI TELECOM JAPAN NEWS AND RETRIEVAL search service, operated by Nihon Keizai Shimbun (Nikkei) Incorporated, provides online, English-language access to Japanese news and business information resources. Its news-oriented data bases include full-text translations of stories scheduled for publication in the next day's issues of *Nihon Keizai Shimbun* and *Japan Times.* As an interesting option, users can select a broadcasting mode that will display news stories as they are entered by NIKKEI TELECOM. In addition, the search service offers backfiles of other publications. A group of numeric data bases provides historical quotations for publicly traded Japanese stocks, and financial information about 10,000 Asian companies.

Subject-oriented Services

While several multidisciplinary information services provide in-depth, multidata base coverage of particular subjects, some online search services are specifically and exclusively designed to support research activities in fields such as medicine, science, engineering, law, and business. The MEDLARS retrieval service offered by the National Library of Medicine is the oldest example of a search service developed to support a single subject or activity. Its main component is the MEDLINE data base, which is also offered by DIALOG, BRS, DATA-STAR, QUESTEL, and other search services; each vendor claims special advantages associated with data base segmentation, the provision of special search facilities, pricing, and the availability of related data bases. Other MEDLARS data bases—such as AIDSLINE, CANCERLIT, and TOXLINE—provide detailed coverage of particular medical specialties. The HISTLINE data base, which covers the history of medicine and related sciences, contains references that are also included in MEDLINE but utilizes different subject headings. CATLINE and SERLINE provide information about the National Library of Medicine's monographic and serials holdings, respectively. The AVLINE data base contains bibliographic references for health-related audiovisual materials and computer software in clinical medicine. Most of the data bases offered by the MEDLARS search service are produced by the National Library of Medicine itself. MEDLARS users also have access to TOXNET, a set of toxicology-oriented data bases dealing with hazardous substances.

The BRS COLLEAGUE information service is designed for physicians, nurses, pharmacists, medical researchers, and related health care professionals. It provides simple, menu-driven access to the BRS health-related data bases, including MEDLINE, EMBASE, MEDICAL AND PSYCHOLOGICAL PREVIEWS, AIDS KNOWLEDGEBASE, SCIENTIFIC AMERICAN MEDICINE, and HEALTH PLANNING AND ADMINISTRATION. BRS COLLEAGUE users can also access BRS data bases in other subject disciplines. For physicians in private practice or those in remote geographic locations, the service's most interesting and potentially useful component is its COMPREHENSIVE CORE MEDICAL LIBRARY, which provides rapid online access to the full text of important biomedical publications and medical reference books. As a valuable feature, BRS COLLEAGUE links bibliographic citations to journal articles in selected medical data bases with the corresponding full text in the COMPREHENSIVE CORE MEDICAL LIBRARY.

Like BRS COLLEAGUE, the PAPERCHASE search service features an intelligently conceived and attractively implemented menu-driven interface designed specifically for untrained users rather than professional information specialists. Operated by Beth Israel Hospital (Boston), PAPERCHASE is intended for physicians, nurses, pharmacists, dentists, physical therapists, and similar health care providers; medical facility administrators, psychologists, social workers, and other professionals with health care interests; and researchers, graduate students, lawyers, and others who require access to biomedical literature. The PAPERCHASE interface recognizes most abbreviations for journal titles, directs users from title words to equivalent terms listed in *Medical Subject Headings,* and automatically unifies variant spellings, plurals, hyphenated words, and other grammatically related forms. While the entire MEDLINE data base is available online, PAPERCHASE initially responds to retrieval queries with references from a core list of 400 clinical journals. As an alternative to the core list, institutional subscribers can enter information about their own holdings so that retrieved references corresponding to those holdings will be displayed prior to other references.

The MEDIS information service, offered by Mead Data Central as part of the NEXIS service described above, combines the MEDLINE data base with the full texts of articles from several dozen biomedical publications, including important medical journals. Other MEDIS offerings include the POISINDEX, DRUGDEX, and EMERGINDEX data bases of acute care information from MICROMEDEX; FDC REPORTS; and the PHYSICIAN DATA QUERY data base of cancer information. The NEXIS service itself is an important source of information about medical and health news.

Outside of the United States, health scientists and researchers can access MEDLINE and related biomedical data bases through DIALOG, BRS, DATA-STAR, QUESTEL, and other multidisciplinary information services. Various national libraries also offer online access to MEDLINE, often supplemented by other information resources. Sweden's MIC/KAROLINSKA INSTITUTE search service, for example, offers a subset of MEDLARS' offerings, plus selected Scandinavian biomedical data bases. The AUSTRALIAN MEDLINE NETWORK, operated by the National Library of Australia, provides online access to MEDLINE, CATLINE, SERLINE, and the HEALTH PLANNING AND ADMINISTRATION data base, plus the AUSTRALASIAN MEDICAL INDEX, which covers biomedical literature from Australia and New Zealand. The most comprehensive non-U.S. source for online access to health-related information, however, is the DIMDI search service operated by the Deutsches Institut für Medizinische Dokumentation und Information, a division of the German Federal Ministry for Youth, Family Affairs, Women and Health. Based in Koln, the DIMDI search service interprets the biosciences broadly to include agriculture, aquatic science, and food science. Its health-related subject coverage combines the best elements of other online services, providing a single system to satisfy the data base access requirements of scientific researchers and health care practitioners.

DIMDI offers most of the MEDLARS data bases plus such useful information resources as EMBASE, BIOSIS PREVIEWS, PSYCINFO, and SPORT for biomedicine and psychology; AGRICOLA, AGRIS INTERNATIONAL, AQUATIC SCIENCES AND FISHERIES ABSTRACTS, CAB ABSTRACTS, and FOOD SCIENCE AND TECHNOLOGY ABSTRACTS for agricultural and food science; and SCISEARCH and ISTP&B (INDEX TO SCIENTIFIC AND TECHNICAL PROCEEDINGS AND BOOKS) for multidisciplinary scientific coverage. Certain familiar data bases are presented in convenient packages. The scientific and technical segments of the CURRENT CONTENTS data base, for example, are implemented as separate files for clinical practice, life sciences, physical sciences, and applied sciences. TOXALL is a "superfile" of toxicology-related citations from various data bases. DIMDI's most distinctive information resources, however, are German-language data bases that deal with biomedicine and related disciplines, such as psychology and physiology. The BIOLIS data base, for example, supplements BIOSIS with sources published in Germany, Switzerland, and Austria. DIAGNOSIS contains information about symptoms, diagnoses, and therapies to assist internists and other physicians. The HECLINET and SOMED data bases cover nonclinical aspects of health care, including industrial toxicology, public health, epidemiology, hospital management, health care planning, medical economics, and medical statistics.

Multidisciplinary search services have long offered online access to scientific and technical information resources. The competitive positions of the ORBIT, ESA-IRS, and CAN/OLE search services, as previously discussed, are principally based on their extensive scientific and technical data bases, some of which are unavailable elsewhere. DIALOG likewise offers impressive coverage of scientific disciplines and an extensive array of data bases pertaining to engineering specialties. Although their sci-tech coverage is less extensive than that of some competing multidisciplinary services, BRS and DATA-STAR each offer important scientific and technical data bases. Several specialized search services, however, concentrate exclusively on scientific and technical information resources. Compared to multidisciplinary services, they offer greater depth of subject coverage. In many cases, their sci-tech offerings are exclusive.

STN INTERNATIONAL is the best-known and most comprehensive example of a specialized sci-tech search service. It is jointly operated by the American Chemical Society in North America, FIZ Karlsruhe in Europe, and the Japan Information Center for Science and Technology. As might be expected, STN INTERNATIONAL provides extensive coverage of chemical information. Its implementation of the CA SEARCH data base from 1967 to the present is conveniently contained in a single file and is more extensive than implementations offered by some other services. The CAOLD data base, which is unique to STN INTERNATIONAL, contains brief references to substances cited in *Chemical Abstracts* prior to 1967. STN INTERNATIONAL also offers CAPREVIEWS, a current awareness data base that contains brief bibliographic information about chemistry-related publications six to eight weeks before the items appear in CA SEARCH. The REGISTRY data base is the world's largest file of chemical substance information. It can be searched by chemical structures, partial structures, molecular formulas, and chemical dictionary terms. For each substance identified, searchers can obtain bibliographic references and abstracts for the 10 most recent citations from the CA SEARCH data base without leaving the REGISTRY file. If the retrieval workstation includes an appropriate graphics-type video monitor, structures can be displayed. Other STN INTERNATIONAL data bases provide noteworthy coverage of patents, materials science, electrical and electronic engineering, computer science, chemical engineering, environmental science, and the life sciences. Some data bases require a knowledge of German for effective searching. Of particular interest to libraries, BIBLIODATA contains references to publications from German-speaking countries collected and registered by the Deutsche Bibliothek since 1972.

The FIZ-TECHNIK information service, which is based in Germany, provides online access to German- and English-language data bases dealing with technology and related topics, such as industrial management. It resembles STN INTERNATIONAL and ESA-IRS, with which it shares some data bases. Subject coverage includes materials science, earth science, fluid engineering, and vehicular engineering, plus several directory-type data bases of European technological companies and components.

The CIS (Chemical Information System) search service, which was originally developed for the National Institutes of Health and the U.S. Environmental Protection Agency (EPA), offers a group of textual and numeric data bases on environmental and toxicological topics. Examples include the CHEMICAL ACTIVITY STATUS REPORT, a directory-type data base of chemicals that the EPA is studying or has studied for regulatory or scientific research purposes; the CHEMICAL CARCINOGENICITY RESEARCH INFORMATION SYSTEM, which contains individual assay results and test conditions for more than 1,000 chemicals; and the CHEMICAL HAZARD RESPONSE INFORMATION SYSTEM (CHRIS), which provides information needed to respond to emergencies associated with the transport of hazardous chemicals. Addressing an important requirement of industrial libraries, safety data sheets for hazardous materials are contained in several data bases.

The HAYSTACK I search service, operated by Information Handling Services (IHS), is an online logistics management system. It offers a useful group of data bases that contain specifications and pricing information about 25 million parts listed in the U.S. Federal Supply Catalog. Most of the data bases are not conveniently accessible through other online systems. Of particular interest to libraries that serve U.S. federal government agencies and government contractors, the HAYSTACK I search service is designed to simplify various engineering and procurement activities, including product design, the development of product specifications, and the identification of alternate procurement sources for specific parts.

The Defense Technical Information Center (DTIC), a component of the Department of Defense's scientific and technical information program, developed the Defense RDT&E Online System (DROLS) to provide access to its special data bases. DROLS' offerings include the TECHNICAL REPORT (TR) data base, which contains bibliographic records for reports submitted to DTIC; the RESEARCH AND TECHNOLOGY WORK UNIT INFORMATION SYSTEM (WUIS), which contains information about ongoing research and technology efforts within the Department of Defense; and the INDEPENDENT RESEARCH AND DEVELOPMENT (IRD) data base, which contains information about contractors' independent research and development activities shared with the Department of Defense. DTIC services in general, and the DROLS data bases in particular, are accessible to the Department of Defense, other government agencies, government contractors, and non-governmental organizations, including libraries. Certain DROLS data bases contain classified information that is restricted to users with appropriate security clearances. DTIC contributes some unclassified technical reports to the NTIS data base, which is widely available through multidisciplinary and specialized search services.

Search services for computer-assisted legal research have been readily available for more than a decade and are widely used by law firms, corporate legal departments, government agencies, academic law libraries, law schools, public affairs organizations, and others who need timely access to laws, legal opinions, and other documents. While several multidisciplinary search services also offer data bases of legal interest, the LEXIS search service, operated by Mead Data Central, and the WEST-LAW search service, operated by West Publishing Company, are the two best-known examples specifically designed for legal research.

LEXIS offers online access to the full text of federal and state court cases, constitutions, codes, rules, and regulations; administrative decisions from selected government agencies; legal publications; and other material of interest to legal researchers. As with the NEXIS service described above, LEXIS data bases are organized into libraries that are subdivided into files of related documents. The General Federal Library, for example, includes files for the U.S. Code and decisions of the U.S. Supreme Court, Courts of Appeals, District Courts, Claims Courts, and Court of International Trade, as well as the *Federal Register, Code of Federal Regulations, Congressional Record,* Comptroller General decisions, and opinions of the U.S. Attorney General. The LEXIS States Library includes statutes, cases, opinions, and administrative decisions from individual states and the District of Columbia. Separate libraries are also provided for individual states. Specialized LEXIS libraries cover admiralty law, banking regulations, bankruptcy law, communication regulations, corporate law, employment law, environmental law, estates and trusts, health law, immigration law, insurance law, patent and trademark law, labor law, public health and welfare, tax and securities law, domestic and international trade regulations, transportation laws and regulations, and military justice. Most LEXIS subject libraries are integrated with the full texts of magazines, newsletters, reports, and other publications available through the NEXIS service, allowing information from those publications to be retrieved without leaving LEXIS. Through agreements with various publishers, LEXIS also offers legal data bases for the United Kingdom, British Commonwealth nations, and France.

West Publishing is a major producer of legal reference works, the contents of which are available online through the WESTLAW search service. WESTLAW offers the full texts of federal regulations, administrative law decisions, and federal and state court decisions, accompanied by editorially prepared headnotes and synopses. WESTLAW data bases are grouped into categories, such as federal materials, state materials, topical materials, texts and periodicals, and news and information. Federal materials include case-law data bases, federal government statutes, rules and regulations, and federal administrative decisions and opinions. The state materials category includes statutes and case law. The topical materials category supports research in such specialized subject areas as antitrust, intellectual property, civil rights, taxation, securities, labor, bankruptcy, and environmental law. WESTLAW also offers an excellent selection of online legal publications and reference data bases, including law reviews, state bar association journals, specialized legal periodicals, and legal directories.

QL QUICKSEARCH, described in the preceding section on multidisciplinary search services, is the principal online source for Canadian legal and taxation information. Its data bases cover federal, provincial, and territorial statutes and case law, plus decisions by Canadian administrative boards. The EUROLEX search service, operated by the European Law Centre Limited, provides online access to United Kingdom law reports, legislation, local government law, industrial relations, and tax law.

Public affairs search services are specifically designed for online legislative tracking and research by law firms, political scientists, issues management specialists, corporate public affairs offices, and government agencies. The ELECTRONIC LEGISLATIVE SEARCH SYSTEM (ELSS), operated by Commerce Clearing House Incorporated, provides online access to information on pending federal and state legislation. Records include notices of bill introductions, committee referrals and actions, hearing notices, floor actions, and presidential or gubernatorial actions. Designed to complement printed looseleaf reference works which provide more detailed information, the ELSS data base can be searched by bill number, subject, jurisdiction, sponsor, date, type of action, and other parameters. Retrieved records contain bill numbers, short titles, sponsor information, summaries, and legislative histories.

The WASHINGTON ALERT SERVICE, operated by Congressional Quarterly Incorporated, provides online access to information about U.S. congressional committee and floor activity to support legislative tracking and other political research. Its data bases contain comprehensive legislative chronologies, complete texts, and voting information for all bills and resolutions. The full text of the *Congressional Record* and all committee reports are also available online. Other data bases describe documents released by congressional committees and support offices. The LEGI-SLATE search service, operated by the *Washington Post,* offers online access to information about congressional legislative activities since 1979. The full texts of bills and resolutions can be retrieved by the names of sponsoring members, date of introduction, stage in the legislative process, words in the text, or subject terms assigned by LEGI-SLATE analysts. Bills and resolutions are normally available online on the same day that printed copies become available from the Government Printing Office. In addition, LEGI-SLATE provides online access to committee and subcommittee schedules and witness lists; house and floor votes; the bills digests produced by the Congressional Research Service at the Library of Congress; and the full texts of committee reports and transcripts of government press briefings.

Although business-oriented data bases are an increasingly important component of the multidisciplinary services discussed above, a growing number of online information services are specifically designed for business applications. While they are often marketed directly to financial planners, corporate strategists, administrative managers, and other end users, they can be effectively utilized by business libraries in the corporate, government, and academic sectors. Library literature contains little information about them, and they are rarely covered in online searching courses taught by library schools; as a result, they are relatively unknown and underutilized.

A few business-oriented information services emphasize data bases that support particular business activities or industries. The HUMAN RESOURCES INFORMATION NETWORK (HRIN), for example, is designed for corporate, government, and institutional personnel directors, training specialists, employment planning specialists, affirmative action officers, compensation analysts, labor relations specialists, and other human resources professionals. It provides online access to news, business, and legal information pertaining to such aspects of human resources management as labor relations and collective bargaining, recruitment and hiring, employee training, day care provisions, and rehabilitation of injured employees. As its name indicates, the AVIATION/AEROSPACE ONLINE information service emphasizes data bases of interest to the aviation industry. The AGRIDATA NETWORK, operated by AgriData Resources Incorporated, offers a group of textual and numeric data bases designed specifically for the agribusiness community, including crop and livestock producers as well as government agencies, public libraries, schools and colleges, trade associations, banks, farm equipment manufacturers, and other organizations and institutions with agricultural missions or interests. AGRISCAN, the AGRIDATA NETWORK's main component, offers news from agricultural publications, wire services, and other sources; general and crop weather data; market prices from major mercantile and commodities exchanges; market advisories; and general financial information, including stock quotations. Other data bases contain agricultural production information dealing with genetics, animal health, nutrition, tillage, conservation, and related topics.

The majority of business-oriented information services are designed to support financial planning and analysis with various combinations of numeric, directory, and full-text data bases. In the manner of early bibliographic search services, some business-oriented services produce their own data bases. This is the case, for example, with Telerate Systems Incorporated, a Dow Jones subsidiary that specializes in financial data bases and decision-support products. Telerate data bases cover exchange rates for more than 100 currencies; fixed-income rates for various instruments on worldwide markets; quotations for stocks, options, futures, and commodities traded on international exchanges; energy market spot prices; prices for municipal bonds, corporate bonds, and Eurobonds; and broker rates for mortgage-backed securities.

Like their multidisciplinary counterparts, however, the largest business-oriented information services offer data bases from many different sources. Examples include ACT Computer Services, ADP Network Services, Control Data Corporation Business Information, Citicorp Database Services, the Conference Board of Canada, DRI/McGraw-Hill, GE Information Services (GEIS), GSI-ECO, Interactive Data Corporation, I.P. Sharp Associates,

Quotron Systems, Reuters Historical Information Division, Shaw Data Services, Warner Computer Systems, and the WEFA Group. As a group, these services offer statistical and company-oriented data bases that are of interest to corporate libraries, particularly those that serve the investment community. Such data bases contain valuable information to support competitive analyses, as well as merger and acquisition activities. They also provide historical economic and forecast information. Popular examples include CITIBASE, the CONSUMER PRICE INDEX (CPI), the PRODUCER PRICE INDEX (PPI), the CANSIM data base of Canadian statistical information, US FLOW OF FUND, and the INTERNATIONAL ECONOMIC INDICATORS.

Several European search services specialize in business information pertaining to particular countries and/or industries. As an example, ABC VOOR HANDEL EN INDUSTRIE C.V. offers HOPPENSTEDT BENELUX, a directory of 78,000 companies in the Low Countries; HOLLAND EXPORTS, which contains information about 9,000 Dutch companies involved in international trade; and the DUTCH DIRECTORY OF BUSINESS SERVICES, which corresponds to the printed *Nederlands ABC-Dienstverleners*. The HELECON search service, operated by the Helsinki School of Economics and Business, provides bibliographic coverage of Scandinavian business publications. GENIOS WIRTSCHAFTSDATEN-BANKEN is perhaps the most comprehensive online source for information about German business. Its offerings, most of which require a knowledge of German for effective searching, provide online directories of German companies plus bibliographic coverage of German business and management publications. Some GENIOS data bases are also available on GBI (GESELLSCHAFT FUR BETRIEBSWIRTSCHAFTLICHE), another business-oriented German search service.

Consumer-oriented Services

As their name suggests, consumer-oriented information services are intended for home computer users rather than corporations, government agencies, and other organizations. Some academic, public, and school libraries, however, make them available for end-user searching. As a group, the consumer-oriented services combine general-interest data bases—such as encyclopedias and reference books, news and weather information, travel directories, and health care guides—with various informational and recreational computer services, including electronic messaging systems, bulletin boards and forums on a variety of topics, software that can be downloaded to customers' computers, large collections of computer games, and online shopping services.

COMPUSERVE, the oldest and best-known consumer-oriented information service, is difficult to categorize. Some of its data bases are obviously suitable for consumers; others, however, are intended for corporate, government, and institutional customers. Of particular interest to public and school libraries, COMPUSERVE's consumer-oriented data bases provide general reference, travel, health, and personal finance information. Examples include ABC WORLDWIDE HOTEL GUIDE, which can be searched by hotel name, chain, location, rates, and amenities; INFOR-MATION USA, a guide to free government publications and services based on the well-known reference book edited by Matthew Lesko; DEPART-MENT OF STATE ADVISORIES, a continuously updated warning service for Americans traveling abroad; HOLLYWOOD HOTLINE, a news data base that covers the entertainment industry; ROCKNET, which contains music news and record reviews; NEW CAR SHOWROOM, a data base of specifications and descriptive information for passenger cars, trucks, vans, and other vehicles; and NEIGHBORHOOD REPORT, which provides demographic profiles for specific zip codes. Familiar data bases include the ACADEMIC AMERICAN ENCYCLOPEDIA and PETER-SON'S COLLEGE DATABASE.

The much-publicized PRODIGY search service, a joint venture of IBM and Sears, features an easily learned user interface, attractive information displays which make effective use of color and graphics, and competitive pricing. Many PRODIGY services are available for a relatively low fixed monthly fee; in addition to user charges, it relies on revenues from advertisements which are displayed with retrieved information. Like other consumer-oriented services, PRODIGY's familiar combination of general-interest data bases, bulletin boards, and related information services will appeal especially to public and school libraries. The ACADEMIC AMERICAN ENCYCLOPEDIA is available, as are various news, weather, and sports information sources. Useful consumer-oriented information includes product reviews, airline schedules, hotel and restaurant reviews, and topical coverage of personal health and fitness, children's learning styles, food and wine, pet care, money management, and other subjects. Online market quotations for stocks, bonds, and mutual funds are derived from several sources, including the DOW JONES NEWS/RETRIEVAL SERVICE. Online trading is possible.

The GENIE (General Electric Network for Information Exchange) search service, operated by General Electric Information Services Company, addresses the same consumer interests as COMPUSERVE and PRODIGY but offers a smaller selection of information resources. Its data bases include GROLIER'S ELECTRONIC ENCYCLOPEDIA; NEWSGRID, a compilation of dispatches from international newswires; NEWSBYTES NEWS SERVICE, which reports important developments in the computer industry; the EASYSABRE data base of airline schedules and fares; the CINE-MAN and HOLLYWOOD HOTLINE data bases of movie reviews; ROCKNET ENTERTAINMENT NEWS, which contains news stories, record reviews, and other information about popular music; and SOAP OPERA SUMMARIES, which contains current and past plot summaries plus related entertainment news. GENIE also provides online bulletin boards and roundtables for the discussion of topics ranging from travel and leisure to religion and ethics. Various computer hardware and software vendors use the GENIE search service to provide online customer support.

Implementation Requirements and Costs

Libraries that utilize online information services will incur both general and search-specific costs. General start-up and ongoing expenses are fixed amounts and are incurred regardless of the volume and nature of searches performed. Examples of such expenses include the cost of equipment purchase or rental, site preparation, searcher training, sign-up fees, and the acquisition of required or desirable operator's manuals, thesauri, and other search aids. Search-specific costs, in contrast, depend on search characteristics for their occurrence and amount. Examples of such variable costs include telecommunication charges, data base access and connect-time charges, online display and offline printing charges, and the cost of professional labor associated with search preparation, execution, and follow-up.

As defined above, online information services are timeshared computer facilities that are accessed via workstations installed at customer sites. Compared to other areas of library automation, online searching involves the simplest equipment requirements and the lowest initial capital investment. To more easily attract customers and broaden their user base by minimizing inconvenient and potentially expensive equipment requirements, all online information services support appropriately configured microcomputers as workstations. As discussed in chapter 3, such microcomputers must be equipped with modems and communications software. Most online information services also support conventional computer terminals that utilize the American Standard Code for Information Interchange. Several services support 3270-type terminals, which transmit the EBCDIC code. European information services can often communicate with videotex terminals. From the library's standpoint, such broad compatibility greatly simplifies the implementation of online information services and permits the addition of new services without the associated procurement of additional equipment. The information services themselves also benefit from such flexibility; by supporting a variety of workstations, they can attract occasional users who could not justify the purchase of a dedicated, special-purpose terminal.

The advantages of microcomputer-based online workstations over conventional computer terminals are widely recognized. While conventional terminals are exclusively intended for communication with remote computers, microcomputer-based workstations can be used for local information processing tasks—such as word processing and spreadsheet operations—as well as for online searching, although a high volume of search activity will typically leave little machine time for other applications. Perhaps the most widely publicized and important advantage of microcomputers for online searching involves the downloading of retrieved records to a hard disk or diskette for local manipulation following a search. A word processing software package can be used to edit the retrieved records and remove irrelevant items prior to printing; alternatively, downloaded records can be transferred to a data management software package for local storage and retrieval. In addition, search statements can be prepared offline prior to establishing a connection with an online search service. For slow typists, this technique can reduce connect-time charges associated with command entry.

As noted above, access to online information services requires a microcomputer equipped with a modem and communication software. Modems are likewise required in terminal installations. By reducing elapsed transaction time, faster modems can correspondingly reduce certain variable search charges discussed below. As an example, the online display of 30 bibliographic citations with abstracts averaging 600 characters per record will require 10 minutes at 300 bits per second (30 characters per second), 2.5 minutes at 1200 bits per second (120 characters per second), and 1.25 minutes at 2400 bits per second (240 characters per second). If telecommunication and data base charges total $60 per hour, a 1200-bit-per-second modem will save $7.25 for such a search when compared to a 300-bit-per-second modem. A 2400-bit-per-second modem will reduce search costs by an additional $1.50. Further savings will result from reductions in professional time required to complete a given search. It should be noted, however, that faster modems only reduce those elapsed-time charges associated with data reception—that is, the portion of an online search when a workstation is displaying, downloading, or printing information. An operator's typing rate and the time required to read and evaluate retrieved information are unaffected by modem speed. Time-dependent search charges are further affected by degraded system response during periods of peak usage. A faster modem can do nothing to improve such degraded response time. As a further constraint, some search services impose higher rates or surcharges for communication at 1200 or 2400 bits per second.

As an alternative to general-purpose software packages, a growing number of online information services offer communications programs designed specifically for use with their systems. The DIALOGLINK package, for example, includes preconfigured parameters that simplify sign-on procedures through major telecommunication networks. It supports the offline preparation of search strategies, as well as the online entry of commands while DIALOG is performing other operations. An account management module tracks online charges for cost accounting and charge-back to users. DIALOGLINK can also produce cost summaries of DIALOG search activity and detailed lists of DIALOG usage by data base. Some software packages combine a communications program with a menu-driven interface that simplifies user access to a specific service. The WILSEARCH program, for example, will automatically select Wilsonline data bases appropriate to user-specified subjects. Data base descriptions can also be displayed. The EZ ACCESS communications program provides menu-driven access to the WESTLAW information service. It is particularly recommended for new or occasional searchers. To facilitate access to the MEDLARS search service, the GRATEFUL MED program provides menus and prompts for novice users but permits the direct entry of commands by experienced searchers.

As with conventional reference services, professional knowledge and search skills are the most important factors that influence the effectiveness of online searching performed by librarians. For librarians who received their graduate degrees before the mid-1970s, online searching represents a new aspect of professional practice requiring additional training. With most multidisciplinary and specialized search services, formal training is desirable. Since the late 1970s, ALA-accredited library schools have offered one or more courses in online searching, but such courses typically emphasize the major North American multidisciplinary services. Although they may be familiar with online search concepts, new library school graduates will often require additional training to use other services effectively. Fortunately, many news- and business-oriented information services are designed for ease of learning and use, and they provide excellent materials for self-instruction. This is the case, for example, with NEWSNET, the DOW JONES NEWS/RETRIEVAL SERVICE, BRS COLLEAGUE, and such consumer-oriented services as COMPUSERVE and PRODIGY.

Where formal training is desired, vendor-sponsored courses typically provide the fastest way to become familiar with a particular information service. Most services offer intensive, introductory seminars of one or two days' duration. These seminars are typically offered in major metropolitan areas or at universities or similar research facilities in small towns. It is customary for a library to train at least two persons in order to provide uninterrupted searching capability during vacations, sick leave, and periods of high demand.

In order to function effectively, online searchers will require some printed support materials. As a minimum, the search area should be equipped with the operator's manuals for all services utilized. In addition to manuals and other documentation specific to a given service, online searchers will require thesauri, subject classification lists, and other search aids published by data base producers. While such search aids may also be available online, it will usually prove less expensive and more convenient to purchase printed copies of the most frequently used materials.

Some online information services require an initial or annual payment for an account number and password, although such fees are typically modest—perhaps $35 to $50. To discourage very occasional users, some services also impose a minimum monthly billing or a monthly account maintenance fee. In a few cases, initial or annual payments are required for use of a particular data base. These payments are independent of any of the search-specific charges described below.

Telecommunications charges are an example of a cost that varies directly with the duration of an online search. As noted above, the use of a modem allows a library to establish an online connection with a remote search service via an ordinary telephone. Some online information services can be reached by direct dialing through the public telephone network. The resulting local or long-distance charges will vary with the geographic location. As an alternative for long-distance communication, however, all online information services can be reached through one or more of the so-called value-added carriers. Examples include TYMNET, operated by BT TYMNET Incorporated; TELENET (SPRINTNET), operated by GTE TELENET Communications Corporation; and the COMPUSERVE NETWORK, operated by CompuServe Incorporated. Several online information services operate their own value-added telecommunications networks, although their geographic coverage may be more limited than that of the independent carriers cited above. Examples include DIALNET, which serves DIALOG's U.S. and European customers in many medium-size and larger cities; BRSNET and ORBITNET, which serve customers in Europe and Australia; MEADNET, which provides access to the NEXIS and LEXIS services; and WESTNET, which provides access to the WESTLAW information service. A growing number of online information services are also accessible via the Internet.

As a group, value-added networks consist of leased telephone lines that link geographically dispersed, timeshared computers with access nodes in medium-size and larger cities. Libraries in areas served by value-added carriers can reach an access node through a local telephone call. They will be charged for the local call plus the ensuing long-distance communication. Most value-added carriers utilize efficient packet-switching transmission techniques to reduce their operating costs. Charges are based on elapsed time, prorated to a specified fraction of a minute or second. For many libraries, rates offered by value-added carriers will prove significantly lower than those attainable through conventional long-distance facilities—assuming, of course, that a network access node is available. Because access nodes, as previously noted, are typically limited to densely populated locations, libraries in rural areas must often make a long-distance telephone call to reach an access node. In such cases, the resulting charges may prove higher than the cost of a direct-dialed long distance call to a given search service. Recognizing this, some search services provide a special inward-WATS number for customers in areas outside of network access nodes.

In-house computing centers and commercial service bureaus have historically based their price schedules on the nature and complexity of computing tasks performed by a given user. In information retrieval applications, for example, operations such as the logical coordination of multiple search terms use considerable system resources and are consequently subjected to higher charges than simpler retrieval commands. Since their inception in the 1970s, however, the majority of online information services have charged users for the amount of time they are connected to a given data base, regardless of the complexity of the retrieval operations performed or the amount of system resources utilized by a given search. Such elapsed-time charges are incurred whether an operator is entering search commands, receiving printed output, or merely sitting at a terminal formulating a search strategy or reviewing displayed information.

Connect-time costs are customarily expressed as an hourly rate, although the searcher is only charged for the fraction of an hour actually spent online. Recognizing that most online sessions are considerably shorter than one hour, some services quote connect-time charges on a cost-per-minute basis. Regardless of the measure used, connect-time charges begin immediately after the online connection to a given service is established, and they end when the online session is terminated. Some specialized information services impose the same connect-time charges for all or most of their data bases. Typically, however, connect-time rates vary from one data base to another and, for a given data base, from one online search service to another. Often, the customer is initially placed in a data base with a relatively low connect-time charge.

Connect-time charges are a composite of a given service's operating charges and profit expectations plus any royalties that must be paid to data base producers. In their price lists, however, most search services present their connect-time charges as a single cost item with no breakdown of individual components. At the time of this writing, data base connect-time charges ranged from about $20 per hour to more than $300 per hour. As might be expected, the not-for-profit information services offer the most attractive pricing, and government-produced data bases, such as ERIC and MEDLINE, have the lowest connect-time charges. Online search services purchase such data bases at relatively low prices, and royalty payments are typically low. Data bases produced by professional and trade associations, universities, and other not-for-profit organizations are generally more expensive to access than their government-produced counterparts but are less expensive than data bases produced by commercial publishers.

Data base connect-time charges likewise vary by subject discipline in a manner that reflects their intended users' ability to pay. Thus, connect-time charges for education data bases are substantially lower than those for business data bases. Connect-time charges for data bases in the humanities and social sciences are generally lower than for those that support scientific and technical activities. The very high charges associated with patent data bases reflect a willingness to pay for the speed and convenience of online patent searching, as well as the importance of timely patent searches for profit-making activities. Connect-time charges are likewise high in fields like chemistry and engineering, where online search costs are a well-established component of research and development budgets.

Some online information services offer discounted connect-time rates to specified customer groups, such as schools, colleges, and their associated libraries. To stimulate system usage during off-peak hours, the consumer-oriented information services popularized the practice of reducing connect-time charges during evenings and weekends. Since many public and academic libraries are open at such times, off-peak discounts offer excellent money-saving opportunities. Some multidisciplinary and specialized information services offer similar economic incentives for searches conducted during designated hours. With some European search services, off-peak discounts conveniently coincide with normal business hours in North America.

As an alternative discount method, some online information services offer substantial reductions to customers willing to guarantee a minimum payment or volume of connect-time activity. Several services also offer prepaid subscription agreements that permit the advance purchase of a given quantity of connect-time at discounted rates. In most cases, the prepurchased connect-time must be used within a specified 12-month period. Unused connect-time cannot be carried over into the next year. Accurate estimation of connect-time usage is obviously critical to the cost-effective use of such subscription pricing. In most cases, a library will be guided by previous usage. Subscription plans are consequently best suited to libraries with an established volume of search activity.

While there has been much discussion of their appropriateness, connect-time charging methods are easily understood and allow the user to make a fairly accurate preliminary estimate of the cost of a given search. As an alternative or supplement to connect-time charges, however, some online information services charge customers for the system resources used during a particular search. Proponents of this charging methodology argue that it more accurately reflects the difficulty of a given search, does not penalize slow typists or terminals, and eliminates charges attributable to telecommunication delays or degraded response time during periods of peak usage. Data base producers and search service operators are also concerned about lost revenues resulting from search techniques that reduce connect-time charges without a corresponding reduction of computer usage. Examples of such techniques include the offline preparation of search strategies and the use of relatively inexpensive data bases for the initial entry of search commands that will subsequently be applied to more expensive data bases.

As a significant complication for librarians who must provide their clients with preliminary estimates of search costs, resource-based charges can prove difficult to conceptualize and even more difficult to predict. Customers of the MEDLARS retrieval service, for example, are charged for individual search statements, disk access operations, characters transmitted or received, citations retrieved, and carriage returns entered in addition to connect-time. Other online information services impose file entry fees and charges for computer resource units. Among the most unusual resource-based pricing plans, the DIMDI search service's connect-time charges are a composite of system time and thinking time. System-time charges begin when the host computer receives a user's command and end when the computer's response has been transmitted. Lower thinking-time charges apply to other portions of an online session. In a radical simplification of pricing, several online information services have abandoned connect-time charges completely in favor of a fixed charge that permits unlimited searching of a given data base in a single online session. Other online information services impose per-search charges which do not vary with elapsed time. Several online information services offer unlimited searching of specified data bases for a fixed monthly or annual fee.

In addition to connect-time costs, many search services charge users for each bibliographic citation or other nonbibliographic record displayed or printed online. Such online display and printing charges vary widely from one service to another and from data base to data base. They may further depend on the specific data elements selected for display. At the time this chapter was written, typical charges ranged from less than 10 cents to more than $10 per retrieved record, the highest rates being associated with full-text and numeric data bases. Lower charges apply when displays are limited to specified fields, such as a title or a bibliographic citation without an abstract. As an alternative to per-record pricing, some information services charge by the number of characters or lines of information displayed or printed. Online display charges also apply to downloading of retrieved records. It is important to note that connect-time charges are incurred while items are being printed or displayed online. Unlike connect-time rates, however, online display charges are rarely subject to discounts.

To reduce online connect-time and avoid display charges, search results can be printed offline at an online information service's computer facilities and mailed or otherwise shipped to the customer. Typical delivery times range from several days to one week. As with online display costs, offline printing charges vary with the search service, data base, and data elements selected. Rates range from about 10 cents to several dollars per full record, including abstracts when present. As with online display charges, the highest rates are associated with full-text and numeric data bases. When a 1200-bit-per-second modem or faster modem is used, the online display and downloading of retrieved records to disks for local printing can prove less expensive than offline printing for data bases with low connect-time and online display rates. By reducing connect-time charges, the subscription and other discount plans discussed above can make that approach more attractive. Such discount plans do not affect the cost of offline printing.

The professional labor of a librarian or other trained information specialist is often overlooked as a cost component in online searching. Unlike the technical services where the workstations used to access bibliographic utilities may be operated by clerical personnel, online searching usually involves the direct participation of professional librarians. Unmediated searching by scientists, faculty members, students, or other end users can be successfully employed in applications with straightforward information retrieval requirements, and several information services have introduced menu-oriented interfaces specifically designed for such situations. Library literature and the experience of practicing professionals, however, continue to confirm the value of a trained intermediary who is conversant with the latest developments in data base structure and search system software and who will conduct presearch interviews, translate the expressed information needs of researchers or other requesters into a logical search strategy and commands appropriate to a particular search service, review search results for relevance, and suggest possible additional searches. As a broad guideline that will necessarily vary with the searcher's experience and the complexity of the search itself, two minutes of preparation and follow-up time are required for each minute spent online. For an online search lasting 15 to 20 minutes, the total professional labor requirements will likely range from 45 to 60 minutes.

Cost Justification

A library's introduction of online searching involves new costs in the sense that the payments that must be made to information services, equipment vendors, the telephone company, and others were not previously included in the library's budget. The introduction of any new library service, whether manual or automated, must normally be justified on the basis of a careful analysis of costs in relation to anticipated benefits. The results of such an analysis form the basis for a cost-justification statement, which, in turn, supports the introduction of the new service as a responsible management decision.

The most common and, from the management standpoint, most persuasive type of justification demonstrates that the costs associated with proposed automation will be lower than those of an existing alternative system, without a corresponding sacrifice of effectiveness. This approach is typically used, for example, to justify the computerization of circulation control, where the cost of an automated system is presumably offset by reductions in clerical labor, lost library materials, and other costs associated with manual circulation methodologies. In the case of online searching, the predominant existing alternative involves the manual searching of printed indexes, abstracting journals, and other reference sources. The typical end product of such manual searching is a typewritten or photocopied list of citations—or factual information in the case of nonbibliographic reference questions—comparable to the list of citations or other information obtained through online retrieval. Library efforts to justify online searching on the basis of reduced cost usually emphasize the economy of online services in the two areas where manual search costs are highest: (1) annual subscriptions to printed indexes and other reference sources; and (2) professional labor.

To create the bibliographic infrastructure essential to manual searching, a library must purchase reference books and subscribe to printed indexing and abstracting journals in anticipation of their future use. There is necessarily some risk that a given reference source will be used only occasionally or not at all, and few libraries have implemented procedures for monitoring the frequency with which their printed indexes and other reference books are consulted. In online searching, however, a library has access to the complete range of data bases offered by a given search service, but it incurs connect-time and offline printing charges only for those information resources that are actually used.

The potential cost advantages of this approach are obvious. If, for example, a library subscribes to an indexing and abstracting journal at a cost of $3,000 per year—plus the expenses of technical processing, shelving, and floor space—and that index is used only once a month, the average cost per use will exceed $250. Assuming that the machine-readable counterpart of that printed index can be accessed online for $65 per connect hour, the annual use cost, based on connect-time charges for 12 searches lasting 20 minutes each, would total just $300. Even allowing for proration of the general expenses associated with an online search, and providing professional labor to assist the user who may have searched the printed index personally, the potential for cost savings through the elimination of subscriptions to infrequently used indexes is considerable. As a result, some libraries have either canceled or considered canceling subscriptions to highly specialized indexes with limited audiences or those that overlap or compete with a more familiar bibliographic resource. Duplicate subscriptions, common in multibranch libraries, are likewise vulnerable to cancellation. Given the ability to satisfy occasional information requirements through online availability, potential subscribers can defer the decision to acquire a given printed index until demand surpasses a predetermined level. For every printed index, regardless of price, there is a break-even point in terms of number of uses below which an available online equivalent will prove less expensive to search.

As might be expected, producers of printed indexes are concerned about the potential loss of subscription revenue resulting from reliance on online data bases. To protect their printed products, a few publishers limit data base access to those who subscribe to their printed counterparts; others offer lower connect-time charges to printed index subscribers. Some publishers further protect their printed indexes by making only a subset of bibliographic information available in data base products offered through online search services. Abstracts included in printed versions, for example, may be omitted from the corresponding online data bases. A few data base producers further provide online access to only the most current information, thus making printed indexes indispensable for retrospective searches. With most data bases, this is the case for those searches that require retrieval of citations to materials published before the late 1960s, when machine-readable data first became available.

While the elimination of subscriptions to infrequently used printed indexes offers potential for cost reduction, many libraries will continue to acquire printed indexes for data bases that are searchable online. This will very likely remain the case, for example, with university-based research libraries where the hours of service are long, direct patron use of indexes is common, and familiarity with and acceptance of searches performed by intermediaries are limited. In such applications, other sources of potential cost reduction must be sought. As discussed in the preceding chapters on circulation control and cataloging, most computer applications are partially or totally justified on the basis of a reduction in labor cost when compared to an alternative manual system. Manual searching is a labor-intensive, time-consuming, and consequently expensive activity. In contrast, available studies of online searching—especially those that compare manual and online searching—emphasize its more efficient use of professional time. But while online searching is less labor-intensive than manual searching, it is not invariably less expensive since professional labor is used differently in the two activities.

In manual searching performed by a librarian, professional labor is involved in all stages of search activity, including the time-consuming process of actually searching printed indexes, bibliographies, and other reference books. In online searching, on the other hand, professional labor is only involved in the formulation of a search strategy and its subsequent confirmation or modification. The search itself is performed by a computer at high speed. During the period of actual online searching, connect-time usage and communication charges accrue on an elapsed-time basis, along with the cost of professional labor. As a result, online searching is the more economical alternative only in those cases where the cost of professional labor associated with a lengthy manual search equals the accumulated online costs.

In order to realize the labor- and cost-saving potential of online search-ing, librarians must analyze individual reference inquiries for character-istics that are likely to prolong, and consequently increase the cost of, a manual search. Exhaustive searches, for example, are often cheaper to perform online than manually. Likewise, searches requiring the logi-cal coordination of multiple subjects or other terms can be very time-consuming to perform manually, but online information services provide retrieval capabilities that make even complex multiterm searches routine. Performed manually, searches requiring the use of multiple printed in-dexes can prove both time-consuming and tiring, since much time and effort are expended in walking to the library shelves to retrieve bound volumes. In online searching, however, multiple data bases—and even multiple online information services—can be quickly and conveniently accessed from the same terminal. The online search services offer search aids that assist the librarian in selecting the appropriate combination of data bases for a given search, and they provide commands that permit the same search strategy to be used with multiple data bases without the reentry of search statements. Several online information services even permit the simultaneous searching of multiple data bases. As a further point in favor of online searching in certain types of situations, some printed indexes—for reasons of organization, typography, or sheer bulk—are difficult to use. Such limitations do not apply to their machine-readable counterparts.

Although online searching usually proves faster and less labor-intensive than manual searching in the situations discussed above, a given library's potential for cost reduction and consequent prospects for cost justification will necesssarily be limited by the amount of professional time currently being spent performing manual searches for researchers and other library users. Literature searching has long been part of the professional respon-sibilities of corporate and government librarians, but public, academic, and school librarians spend little, if any, time performing literature searches for library users. Historically, the academic librarians' argument for faculty status has been based, in part, on the provision of instruction in the use of bibliographic sources rather than on the actual performance of literature searches or the provision of factual information. Trained as teachers, many school librarians similarly view their reference role as primarily instructional.

It appears, then, that outside of those special libraries with significant ongoing expenditures for manual searching, there is little potential for the cost justification of online searching through labor reduction. Recognizing this, some academic and public libraries ask their users to acknowledge the personal benefits of an online search by paying some or all of the costs. Critics of such user charges view them as a potential threat to the Amer-ican tradition of free library service in the public sector. These critics warn that the imposition of user charges will deny access to information to those unable to afford the comparatively high costs associated with online searching. As an economic rather than a philosophical objection, others note that the collection of fees can itself be a costly procedure that involves substantial amounts of paperwork, cash handling, accountability procedures, and periodic audits. These activities, in turn, increase the cost of online searches.

As a further point, some observers object to the view that online searching, or any form of library automation, is a direct substitute for previously manual activities. Although academic, public, and school libraries have historically emphasized collection development rather than the provision of information services characteristic of special libraries, the needs of library users in the years ahead are likely to be best addressed by cooperative collection development accompanied by increased funding for information services. If such is the case, the productivity potential of online searching can enable a library to increase the amount of services it provides without corresponding increases in its professional staff.

While the justification of online searching on the basis of cost reduction is often the preferred approach, information systems professionals also recognize the possibility of cost justification based on enhanced function or "added value." In this approach, the higher cost of online searching (if any) is accepted as the price of improved performance relative to the manual searching of printed indexes—assuming, of course, that such improved performance is warranted. Comparison of the two search methodologies reveals that online searching is not merely faster than its manual counterpart but that it also offers capabilities that yield results not readily obtainable in manual searching. With some data bases, for example, online searches can be based on retrieval parameters that are not available in the corresponding printed indexes. The best-known example of such enhanced searching capabilities is the distinction between major and minor descriptors in MEDLINE, ERIC, NTIS, and other data bases. Items indexed for inclusion in those data bases are assigned six to 10 subject descriptors. To save space in the printed indexes, however, items appear under only those three or four subject descriptors that represent the major facets of a given article or report. The minor descriptors assigned to a given item are only searchable in the online data bases.

In addition to retrieval by assigned descriptors, most online search services permit the searching of the entire machine-readable text of citations, abstracts, and other stored data. Thus, a subject search based on assigned descriptors can be enhanced by a free-text search of one or more specified keywords in article titles or abstracts.

As another indication of added value, online data bases are often more up-to-date than their printed counterparts. A library's receipt of successive issues of printed indexes and bibliographies is often delayed by production and distribution problems. Once issues are received, backlogs in technical processing or the serials department may further delay their availability to library users. Since many searches require access to recent citations, such delays can limit the effectiveness of printed indexes. The creation of machine-readable data bases on magnetic tape, however, is not subject to delays inherent in the printing of paper reference sources. While the various online information services update their data bases on different schedules, new data can usually be accessed online within a very short time following their receipt by a given service. In addition, many online data bases are updated more frequently than their printed counterparts. Thus, a printed index may appear quarterly while its machine-readable counterpart is updated monthly or even weekly.

As a final point of added value compared to printed reference sources, online data bases offer more flexible physical access. Librarians and information specialists have long recognized that the use of a library or other information resource varies inversely with the potential user's distance from that resource. Special libraries, for example, often have difficulty providing adequate information services to users in geographically dispersed corporate or institutional facilities, while academic libraries can experience similar problems with branch campuses. Unlike printed indexes, which must be used in a library or similar physical setting, online data bases can be accessed from any compatible terminal in any physical location. Given the pervasiveness of terminals and microcomputers—along with the availability of portable models—a librarian can, in effect, take part of the library directly to the user. Alternatively, an online information service, a library-based terminal, and a remote terminal at a user's location can all be linked by means of a conference telephone call. Once the user's information requirements are confirmed by voice contact, search statements are entered at the library's terminal and the search output is simultaneously displayed at both workstations. The searcher and remote user can discuss the progress of the search via a separate telephone line.

CD-ROM as an Online Alternative

As described above, online information services emerged during the 1970s as a simpler, more cost-effective alternative to the in-house implementation of computerized information retrieval systems based on the direct procurement of machine-readable data bases from their producers. With their prewritten retrieval software and usage-based pricing plans, online information services facilitated the rapid implementation of computer-based reference activities. As an additional advantage, high capital investments for hardware procurement and software development were avoided; as previously noted, startup costs associated with online information services are modest.

While online information services remain the dominant approach to computer-based reference service for most libraries, there has been a renewal of interest in in-house implementations of specific data bases. Such in-house implementations are sometimes described as "local online" to distinguish them from the remote, timeshared access provided by online search services. They may involve the procurement of popular bibliographic data bases on magnetic tape for installation on a library's own computer equipped with custom-developed or prewritten retrieval software. Some of the integrated library systems described in chapter 6 can support the local installation of such bibliographic data bases. More commonly, however, librarians are interested in CD-ROM editions of particular data bases as an alternative to online information services.

As previously defined, CD-ROM and other read-only optical discs are electronic publishing media. More specifically, they permit a form of electronic publishing that is often described as optical publishing—a phrase that denotes the recording and dissemination of machine-readable information on optical storage media. Other forms of electronic publishing employ different dissemination methodologies, including the distribution of information on floppy disks or timeshared access to information recorded on hard disk drives. With their high storage capacities, read-only characteristics, and economical replication through mastering techniques, CD-ROM discs are particularly well suited to the distribution of large computer-processible data bases, reference books, and other voluminous information products.

CD-ROM information products can be divided, by their intended audiences, into two broad categories: (1) private implementations, intended for controlled release to closed user groups; and (2) reference- and research-oriented products intended for public sale. Online public access catalogs were described in chapter 6 as an example of private CD-ROM implementations for closed user groups. The number of publicly available CD-ROM data bases has increased steadily since the 1980s. Such data bases are typically accompanied by information retrieval software that is supplied on diskettes. In most cases, the software, and its associated CD-ROM data base, are intended for IBM-compatible or Macintosh microcomputers. Unlike online systems, which often require formal training for effective searching, most CD-ROM retrieval programs are designed for casual users who will receive little or no instruction. As such, they make extensive use of menus, prompts, and help screens to simplify retrieval operations. Recognizing that elaborate menu systems intended for novice users can prove tedious to experienced searchers, many retrieval programs also provide command-oriented shortcuts for specific operations. Most programs also make use of function keys to minimize typing. Graphical user interfaces, which feature pulldown menus, dialog boxes, and multiwindow displays, are increasingly common.

CD-ROM producers include conventional publishers and data base creators—like Grolier, R.R. Bowker, and the Information Access Company—who are seeking new outlets for their products; companies, like SilverPlatter, that were formed specifically to market CD-ROM versions of existing data bases produced by government agencies and commercial firms; and online information service operators, such as DIALOG and H.W. Wilson Company, that offer CD-ROM products as a local adjunct to their timeshared services. To obtain a reasonable amortization of data preparation and mastering costs, CD-ROM producers typically emphasize popular information resources with well-established audiences, and some well-known data bases have even attracted multiple producers.

Aimed at the large and potentially lucrative public and school library markets, various CD-ROM information products index or abstract articles contained in general-interest periodicals. Examples include the INFO-TRAC MAGAZINE INDEX PLUS, GENERAL PERIODICALS INDEX: PUBLIC LIBRARY, and TOM data bases from Information Access Company; EBSCO's MAGAZINE ARTICLE SUMMARIES; the WILSONDISC implementations of the *Readers' Guide to Periodical Literature* and *Readers' Guide Abstracts;* and PERIODICAL ABSTRACTS ONDISC from University Microfilms International. CD-ROM versions of encyclopedias, dictionaries, and other general reference works likewise appeal to public and school libraries. The concept of an electronic encyclopedia predates CD-ROM technology; its advantages were discussed by Vannevar Bush and Arthur C. Clarke, among others. Grolier's ACADEMIC AMERICAN ENCYCLOPEDIA, as previously noted, is offered by various online information services. The compact disc implementation, now known as GROLIER'S NEW ELECTRONIC ENCYCLOPEDIA, was one of the earliest CD-ROM information products. Other examples include World Book's INFORMATION FINDER, COMPTON'S MULTIMEDIA ENCYCLOPEDIA, and the HUTCHINSON ELECTRONIC ENCYCLOPEDIA. A CD-ROM edition of MERRIAM-WEBSTER'S NINTH NEW COLLEGIATE DICTIONARY includes pronunciations. The FINDIT WEBSTER CD-ROM from Innotech Incorporated contains 85,000 English-language entries derived from citations in *The New York Times.* The AMAZING MOBY CD-ROM contains entries for more than one million English words and phrases. A CD-ROM edition of the *Oxford English Dictionary* was introduced in 1988.

Encyclopedias and dictionaries are examples of CD-ROM information products with potentially broad appeal; others include Microsoft Corporation's BOOKSHELF, a much-publicized collection of useful reference books designed for integration with word processing software and other computer applications; the GUINNESS DISC OF WORLD RECORDS, produced by Pergamon Compact Solutions; and the various CD-ROM implementations of the Bible, produced by Ellis Enterprises, Innotech, Tri Star Publishing, the Foundation for Advanced Biblical Studies, Deutsche Bibelgesellschaft, and other companies. Many CD-ROM reference products, however, are designed to support specialized research in particular subject areas. A number of CD-ROM reference products address the information requirements of biomedical researchers and healthcare professionals. The best-known examples are the various CD-ROM implementations of the MEDLINE data base. Elsevier Science Publishers and SilverPlatter offer a CD-ROM implementation of EMBASE, the machine-readable counterpart of the printed *Excerpta Medica.* Subsets are available for selected medical specialties, including cardiology, gastroenterology, obstetrics and gynecology, pathology, and radiology. Specialized CD-ROM products containing information about specific diseases include implementations of the CANCERLIT data base; the PEDIATRIC INFECTIOUS DISEASE JOURNAL; the COMPACT LIBRARY: AIDS and COMPACT LIBRARY: VIRAL HEPATITIS discs from the Massachusetts Medical Society; and the COMPUTER CLINICAL INFORMATION SYSTEM, a data base of poisons and their emergency treatments. CD-ROM editions are available of standard medical reference books and journals; examples include the PHYSICIAN'S DESK REFERENCE disc, which also includes machine-readable versions of the *Merck Manual,* the *Oxford Textbook of Medicine, Renal Tumors of Children,* the *Journal of the American Medical Association,* and the *New England Journal of Medicine.*

Scientific and technical data bases, the historical mainstay of online search services, are increasingly available in CD-ROM implementations. Examples include SilverPlatter's implementation of BIOLOGICAL AB-STRACTS, the BIOLOGICAL AND AGRICULTURAL INDEX from H.W. Wilson, the CD-ROM edition of the SCISEARCH data base from the Institute for Scientific Information, and the LIFE SCIENCES COLLECTION from Compact Cambridge. Available agricultural data bases include AGRIS, AGRICOLA, CAB ABSTRACTS, FSTA (Food Science and Technology Abstracts), and TROPAG, a tropical agriculture data base. Among general scientific and technical data bases, the APPLIED SCIENCE AND TECHNOLOGY INDEX and the GENERAL SCIENCE INDEX are available in CD-ROM implementations from H.W. Wilson. The MCGRAW-HILL CD-ROM SCIENCE AND TECHNICAL REFERENCE SET combines the contents of two printed publications: the *Concise Encyclopedia of Science and Technology* and the *Dictionary of Scientific and Technical Terms;* it provides broad coverage of biology, the physical sciences, and engineering. The SCI-TECH REFERENCE PLUS CD-ROM from R.R. Bowker includes scientific and technical citations from the BOOKS IN PRINT and ULRICH'S data bases, biographical entries from the AMERICAN MEN AND WOMEN OF SCIENCE data base, laboratory information from the DIRECTORY OF AMERICAN RESEARCH AND TECHNOLOGY, and corporation data from the CORPTECH data base.

For engineering libraries, subsets of the INSPEC and COMPENDEX PLUS data bases are available on CD-ROM, as are METADEX and GEOREF. John Wiley and Sons offers CD-ROM implementations of the KIRK-OTHMER ENCYCLOPEDIA OF CHEMICAL TECHNOLOGY and the MARK ENCYCLOPEDIA OF POLYMER SCIENCE AND ENGINEER-ING. Patent information resources include the CASSIS CD-ROM, an implementation of the U.S. Patent Office data base; ESPACE, a CD-ROM version of the European Patent Office data base; the AUTOMATED PATENT SEARCHING (APS) system from Chadwyck-Healey; the CLAIMS/PATENT CD from SilverPlatter; and the FULL-TEXT patent data base from MicroPatent.

Designed for financial analysts, researchers, business librarians, and others who need access to information about publicly held companies, COMPACT DISCLOSURE was one of the earliest CD-ROM information products. Other CD-ROM sources of company information include the CD/CORPORATE, CD/CORPTECH, CD/PRIVATE+, CD/BANKING, and CD/INTERNATIONAL data bases from Lotus Development; the SPECTRUM OWNERSHIP and CORPORATE SNAPSHOTS data bases from Disclosure; CORPORATE INDUSTRY RESEARCH REPORTS (CIRR) from Bowker Business Research; COMPUSTAT PC PLUS and S&P CORPORATIONS from Standard and Poor's; and the MILLION DOLLAR DIRECTORY from Dun's Marketing Service. Useful company information can also be found in the CD-ROM editions of such bibliographic data bases as ABI/INFORM, F&S INDEX, and COMLINE NEWS. With their high capacities, CD-ROM discs are well suited to the publication of statistical and demographic data bases produced by government agencies and other organizations. Examples of business-oriented statistical information products include the various collections of federal, state, and county statistics produced by Slater Hall; the AGRI/STATS, CONSU/STATS, ECON/STATS, FOOD/STATS, and LABOR/STATS discs from Hopkins Technology; the INTERNATIONAL FINANCIAL STATISTICS and MAIN ECONOMIC INDICATORS data bases from DSI-Data Service and Information; the STATISTICAL MASTERFILE from Congressional Information Service; and various CD-ROM compilations published by the U.S. Department of Commerce.

West Publishing offers CD-ROM editions of various legal data bases. LEGALTRAC is a CD-ROM implementation of the *Legal Resources Index*. The Search Master Tax Library is a CD-ROM data base of federal and state tax codes produced by Matthew Bender and Company. Various state legal codes are available in CD-ROM implementations. Examples include NEW MEXICO LAW ON DISC, the DELAWARE CODE ANNOTATED, and the VIRGINIA STATE LEGAL CODE, all published by the Michie Company. The PAIS data base, which provides bibliographic coverage of many legal and public affairs publications, has been available on CD-ROM since the late 1980s. The LAWBASE CD-ROM, which contains decisions of the Swiss Federal Court, is typical of European titles for the legal market. Other examples include the REPERTORIO DEL FORO ITALIANO, which contains excerpts from Italian case law and bibliographic citations pertaining to legal questions; RECHTSSPRECHUNG DES BUNDESFINANZHOFS, the CD-ROM counterpart of the online JURIS DATANBANKEN; and the CD-ROM edition of LEGAL DATABANK, produced by Kluwer Datalex.

As is the case with data bases offered by online search services, researchers in the social sciences and humanities are served by a smaller number of CD-ROM products than their scientific, business, and professional counterparts. PSYCLIT (Psychological Abstracts) and the ERIC data base, however, were among the earliest and most widely publicized CD-ROM products. Other CD-ROM data bases of interest to social scientists include the SOCIAL SCIENCES CITATION INDEX from the Institute for Scientific Information; the SOCIAL SCIENCES INDEX from H.W. Wilson; SOCIOFILE (Sociological Abstracts); the CROSS-CULTURAL CD, a series of textual extracts from sociological and anthropological publications; and PSYNDEX, which provides bibliographic coverage of German-language publications on psychology. ABC-CLIO offers CD-ROM editions of its HISTORICAL ABSTRACTS and AMERICA: HISTORY AND LIFE data bases. The U.S. HISTORY ON CD-ROM collection contains the full texts of more than 100 American history books.

Intended for general readers as well as scholars, machine-readable compilations—the equivalent of huge anthologies—of literary works have been issued by various CD-ROM publishers. Examples include the SHAKESPEARE ON DISC and SHERLOCK HOLMES ON DISC collections from CMC ReSearch. The GREATEST BOOKS EVER WRITTEN is a CD-ROM collection of literary classics from ancient times to the present. The LIBRARY OF THE FUTURE SERIES, from World Library Incorporated, contains the complete texts of more than 450 literary, historical, philosophical, and religious works. DISCLIT: AMERICAN AUTHORS, produced by G.K. Hall and OCLC Electronic Publishing, contains the texts of 143 volumes from Twayne's United States Author Series. Chadwyck-Healey's ENGLISH POETRY FULL-TEXT DATABASE contains the works of 1,350 poets from 600 A.D. to the early twentieth century.

While bibliographic, financial, and statistical data bases account for the majority of available CD-ROM products, considerable attention has been given to surveying, military command and control, and other geographic applications involving mapping data. The GEODISC U.S. ATLAS, produced by GeoVision Incorporated, permits the retrieval and display of maps identified by geographic region or gazetteer entry. DeLorme Mapping Systems, a well-known publisher of detailed state atlases, has produced a CD-ROM world atlas. Produced by Chadwyck-Healey Incorporated, the SUPERMAP CD-ROM system permits the retrieval, tabulation, and mapping of U.S. and Australian census data.

Many librarians report heavy utilization and favorable experiences with CD-ROM information products. Because many of the same data bases are offered by online information services and in CD-ROM editions, the competitive relationship of the two approaches to automated reference has attracted considerable attention. Leaving the issue of equivalent performance temporarily aside, CD-ROM systems are widely advertised as less expensive replacements for online information services, but cost-effectiveness depends on the volume and characteristics of searches performed in a particular application. Any cost advantage enjoyed by one or the other technology is largely determined by the different role of fixed and variable charges in CD-ROM and online information services.

As with online information services, CD-ROM users will incur fixed costs associated with equipment procurement, site preparation, training, the procurement of search aids, and annual maintenance charges. Such costs are typically comparable to their online counterparts. In a marked departure, however, from the variable, usage-based charges associated with online information services, CD-ROM data bases are sold by subscription. A library or other customer pays a fixed annual fee, which permits unlimited searching without additional charges for connect-time, display, or printing. Given this difference, the potential economic advantage of CD-ROM over online information services is clear: a CD-ROM data base will prove less expensive than its online counterpart when, and if, the total variable charges for searching a given data base in a particular year exceed the annual cost of a CD-ROM subscription to that data base.

From the cost standpoint, CD-ROM is best suited to data bases that are searched frequently; online information services remain the preferred approach for data bases that are searched occasionally. The break-even point for justification of a CD-ROM subscription varies with search characteristics and can only be determined in the context of specific applications. For some data bases, CD-ROM can prove less expensive than online information services for data bases that are searched just three or four times per month.

Such cost comparisons necessarily ignore non-economic factors which can limit CD-ROM's utility as an alternative to online information services in certain situations. As a potentially significant constraint, the number of CD-ROM information products—while increasing steadily—remains smaller than the number of data bases available through online information services. As a further limitation, many CD-ROM data bases are updated by replacement at specified intervals, usually quarterly but occasionally semiannually or annually. In most cases, however, data base creators issue new records at monthly or more frequent intervals, and online information services may add such new records to their data bases soon after receipt. Delays inherent in CD-ROM production typically prohibit such frequent updating. Since many tasks require information that is as current as possible, CD-ROM systems cannot entirely replace online services, even where cost comparisons indicate that CD-ROM subscriptions are more economical. In a conceptually interesting hybrid implementation, however, online searching can be used for tasks requiring the most current information, while a supplemental CD-ROM subscription supports retrospective searches based on data base backfiles.

Differences in the coverage and content of online and CD-ROM implementations of a given data base may affect their performance in specific applications. In particular, some CD-ROM editions of bibliographic data bases do not contain as many older citations as their online counterparts. As an example, backfile coverage for DIALOG's ONDISC implementation of the NTIS data base begins in 1980, while the DIALOG online implementation includes backfile records dating from 1964. Similarly, Cambridge Scientific Abstracts' CD-ROM editions of the LIFE SCIENCES COLLECTION and AQUATIC SCIENCES AND FISHERIES ABSTRACTS include backfiles since 1982, but bibliographic citations contained in their online DIALOG counterparts date from 1978. SilverPlatter's CD-ROM edition of the PSYCLIT data base includes backfiles since 1974, but DIALOG's online implementation of PSYCINFO includes citations since 1967. As a further limitation, the PSYCLIT disk omits technical reports and dissertations which are included in the online PSYCINFO data base.

Constrained by the performance limitations of microcomputer-based workstations, CD-ROM searches involving broad terms or complex combinations of search terms and logical operators can take longer to complete than the same searches performed through mainframe-based online services, although advances in microcomputer technology and software improvements will narrow and possibly eliminate the disparity. As an additional complication, the time-consuming local printing of large numbers of retrieved citations can monopolize CD-ROM workstations, necessitating additional subscriptions and equipment, which can significantly increase CD-ROM costs. To minimize the potential for abuse, some libraries limit CD-ROM users to a specified amount of search time or printing activity. As previously described, online search services address this problem through offline printing of citations.

The Problem of Document Delivery

Used in this context, the term *document delivery* denotes the process whereby libraries provide users with access to the books, articles, reports, and other documents indexed in machine-readable data bases. Considerable available evidence suggests that the introduction of automated reference services is accompanied by a significant increase in the demand for, and consequently the cost of, document delivery. Paradoxically, online searching gives librarians the ability to quickly retrieve large numbers of potentially relevant bibliographic citations, but rising subscription prices and retrenched acquisitions budgets make it increasingly unlikely that a given library's collection will contain the documents identified in an online search, thereby prompting an increase in interlibrary loan activity.

Even assuming that existing interlibrary loan staffs can accommodate such increases within a given library, there is some question whether conventional interlibrary loan provides a sufficiently rapid response to users' document delivery demands. The several weeks usually required to complete an interlibrary loan transaction can quickly offset any speed advantage gained through an online search. In addition, users of automated reference methodologies may be more conscious and thus less tolerant of the delays inherent in conventional interlibrary loan methodologies. In the typical time-consuming manual bibliographic search, as performed by a researcher or other library user, citations are retrieved gradually and interlibrary loan requests submitted in small batches at regular intervals. While the loan requests are being processed, the search for additional citations continues. But the citations resulting from an online or CD-ROM search are made quickly available in their entirety. If a substantial number of retrieved citations must be obtained from other libraries, the user's work will slow down or even stop. In many cases, existing interlibrary loan channels will be glutted by a large volume of requests submitted in a short interval, further increasing the time required to complete a given loan transaction.

Efforts to address this problem have been directed toward the development of alternative document delivery methodologies. There have, for example, been several successful attempts to facilitate library resource sharing and increase the speed of interlibrary loan processing through technological intervention. As discussed in the preceding chapter, many individual libraries and multilibrary systems use bibliographic utilities or computer-produced union catalogs to provide more convenient and timely access to collection-related information of potential use in interlibrary loan processing. The bibliographic utilities include libraries' holdings information in their data bases. These holdings data can be quickly searched online. The bibliographic utilities likewise support interlibrary loan subsystems or other forms of computer-based, subscriber-to-subscriber communication for interlibrary loan purposes. Such systems automatically route interlibrary loan requests to appropriate holding libraries.

But while services offered by bibliographic utilities can expedite the identification of source libraries and the submission of interlibrary loan requests, they do nothing to promote the rapid delivery of requested materials by the source libraries. Addressing this requirement, some libraries have installed facsimile transceivers. As discussed in chapter 4, facsimile technology permits the electronic transmission of encoded document images and their reconstruction as paper copies at remote locations. Previously tried and abandoned as unreliable and impractical by libraries in the 1960s, facsimile devices are now faster, more versatile, and more reliable than their unsatisfactory predecessors. Using ordinary telephone lines, documents can be transmitted from one location to another at sub-minute speeds. But while facsimile transmission can reduce the disparity between the high speed of online searching and the comparative slowness of interlibrary loan, the disparity between long-distance telephone rates and conventional postal delivery charges limits its use to applications where rapid document delivery is essential.

As an alternative to interlibrary loan, data base producers and other companies—sometimes working in conjunction with online search services—have developed various fee-based document delivery packages and services. The Original Article Tear Sheet (OATS) service, operated by the Institute for Scientific Information, is one of the oldest and best known of these document ordering services, and it was the first to be accessible through online search services. Once a deposit account has been established, online searchers can place orders for specified documents through their terminals. The orders are transmitted to the Institute for Scientific Information, which mails copies of the indicated documents to the requester. Similar online document fulfillment services are offered by many other companies. Depending on the service selected and the item ordered, the charge for a given document may or may not compare favorably with the cost of borrowing it through conventional interlibrary loan or other channels. The order fulfillment time is, however, much shorter in most cases.

To minimize document delivery activity by enabling researchers and other users to make more knowledgeable assessments of the probable relevance of retrieved citations, the content of many data bases is enhanced by abstracts. With some data bases, such as ABI/INFORM, the abstracts are sufficiently detailed to satisfy some information requirements. Problems of document delivery are eliminated, however, where online data bases include the full text of indexed documents. Thus, a searcher working at an online terminal can retrieve entire documents as well as document surrogates. While such capabilities were once unusual, they are increasingly commonplace; a growing percentage of data bases offered by online information services include a full-text component, and some services—such as NEXIS, LEXIS, WESTLAW, VU/TEXT, and NEWS-NET—emphasize full-text information resources. As an alternative to full-text data bases, which contain information in character-coded form, several organizations are experimenting with electronic document imaging technology for on-demand delivery of library materials. The images, which may be created by scanning the required documents at the time a request is received or by storing previously scanned pages on optical disks in anticipation of retrieval, are transmitted to requesters on demand via facsimile.

Other vendors offer prepackaged document collections for sale to libraries. Following a pattern established by ERIC and NTIS, several publishers support their machine-readable data bases with document collections offered for sale, partially or completely, on microfilm or microfiche. The Congressional Information Service, for example, offers microfiche copies of documents indexed in the CIS INDEX and ASI data bases, while Information Access Company sells a microfilm collection of items indexed in the MAGAZINE INDEX. By purchasing these microform collections, a given library can assure its users access to most or all of the documents retrieved during an online search. Substituting optical disks for microfilm, the ADONIS BIOMEDICAL COLLECTION, a cooperative venture of the British Document Supply Centre and a group of scientific publishers, produces CD-ROM discs containing articles from more than 200 biomedical journals indexed in widely used data bases. The GENERAL PERIODICALS CD-ROM from University Microfilms International combines indexing and abstracting information with electronic images of selected articles.

SUMMARY

The computer-based handling of ready-reference questions and literature searches depends on the availability of machine-readable reference sources. Since the late 1960s, many publishers of printed indexing and abstracting journals and bibliographic reference tools have offered machine-readable versions of their products for use by libraries and other organizations. Historically, these bibliographic data bases have been most widely encountered in scientific and technical disciplines, but much recent attention has been given to their availability in the social sciences, humanities, and business. In addition to those data bases that correspond to established printed publications, a growing number of reference services have been developed specifically for use in computer-based systems and have no printed counterparts. While the earliest machine-readable data bases developed to support the reference activity were bibliographic in character, nonbibliographic directory-type and numeric data bases are increasingly available.

During the late 1960s and early 1970s, a number of libraries purchased machine-readable bibliographic and nonbibliographic data bases for processing on in-house computers using custom-developed information retrieval software. However, most libraries lacked access to the hardware and software resources required to implement such systems. Through the early 1970s, the needs of these libraries were addressed by fee-based search services operated by the producers of machine-readable data bases or other organizations. Such services, like their in-house counterparts, customarily operated in the offline, batch processing mode and have since been replaced by services offering online data base searching.

Online information services can be divided into two broad groups: (1) multidisciplinary services that provide data base coverage of a varied range of subjects for a broad clientele; and (2) specialized services that provide access to one or more data bases relevant to a single subject discipline, profession, or activity. While they differ in the number and type of data bases offered and the specific retrieval capabilities supported, both types of services share a common operating methodology: they purchase or otherwise obtain bibliographic and nonbibliographic data bases in machine-readable form from their producers, convert the data bases to a form required for storage on their computers, and allow libraries or other subscribers to perform various retrieval operations on such data using prewritten data base management software. Some services also offer private file capabilities which allow libraries to establish their own data bases. Like general-purpose data base management systems, the software provided by these online information services features a nonprocedural query language that permits a user working at an online terminal to initiate literature searches or other information retrieval operations by entering specified commands. These query languages are easily learned but provide powerful information-processing capabilities.

Libraries using information search services must be equipped with terminals or appropriately configured microcomputers. For long-distance telecommunications, most libraries use one of the value-added carriers in preference to the conventional telephone networks. Internet access is increasingly a possibility. Staff training and the procurement of printed manuals and other search aids are required before searching can begin.

Most online search services assess usage charges on the basis of connect-time, with varying rates for different data bases. Additional charges are levied for the online or offline printing of retrieved citations or other data. Cost justification when compared to a manual reference system typically depends on a combination of cost reduction and perceived added value in online search capability. The two major areas of potential cost reduction are (1) the elimination of subscriptions to infrequently used printed indexes and (2) the reduction of professional labor devoted to literature searching or other reference tasks. The added-value approach to cost justification emphasizes the superior results obtainable with online searching.

As a possible alternative to online searching, an increasing number of data bases are available on CD-ROM disks. Accompanied by information retrieval software, such CD-ROM products support data base searching at local microcomputer workstations. Offered on a subscription basis, they can prove less expensive than online searching for data bases that are accessed frequently, although a lack of timeliness and other performance limitations may make them unsuitable for some applications.

Because they provide libraries with greatly improved ability to rapidly retrieve large numbers of potentially relevant bibliographic citations, automated reference services can result in significant increases in the demand for document delivery. Such demands are increasingly difficult to accommodate at a time of rising subscription rates and retrenched collection development, thus prompting an increase in interlibrary loan activity. Because existing interlibrary loan methodologies cannot usually accommodate this increased demand, considerable attention has been given to the development of alternative document delivery systems. Examples include facsimile transmission, electronic document ordering, the purchase of entire document collections on microforms or optical disks, and online availability of documents themselves, either in character-coded, full-text formats or as electronic images.

ADDITIONAL READING

ALLEN, B. "The Effects of Academic Background on Statements of Information Need." *Library Quarterly* 60 (2): 120–38 (1990).

ALLEN, G. "CD-ROM Training: What Do the Patrons Want?" *RQ* 30 (1): 88–93 (1990).

———. "Database Selection by Patrons Using CD-ROM." *College and Research Libraries* 51 (1): 69–75 (1990).

BAILEY, C. "The Intelligence Reference Information System Project: A Merger of CD-ROM LAN and Expert System Technologies." *Information Technology and Libraries* 11 (3): 237–44 (1992).

BARBUTO, D., and CAVALLOS, E. "End-user Searching: Program Review and Future Prospects." *RQ* 21 (2): 214–28 (1991).

BATES, M. "How to Use Information Search Tactics Online." *Online* 11 (2): 47–54 (1987).

BATES, M., et al. "An Analysis of Search Terminology Used by Humanities Scholars: The Getty Online Searching Project, Report Number 1." *Library Quarterly* 63 (1): 1–38 (1993).

BAUMOL, W., and BLACKMAN, S. "Electronics, the Cost Disease, and the Operation of Libraries." *Journal of the American Society for Information Science* 34 (2): 181–91 (1983).

BELL, G. "Online Searching in Industry versus Academia: A Study in Partnerships." *Online* 14 (5): 51–56 (1990).

BELL, S. "Online without the Line: Cellular Technology for Searching on the Go." *Online* 15 (5): 15–25 (1991).

BENNETT, G. "RLIN: Mud and Stars—A Bibliographic Essay on the Use of the Research Libraries Information Network at the Reference Desk." *RQ* 25 (4): 476–82 (1986).

BESSER, H. "Visual Access to Visual Images: The UC Berkeley Image Database Project." *Library Trends* 38 (4): 787–808 (1990).

BOSS, R. "Accessing Electronic Publications in Complex LAN Environments." *Library Technology Reports* 28 (3): 275–388 (1992).

BOURNE, C. "On-line Systems: History, Technology, Economics." *Journal of the American Society for Information Science* 31 (2): 155–60 (1980).

BURRIS, A., and MOLINEK, F. "Establishing and Managing a Successful End-user Search Service in a Large Special Library." *Online* 15 (2): 36–39 (1991).

BUTLER, M. "Full-text CD-ROM Libraries for International Development." *Microcomputers for Information Management* 7 (4): 273–91 (1990).

CAWKELL, A. "Electronic Document Supply Systems." *Journal of Documentation* 47 (1): 41–73 (1991).

CLARK, K., and GOMEZ, J. "Faculty Use of Databases at Texas A&M University." *RQ* 30 (2): 241–48 (1990).

COOPER, L., and THARP, A. "Inverted Signature Trees and Text Searching on CD-ROMs." *Information Processing and Management* 25 (2): 161–69 (1989).

CRAWFORD, G. "The Effects of Instruction in the Use of PsycLIT on Interlibrary Loan." *RQ* 31 (3): 370–76 (1992).

DAVIDOFF, D., and GADIKIAN, R. "If It's Not Here, I Can't Be Bothered: Limiting Searches to In-house Journals." *Online* 15 (4): 58–61 (1991).

DENTON, B. "E-mail Delivery of Search Results via the Internet." *Online* 16 (2): 50–53 (1992).

DONEL, J., and HOLBO, R. "The CD-ROM Network Experiment at Oregon State University." *Online* 17 (1): 104–106 (1993).

HAGEE, J., and BOEWE, K. "Downloading and Printing Search Results from Online Databases." *Information Technology and Libraries* 11 (3): 305–307 (1992).

HOWDEN, N., and DILLARD, J. "Technology Used in Online Searching." *Special Libraries* 82 (3): 288–94 (1991).

JACKSON, K. "Loading Wilson Indexes Locally: The Texas A&M Experience." *Online* 14 (3): 42–45 (1990).

KEAYS, T. "Searching Online Database Services over the Internet." *Online* 17 (1): 29–33 (1993).

LADNER, S., and TILLMAN, H. "Using the Internet for Reference." *Online* 17 (1): 45–51 (1993).

LEACH, S., and SPENCER, M. "The Perfectly Organized Search Service." *Online* 17 (1): 104–106 (1993).

MEYER, R. "Management, Cost, and Behavioral Issues with Locally Mounted Databases." *Information Technology and Libraries* 9 (3): 226–41 (1990).

MITCHELL, M., and SAUNDERS, L. "The Virtual Library: An Agenda for the 1990s." *Computers in Libraries* 11 (4): 8–10 (1991).

MONDSCHEIN, L. "SDI Use and Productivity in the Corporate Research Environment." *Special Libraries* 81 (3): 265–79 (1990).

O'LEARY, M. "Standalone Online Sources: The Challenge of the Niche Database." *Online* 15 (6): 56–60 (1991).

PRIORE, C., and MILLER, R. "Local Holdings Searching in CD-ROM Databases." *Information Technology and Libraries* 11 (3): 307–309 (1992).

QUINT, B. "Inside a Searcher's Mind: The Seven Stages of an Online Search." *Online* 15 (3): 13–18; 15 (4): 28–35 (1991).

ROPIQUET, S., ed. *CD ROM: Optical Publishing.* Redmond, Wash.: Microsoft Press, 1987.

SAFFADY, W. "The Availability and Cost of Online Search Services." *Library Technology Reports* 28 (2): 115–268 (1992).

SARACEVIC, T., and KANTOR, P. "Online Searching: Still an Imprecise Art." *Library Journal* 116 (10): 47–51 (1991).

SAULE, M. "User Instruction Issues for Databases in the Humanities." *Library Trends* 40 (4): 596–613 (1992).

SCHUMAN, B. "The 'Hometown' Syndrome: Will the First System You Learn Always Be Your Favorite?" *Online* 16 (2): 54–58 (1992).

SCOTT, R., and SCOTT, N. "Online Searching at 9600 Baud." *Online* 15 (6): 33–37 (1991).

SMITH, M. "Infoethics for Leaders: Models of Moral Agency in the Information Environment." *Library Trends* 40 (4): 553–70 (1992).

SMITH, S., and SMITH, J. "Online Searching in the Small College Library: Ten Years Later." *Online* 15 (1): 37–40 (1991).

STEFFEY, R. "The NOTIS Multiple Database Access System: A Look behind the Scenes." *Online* 14 (5): 46–49 (1990).

THIEL, T., et al. *CD-ROM Mastering for Information and Image Management.* Silver Spring, Md.: Association for Information and Image Management, 1990.

TURNER, P. "The Effects of Baud Rate, Performance Anxiety, and Experience on Online Bibliographic Searches." *Information Technology and Libraries* 34 (1): 34–42 (1990).

8

Automated Acquisitions and Serials Control

Although the two activities discussed in this chapter are often relegated to separate departments within a given library, they share an important function: the procurement of library materials. This chapter will follow common library practice in using the term *acquisitions* to collectively denote those tasks that support the procurement of library materials that are published on a nonrecurring basis, including books, technical reports, government publications, and audiovisual materials. The acquisition of journals, magazines, and other periodical publications is considered a facet of serials control, the scope of which extends to such activities as the cataloging and binding of serial publications.

This distinction between acquisitions and serials control is rarely unequivocal, however, since annuals or irregularly published materials may be treated as monographs in one library and as serials in another. Regardless of the type of material involved, it is important to distinguish those tasks that support the acquisition of serial and nonserial publications from the professional activities associated with collection development. Such activities include the formulation of collection development policies and the evaluation and selection of library materials. Acquisition tasks, whether for serial or nonserial publications, are procurement-oriented and begin once the decision to add a given item to the library's collection has been made.

Since acquisitions and serials control result in the addition of materials to library collections, they would seem to be more appropriately discussed at the beginning rather than at the end of a survey of library automation. They are discussed here, however, because an understanding of prevailing approaches to automated acquisitions and serials control requires some familiarity with the systems and services described in the preceding chapters. This chapter begins with an overview of acquisitions work steps and their potential for automation, followed by a survey of automation alternatives ranging from custom-developed software to turnkey acquisitions systems. Serials control systems are discussed in later sections.

COMPUTER-BASED ACQUISITIONS

As with automated circulation control and catalog production, libraries have had more than two decades of experience with automated acquisitions. Book ordering systems—using keypunch equipment, card sorters, and tabulating machines—were developed in the late 1950s by public and academic libraries in Illinois, Indiana, and Missouri. In the early 1960s, batch processing, computer-based acquisitions systems were developed by a number of academic libraries, including those at the University of Michigan, Yale University, Pennsylvania State University, the Washington University School of Medicine, and the Claremont Colleges. In the late 1960s and early 1970s, several academic libraries implemented online acquisitions systems, perhaps the most widely publicized being the Book Order and Selection System (BOSS) at the University of Massachusetts, the Library On-Line Information and Text Access (LOLITA) system at Oregon State University, and the acquisitions subsystem within the previously discussed BALLOTS system at Stanford University. The first minicomputer-based turnkey acquisitions system, developed by CLSI, was installed in 1972 at the Cleveland Public Library.

But despite these promising beginnings, automated acquisitions systems failed to attract the widespread library and vendor interest given to the automation of circulation control, cataloging, and reference service during the mid- to late 1970s. Since the late 1970s, however, interest in automated acquisitions has increased steadily, especially among librarians and vendors who have previously implemented automated circulation or cataloging systems. This interest is motivated by increased library awareness of certain problems and limitations inherent in manual acquisitions systems.

Acquisitions funds represent a large and important component of the typical library budget, and library administration is accountable for their responsible expenditure. As with circulation control, manual acquisitions systems cannot readily generate the financial and statistical information essential to scientific planning and management. In libraries where book budgets are allocated annually, for example, certain acquisitions funds may remain characteristically underspent over a period of many months, necessitating intensified expenditures at the year's end, a situation that is not conducive to prudent selection practices. Similarly, certain funds may be expended too quickly, leaving little reserve for important materials published later in the year.

In either case, periodic reports of fund status can alert subject bibliographers and library administrators to exceptional situations requiring attention and possible corrective action. While such reports can be produced manually, the available labor in most manual acquisitions systems is fully occupied in paperwork processing and related work routines pertaining to book orders. As with circulation control, library interest in automated acquisitions is in large part motivated by a desire to improve the quality of management decision making, while making more money available for collection development and professional services by reducing clerical support requirements. Cost reduction aside, many librarians perceive an added value in the potentially faster paperwork processing and earlier ordering and receipt of materials permitted by a computer-based system.

As discussed below, the automation of acquisitions also contributes to the development of integrated library systems in which a single bibliographic data base serves the various information-processing requirements of technical services, reference, and administrative applications. Bibliographic data, captured in machine-readable form at the time an item is ordered, can later be enhanced or modified to support circulation control, cataloging, or other activities, thereby eliminating some duplication of data entry, recordkeeping, and other work routines. The automation of acquisitions likewise permits the integration of a library's in-process and catalog files, thus facilitating access to bibliographic information about items on order or awaiting cataloging.

Application Overview

While differences in purchasing practices and procurement regulations may lead to local variations in acquisitions systems, certain basic characteristics and work steps are commonplace. Depending on the type of library involved, a request to purchase a specific item may be transmitted to the acquisitions department by subject bibliographers, other library staff members, library users, or other persons or groups. Typically, the library's own acquisitions files and catalog are first consulted to determine whether the item is on order or already in its collection. Assuming that the item is not already owned or that an additional copy will be purchased, the bibliographic information in the request must be verified, the item's availability determined, and a vendor selected. In a manual circulation system, bibliographic verification relies on the printed library catalogs discussed in chapter 6 and such trade bibliographies as *Books in Print* or the appropriate comparable sources for nonbook materials. As an alternative, some book jobbers provide their customers with lists of available titles in hard copy or on microfiche.

Once a vendor has been selected, a purchase order is typed and issued. Libraries that are not responsible for their own purchasing operations will type a requisition for transmittal to a corporate or institutional purchasing department, which then issues a purchase order. In either case, the appropriate procurement documents are typically prepared in multiple copies, several of which are retained by the acquisitions department for inclusion in an outstanding order file arranged by title, a vendor file arranged by vendor name, and a fund file arranged by fund number or name. Additional files may be maintained in specific situations. When an item is received, the corresponding documents are removed from files and updated as required to reflect the full or partial receipt of an order. Payment is then authorized and a check issued. In the case of libraries that are not authorized to write checks, a payment voucher is typed for transmittal to a corporate or institutional disbursements department.

Automated acquisitions systems retain these basic characteristics but replace typing, filing, and related manual work steps with data entry, online searching, and other computer-oriented work routines. If the library has an online catalog or master circulation file, for example, it can be searched to determine whether a given item is already owned. Bibliographic verification can be automated similarly by searching the shared cataloging data bases maintained by bibliographic utilities or the MARC-derivative data bases offered by online information services or published as CD-ROM information products. As the machine-readable counterparts of printed library catalogs, such data bases can simplify preorder searching by providing access to bibliographic records by a variety of retrieval parameters.

The various machine-readable data bases produced by R.R. Bowker are particularly useful for acquisitions-oriented bibliographic verification. Available through several online search services, the BOOKS IN PRINT data base is the machine-readable counterpart of several printed trade bibliographies, including *Books in Print, Subject Guide to Books in Print, Forthcoming Books, Subject Guide to Forthcoming Books, Paperbound Books in Print,* and *Scientific and Technical Books & Serials in Print.* Updated monthly, it provides bibliographic and ordering information, including International Standard Book Numbers and prices, for more than 1.3 million records. Data base records cover all books currently in print, books that are about to be published, and books declared out-of-print or indefinitely out-of-stock since 1979. The BRITISH BOOKS IN PRINT data base, produced by J. Whitaker and Sons, provides similar coverage for books published in the United Kingdom. It is accessible through DIALOG, BLAISE-LINE, and other online information services.

Since 1985, Bowker has offered a CD-ROM implementation of the BOOKS IN PRINT data base. Called BIP PLUS, it includes more than 800,000 records from *Books in Print, Subject Guide to Books in Print, Books in Print Supplement,* and *Forthcoming Books.* Menu-driven software permits convenient retrieval of bibliographic records by author, title, publisher, publication date, ISBN, LC card number, subject, edition, language, price, and other parameters. If desired, retrieved records can be displayed in a format suitable for the printing of a temporary catalog card for items on order, omitting classification numbers, places of publication, and some tracings. An operator can augment retrieved records and format them for transmission to electronic ordering systems operated by Baker and Taylor, Ingram, Blackwell/North America, Brodart, and others. In early 1988, Bowker began packaging the CD-ROM edition BOOKS IN PRINT with BOOK REVIEWS PLUS, a data base of book reviews from *Publishers Weekly, Library Journal, School Library Journal, Choice,* and *Booklist.* Bowker also offers BOOKS OUT OF PRINT PLUS as a separate CD-ROM product. In the United Kingdom, J. Whitaker and Sons offers BOOKBANK, a CD-ROM implementation of the BRITISH BOOKS IN PRINT data base described above. For bibliographic verification of German-language imprints, Online Computer Systems and Buchhandler Vereinigung have produced a CD-ROM version of the VERZEICHNIS LIEFERBARER BUCHER data base. It is modeled on BIP PLUS.

Whether bibliographic verification is performed by manual or automated methodologies, automated acquisitions control typically employs a combination of three data files: (1) an order file, sometimes called an "in-process file," contains one record for each item purchased; (2) a vendor file contains one record for each publisher, book jobber, or other procurement source; and (3) a fund file contains one record for each account which supports the purchase of library materials. While specific details will necessarily vary from one system to another, most order files contain a combination of bibliographic and order-specific data, including author, title, and imprint information; an edition statement; an ISBN, LC Card Number, or other unique numerical identifier; an order number; the order date; a fund account number; a vendor number, code, or similar identifier; the number of copies ordered; the price, both list and net, plus discounts and service charges; the currency type; the estimated receipt date; the ordering branch, department, or agency; the name of the requester, bibliographer, or other person responsible for the order; and a status code or other information that permits the tracking of an item at various stages of the acquisitions process. Most systems likewise reserve a field for a designation of the order type, such as a firm order, standing order, prepayment, approval item, gift, exchange, membership acquisition, or deposit account. Some systems also include a text field for free-form messages intended for acquisitions clerks, catalogers, or others. With some automated acquisitions systems, the order file contains additional bibliographic data fields; alternatively, order records may be linked to detailed bibliographic records maintained in a separate file.

As noted above, vendor files contain one record for each publisher, book jobber, book dealer, sales agent, or other procurement source. To accommodate gifts and exchanges, the vendor file may also include donor records. Again subject to variation from installation to installation, commonly encountered data fields include the vendor's name, address, telephone number, and fax or telex number; an assigned numeric or other coded identifier which links specific order records to the vendor file; pertinent contract numbers and dates; applicable discount schedules; a claim period indicator, which specifies the intervals at which notices will be sent for overdue orders; and the total volume of vendor activity—as an item count or dollar value—for a specified period of time. Some vendor files also incorporate performance statistics, such as the average time each vendor requires to fill an order and the number of claims or cancellations experienced in a specified period of time.

Most fund files contain one record for each account or other budgetary unit established by the library for acquisitions purposes. These funds may reflect subdivisions of a library's collections, academic departments within a college or university, branch libraries within a public library system, special accounts established for the purchase of particular types of materials, or gifts from specific individuals or groups. For each fund file record, typical data fields include the account number, a brief account description, the original dollar amount allocated at the beginning of the budgetary cycle, total expenditures since the beginning of the budgetary cycle, encumbrances associated with items ordered but not received, and the current fund balance.

Some automated acquisitions systems also include a requester file, which contains names, addresses, and other pertinent information for persons or organizations, including branch libraries, who may initiate acquisition requests. It is often used to print notification slips when requested material is received by the acquisitions department or as other information about the status of requested items becomes available. In some cases, the requester file and vendor file are merged in a master name and address file, although vendor records may contain more information than requester records. A few automated acquisitions systems maintain invoice files to permit the retrieval of information by invoice number in answer to questions about the payment status or history of particular transactions. Similarly, some systems feature an online desiderata file, which contains records for items being considered for purchase. In the case of antiquarian or out-of-print items, lists of desiderata records may be printed for circulation to book dealers and other procurement sources.

Vendor, fund, and requester files are typically established in advance of system operation. Their information content is typically converted to machine-readable form by the key-to-disk methodologies described in chapter 1. In most cases, this information is derived from files of source documents used in the automated system's manual predecessor. Such files can be updated as required to incorporate records for new vendors, funds, or requesters. Records in the order file are created as items are ordered. Most of the sources used for preorder searching provide author, title, and other bibliographic data sufficient to establish a preliminary cataloging record for an item.

Some of the acquisitions systems discussed later in this chapter will accept machine-readable records transferred from data bases maintained by bibliographic utilities, CD-ROM cataloging support systems, online public access catalog systems, turnkey circulation systems, or other sources. This machine-readable information may be entered into the system through magnetic tape—such as the archival tapes produced by bibliographic utilities—or, where available, through an online interface. In most cases, additional information must be contributed to complete the master order record. Keystroking methodologies are typically used to convert this additional information to machine-readable form. In the absence of an appropriate source of pre-existing machine-readable data, the entire order record for a given item can be converted to computer-processable form through keystroking or, less commonly, optical character recognition methodologies.

This data entry activity is the computer-based counterpart of the typing of purchase orders and related procurement documents in a manual acquisitions system. While some batch-oriented systems with offline components may remain in use, automated acquisitions systems are increasingly designed for online operation. To simplify data entry, video terminals display formatted screens with labeled fields, although newly entered records are seldom added to data files in real time. In most cases, newly created records or modifications to existing records are stored in temporary disk files for later batch processing.

One of the principal advantages of automated acquisitions is the substitution of computer-based file maintenance for the labor-intensive sorting, filing, and other paper-handling procedures associated with manual acquisitions systems. When an order record is entered, most systems will automatically encumber the estimated purchase price in the indicated fund account. Most systems will likewise produce claiming and cancellation notices, thereby eliminating a time-consuming work step encountered in manual systems. As items are received, order records are searched and their status updated to reflect full or partial shipments. When an order is closed, the corresponding records can be automatically purged from the online order file to a historical file on magnetic tape, while the bibliographic information associated with a received item can be automatically transferred to a cataloging or circulation data file for revision and enhancement as required.

Superior file-inquiry and order-tracking capabilities further distinguish automated acquisitions systems from their manual counterparts. The most advanced systems permit the online retrieval of order records by such parameters as the order control number, the purchase order number, the order date, the vendor name or code, the requester name or code, the fund number, or such bibliographic information as author, title, partial title, or publisher. Retrieved records typically include brief bibliographic data, accompanied by a summary of the order's essential characteristics and status, including vendor and fund information. Such online inquiry capability is especially useful in minimizing inadvertent duplicate orders by libraries where acquisitions responsibilities are dispersed among multiple persons, departments, or branches. Users can often request more detailed displays, which may include the number of copies ordered, the price, the payment type, the currency type, the vendor's discount, and the specified cancellation date. Vendor records can usually be accessed by vendor code and name. Fund records are typically retrievable by account number, although some systems permit retrieval by fund balance.

In addition to supporting online inquiries, the typical automated acquisitions system will generate three broad groups of printed output products: procurement documents, notices, and reports. The most important examples of the first group are purchase orders and payment documents, both of which are customarily produced in the batch mode at predetermined intervals. In addition to printing purchase orders on library-designed paper forms, some automated acquisitions systems can record purchase order information in machine-readable form on magnetic media for input to computer systems maintained by publishers, book jobbers, or other vendors. The Book Industry Systems Advisory Committee (BISAC) of the Book Industry Study Group Incorporated has developed a format for the recording of such computer-processible purchase order data. That format uses the International Standard Book Number as the primary identifier for ordered items, with modified author/title information to be substituted in cases when an ISBN is unavailable. The format also specifies the essential data to be provided in a given order, including the customer identification, preferably in the form of a Standard Address Number (SAN); purchase order number; date; and price. The BISAC format can also be used for electronic transmission to online ordering systems.

The claiming of overdue orders has a direct counterpart in the circulation activity. As previously discussed, most automated acquisitions systems will print claiming and cancellation notices to vendors at predetermined intervals and arrival notices to requesters when items are received. With some systems, librarians must specify an anticipated arrival date for orders; in other cases, the system will use the performance statistics stored in vendor records to calculate an arrival date. Most systems can generate lists of overdue orders for operator examination prior to the printing of claiming notices. Some systems will also print routing slips for received materials.

Although online inquiry can be used to quickly determine the status of a given order or fund balance, most automated acquisitions systems rely on printed reports to provide aggregate financial, statistical, or other information on a regularly scheduled or demand basis. Examples include fund status summaries, arranged by account number; fund history reports, listing closed orders by title within each account; lists of daily accounting transactions; charts of accounts; purchase order lists arranged by title, vendor, fund, workstation, or other parameters; claimed item lists; lists of canceled orders; lists of open orders; lists of orders outstanding longer than a specified period of time; lists of orders received but not invoiced after a specified number of days; vendor rosters, including discounts and performance statistics; lists of newly acquired items arranged by author, title, classification number, or other parameters; and lists of ordered items on hold for requesters. Some automated acquisitions systems will also issue checks or payment vouchers. A few systems can generate electronic payment information for use by corporate or institutional disbursement departments.

Implementation Alternatives

Unlike automated circulation control and, to a greater extent, automated cataloging, where one or two approaches to automation are dominant, at least four different implementation alternatives are available to libraries considering automated acquisitions: (1) an acquisitions software package can be custom-developed to an individual library's specifications; (2) a library can purchase a prewritten acquisitions-specific software package; (3) acquisitions can be implemented as an application module within a multifunction integrated library system; and (4) several bibliographic utilities and book jobbers offer online acquisitions systems that subscribers can access on a timesharing basis.

Customized software development is, of course, an alternative in every computer application. Customized acquisitions systems may be implemented on computing equipment owned and operated by the library itself; on centralized computers operated by a university, government agency, corporation, school system, or other organization with which the library is affiliated; or on equipment operated by a computer service bureau. In the last of these approaches, the service bureau may also be responsible for the development of customized software through a contract with the library. As noted earlier in this chapter, a number of libraries developed customized acquisitions systems during the 1960s and early 1970s, and some of those systems remain in operation. For the most part, they are implemented on mainframes or minicomputers operated by a university, municipality, corporation, or other organization with which a given library is affiliated. Since the mid-1980s, various small- to medium-size libraries have utilized microcomputer-based data base management programs to develop acquisitions systems.

Compared to the other implementation alternatives discussed in this section, custom-developed acquisitions systems offer one important advantage: hardware components can be selected and programs written to the library's specifications, thereby minimizing the need to compromise on desired features. But while the selection of appropriate hardware components rarely poses problems, customized software development can prove to be a time-consuming and expensive activity that can result in significant delays in implementation and substantial, often unanticipated costs. Post-implementation costs will likewise be incurred by the continuing requirement for software modification or other maintenance to address changing application requirements. As a result, customized development of acquisitions systems is often viewed as an implementation alternative of last resort, to be seriously considered only in those situations where other approaches to automated acquisitions are clearly unacceptable.

The purchase of prewritten acquisitions software can minimize the worst implementation problems associated with customized system development. As a potential constraint for libraries that must use existing mainframe or minicomputer systems operated by institutional or corporate data processing centers, such prewritten programs are invariably designed for operation on particular hardware configurations equipped with specific systems software. Assuming compatibility with a library's existing computer installation, prewritten acquisitions software can be obtained from several sources, including libraries that have undertaken customized software development. More commonly, however, prewritten acquisitions software is purchased from commercial vendors. Some of the most versatile products are designed for microcomputer-based implementations in standalone and local area network configurations.

As an example, the MATSS acquisitions system from Midwest Library Service is designed for IBM-compatible microcomputers. It maintains order, vendor, and fund files as described above. Order records can be key-entered or downloaded from other systems. MATSS provides interfaces to bibliographic utilities, including OCLC, RLIN, and WLN. It also supports record transfers from such CD-ROM information products as Bibliofile, WLN's LASERCAT, and BIP PLUS. Checks by author, title, ISBN, and LCCN prevent duplicate ordering of items already owned or on order. For status inquiries or other purposes, order records can be retrieved by author, title, ISBN, LCCN, purchase order number, and a unique MATSS record number. Order records can be deleted to reflect cancellations or received items. Orders can be produced in printed or BISAC electronic formats. Vendor and fund files are automatically adjusted when orders are placed. Canceled orders are automatically unencumbered. Order records include a currency code and exchange rate with a default currency. Foreign encumbrances are recalculated when exchange rates fluctuate. The MATSS program monitors vendor performance by several parameters. Printed order forms, reports, and notices can be produced in a variety of formats.

The MATSS program is menu-driven and relies on function keys to initiate commonly encountered operations. Profiles defined by a library-appointed system supervisor determine which menu options and program capabilities are available to specific users. While MATSS is a microcomputer-based product, large implementations involving hundreds of workstations are possible in networked configurations.

As an alternative to acquisitions-specific programs, most integrated library automation systems support an acquisitions module as a standard or optional feature. As described in chapter 6, such integrated systems are available as prewritten software packages for implementation on customer-supplied computer systems or as turnkey combinations of preconfigured hardware and prewritten software. In either case, developers of integrated systems view acquisitions as an essential component; it is the entry point for data that will subsequently be enhanced by the software package's cataloging and circulation modules. Integrated systems consequently provide convenient support for the creation of brief bibliographic records at the time items are ordered.

While there is some variation from product to product, the acquisitions modules associated with integrated library systems support the broad range of capabilities associated with acquisitions-specific programs described above. The most versatile systems are highly parameterized—that is, they allow a given library, or individual branches in a library system, to specify file contents, document formats, report contents, frequency of output production, time periods for automatic claiming of unreceived orders, and other operating conditions. Most systems can likewise accommodate a variety of order conditions, including rush orders, gifts, exchanges, standing orders, approval plans, multiple-copy and multiple-volume orders, and prepaid orders. In terms of accounting capabilities, the most sophisticated systems permit multifund encumbrances; automatic checking for overexpenditures in funds; and automatic currency conversions.

As a potentially significant advantage of multifunctional implementations, an acquisition application module can often utilize an integrated system's master bibliographic data base for pre-order searching. While this capability does not eliminate the use of external sources for bibliographic verification, it can prove especially convenient in multilibrary or multibranch installations where the automated system maintains a union catalog of holdings or where individual catalog data files are accessible by all participants. To facilitate data entry by minimizing keystroking requirements, integrated software packages usually permit the transfer of data from bibliographic records to order records.

Similarly, the acquisitions activity can generate preliminary circulation records for items on order. If desired, such items can be "checked out" to vendors and "checked in" on receipt. Certain nonbibliographic data generated by the acquisitions activity may also prove useful in circulation control. If a borrower is to be billed for a lost item, for example, information about its original purchase price is available. As a convenience to users, the integration of acquisitions and circulation in a single system allows holds to be placed on items that are on order.

Certain acquisitions tasks may likewise be facilitated by their integration with circulation capabilities. The potential contribution of automated circulation control to collection development was noted in chapter 5. As an example of circulation-related information of significance for acquisitions, an excessive number of holds placed on a circulating item may indicate the need to acquire additional copies. Similarly, in some libraries the weeding of collections, whether for removal to storage or discarding, is the responsibility of the acquisitions department. Such weeding can be most knowledgeably performed on the basis of accurate, up-to-date circulation statistics.

While the prewritten software packages and turnkey systems described above offer the advantages of self-contained operation by a library itself, they typically require a substantial capital investment in computing resources. This capital investment can be reduced if automated acquisitions capabilities are obtained on a timesharing basis through a bibliographic utility. WLN, the first bibliographic utility to offer such capabilities, implemented its acquisitions subsystem in 1978. It supports pre-order searching and bibliographic verification through the WLN data base of cataloging records, online order entry, retrieval of records by multiple access points, full fund accounting with an unlimited number of accounts, and automatic production of routing slips. Order and accounting profiles, which specify options to be applied to particular acquisitions functions, are established for each system participant. To prepare an order, a library searches the WLN data base for an appropriate bibliographic record. Retrieved information is automatically transferred to an acquisitions workform. The terminal operator enters a vendor identifier, account number, invoice number, shipping address, quantity, and other information required to complete an order.

The WLN acquisitions system can accommodate regular purchases, standing orders, membership and depository account items, information requests, exchanges, and other types of transactions. To simplify data entry, default values for specific fields can be established on a session-by-session basis. Order records are linked to bibliographic records and stored in an in-process file that can be searched by purchase order number or retrieved by any of the parameters supported by the WLN online cataloging system. WLN was the first bibliographic utility to offer electronic overnight transmission to cooperating vendors. Purchase orders can also be printed from in-process records in batches at regular intervals. In-process records can be updated online by adding, deleting, or changing bibliographic or order information. Automatic claiming intervals can be specified, and claim notices will be printed automatically. When the order cycle is completed, a receiving report is produced, and the order record is transferred to an offline history file.

The WLN acquisitions system maintains an account status file, which contains identifying numbers, descriptions, original allocation amounts, outstanding encumbrances, disbursements, and balances for each library's acquisitions accounts. Password control provides access to specific accounting functions. Account status information, transaction reports, and account history reports are printed periodically. The acquisitions system can also generate processing slips, requester notification cards, vendor lists, vendor reports, lists of outstanding purchase orders, and lists of aged orders and other exceptional conditions.

Designed for the varied acquisitions requirements of large research libraries, the RLIN acquisitions system supports selection decisions, unitary procurements, extended procurements, direct accessions, and expected material. It can accommodate regular orders, prepaid orders, blanket orders, deposit accounts, gifts, exchanges, approval plans, publications received through memberships, and other procurement situations. Users can track the status and location of specific items from the time of the original order through claiming, and receipt or cancellation. Claims can be generated automatically or on demand. Order forms, claims, cancellation notices, and various management reports can be printed locally or at RLIN headquarters.

The Utlas ACCORD (Acquisitions par CATSS/CATSS Ordering) system is an online order entry and preparation program that permits the creation of CATSS records for library materials at the time they are ordered. Once created, the records can be used to generate purchase orders for the indicated materials. To facilitate order preparation and vendor selection, the CATSS data base incorporates several acquisitions-oriented source files, including *Books for College Libraries* and the UMI Article Clearinghouse's list of papers from journals, conference proceedings, and newspapers. In addition, the Utlas cataloging source files and contributed cataloging records described in chapter 6 provide a very large and useful repository of information to support bibliographic verification and other pre-order activities.

Before creating an order, the ACCORD user searches the CATSS data base for cataloging records that match the materials to be ordered. Records retrieved in this manner can be edited to meet local requirements and converted to order records through the addition of field values that indicate the vendor, price, date, number of copies, and other order-specific information. If no appropriate CATSS record is located, a skeletal order record containing brief bibliographic data can be entered online. Whether derived from CATSS records or key-entered, order records are stored in a library's own file with the CATSS data base. Specific fields can be updated to reflect the item's progress through various stages of ordering, receipt, and cataloging. Incomplete records contain codes that identify them as items on order.

ACCORD utilizes Utlas's electronic messaging facility for transmission of orders to various U.S. and Canadian publishers and distributors. Librarians can also send free-form messages to vendors. For vendors that are not accessible through electronic messaging, ACCORD will print purchase orders. To claim an item, an ACCORD user searches the CATSS data base, retrieves the appropriate order record, and enters a claiming message and date. The ACCORD program will automatically generate an online or printed claiming message.

As previously noted, timeshared access typically involves lower initial costs than those encountered with turnkey implementations, prewritten software, or custom-developed software. In libraries that subscribe to a bibliographic utility or CD-ROM system for cataloging support, the acquisitions department may already have workstations for bibliographic verification, thus minimizing or eliminating the need for additional equipment purchases. Because charges are incurred as the acquisitions system is used, the timeshared approach is especially attractive for libraries with a modest annual volume of acquisitions activity. In most cases, the library will pay charges ranging from two to three dollars per order for data entry and output production.

Regardless of the volume of a given library's ordering activity, the availability of a large shared cataloging data base for bibliographic verification is a further advantage of automated acquisitions subsystems offered by bibliographic utilities. The ability to transfer bibliographic data from cataloging records can significantly improve productivity in the entry of order data, while the immediate online availability of holdings information for other libraries is useful in cooperative collection development. With some bibliographic utilities, a workstation operator can also determine whether another institution has a given item on order. The use of a single system for acquisitions and cataloging also simplifies staff training requirements and promotes the integration of technical services operations.

As disadvantages, the automated acquisitions subsystems offered by bibliographic utilities are vulnerable to the slow response time that is a potential problem for all timesharing systems, especially successful ones which attract many subscribers. Some libraries may also find that a given system does not meet the requirements of local auditing or accounting practices, or that a particular bibliographic utility cannot provide all of the services required to complete a given transaction. Compared to prewritten acquisitions software and acquisitions modules supported by integrated library automation systems, the bibliographic utilities typically provide less flexibility in the production of information or statistical reports suited to a particular library, although certain types of financial reports, such as fund activity and history reports, are routinely offered. None of the bibliographic utilities provides check-writing capabilities. As with prewritten acquisitions software, long-established local ordering and procurement practices may have to be modified, although the resulting inconvenience can have a positive impact. While modifications to established procedures will require some initial restructuring and retraining, they may ultimately result in beneficial work simplification.

Libraries that use a bibliographic utility for automated acquisitions must typically provide the utility with fund names and balances, general ordering instructions, format specifications for procurement documents, claiming instructions, and similar background information. As the previous examples indicated, the bibliographic utilities provide formatted screens, or online workforms, for the simplified entry of order data. If a search of the cataloging data base or other libraries' acquisitions files retrieves an existing record for an item on order, specified bibliographic data elements can be automatically transferred to the acquisitions workform, thereby minimizing required keystroking. If no existing record is retrieved, an original acquisitions record can be created.

As with other automated acquisitions systems, order records enter an in-process file that is maintained automatically. Inquiries about specific order records are usually accomplished in the same manner as searches for cataloging records. The utilities usually provide an online directory which contains name and address information for publishers, jobbers, associations, and other organizations involved in the book ordering and delivery process. When entering order information, the workstation operator need only type the code for a given vendor into the order form, and the system will print full addresses on procurement documents and other printed products.

As an alternative to the bibliographic utilities, several book jobbers— including Brodart, Baker and Taylor, and Blackwell North America—offer software and timesharing services for online book ordering. As previously defined, book jobbers are companies that specialize in the sale of books and other materials to libraries. Used in this context, online ordering denotes those systems that not only automate the creation and maintenance of acquisitions records but also transmit orders electronically, typically to the vendor that operates the acquisition support system. Since jobbers sell books, their online ordering systems are designed to expedite delivery to customers, although they may also help libraries manage their acquisitions operations by maintaining records and preparing purchase orders for materials to be acquired from other vendors.

Such systems provide timeshared access to book jobbers' computer systems. Like the timeshared services offered by bibliographic utilities, this approach to automated acquisitions requires a very small capital investment in equipment. A terminal or microcomputer-based workstation is installed at the customer's site. Depending on the service, libraries may pay a fixed monthly or annual subscription fee for unlimited connect-time; alternatively, they may incur connect-time charges based on actual usage. In the manner of bibliographic utilities, most systems support formatted screens to simplify order entry. File maintenance and fund accounting are performed automatically, and online inquiries about the status of a given order are supported. Because the book jobbers' data bases contain inventory information, the availability of a given item can be immediately determined. If the book jobber has the item in stock, it can be ordered electronically. Alternatively, purchase orders for items to be ordered from other vendors can be produced on local printers. Libraries receive periodic printed reports that reflect their acquisitions and fund accounting activities.

COMPUTERIZED SERIALS SYSTEMS

As used in this section, the term *serials* denotes those publications that are issued in successive parts on a recurring basis, usually, but not necessarily, at regularly scheduled intervals. In addition to scholarly journals, popular magazines, and other periodical publications, the term encompasses newspapers, the proceedings and transactions of professional societies, newsletters, and numbered monographic series. Unlike multivolume books, which may likewise be issued in successive parts, serials are characteristically open-ended. The publication of successive issues is expected to continue indefinitely, although external circumstances may force the eventual suspension of a given serial.

Bibliographic Control Systems

Current serials automation efforts are directed at two types of activities: (1) the bibliographic control of serials; and (2) processing and management of serials collections in individual libraries or multilibrary systems. The task of bibliographic control, the focus of this discussion, is the establishment of definitive bibliographic information about serial publications, including their titles, publishers, dates, publication frequency, language, and subscription prices; the sources that index them; and the libraries that subscribe to them. Such information is essential to the acquisition and cataloging of serials, the formulation of cooperative collection development strategies, the fulfillment of interlibrary loan requests, and other library activities.

Performed manually, the bibliographic control of serials at the national and international levels is primarily accomplished by such printed sources as Ulrich's *International Periodicals Directory* and *Irregular Serials and Annuals,* both of which are published by R.R. Bowker. For computer-based searching, they are available as machine-readable data bases through DIALOG and other online information services. Bowker also offers a CD-ROM implementation called ULRICH'S PLUS. Taken together, the Bowker serials data bases contain bibliographic, ordering, and subject information for more than 100,000 regularly and irregularly published magazines, journals, newsletters, yearbooks, annual reviews, conference proceedings, and other serials from 65,000 sources in more than 180 countries. They also include information for several thousand additional serials which have ceased publication since 1974. The online and CD-ROM implementations can be used to verify titles, determine publishers' names and addresses, and obtain other information about specific serials. Data base records contain essential bibliographic data plus information about current status, publication frequency, and indexing sources for serial publications. Depending on the implementation, serial records can be searched by a variety of parameters, including title, alternate title, title keywords, subject, International Standard Serial Number (ISSN), Dewey Decimal number, publisher, and country of publication.

The Bowker serials data bases, their printed counterparts, and other printed sources, such as *New Serial Titles,* provide much useful information about serial publications. They do not provide the complete bibliographic data required for cataloging serials. The ULRICH's data base, for example, provides the Dewey classification number for a given serial title but not the Library of Congress classification number. Since the 1960s, librarians have advocated the creation of a comprehensive, machine-readable data base to serve as a registry of, and authoritative source of bibliographic information about, serials published throughout the world. Established in the early 1970s with funding from UNESCO and the French government, the International Serials Data System (ISDS) and the International Centre for the Registration of Serials, located in Paris, were the first agencies charged with responsibility for the development of an international file of machine-readable data pertaining to serials.

Each ISDS serial record contains 25 data elements, including the original title, variant title, imprint, publication status, starting date, frequency, language of publication, and classification numbers. As part of its registry function, the ISDS is responsible for the assignment of the International Standard Serial Number (ISSN) and key-title to each serial record it processes. Like its counterpart, the International Standard Book Number (ISBN), the ISSN is a standard code for the unambiguous identification of a given serial publication. The key-title is a distinctive title assigned to a given serial record. It is typically derived from information appearing on the serial's title page. The ISDS data base, which contains more than 600,000 serial records, has more than doubled since the mid-1980s. A CD-ROM implementation, called ISDN COMPACT, was introduced in 1992.

The ISDS works through a network of national centers which register serials in their own countries. At the time of this writing, there were 52 national centers. In the United States, the ISDS center is the National Serials Data Program (NSDP), which is located in the Library of Congress. Operational since 1973, the NSDP is charged with responsibility for the development of an authoritative automated bibliographic resource upon which serials processing systems can be built in the United States' three national libraries (the Library of Congress, the National Library of Medicine, and the National Agricultural Library), and other research libraries as well. As part of its ISDS involvement, the NSDP assigns ISSNs and key-titles to U.S. serial publications. It also maintains an authority file for corporate entries. For Canadian serials, a comparable role is played by the ISDS Canada Center, which is housed in the National Library of Canada.

In addition to its involvement with the National Serials Data Program, the Library of Congress has developed a MARC format for serial publications and offers machine-readable serials cataloging records on magnetic tape through the Cataloging Distribution Service. First published in 1969 and subsequently revised, the MARC serials format—sometimes termed MARC-S—is essentially a modified and somewhat enhanced version of the basic MARC II format. It includes variable fields for ISSN, Dewey and LC classification numbers, title, key-title, variant forms of title, former titles, and other cataloging data appropriate to serial records. A field is likewise provided for library holdings information, with subfields for the NUC symbol for the holding library, the inclusive dates, and a retention statement. A similar format for machine-readable serials cataloging records has been adopted by the National Library of Canada.

During the early 1970s, representatives of research libraries and library-related agencies held several formal and informal meetings to share their concern that a lack of communication among producers of machine-readable serials data bases would result in redundant conversion efforts as well as incompatibilities in data format and content. (The ISDS serials record, for example, employs only a subset of the MARC-S data elements.) The CONSER program was the outcome of these concerns. The acronym CONSER originally stood for Conversion of Serials; it has since been changed to Cooperative Online Serials. The purpose of CONSER is to establish and maintain a high-quality machine-readable data base of serials cataloging records. It was initially funded by a grant from the Council on Library Resources. The OCLC computer facility was selected as the host site for the CONSER data base.

When the initial grant expired, OCLC assumed responsibility for the daily administration of the program, while the Library of Congress provides the staff funding necessary to authenticate serial records for inclusion in the CONSER data base. As used in this context, authentication denotes the process of certifying that the data content and content designators in a given serials record meet the cataloging standards established by CONSER participants, which include the Library of Congress, the National Library of Canada, the National Library of Medicine, the National Agricultural Library, the New York State Library, the State University of New York, the University of Minnesota, Yale University, Cornell University, the University of California, the University of Florida, Harvard University, and the Boston Theological Institute.

As described in chapter 6, the OCLC data base contains records contributed by libraries of all types and catalogers of varying levels of knowledge and expertise. Regardless of the quality controls provided at the local library level, cataloging errors are possible. In addition, the OCLC data base contains duplicate serials records, some of which are the result of the batch loading of large bibliographic files, such as the serials portion of the LC MARC data base, the Minnesota Union List of Serials (MULS), and the Pittsburgh Regional Union List. As a further complication, titles, publishers, publication frequency, or other information about serials may—and often does—change over time, necessitating corresponding changes in cataloging records.

Working at OCLC terminals, CONSER participants can add, change, or delete the bibliographic content of existing serials cataloging records in the OCLC data base. They can also input original cataloging records. After editing or input, the participant sends a copy of the record to the Library of Congress or the National Library of Canada for authentication. Records are also routed to the National Serials Data Program or ISDS Canada for the authentication of the ISSN and key-title. Once authenticated, CONSER records are said to be "locked" and can only be changed by the authenticating agency.

As a result of CONSER activity, OCLC has deleted a significant number of duplicate records from its data base, thus making the correct records easier to access. Authenticated CONSER records are issued in machine-readable form through the Library of Congress MARC Distribution Service on weekly tapes. They are consequently made available to other bibliographic utilities. It should also be noted that all of the bibliographic utilities, including OCLC, maintain non-CONSER serials records and that such records can prove very useful for bibliographic control purposes. Because holdings information is associated with these serials records, the bibliographic utilities provide online access to a national union list of serials.

Authenticated CONSER records are distributed by the Library of Congress as part of the serials portion of the LC MARC data base. Libraries can access them through bibliographic utilities and CD-ROM cataloging support products, which incorporate them into their data bases. The LC Cataloging Distribution Service also offers SERIAL RESOURCE RECORDS, a magnetic tape service that distributes CONSER records that are in the process of being authenticated, and CDMARC SERIALS, a CD-ROM implementation of the CONSER data base, which supports retrieval of CONSER records by a variety of parameters. The former is issued monthly, the latter quarterly. CONSER records appear in human-readable form in *New Serial Titles,* an LC publication that serves as a union list for titles cataloged by CONSER members. Various cumulations cover the period from 1971 to the present. CONSER records are also published on COM-generated microfiche by the National Library of Canada.

Serials Processing Systems

In terms of their utility for local serials processing and management, the computer-based national and international bibliographic control systems described above can facilitate the verification of serials data for acquisitions or interlibrary loan purposes. They can also simplify the search for LC or other cataloging copy. They do not, however, provide automated support for ordering, claiming, or other aspects of serials collection management at the local library level. Since the 1960s, library interest in automated serials processing systems has been motivated by the same factors that have encouraged the development of automated approaches to acquisitions, circulation control, cataloging, and reference service. Their principal motivation is the desire for cost reduction and improved operating efficiencies which permit the performance of increased work without comparable growth of staff.

The cost of acquiring and maintaining serial publications represents a significant percentage of many libraries' budgets. In technical, medical, and business libraries, for example, serials typically constitute the major collection component, and ordering, claiming, binding, and related paper-work processing tasks can require many hours of labor. Even in academic and public libraries, where the ratio of serial to monographic publications is usually lower, serials departments may have large staffs. At a time of simultaneously rising subscription prices and diminished library budgets, operational economies are essential if a given library's serials collection is to be maintained at its present level, let alone increased.

Although library interest is high and cost-reduction potential con-siderable, the widespread development and implementation of effective computer-based serials processing systems have historically been im-peded by complications associated with certain characteristics of serial publications. Circulation control, cataloging, and, to a lesser extent, ac-quisitions are characterized by a well-defined, predictable sequence of work steps performed in a predetermined order on a regular basis. Serials processing tasks, on the other hand, are complicated by a variety of exceptional circumstances that must be anticipated in the design of any automated system. While bibliographic and other data pertaining to monographs remain relatively stable once entered into computer storage, it is a rare serials record that will not eventually require some change in title, publisher, issuing agent, frequency of publication, numbering se-quence, or other attributes. Such changes can render obsolete a computer-printed union list, complicate the development of an automated claims production system, or alter previously established binding practices for a given serial. While computer systems can be designed to accommodate such changes and exceptional conditions, they complicate the design effort and increase the cost of automated serials implementations.

Despite these complications, a number of libraries and vendors have developed systems that automate one or more aspects of serials process-ing, including the production of serials holdings lists for single or multiple libraries, ordering, check-in, claiming, and the routing of received issues to designated persons. Of these, systems that produce serials lists are perhaps the most straightforward and widely implemented. While records for serial publications can be incorporated into a general card, book-form, or online catalog, many libraries maintain separate book-form lists which presumably provide more convenient and detailed access to information about their serials collections. Such serials lists may reflect the collections of a single library or, as a union list, the serials holdings of multiple libraries in a given system, consortium, or geographic area. Such union lists have long proven indispensable to the formulation of cooperative serials acquisitions programs and the efficient processing of interlibrary loan requests. From the library user's standpoint, they provide informa-tion about the availability of resources outside of the local collection.

Although book-form serials lists have been produced by conventional typewriting and typesetting methodologies, a substantial amount of cler-ical time and effort is required to incorporate new entries and to modify specified information within existing entries. Automation can greatly simplify these tasks. Where ordering, claiming, or other aspects of serials processing will not be automated, a microcomputer-based data management program can be used to maintain a data base of serials records and print alphabetical or other lists of all or selected titles. Such programs enable an operator to easily define the fields to be included in serials records. In a union list application, for example, such fields might include the title; the call number, if serials are classified; a holdings statement, indicating volume numbers, issue numbers, and dates; the language of publication; and the branch or individual library location where a given title is held. While constraints may be placed on the number of fields and on the number of characters in a given field, most data management programs are flexible enough to accommodate a wide range of applications. With records formatted in this way, the operator can select those records or combinations of records that meet stated criteria in order, for example, to produce lists of serials in a particular language, lists of serials held in a particular branch or library location, or lists of serials in a particular language in a particular location. Conventional alphabetical title or call number lists can likewise be generated.

As an alternative to data management programs, many word processing software packages include list management modules that are appropriate for serial records management and list production. Depending on the capabilities of the particular software package and hardware utilized, lists of serials can be printed on paper in a variety of formats, including single- or double-column, with or without justified margins and proportional spacing.

List production capabilities are likewise offered by companies and organizations that provide computer-based serials processing services to libraries. Among the bibliographic utilities, for example, WLN subscribers can order printed lists reflecting the serials holdings of one or more libraries. The OCLC Union List component likewise provides serials holdings lists arranged in a variety of formats. Among private companies, F.W. Faxon offers a union list production service to its library customers. The list is compiled in alphabetical order. Each entry contains the full serial title, a holdings code, the publication frequency, the number of subscriptions in each holding library, and other data. Faxon stores a machine-readable version of the list to simplify future updates and modifications. Libraries participating in the production of a given union list also receive individualized lists of their own serials holdings.

Depending on application characteristics and the types of output peripherals available, a union or other list of serials may be produced in hardcopy form via impact or nonimpact printers, or recorded on microfilm or microfiche via COM. The microform option is particularly attractive for very long lists that will be mailed or otherwise distributed to a number of locations. Microfiche was selected as the output medium for the California Union List of Periodicals (CULP), which contains information about 63,000 periodicals representing the holdings of more than 700 California libraries. COM has also been used for many smaller projects. Several union lists of serials can be accessed through the online information services discussed in chapter 7; examples, both offered by CAN/OLE, include the CISTI CATALOGUE OF SERIALS and the CANUCS union list of social sciences and humanities serials held by Canadian libraries. CD-ROM is also a possibility for the distribution of union lists of serials, but few applications will require the formidable storage capacity that CD-ROM provides. For libraries that implement a CD-ROM public access catalog of the type described in chapter 6, a list of serials might be appended as a related application.

As an alternative to a self-contained implementation, a computer-printed serials list can be produced from a master machine-readable serials data file that is designed to support acquisition, check-in, claiming, or other control activities. This file, which is comparable in purpose and scope to the master data files that support automated circulation control and acquisitions, usually contains a combination of bibliographic, holdings, ordering, and binding data for each serial owned by a given library. While file structure and content vary, most systems maintain some combination of the following information about serial publications: title, imprint, holdings (volumes and issues), subscription terms, renewal dates, branch or library location, cost, vendor identifier, number of copies, media type, call number (if serials are classified), and the International Standard Serial Number, CODEN, or other unique identifiers. Typical binding information includes the frequency of binding, spine title, binding source, binding type, cover color, and lettering color. Depending on the system, serials data records may be key-entered, loaded from magnetic tapes obtained from bibliographic utilities or other sources, or transferred through an online interface from an external data base. Serials records may be retrieved by title, author/title keywords, ISSN, order numbers, or other parameters. In computer-based serials systems that support acquisitions, the master data file coexists with vendor and fund files of the type described above.

As with conventional book acquisitions, computers can be used to simplify recordkeeping and minimize or eliminate the labor-intensive sorting, filing, and other paper-handling work routines associated with manual serials processing. Most serials control systems support some combination of order preparation, check-in of received issues, claiming of missing issues, preparation of bindery orders, and report production. Order and renewal preparation are typically performed online, although purchase orders and renewal orders may be printed in batches. Received issues are checked in at terminals by retrieving the appropriate serials record and modifying designated holdings fields. The most flexible systems simplify data entry by displaying information about an expected issue, including the volume and issue number, cover date, and number of copies anticipated. The workstation operator simply modifies those data elements requiring correction. When all modifications are completed, the new record enters the serials data file.

Applying predictive algorithms to information about the frequency of publication stored in serials records, some automated systems will generate claiming notices without library intervention. The library specifies the periodicity for successive issues and the number of days after the anticipated receipt when claiming notices are to be sent. When overdue issues are to be claimed, the system searches the serials data file for issues that have not arrived according to their previously defined frequencies. Based on information stored in serials holdings records, most serials control systems will also prepare bindery orders, print instruction slips, check in items on their return from binding, and print claiming notices for items that have not been returned on schedule.

Automated serials control systems can be implemented in several ways. They can be custom-developed for specific libraries, accessed on a time-sharing basis, or purchased as prewritten products for local operation. As with monographic acquisitions, various academic, public, and special libraries developed customized serials control systems during the 1960s and 1970s. Several such systems remain in use. Perhaps the earliest and most widely discussed example is the PHILSOM system, which was developed in 1962 by the Washington University School of Medicine Library in St. Louis. It has been enhanced over the years to take advantage of ongoing developments in computer technology and to accommodate changing application requirements. PHILSOM supports online retrieval and real time updating of serials records. It can produce a variety of printed output, including serials catalogs and union lists, claiming lists, subscription renewal lists, and financial reports. Other libraries that have custom-developed serials control systems include the University of California at San Diego, where an automated serials checking system was implemented as early as 1961; the UCLA Biomedical Library; the San Francisco Public Library; the University of Massachusetts; the University of Arizona; the University of Washington; Brigham Young University; and the Université Laval in Quebec, one of the first libraries to implement an online serials control system.

As an alternative to the time and expense associated with custom-developed systems, libraries can obtain access to serials control capabilities on a timesharing basis through serials subscription services such as F.W. Faxon and EBSCO. Faxon's LINX system, for example, can be accessed through dial-up or leased telephone lines. Introduced in the early 1980s, it provides online access to a data base of more than 200,000 bibliographic records for serials titles and monographic series, including the serials portion of the LC MARC data base as well as serials records authenticated by the CONSER program. Records can be retrieved by various parameters, including ISSN, title, title keywords, and publisher. The LINX service also maintains information about the serials subscriptions and holdings of Faxon's customers. It routinely identifies serial records that may require claiming action. Faxon will automatically handle claims for titles ordered through it. Libraries are responsible for claims for serials purchased from other sources. LINX customers can also obtain online access to payment histories and other financial information for serial subscriptions. An electronic messaging subsystem permits communication with Faxon's staff.

EBSCONET, a timeshared serials ordering system developed by EBSCO Subscription Services, likewise provides online access to a large data base of serials records, including annuals, irregular serials, and discontinued publications. Each record includes the serial's title, ISSN, publisher, country of publication, language, LC and Dewey classification numbers, frequency, and other information. Records can be accessed by ISSN, keywords, classification numbers, and other parameters. EBSCONET supports online ordering, claiming, and subscription renewal; electronic invoicing; electronic message transmission between customers and EBSCO; and electronic data interchange (EDI) for transfer of serials records to local library automation systems. EBSCO also offers a CD-ROM implementation of its serials data base.

Several organizations have developed prewritten software packages and preconfigured turnkey systems designed specifically for serials management. As an example of the former approach, the Microlinx program from F.W. Faxon operates on IBM-compatible microcomputers. It supports automated check-in, claiming, printing of bindery slips, and routing of received issues. It can also generate various reports, including serials holdings lists. To minimize data entry requirements and facilitate implementation, Microlinx customers receive a data base that contains bibliographic and financial records for serials that they have ordered from Faxon.

Despite their impressive capabilities, self-contained serials management products have limited appeal. Rather than implementing serials control as a standalone function on a separate system, many libraries want to integrate it with other automated activities. Recognizing this, most integrated library automation systems offer a serials management module. Implementation patterns and functionality vary from product to product. The INNOVACQ product line, for example, originated as a turnkey system for acquisitions and serials control to which circulation and online catalog access were subsequently added. As might be expected, its serials management capabilities are very well developed. Certain integrated library automation systems intended for corporate, government, and medical libraries likewise provide excellent serials control features. With some integrated library automation systems, however, serials management capabilities appear to have been added as an afterthought to be responsive to requests for proposals that demand a comprehensive, multifunctional system. In such cases, the serials module lacks the functionality of the integrated system's other application components.

Some integrated library automation systems treat serials control as a specialized form of acquisitions. The NOTIS acquisitions subsystem, for example, was specifically designed for compatibility with serial publications. As with monographic purchases, the workstation operator prepares an order by entering essential bibliographic information, a vendor identifier, a fund account number, shipping instructions, and an action date for future claiming notices. When individual issues are received, the appropriate record is retrieved and the record modified. Daily lists of expired action dates indicate that claiming notices are required.

SUMMARY

While they are customarily handled by separate departments within a library, acquisitions and serials control share a common function: the procurement of library materials. Both functions have been automated since the 1960s. Until recently, however, they have received less attention than other aspects of library automation.

Among the motives for automated acquisitions are the desire for improved decision making through statistical analysis and other reporting of acquisitions activity, and the increasing library interest in the establishment of integrated systems in which a bibliographic record is created at the time an item is ordered. Preorder searching and related bibliographic verification activities can be automated by using data bases offered by the bibliographic utilities, online information services, and CD-ROM publishers discussed in preceding chapters. Especially relevant is the BOOKS IN PRINT data base, which is available through online information services and in a CD-ROM implementation.

Libraries considering the automation of acquisitions activities can select from at least four different implementation alternatives: a custom-developed system; an acquisitions-specific prewritten software package or turnkey system; an acquisitions module supported by a multifunctional, integrated library system; and timeshared acquisitions support services offered by bibliographic utilities and book jobbers. Each alternative has advantages and disadvantages. Customized systems can be developed to individual library specifications, but are expensive and time-consuming to create. Prewritten acquisitions-specific software and the acquisitions application modules supported by integrated library automation systems can minimize the delays and other implementation problems associated with customized software development. The integration of acquisitions with cataloging and circulation in a single system offers several important advantages, including the ability to establish a preliminary bibliographic record at the time an item is ordered.

To reduce capital investments in hardware and software procurement, automated acquisitions capability can be obtained on a timesharing basis through a bibliographic utility or book jobber. Because charges are incurred as the acquisitions capability is used, this approach is especially attractive to libraries with a modest annual volume of acquisitions activity. Use of a bibliographic utility for acquisitions offers other advantages as well. The transfer of bibliographic data from cataloging records can facilitate the entry of order information, and the immediate online availability of holdings information for other libraries supports cooperative collection development. The use of a single system for acquisitions and cataloging also simplifies staff training requirements. The timeshared acquisitions systems offered by booksellers typically feature access to inventory information and online ordering capabilities.

Current serials automation activities are directed toward two types of tasks: the bibliographic control of serial publications and the management of serials collections in individual libraries. The task of bibliographic control is the establishment of definitive bibliographic information about serial publications. Among automated approaches to this task, R.R. Bowker offers machine-readable versions of its various printed guides to serial publications, including *Ulrich's International Periodicals Directory*.

The International Serials Data System (ISDS) and the International Centre for the Registration of Serials are charged with responsibility for the establishment and maintenance of a comprehensive, machine-readable registry of bibliographic information about serials published throughout the world. As part of its registry function, the ISDS is responsible for the assignment of the ISSN and key-title to each serial record it processes. The ISDS works through a network of national centers which register serials in their own countries. In the United States, the ISDS center is the National Serials Data Program at the Library of Congress.

The Library of Congress has also developed a MARC format for serial publications, and participates in the CONSER program. The purpose of the CONSER program is to establish and maintain a high-quality, machine-readable data base of serials cataloging records. Records submitted for inclusion in the CONSER data base are authenticated by the Library of Congress and the National Library of Canada. The data base itself is maintained by OCLC, and CONSER records are disseminated through the LC Cataloging Distribution Service.

Turning to the management of local serials collections, a number of libraries and several vendors have developed systems that automate one or more aspects of serials processing, including union list production, ordering, check-in, claiming, and the routing of received issues to designated persons. Systems that produce union or other lists of serials are straightforward and widely utilized. They can be easily implemented through data management software or word processing systems.

A number of libraries developed customized serials control systems during the 1960s and 1970s. One of the most famous of these is the PHILSOM system developed by the Washington University School of Medicine Library. As an alternative to the time and expense involved in customized system development, libraries can obtain access to serials control capabilities on a timesharing basis through subscription service companies, such as F.W. Faxon and EBSCO. Serials-specific software packages and turnkey systems have been developed, but many libraries prefer an integrated system that incorporates serials management capabilities. Most integrated library automation systems offer a serials management module.

ADDITIONAL READING

ANABLE, R. "CONSER: Bibliographic Considerations." *Library Resources and Technical Services* 19 (3): 341–48 (1975).

BAILEY, C. "Network-based Electronic Serials." *Information Technology and Libraries* 11 (1): 29–35 (1992).

BARRON, L. "Concerning CONSER: Accomplishments and Aspirations." *Serials Librarian* 19 (3): 171–81 (1991).

BARTLEY, L., and REYNOLDS, R. "CONSER: Revolution and Evolution." *Cataloging and Classification Quarterly* 8 (3): 47–66 (1988).

BARTLEY, L., et al. "Automation of Serials Cataloging." *Serials Librarian* 12 (1): 131–68 (1987).

BECKETT, C. "Exchanging Data in the Serials Industry." *Serials* 4 (3): 21–28 (1991).

BOSS, R. "Automated Acquisitions Systems." *Journal of Library Automation* 13 (3): 156–64 (1980).

———. "Technical Services Functionality in Integrated Library Systems." *Library Technology Reports* 28 (1): 5–109 (1992).

BOSS, R., and MCQUEEN, J. "The Uses of Automation and Related Technologies by Domestic Book and Serials Jobbers." *Library Technology Reports* 25 (2): 125–251 (1989).

BOSS, R., and MARCUM, D. "Online Acquisitions Systems for Libraries." *Library Technology Reports* 17 (2): 115–202 (1981).

BOSTIC, M. "Serials Claiming." *Serials Librarian* 10 (2): 185–94 (1985).

BOWDEN, V., and SWANNER, S. "Implementing Change: The Installation of an Integrated Library System at UTHSCSA." *Bulletin of the Medical Library Association* 73 (3): 271–77 (1985).

BRADLEY, I. "International Standard Serial Numbers and the International Serials Data System." *Serials Librarian* 3 (2): 243–53 (1979).

CHICKERING, S., et al. "A Conversion of Serials Records: OCLC LDR to VTLS US-MARC Format." *Information Technology and Libraries* 9 (3): 263–71 (1990).

CHRIST, R., and LIN, S. "Serials Retrospective Conversion: Project Design and In-house Implementation." *Cataloging and Classification Quarterly* 14 (3): 51–73 (1992).

CLARK, C., and FEICK, C. "Monographic Series and the RLIN Acquisitions System." *Serials Review* 10 (3): 68–72 (1984).

COE, G., et al. "Book Distributors and Automation: A Complete Package." *Library Technology Reports* 26 (4): 497–501 (1990).

COLLVER, M. "Organization of Serials Work for Manual and Automated Systems." *Library Resources and Technical Services* 24 (3): 307–16 (1980).

COPELAND, N. "Retrospective Conversion of Serials: The RLIN Experience." *Serials Review* 14 (3): 23–28 (1988).

DANIELS, M. "Automated Serials Control: National and International Considerations." *Journal of Library Automation* 8 (2): 127–46 (1975).

DEGENER, C., and WAITE, M. "Using an Automated Serials System to Assist with Collection Review and Cancellations." *Serials Review* 17 (1): 13–20 (1991).

DYER, H. "Microcomputer based Serial Systems." *Serials* 4 (2): 40–46 (1991).

EVANS, K. "MARC Format Integration and Seriality: Implications for Serials Cataloging." *Serials Librarian* 18 (1): 37–45 (1990).

FARRINGTON, J. "Selecting a Serials System: The Technical Services Perspective." *Library Resources and Technical Services* 32 (4): 402–406 (1988).

FRASER, A., et al. "Serials Librarians/Serials Suppliers: Bridging the Communications Gap in the Technological Environment." *Australian and New Zealand Journal of Serials Librarianship* 1 (1): 45–55 (1990).

FURLONG, E. "A Case Study in Automated Acquisitions: Northwestern University Library." *Journal of Library Automation* 13 (2): 222–40 (1980).

GADZIKOWSKI, C. "Octanet/PHILSOM: Using a Serials Control System for Interlibrary Loan." *Technical Services Quarterly* 1 (3): 45–53 (1984).

GELLATLY, P., ed. *The Management of Serials Automation: Current Technology and Strategies for Future Planning.* New York: Haworth Press, 1984.

GEYER, E., and BOTTA, G. "REMO: Automated Serials Management in a Medium-sized Medical Library." *Serials Librarian* 16 (1): 39–64 (1989).

GOLDBERG, T., and BURTON, P. "Building a Serials Database on NOTIS at the University of Louisville." *Serials Librarian* 18 (3): 115–28 (1990).

HAWKS, C. "Internal Control, Auditing, and the Automated Acquisitions System." *Journal of Academic Librarianship* 16 (5): 296–301 (1990).

HEATH, B. "Detroit Area Library Network: Bringing up Acquisitions." *Resource Sharing and Information Networks* 7 (1): 91–97 (1991).

INTER, S. "A New Paradigm for Access to Serials." *Serials Librarian* 19 (3): 151–61 (1991).

JOHNSON, M. "Medical Periodicals Control—Evolution into Networking." *Technical Services Quarterly* 1 (3): 37–43 (1984).

KARCH, L. "Serials Information on CD-ROM: A Reference Perspective." *Reference Services Review* 18 (2): 81–86 (1990).

KHOO, C., et al. "Serials Fiscal Control Using a Flat-file Database Management System on a Microcomputer." *Serials Librarian* 20 (1): 91–105 (1991).

LYNCH, C. "Serials Management in the Age of Electronic Access." *Serials Review* 17 (1): 7–12 (1991).

MCCLARE, C. "Serials Reference Services at the National Library of New Zealand." *Serials Librarian* 20 (4): 35–45 (1991).

MCLAREN, M. "Full Acquisitions Systems." *Library Acquisitions: Practice and Theory* 14 (3): 247–50 (1990).

MILLER-MCIRVINE, R. "Challenges for Serials Automation." *Library Resources and Technical Services* 33 (2): 166–71 (1989).

MYERS, A. "Acquiring Minds Want to Know: Integrating Automated Acquisitions with Other Library Functions." *Law Library Journal* 83 (3): 479–91 (1991).

NELSON, B. "Automated Acquisitions in Small Academic Libraries." *Library Acquisitions: Practice and Theory* 13 (4): 351–59 (1989).

NEWELL, A. "Automated Serials Control for Special Libraries: An Overview of Available Systems." *Australian and New Zealand Journal of Serials Librarianship* 2 (4): 7–16 (1991).

OSMUS, L. "Serials Cataloging from the Union List Standpoint." *Serials Librarian* 12 (1): 101–16 (1987).

ROLLINS, G. "Creating Bibliographic Records in the GEAC Acquisitions Module Efficiently." *Library Acquisitions: Practice and Theory* 15 (4): 427–31 (1991).

SIMMONS, P. "Serial Records, International Exchange, and the Common Communication Format." *IFLA Journal* 16 (2): 198–203 (1990).

SMITH, S. "Linking Approval Plans and Automated Library Acquisitions Systems." *Library Acquisitions: Practice and Theory* 11 (2): 215–16 (1987).

STAKOWSKI, R. "Automated Acquisitions and OCLC: A Brief History, Present Concerns, Future Options." *Technical Services Quarterly* 8 (3): 59–68 (1991).

STEELE, P. "Automated Serials Control Using NOTIS." *Serials Review* 9 (1): 64–73 (1983).

VAN AVERY, A. "Recat vs. Recon of Serials: A Problem for Shared Cataloguing." *Cataloging and Classification Quarterly* 10 (4): 51–68 (1990).

VAN HOUTEN, S. "The PHILSOM Automated Serials Control System: An Introduction." *Serials Review* 7 (3): 93–99 (1981).

WALLBRIDGE, S. "CONSER and OCLC." *Serials Review* 6 (3): 109–11 (1980).

WANG, C. "Automating Acquisitions for Departmental Libraries: System Analysis and Requirements." *Journal of Library Administration* 7 (1): 61–73 (1986).

ZAGER, P., and SMADI, O. "A Knowledge-based Expert Systems Application in Library Acquisitions: Monographs." *Library Acquisitions: Practice and Theory* 16 (2): 145–54 (1992).

ZAJANC, J. "Factors to Consider in Automating Serials." *Serials Librarian* 10 (1): 7–12 (1986).

Index

375